AUGUSTINE OF HIPPO
PHILOSOPHER, EXEGETE, AND THEOLOGIAN

AUGUSTINE OF HIPPO
PHILOSOPHER, EXEGETE, AND THEOLOGIAN

A SECOND COLLECTION OF ESSAYS

By

ROLAND J. TESKE, SJ

MARQUETTE
UNIVERSITY
PRESS

MARQUETTE STUDIES IN PHILOSOPHY
NO. 66
ANDREW TALLON, SERIES EDITOR

© 2009 Marquette University Press
Milwaukee, Wisconsin 53201-3141
All rights reserved.
www.marquette.edu/mupress/

LIBRARY OF CONGRESS CATALOGING-IN-PUBLICATION DATA

Teske, Roland J., 1934-
Augustine of Hippo : philosopher, exegete, and theologian : a second collection of essays / by Roland J. Teske.
   p. cm. — (Marquette studies in philosophy ; no. 66)
Includes bibliographical references (p.   ) and index.
ISBN-13: 978-0-87462-764-0 (pbk. : alk. paper)
ISBN-10: 0-87462-764-8 (pbk. : alk. paper)
1. Augustine, Saint, Bishop of Hippo. I. Title.
BR65.A9T438 2009
270.2092—dc22
                         2009008574

∞The paper used in this publication meets the minimum requirements of the American National Standard for Information Sciences— Permanence of Paper for Printed Library Materials, ANSI Z39.48-1992.

MARQUETTE UNIVERSITY PRESS
MILWAUKEE

The Association of Jesuit University Presses

TABLE OF CONTENTS

Dedication 7

Acknowledgments 9

Introduction 11

AUGUSTINE AS PHILOSOPHER

Ultimate Reality according to Augustine of Hippo 21

Augustine, Flew and the Free Will Defense 39

Platonic Reminiscence and Memory of the Present in St. Augustine 61

Augustine of Hippo on Seeing with the Eyes of the Mind 77

St. Augustine's Epistula X: Another Look at 'Deificari in otio' 97

AUGUSTINE AS EXEGETE

St. Augustine, the Manichees, and the Bible 111

The Criteria for Figurative Interpretation in St. Augustine 127

St. Augustine and the Vision of God 145

St. Augustine on the Good Samaritan 167

St. Augustine's Use of 'Manens in Se' 193

AUGUSTINE AS THEOLOGIAN

St. Augustine on the Humanity of Christ and Temptation 215

Augustine, Maximinus, and Imagination 235

The Definition of Sacrifice in the *De ciuitate Dei* 253

The Image and Likeness of God in St. Augustine's *De Genesi ad litteram liber imperfectus* 271

Bibliography 281

Index of Names 293

IN LOVING MEMORY OF
MARY ANN WENDLING TESKE
1918–2008

ACKNOWLEDGMENTS

The articles in this volume were previously printed elsewhere. I thank the editors of the books and journals in which they were first published and acknowledge that they retain the copyright to them.

"Ultimate Reality according to Augustine of Hippo," *The Journal of Ultimate Reality and Meaning* 18 (1995): 20–33.

"Augustine, Flew and the Free Will Defense," *Proceedings of the Jesuit Philosophical Association* (1980): 9–27.

"Platonic Reminiscence and Memory of the Present in St. Augustine," *New Scholasticism* LVIII (1984): 220–235.

"Augustine of Hippo on Seeing with the Eyes of the Mind," in *Ambiguity in Western Thought*, ed. Craig J. N. de Paulo, Patrick Messina, and Marc Stier (New York: Peter Lang, 2005), pp. 72–87 and 221–226.

"St. Augustine's Epistula X: Another Look at 'Deificari in otio,'" *Augustinianum* 32 (1992): 289–299.

"St. Augustine, the Manichees, and the Bible," in *Augustine and the Bible*, ed. P. Bright, Notre Dame, IN: Notre Dame University Press, 1999. Pp. 208–221.

"The Criteria for Figurative Interpretation in St. Augustine," in *De doctrina christiana: A Classic of Western Culture*, ed. by D. W. H. Arnold and P. Bright. Notre Dame: University of Notre Dame Press, 1995. Pp. 109–122.

"St. Augustine and the Vision of God," in *Augustine: Mystic and Mystagogue*, ed. F. Van Fleteren, J. Schnaubelt, and J. Reino (New York: Peter Lang, 1994). Pp. 287–308.

"St. Augustine on the Good Samaritan," in *Augustine the Exegete*, ed. F. Van Fleteren and J. Schnaubelt (New York: Peter Lang, 2001), pp. 347-367.

"St. Augustine's Use of '*Manens in Se*,'" *Revue des études augustininnes* 39 (1993): 391–307.

"St. Augustine on the Humanity of Christ and Temptation," *Augustiniana* 54 (2004): 261–277.

"Augustine, Maximinus, and Imagination," *Augustiniana* 43 (1993): 27–41.

"The Definition of Sacrifice in the *De ciuitate Dei*," in *Nova Doctrina Vetusque: Essays on Early Christianity in Honor of Fredric W. Schlatter, SJ*, ed. Douglas Kries and Catherine Brown Tkacz (New York: Peter Lang, 1999). Pp. 153–167.

"The Image and Likeness of God in St. Augustine's *De Genesi ad litteram liber imperfectus*," *Augustinianum* XXX (1990): 441–451.

INTRODUCTION

This volume contains a group of previously published articles on Augustine of Hippo that were written over past three decades. The articles are grouped according to their principal focus. Some were written principally on philosophical aspects of Augustine's thought, which is quite in accord with my academic background and work. But others deal with Augustine's interpretation of scripture, a topic that loomed large in Augustine's writing and work as a pastor in Hippo and that I could not avoid in coming to terms with Augustine's thought. Finally, some clearly take up theological topics, such as the humanity of Christ, the meaning of sacrifice, the Arianism of Maximinus, our being made to the image of God in Augustine's second commentary of Genesis. The volume is subtitled a 'Second Collection' since I have already published a volume of previously published articles on Augustine and the present volume accordingly represents a second collection of such articles, which like the second collection at Mass may be slimmer than the first or equally rich.

AUGUSTINE AS PHILOSOPHER

"Ultimate Reality according to Augustine of Hippo" can serve as an introduction to the thought of the bishop of Hippo since it touches upon his life and works, his Neoplatonism, his hierarchical view of the universe with the God, who exists in the highest manner at its summit. Although Augustine was greatly indebted to the great Neoplatonist philosophers, Plotinus, whom he regarded as Plato *redivivus*, and Porphyry, and although he insisted that they came to know God as the cause of existing, the source of understanding, and order of living, he also saw the limitations of these great philosophers who failed to recognize the work of Christ in his incarnation, life, death, and resurrection. Like much of what I have written on Augustine, the present article emphasizes his debt to the great Platonists for his concept of God and the soul as incorporeal or non-bodily beings and of God as non-temporal.

"Augustine, Flew and the Free Will Defense" was one of the first articles I wrote on Augustine. In the context of Antony Flew's argument against Alvin Plantinga's version of the free will defense of God on the problem of evil in the world, I tried to show that Augustine has a version of the free will defense in book two of *De libero arbitrio* and that Augustine's version of the argument avoids at least some of the problems that Flew points to in Plantinga's version of the argument. The crux of Augustine's argument is that free will, though not one of the great goods, like justice, which cannot be misused, is a good and one necessary for our being able to attain the highest good, namely, happiness in the vision of God. The evil, however, with which Augustine is most concerned is the evil of sin, not with the evil that human beings cause by the misuse of their freedom. Furthermore, Augustine sees that moral evil or the evil of sin lies in the will rather than in anything that the will produces. Moral goodness and moral evil consist in turning to God and turning away from God, that is, in loving God and our neighbor or in not loving God and our neighbor, and without free will one could not love God and neighbor. Such love is the great good that free will makes possible, even if free will also means that we can go wrong and turn away from the love of God and neighbor. That is, Augustine's version of the free will defense basically claims that the creation of creatures capable of love, which has to be free if it is to be love, is what counterbalances the existence of moral evil or sin.

In "Platonic Reminiscence and Memory of the Present," I took on Etienne Gilson's claim that Augustine replaced the Platonic doctrine of a memory of the past with his own doctrine of a memory of the present. The elimination of the Platonic memory of the past means that the soul does not now remember what it saw in some previous existence before coming to be in these present bodies. Although Augustine clearly does use memory to refer to the mind's contemplation of things whose existence is not past, but present, he is also clear in some of his earlier writings that knowing is remembering. And in Letter 7 he claims that those who reject present memory of intelligible things that we saw in the past, that is, before the fall into these bodies, are misinterpreting Socrates's famous discovery. Even in *De trinitate* where he has given up any memory of our previous happiness, he insists that the soul does not now remember its previous happiness in Adam or elsewhere, since that has been completely forgotten. One cannot, however, forget something that one did not previously experience.

"Augustine of Hippo on Seeing with the Eyes of the Mind" was originally presented as the inaugural address for the Donald J. Schuenke Chair in Philosophy, which I have been privileged to hold during the past years. In the lecture I pointed to the difference between what I called Augustine's 'official account' of what intellectual knowing is and what I called his 'unofficial account' of such knowing. While the official account, that is, the account that he gives when describing what it is to know intellectually, entails that the eyes of the mind see intelligible objects in an intelligible world without any role for the senses. The official account, I claimed, runs into a number of problems, which are inevitable for someone who takes intellectual knowing to be a seeing of intelligible objects with the eyes of the mind. But his unofficial account of knowing is much more plebeian and often seems to be merely an ability to grasp and articulate concepts of intelligible realities, more the sort of thing that we might describe as insights, such as the grasp of what it is to be non-bodily or non-temporal.

"St. Augustine's Epistula X: Another Look at 'Deificari in otio'" examines the phrase from Augustine's early letter to his friend, Nebridius, in which Augustine describes the life of philosophy that he and his friend had hoped to live together. The phrase is interesting since it is one of the few times that Augustine spoke of our deification or becoming godlike. Although some scholars have regarded that expression as a mark of selfishness and presumption and as purely philosophical rather than Christian, I argue that the phrase need not and probably should not be so regarded and that the leisure that Augustine and Nebridius desired can be understood as Christian, although the letter to Nebridius is quite philosophical in its tone, perhaps because of Nebridius' penchant for philosophy.

AUGUSTINE AS EXEGETE

The second cluster of articles are concerned with Augustine as biblical exegete. In "St. Augustine, the Manichees, and the Bible," I first looked at the role of the Bible in Augustine's conversion to Manichaeism. Augustine had considerable trouble with the style of the Old Latin version of the scriptures, with the anthropomorphism of the Old Testament, and with the supposed immorality of the Hebrew patriarchs. Secondly, I examined the Bible that he knew as a Manichee. He would have rejected the entire Old Testament and a good deal of the New, which the Manichees found unacceptable, either because it quoted the

Old Testament or because it contained other content opposed to their beliefs, such as the genealogies of Christ or the coming of the Holy Spirit on Pentecost. Thirdly, I turned to his use of the Bible against the Manichees where I dealt with the canon of the scriptures, the proper approach to the biblical text, and figurative interpretation of the Bible.

"The Criteria for Figurative Interpretation in St. Augustine" is closely related to the previous article since Ambrose's figurative interpretation of scripture was one of the key factors in Augustine's return to the Catholic Church in 386–387. I examine two criteria that Augustine used for having recourse to a non-literal or figurative interpretation of the biblical text. The first criterion is what I call, following J. Pépin, the absurdity criterion according to which one must have recourse to a figurative interpretation when the literal interpretation of the text leads to absurdity or something unworthy of God. But there is also a second criterion of figurative interpretation, namely, that everything scripture that does not refer to faith and morals must be regarded as figurative. The article examines Augustine's reasons for moving to the second criterion that clearly maximizes the extent of figurative interpretation and points out some of the interpretations to which the maximizing second criterion leads.

"St. Augustine and the Vision of God" originated from my interest in some passages in the early Augustine in which he spoke of some persons who were able to attain in this life a vision of God beyond which no one cannot go even in the hereafter. I found that such statements in Augustine's early works were not simply examples of his initial enthusiasm for Neoplatonism and that he did not abandon such views in his later works. In *De Genesi ad litteram* and in *Epistola* 147 he in fact spelled out the psychology and theology of such a vision of God in the very substance by which he is God, a vision that he thought Moses and Paul enjoyed as well as some of the great Neoplatonist philosophers.

"St. Augustine on the Good Samaritan" examines Augustine's interpretation of the parable of the good Samaritan in which, following many of the other Fathers of the Church, he sees the good Samaritan as Christ and the man left half-dead on the road as the whole human race injured by sin. Although modern exegetes have regarded such a Christological interpretation of the parable as far-fetched, I argue that there is much to be said in favor of the traditional patristic interpretation, which certainly is an interesting way of reading the parable and one thoroughly in accord with the faith. Given the Christological interpretation, the punch line of the parable, "Go and do likewise," really tells us to love our neighbor as Christ has loved us.

"St. Augustine's Use of '*Manens in Se*'" examines Augustine's use of the Wisdom 7:27b, which states that wisdom, "remaining in itself, renews all things." After looking at all the quotations and allusions to the verse that I could find, I concluded that Augustine used the verse most frequently, although not exclusively, in speaking of the Word, which, though it remains immutable in itself, entered into activity in creation and in human history. Although Augustine did not find in Plotinus that the Word of God personally entered human history, he did find in Plotinus that the immutable God, while remaining in himself, could act in the world. Hence, the article illustrates another way in which Plotinus helped Augustine toward an understanding of the God of the Christian faith.

AUGUSTINE AS THEOLOGIAN

The final cluster of articles is more theological than the previous two. "St. Augustine on the Humanity of Christ and Temptation" took its origin from some of the things that Marilyn McCord Adams said in his 1999 Aquinas Lecture, *What Sort of Human Nature? Medieval Philosophy and the Systematics of Christology*, in which she pointed to the varied understanding of Christ's human nature among medieval theologians. At that time I was making translations of Augustine's anti-Pelagian works and was intrigued by some of the things of which Julian accused Augustine. As a result I turned to his use of various biblical texts on Christ's temptations. I found, for example, that Augustine interpreted Christ's words on the cross, "My God, my God, why have you abandoned me?" as something that Christ spoke in the person of his body since he himself, being God, could not have felt abandoned by God. Similarly Julian accused Augustine of a form of Apollinarism because he seemed to make Christ immune from any sort of sexual temptations. I suggest that the human nature that Christ assumed in Augustine's Christology was the human nature that existed in Adam before the fall rather than the human nature in which we are now born after the fall.

"Augustine, Maximinus, and Imagination" originated with my translations of the *Collatio Maximini* and the *Contra Maximinum*, works in which Augustine debated the Arian bishop, Maximinus, and then followed up the debate with two books of further refutation. Maximinus was most probably a Goth and represented the later Homoian Arianism, which acknowledged Christ as God, but as one less than the Father. Augustine accused the Arians of thinking of the Trinity in terms of "carnal thought," that is, they pictured the three persons in bodily terms with the imagination rather than by the intellect. Thus he claimed that they interpreted John 5:19 by imagining the Father as a master craftsman and the Son as his apprentice, who can do nothing he has not seen the Father do. Maximinus's insistence upon sticking with biblical language and his eschewing of all philosophy left him, I argue, with no way to think of God and of the three persons as nonbodily. Hence, he pictured them as one next to the other and distinguished them as greater and lesser. In conclusion I argued that some contemporary theologians who bemoan the Hellenization of Christianity fail to realize the sort of alternative that the Church would have faced without the spiritualist metaphysics that Augustine and others learned from Neoplatonism.

"The Definition of Sacrifice in the *De ciuitate Dei*" examines Augustine's definition of sacrifice, which has been the subject of considerable controversy. In fact one distinguished theologian, namely, Guy de Broglie, has argued that Augustine did not intend to offer a definition of sacrifice in that work and did not offer one. Augustine's claims that "what everyone calls a sacrifice is a sign of the true sacrifice" and that "mercy is the true sacrifice" do seem to call into question the death of Christ on Calvary and the Mass, actions that the Church has consistently called sacrifices. In the article I found that I agreed with the views of Yves de Montcheuil, which puts a more favorable interpretation on Augustine's words. He sees the words of Augustine as a definition of sacrifice and claims that the sacrifice of Calvary is the one universal work of mercy that is represented in the Eucharistic sacrifice and unites redeemed mankind to God. On the other hand, I should perhaps have been more sensitive to Augustine's minimizing of the role of any external signs or realities, including the external sacrifice of Christ's body on Calvary and the sacraments is conferring grace.

"The Image and Likeness of God in St. Augustine's *De Genesi ad litteram liber imperfectus*" examines Augustine's early interpretation of the image of God, one that he soon abandoned. In this early commentary on Genesis, which Augustine had left unfinished, he interpreted

INTRODUCTION

our being made to the image of God as our being made unto the image of Christ who is the Image of God. Augustine then broke off this first literal commentary with the next verse about God creating them male and female. I suggest that it may have been due to the fact that maleness and femaleness have to be understood in terms of the body, while Augustine at that time thought that prior to sin Adam and Eve did not have bodies, although Augustine's stated reason has to do with the plural verb and "our image" indicating that we were made to the image of the Trinity, which is non-bodily.

In conclusion, I hope that the greater availability of these articles published together will be of benefit to students of the thought of Augustine of Hippo who continues to be the Father of the Church who has formed Western Christian thought for the past sixteen centuries and who will surely continue to do so in the years ahead.

AUGUSTINE AS PHILOSOPHER

ULTIMATE REALITY ACCORDING TO AUGUSTINE OF HIPPO

I. AUGUSTINE'S LIFE AND WORKS

Augustine was born on November 13, 354 in the North African town of Thagaste, now Souk Ahras in Algeria, the son of Monica, a Christian, and Patricius, a pagan. He received his early education in Thagaste and then in neighboring Madaura, later moving to the port city of Carthage for more advanced studies where he became a teacher of rhetoric. At Carthage he fell in love with philosophy, encountered intellectual difficulties with Christianity, and abandoned the faith of Monica. In his search for wisdom he became a "hearer" among the Manichees, and he remained for at least nine years in that dualistic gnostic sect, which promised him knowledge without having to believe. In order to find a better teaching situation he moved first to Rome and then to Milan where he came in contact with Ambrose, the bishop, whose preaching offered him some solutions to his problems with the Catholic faith. In Milan he also encountered a group of Christians, including Ambrose, who were strongly influenced by Neoplatonist thought and who brought him into contact with the writings of Plotinus and possibly of Porphyry. These works allowed him to conceive of God and the soul as non-bodily realities and provided him, at least to a large extent, with solutions to his intellectual difficulties with Christianity. Having dismissed his mistress, the mother of his son, Adeodatus, and determined to live a life of celibacy, Augustine was baptized in Milan at the Easter Vigil of 387. Monica, who had followed him to Rome and to Milan, died in the same year while she and Augustine were awaiting at Ostia a ship to return them to Africa. Once back in Africa Augustine founded a monastery at Thagaste and then at Hippo, after he was pressed into ordination to the priesthood in 391. He was consecrated bishop in 395 and succeeded Valerius in 396 as bishop of Hippo where he presided over the church until his death in 430.

Augustine's writings are many and voluminous. Electronic data bases have recently made his four and one half million extant words readily available. In his own *Revisions*, which he wrote shortly before his death, Augustine surveyed his books, amending or defending them as needed, and listed ninety four works. He was still to write more, and he made no mention of his Letters, of which approximately 300 are extant, or of his Homilies and Sermons, of which over 500 have come down to us. His best known writings are his *Confessions*, in which he recounts in the form of a prayer to God his own past life and his return to him, and *The City of God*, which he wrote as a defense of the Christian faith against the pagans in the face of the fall of Rome to Alaric's forces in 410. His *The Trinity* marked a peak in systematic theology that would remain without rival until at least the time of Thomas Aquinas. Augustine's writings were most often products of controversies with various heretical groups, such as the Manichees, the Donatists, the Arians, and the Pelagians. Augustine's many anti-Pelagian works earned his the title: *Doctor Gratiae*—Teacher of Grace. He is commonly recognized as the greatest of the Western Fathers of the Church. Even in his own lifetime St. Jerome, with whom he had once fiercely quarreled, called him "the second founder of the faith."

II. AUGUSTINE AND NEOPLATONISM

Toward the beginning of the twentieth century Prosper Alfaric touched off a storm of protest when he claimed that both morally and intellectually Augustine of Hippo was converted to Neoplatonism in 386 rather than to the Gospel,[1] even adding that, if he had died shortly thereafter, he would have been remembered as a committed Neoplatonist, slightly tinged with Christianity.[2] Others, e.g., Charles Boyer, argued strongly that Augustine became a Christian rather than a Neoplatonist, often minimizing the influence of Plotinus and Porphyry upon his intellectual development.[3] Pierre Courcelle brought the dispute to an end, at least to a large degree, by the discovery that in the

---

1 Prosper Alfari, *L'évolution intellectuelle de saint Augustin: I. Du manichéisme au néoplatonisme* (Paris: Nourry, 1918), p. 399.

2 Ibid., p. 527.

3 See Charles Boyer, Christianisme et Néoplatonisme *dans la formation de saint Augustin* (Paris: G. Beauchesne, 1920), p. 203, and John J. O'Meara, *Saint Augustine. Against the Academics* (Westminster, MD: Newman, 1950), p. 21.

Milanese Church, in which Augustine was baptized by St. Ambrose at the Easter vigil in 387, there was a group of Christians, including their bishop, who were strongly influenced by Neoplatonism so that Augustine could be seen as having been converted both to Neoplatonism and to the Christian faith rather than to one or the other.[4]

That the Neoplatonists strongly influenced Augustine at the time of his Baptism and continued to influence him even in his mature years, as a Christian bishop has been commonly recognized and can be illustrated from such texts as the following. In his earliest surviving work, Augustine reminds Romanianus, his patron and a man he had led to Manichaeism, of how his reading of Cicero's *Hortensius* had, when he was but nineteen, set him afire with the love for philosophy. But thirteen years later, when the books of the Platonists let fall, he adds, "a few drops of oil upon that little flame, they stirred up an incredible blaze—incredible, Romanianus, incredible—perhaps more than you would believe of me. What more can I say? More than I would believe of myself."[5]

His early enthusiasm for Neoplatonism was such that, a few years later in *The True Religion* IV, 7, he did not hesitate to say that, if the great Platonists "could again live this present life with us, they would surely see by whose authority human beings are more readily helped, and with the change of a few words and ideas (*paucis mutatis verbis atque sententiis*) they would become Christians, as several Platonists of recent and our own times have done." As an example of such conversions to the Christian faith, Augustine surely had in mind Marius Victorinus, who translated into Latin Plotinus's *Enneads* and whose conversion to Christianity, described in *Confessions* VIII, served as a model for Augustine's own conversion. If such praise for Neoplatonism can be dismissed as part of Augustine's early enthusiasm for "the books of the Platonists" or "of Plotinus,"[6] his statement in *The City of God* VIII, 5, that "none have come closer to us than the Platonists" must be taken seriously as his mature view.

I have argued elsewhere that the union of Neoplatonism and the Christian faith in Augustine spelled the birth of Christian metaphysics

---

4 Pierre Courcelle, *Recherches sur les "Confessions" de saint Augustin* (Paris: E. de Boccard, 1950), p. 230.

5 *Answer to the Academics* II, ii, 5.

6 *Confessions* VII, ix, 13, and *The Happy Life* I, 4.

in the Latin West.[7] That claim is, I believe, correct, though it needs to be carefully understood. The union of Neoplatonism and Christian faith did not mean for Augustine a mingling of the two such that there resulted a *tertium quid* in which neither preserved its identity. Rather, the Christian faith was always for Augustine the norm or standard in accord with which he adopted elements of Neoplatonism or of what he took to be Neoplatonism, not to dilute or falsify, but to understand the Christian message.[8] Given such necessary qualifications, it was Neoplatonism I contend that provided the framework within which Augustine articulated for himself—and for the Church in the West for centuries to come—an understanding of the Christian faith. In providing that framework, Neoplatonism—at least to a large extent—provided Augustine with his view of what is ultimately real and the source of meaning.

III. A HIERARCHICAL UNIVERSE

As the basis of his presentation of Augustine's view of reality, Vernon Bourke took the three-tiered structure of the universe: "At the top is God, in the middle is the human soul, and at the bottom is the world of bodies."[9] Augustine expressed this hierarchical view in many texts.[10] For example, in *Letter* 18, written in 390 to his friend, Caelestinus, to whom Augustine had sent some of his early anti-Manichaean writings, he describes his three-tiered view of reality as "this small, but precious gem" (*hoc quiddam grande et breve*). At the lowest level there is "a nature that can change in both place and time, such as body." Next comes "a nature that can in no sense change in place, but can change in time, such as soul." Finally, at the top of the hierarchy there is "a nature that cannot change in either place or in time, and that is God."[11]

---

7 Roland J. Teske, "St. Augustine as Philosopher. The Birth of Christian Metaphysics." The Saint Augustine Lecture 1992. *Augustinian Studies* 23 (1992): 7–32, here 20–21.

8 James J. McEvoy, 1992. "Neoplatonism and Christianity: Influence, Syncretism, or Discernment?" in *The Relationship between Neoplatonism and Christianity*, ed. by Thomas Finan and Vincent Twomey (Dublin: Four Courts, 1992), pp. 155–170, here pp. 165–170).

9 Vernon J. Bourke, *Augustine's View of Reality*. The Saint Augustine Lecture 1963 (Villanova: Villanova Press, 1964), p. 3.

10 Ibid., pp. 27–28.

11 *Letter* 18, 2.

For Augustine being clearly has degrees so that some things are more than others. In the same *Letter* 18, he goes on to explain that "everything that we say is is insofar as it remains and insofar as it is one." Thus natures are more in proportion to their sameness or oneness. He adds, "You surely see in this division of natures what is in the highest manner (*summe sit*), what is in the lowest manner and yet is, and what is in the middle, more than the lowest and less than the highest." He further explains, "The highest is beatitude itself; the lowest can be neither happy nor unhappy, but the middle one lives unhappily by turning down toward the lowest and lives happily by conversion to the highest." He adds a brief mention of Christ of the sort, which, taken by itself, would seem to support Alfaric's view, "One who believes Christ does not love the lowest, is not proud over the intermediate, and thereby becomes suited to be happy by clinging to the highest." For the young Augustine this stance toward the hierarchy of sameness seems to sum up the whole task of the Christian's life: "And this is the whole of what we are commanded, admonished, and set afire to do." The idea of a three-tiered universe and the conviction that the human soul attains happiness only by clinging to its God remained basic to Augustine's view of reality from the time of his conversion until his death in 430.

IV. HE WHO IS IN THE HIGHEST MANNER

Augustine's hierarchy in ascending order of bodies, souls, and God is obviously one of decreasing changeability so that the highest is utterly unchanging and unchangeable. The God to whom Augustine comes in his ascent of the mind to God in *Free Choice* II is the immutable Truth, he who truly is (*vere est*),[12] for to be truly is to be immutably. "To be is the name of immutability. For everything that is changed ceases to be what it was and begins to be what it was not. Only he who is not changed has true being, pure being, genuine being."[13] So too, a favorite Augustinian term for God is "the Selfsame"—at once the Psalmist's *Idipsum* and the Platonist's τὸ αὐτόν.[14]

---

12 Roland J. Teske, "The Aim of Augustine's Proof that God Truly Is," *International Philosophical Quarterly* 26 (1986): 253–268, here 262–263)

13 *Sermon* 7, 7.

14 James Swetnam, "A Note on *In Idipsum* in St. Augustine," *The Modern Schoolman* 30 (1953): 328–231.

The simplicity of God, which Augustine understood in Plotinian terms, underlies divine immutability.[15] "There is, then, one Good, which is simple and, for this reason, immutable, namely God."[16] The simplicity of God's nature means "that, insofar as he is said to be something in himself, not in relation to another, he is what he has. Thus he is said to be living in himself, because he has life, and is himself life," with no distinction between what he is and what he has.[17] As simple, he does not have anything that he could lose; "no accident is present in God, because there is nothing that can be changed or lost."[18] Augustine is well aware that the Scripture says that God is "multiple, because he has many qualities in himself, but he is those qualities which he has, and he is all of them, while being one."[19] God exists as simple, "because his being is not one thing and his living another, as if he could be not living. Nor is his knowing one thing and his being happy another, as if he could know without being happy. Rather, what for him is to live, to know, to be happy—that is for him to be."[20] It is especially the simplicity of God that accounts for our inability to think anything worthy of him, though we ought always to think of him, and that accounts for our inability to say anything adequate of him, though we ought always to praise him by speaking well of him (*bene dictio*), that is, by blessing him.[21]

Augustine clearly acknowledges that he learned from the Platonists to think of God and of the soul as non-bodily. He says of himself as late as his first stay in Rome, "I wished to meditate on my God, but I did not know how to think of him except as a vast corporeal mass, for I thought that anything not a body was nothing whatsoever. This was the greatest and almost the sole cause of my error. As a result, I believed that evil is some substance. ..."[22] Shortly afterward, having taken a post in Milan, he heard Ambrose, the bishop of Milan, and Theodorus, a Christian Neoplatonist, speaking of God and the soul as if they were

---

15 W. Gundersdorf von Jess, "La simplicidad de Dios en el pensamiento agustiniano," *Augustinus* 19 (1974): 45–52.

16 *The City of God* XI, 10.

17 Ibid.

18 *The Trinity* V, iv, 5.

19 *The City of God* XI, 10.

20 Ibid. VIII, 6.

21 *The Trinity* V, i, 1.

22 *Confessions* V, x, 19–20.

not bodily. He wrote to Theodorus, "I noticed—often in the words of our priest and at times in yours—that, when one thinks of God, one should think of nothing bodily, and the same holds for the soul, since it is the one thing in the world closest to God."[23] Looking back on his youth from the vantage point of the Christian Neoplatonism he learned in Milan, Augustine admits, "And I had not known that God is a spirit, who does not have members with length and breadth and who does not have any mass. For a mass is smaller in a part than in the whole, and if it is endless, it is smaller in a part marked off in a certain space than in its endless extent. A mass is never whole everywhere, as a spirit is, as God is."[24]

Unlike every bodily mass, which is never whole in all its parts, Augustine's God is omnipresent—not merely in the sense that he is present everywhere, like air extending endlessly, as some have thought, but in the sense that he is present everywhere and present as a whole wherever he is.[25] Hence, Augustine can address his God with the words, "You, most high and most near, most hidden and most present, who do not have some larger members and some smaller, but you are everywhere whole (*ubique totus*), and never confined in place. ..."[26] Though the Christian prays, "Our Father, who art in heaven," Augustine warns that one should not think that God, "who is whole everywhere by his incorporeal presence, is there and not here. ..."[27] So too, in the opening paragraphs of the *Confessions*, Augustine forces his reader to confront the paradoxes of God's omnipresence. He invokes—calls into himself—the God who fills heaven and earth, though, as Augustine says in prayer, "I do exist, and yet would not be, unless you were in me. ... To what place do I call you, since I am in you? Or from what place can you come to me?"[28]

God's absolute immutability implies eternity, not merely in the sense of duration without beginning or end, but in the sense that there is neither past nor future, but only the present in God. As God's omnipresence means that he is whole everywhere (*totus ubique*), his eternity

---

23 *The Happy Life* I, 4.

24 *Confessions* III, vii, 12.

25 *Letter* 118, 4.

26 *Confessions* VI, iii, 4.

27 *Letter* 120, 3.

28 *Confessions* I, ii, 2.

means that he is whole all at once (*totus simul*). "He is, and he truly is, and by reason of the fact that he truly is, he is without beginning or end."[29] While past and future are found in all motion, there is neither past nor future in the truth which remains, "Examine the changes of things and you will find 'Was' and 'Will be.' Think of God, and you will find 'Is,' where 'Was' and 'Will be' cannot be."[30] Or, as he puts it in language no less difficult in Latin than in English, "There is in him only 'Is'; there is no 'Was' and no 'Will be,' since what was is no longer and what will be is not yet, but whatever is in him is only 'Is.'"[31] Not merely was Augustine the first Christian thinker, at least in the Latin West, to come to a philosophically articulated concept of God and the soul as non-bodily, but he was the first—except possibly for Gregory of Nyssa in the East—to come to a concept of divine eternity as *tota simul*, as having neither past nor future, but only the present.[32] And so well did he teach the Latin West to think of God as non-bodily and non-temporal that it is often assumed that these ultimately Neoplatonic doctrines are explicitly contained in the New Testament.[33]

Augustine's God is in himself absolutely immutable; he is unchanging and unchangeable in his being, knowledge, or will. "For, as you are in the fullest sense, you alone know, who are unchangeably, who know unchangeably, who will unchangeably."[34] Yet, he is a God who acts in the world, bringing about newness without any newness in himself, changing other things while remaining in himself unchanged. In his *Confessions* Augustine addresses his God as "immutable, yet changing all things, never new, never old, yet renewing all things ... ever acting, ever at rest, gathering without being in need, filling and protecting, creating, nourishing, perfecting, seeking, though you lack nothing."[35] In fact, Augustine claimed to read in the books of the Platonists that the Son of God "remains unchangeably before and above all times and that souls receive from his fullness so that they might be happy and are

---

29 *Homilies on the Psalms* CXXXIV, 9.

30 *Homilies on the Gospel of John* XXXVIII, 10.

31 *Homilies on the Psalms* CI, sermon 2, 10.

32 Roland J. Teske, "St. Augustine as Philosopher," here 19–20.

33 François Masai, "Les conversions de saint Augustin et les débuts du spiritualisme en Occident," *Moyen âge* 67 (1961): 1–40, here p. 13.

34 *Confessions* XIII, xvi, 19.

35 Ibid. I, iv, 4.

renewed by sharing in the wisdom that remains in itself so that they might be wise."[36] He finds both in words of Scripture concerning Wisdom, which "while remaining in itself, renews all things" (Wis 7:27), and in similar words of Plotinus the doctrine that the ultimate reality can remain immutably in itself, while being the source of change and newness in other things.[37]

Despite the decidedly Neoplatonic features of Augustine's God, it is this same God who is active in the world and has revealed himself in history. When Moses asked the Lord his name, "the Lord said to him, 'I am who am,' and he repeated, 'He who is sent me to you.' He did not say: 'I am God,' or: 'I am the maker of the world,' or: 'I am the creator of all things' ... but only: 'I am who am.'"[38] Augustine interprets the name of God in Exodus 3:14, "He who is," in terms of absolute immutability that makes God unlike any creature: "Perhaps it was," Augustine comments, "much even for Moses, as it is much for us—and far more for us—to understand the meaning of 'I am who am' and 'He who is sent me to you.'"[39] If Moses could not grasp the meaning of "He who is," then much less could the people to whom he was sent. "For," Augustine adds, "what mind can grasp, 'I am who am'?" For this reason, Augustine explains that God, whose proper name is the incomprehensible "He who is," added in his mercy, "I am the God of Abraham, and the God of Isaac, and the God of Jacob."[40] Having said to Moses what he is in himself, he also indicated who he is for us, namely, the God who revealed himself to the Jewish people and in Jesus Christ.

V. WHAT THE NEOPLATONISTS SAW

In *The City of God* VIII, 6, Augustine examines the various philosophical views of God known to him from the ancient world; for him the Platonists surpass all others, inasmuch as

> these philosophers ... saw that God is not a body and, therefore, passed beyond all bodies in their search for God. They saw that whatever is changeable is not the sovereign God and, therefore,

---

36 Ibid. VII, ix, 14.

37 Roland J. Teske, "St. Augustine's Use of '*Manens in Se*,'" *Revue des études augustiniennes* 39 (1993): 291–307.

38 *Homilies on the Gospel of John* XXXVIII, 8.

39 Ibid.

40 Ibid.

passed beyond every soul and all changeable spirits in their search of the sovereign God.

Not merely did these great philosophers ascend to the immutable God, but "they saw that which is."[41] In the books of those philosophers, Augustine tells us, he found that they even saw that God has an only-begotten Son through whom all things were made; "they saw that which is, but they saw it from afar," because in their pride they did not glorify God or give him thanks.[42]

According to Augustine, Plato brought philosophy to its perfection and divided it into three parts: moral, natural, and rational. In these respective parts Plato located "the end of all actions, the cause of all natures, and the light of all reasons."[43] Each of the parts of philosophy had to do with God, for God is the creator of all else, the light of every mind, and the source of human happiness. Augustine tells us that the great Platonists came to know "the true God" as "the author of things, the source of the light of truth, and the bestower of beatitude."[44] Or in other words he claims that the Platonists found in God "the cause of existing, the source of understanding, and the order of living," and points out that these titles correspond to the three divisions of philosophy: natural, rational, and moral.[45] They searched after and found "God without whom no nature subsists, without whom no instruction teaches, without whom no action is profitable." That is, Augustine found—or at least thought he found—in the God of the Neoplatonists "the one God, the author of this universe, who is not only non-bodily above all bodies, but also incorruptible above all souls: our principle, our light, our good."[46] The reason why the Platonists are preferable to all others is that: "they knew God; they found the cause of all that has been made, the light for perceiving the truth, and the fountain for drinking in felicity."[47]

41 Ibid., II, 3.

42 See Goulven Madec, "Connaissance de Dieu et action de grâces. Essai sur les citations de l'*Ép. aux Romains* I, 18–25 dans l'oeuvre de saint Augustin." *Recherches augustiniennes* 2 (1962): 273–309, here pp. 284, 308–309).

43 *The City of God* VIII, 5.

44 Ibid.

45 Ibid. VIII, 4.

46 Ibid. VIII, 10.

47 Ibid.

Further to spell out Augustine's view of ultimate reality and meaning, one can hardly do better, at least if one prescinds from articles of the Christian faith, than to follow the triadic pattern he so often employed in the texts just cited from *The City of God* as a guide to the principal contribution of the Neoplatonists. Hence, let us turn to God as cause of existing, the source of understanding, and the order of living.

A. THE CAUSE OF EXISTING

Despite the doctrine of a necessary emanation of all else from the One that is found in Plotinus, Augustine held that God created the world out of nothing, neither out of himself nor out of some matter that he did not create. In Manichaeism, with which Augustine was associated as a "hearer," or layman, for nine years before the conversion leading to his Baptism in 387, Augustine had known an account of the origin of things and an explanation of the evil in the world that he once found attractive. In that account the good God made the world, but made it out of an evil matter that he himself did not make,[48] while human souls were seen as particles of God—literally divine, because made from the nature of God—trapped in the prisons of their bodies. Augustine came to see that the changes obviously present in human souls as clear evidence that they are not what God is. Writing to Paul Orosius in 415, Augustine says, "I have argued many times against the Manichees that, although the soul is immortal in its own way, it is proved to be changeable for the worse by its failure and for the better by its progress. This argument shows with utter clarity that the soul is not the substance of God."[49] Everything other than God, Augustine saw, was made by God, but made out of nothing. "A creature is said to be from God not in the sense that it has been made from his nature; it is said to be from him for the reason that it has him as the source of its being, not so that it was born from or has proceeded from him, but so that it was created, established, made. ..."[50] Some things God made out of other things that he had created, as in the Genesis account he made the man from the dust of the earth and the woman from the man's rib; other things he made "out of no other thing, that is, from nothing

---

48 *Heresies* XLVI, 4.
49 *To Orosius in Refutation of the Priscillianists and Origenists* I, 1.
50 *The Nature and Origin of the Soul* II, iii, 5.

whatsoever," such as "heaven and earth, or rather the whole matter of this whole earthly mass created with the world."[51]

The influence of Platonism upon Augustine's view of creation, as well as the correction of that view by the rule of faith, is well illustrated by Augustine's discussion of the Platonic ideas in a brief question that was to bear a decisive influence upon the later Middle Ages. As he saw it, the rationality of the created world is guaranteed by the divine ideas in accord with which God created it. Though Plato, Augustine concedes, first used the term, "ideas," the reality was, he suspects, known to other wise men. Regardless of their name—for one can call them "forms" or "species" or "patterns" (*rationes*) in Latin—"the ideas, which are principles, are certain stable and immutable forms or patterns of things; they are not themselves formed and, for this reason, are eternal and existing always in the same way and are contained in the divine mind."[52] God, after all, did not create the universe without reason, and each creature has its own reason or pattern, which must be located in the mind of the creator, since he did not look to a pattern external to himself in creating.

> But if these patterns of all things created or to be created are contained in the divine mind, and nothing can be in the divine mind save what is eternal and immutable, and Plato called these principal patterns ideas, not only are there are ideas, but they are true, because they are eternal and remain the same and immutable.[53]

Hence, it is by participation in these ideas that there comes to be whatever exists.

As the intelligibility of the world is guaranteed by the ideas, in accord with which God creates the universe of creatures, so its goodness follows upon his goodness. In the *Timaeus* 29e Plato said of the Demiurge, "He is good, but one who is good never has any envy whatsoever of anyone." Augustine most probably encountered this theme of the generosity of the good in Plotinus.[54] It is a theme that recurs frequently in Augustine, especially when he discusses why God created

---

51 Ibid.

52 *Eighty-Three Different Questions* 46.

53 Ibid.

54 Du Roy, *L'intelligence de la foi en la trinité selon s. Augustin. Genèse de sa théologie trinitaire jusqu'en 391* (Paris: Etudes augustiniennes, 1966), p. 474.

the world. Though he at times simply answers, "Because he willed to," he at other times answers, "Because he is good."[55] In fact, he appeals to the divine goodness, even to the point that at times it sounds as though, given his goodness, God could not have not created the world and its full panoply of beings from the highest to the lowest.[56] In *The Trinity* XI, v, 8, he says, "God made all things very good, for no other reason than that he himself is supremely good." So too, in *The Literal Meaning of Genesis* IV, xvi, 27, he argues that, if God "could not make good things, he would lack power; if, however, he could and did not, he would have great envy. Hence, because he is almighty and good, he made all things very good." At times Augustine verges toward a Leibnizian optimism. He tell Evodius in *Free Choice* III, v, 13 that

> God, the maker of all good things, has already made anything better that occurs to you with true reason. ... there can be something in the nature of reality that you do not think of with your reason. But there cannot fail to be what you think of with true reason. For you cannot think of something better in creation that has escaped the artisan of creation.

Hence, Augustine says to God in his *Confessions* that things of this world cry out to us that they have been made. "The voice by which they speak is their presence to our senses. And so, you, Lord, who are beautiful made them, for they are beautiful; you who are good made them, for they are good; you who are made them, for they are," and yet compared to God they are not, nor are they good, nor are they beautiful.[57]

B. THE SOURCE OF UNDERSTANDING

As early as his *Soliloquies*, written at Cassiciacum before his Baptism in Milan, Augustine speaks of God as a certain ineffable and incomprehensible light of minds.[58] Augustine conceived of human knowing as a kind of seeing, not a seeing with the eyes of the body, but a seeing

---

55 Robert-Henri Cousineau,, "Creation and Freedom: An Augustinian Problem: 'Quia voluit'? or 'Quia bonus'?" *Recherches augustiniennes* 2 (1963): 253–271.

56 Roland J. Teske, "The Motive for Creation according to Saint Augustine," *The Modern Schoolman* 65 (1988): 245–253.

57 *Confessions* XI, iv, 6.

58 *Soliloquies* I, xiii, 23.

with the eyes of the mind. God, as the light of minds (*lux mentium*), stands to the eyes of the mind as the sun stands to the eyes of the body.[59] As the sun illumines sensible things so that they are visible and the sun is itself visible, so God illumines intelligible things, such as the intellectual disciplines, so that they can be understood by the eyes of the mind, and God himself is intelligible.[60] Augustine tells us that, after reading the books of the Platonists, he entered into himself and saw by the soul's eye an unchangeable light above his mind. "It was not this ordinary light … nor a greater light of the same kind. … Not such was that light, but different, far different from all other lights. … It was above my mind, because it made me, and I was beneath it, because I was made by it. He who knows the truth knows that light."[61] God, the eternal truth, is "the intelligible light in which and by which and through which are intelligibly bright all things which are intelligibly bright."[62]

Just as for bodily seeing one needs eyes that are healthy and open and that look at what is to be seen, so the mind has its own eyes that are made healthy by faith and whose look or gaze is reason.[63] Moreover, as our bodily seeing is impeded by fog or clouds, which prevent our seeing or filter the light, so the eyes of the mind have their own clouds: images or phantasms, that have to be swept away like "pesky flies from the interior eyes." Then, in thinking of God, spiritual people "may become used to the purity of that light, and by it as a witness and judge they may prove that these bodily images rushing upon their inner gazes are utterly false."[64] Once Augustine pleads for a person who can think without images, "Give me someone who can see without any imagining of carnal objects of sight; give me someone who can see that the principle of everything one is the One alone, from which everything one is."[65]

Besides the seeing with the eyes of the body, Augustine distinguishes two further levels of seeing or vision. There is spiritual vision by which we see "not bodies, but likenesses of bodies," that is, images in

---

59 Ibid. I, vi, 12 .

60 Ibid. I, viii, 15 .

61 *Confessions* VII, x, 16.

62 *Soliloquies* I, i, 3.

63 *The Greatness of the Soul* XXVII, 53.

64 *Homilies on the Gospel of John* CII, 4.

65 *The True Religion* XXXIV, 64.

the mind, and there is the intellectual vision by which we see intelligible realities with the eyes of the mind, such as "charity, joy, peace ... and God himself, from whom and through whom and in whom are all things."[66] How we are to understand such a vision of God remains one of the most disputed areas of Augustinian studies, with scholars divided about what it means to see things in God or in the divine light.[67] Though in many texts Augustine seems merely to say that human beings see intelligible things in God in a sense analogous to that in which we see sensible things in the sunlight, that is, by means of light of the sun, at other times he seems to say that we see the divine ideas themselves or see the eternal truth, namely, God himself. For example, in discussing the divine ideas, he comments that only the rational soul among God's creatures "surpasses all things and is next to God, when it is pure" so that, illumined by the intelligible light, it can "see, not through bodily eyes, but through its ... intelligence, those patterns, by whose vision it becomes blessed."[68] So too, he says, "In that eternal truth by which all temporal things have been made, we see by the sight of the mind the form in accord with which we are and in accord with which we do something—either in ourselves or in bodies—with true and right reason."[69] What is clear is that Augustine thought that the divine truth served as the norm or rule by which the truth we attain is judged and that certitude and truth of human knowledge is a participation in the truth, which is God.

C. THE ORDER OF LIVING

As the highest good, God is the source of human happiness. In Cicero's *Hortensius*, a work written as an exhortation to the life of philosophy, which Augustine read at the age of nineteen and which set him afire with the love of wisdom, Augustine read that "we all certainly want to be happy."[70] The statement appears again and again in

---

66 *The Literal Meaning of Genesis* XII, xxiii, 49 and xxiv, 50.

67 Ronald H. Nash, *The Light of the Mind: St. Augustine's Theory of Knowledge* (Lexington: University of Kentucky, 1969), pp. 94–124.

68 *Eighty-Three Different Questions* 46.

69 *The Trinity* IX, vii, 12.

70 *The Happy Life* II, 10.

Augustine's writings,[71] and the desire for happiness is arguably at the very heart of Augustine's thought.[72] In a very early work, *The Happy Life*, Augustine claims that, in order to be happy, one must have what one wants, provided, of course, one wants what is good and has no reason to fear the loss of that good against his will. Hence, only one who has the unchangeable good, namely, God, can be happy, for one who has God can only lose him by willingly turning away from him in sin.

Moral philosophy investigates the highest good to which we refer all we do and which we seek, not for the sake of something else, but for its own sake. Once we have attained it, we seek nothing else for our happiness.[73] Plato, Augustine says, "calls God the highest good; hence, he would have a philosopher be a lover of God. And since philosophy leads to the happy life, one who loves God will be happy in the enjoyment of him."[74] Indeed, Augustine claimed that happiness was the only reason for being a philosopher,[75] and defined happiness as "joy in the truth" (*gaudium de veritate*), the truth, of course, being God himself.[76]

In some of his earliest writings Augustine thought that some few human beings could attain, even in this life, a wisdom that entailed a beatitude, beyond which one could not go even in the next.[77] However, he soon came to a deep appreciation of the wounds that human nature had suffered from sin that left it in need of healing, a healing of the ignorance and weakness that would be complete only in the next life.[78] Though the great Neoplatonists came to the knowledge of the true God, though they saw the goal, saw that which is, they saw it only from afar and scorned the humble way to return to their fatherland, namely, through faith in the cross of Jesus Christ, the one mediator between God and human beings. "They were able to see that which is, but they

---

71 See Werner Bierwaltes,, *Regio Beatitudinis: Augustine's Concept of Happiness*. The St. Augustine Lecture 1980 (Villanova: Villanova University Press, 1981), p. 34).

72 See Etienne Gilson, *The Christian Philosophy of St. Augustine*, tr. L. E. M. Lynch (New York: Random House, 1960), p. 115.

73 *The City of God* VIII, 8.

74 Ibid.

75 Ibid. XIX, 1.

76 *Confessions* X, xxiii, 33.

77 *On Order* II, ix, 26.

78 *Nature and Grace* XIX, 21–XXI, 23 and XXXV, 41.

saw it from afar. They refused to hold to the humility of Christ. They contemned the cross of Christ, the ship on which they might safely come to that which they were able to see from afar."[79] Though they had to cross the sea, they rejected the wood (*lignum*)—the wood of a ship, the wood of the cross. Despite Augustine's harsh criticism in his mature years for the Platonists, who in their pride rejected the way of humility, namely, faith in the humanity of the savior, he never denied the greatness of their achievement: they came to see the God who is. "They were able to see that which is, but they saw it from afar."[80]

Even when he stresses the need for the humble way of faith, which they rejected, he thinks of the relation between faith and vision in a Platonic framework. Twice Augustine cites the words of Plato in *Timaeus* 29c, "As eternity stands to what has come to be, so truth stands to faith."[81] The statement is, Augustine tells us, perfectly true. He is saying that, as the eternal being of God stands to the world of change and becoming, so the vision of the truth stands to faith in temporal events. Though the vision of the eternal truth is the goal, the way to the truth is faith in the humanity of Christ. As Plato's πίστις had as its object what comes to be, so Christian faith is directed toward the temporal events that are the life, death, and resurrection of Jesus. As Plato's ἐπιστήμη had as its object the eternal and really real, so the vision of God, to which the Christian looks forward in hope, will be the contemplation of the eternal being of God. For the Christian, Christ is in his humanity the way, as he is in his divinity the truth. "Because we believe that what had come to be in him has passed over to eternity, so too, when faith has come to the truth, what has come to be in us will also pass over."[82] Even when he was articulating the Christian's participation in the "passing over of the Lord" (*transitus Domini*), Augustine did so within the Platonic categories of temporal becoming and eternal being, of faith in the former to be replaced by vision of the latter.[83] For Christ is at once the way and the truth, both our knowledge as

---

79 *Homilies on the Gospel of John* II, 4.
80 Ibid.
81 *The Trinity* IV, xviii, 24 and *The Agreement of the Evangelists* I, xxxv, 53.
82 *The Trinity* IV, xviii, 24.
83 Roland J. Teske, "The Link between Faith and Time in St. Augustine," in *Augustine: Presbyter Factus Sum*. Collectanea Augustiniana II, ed. by E. Muller, J. Lienhard, and R. Teske (New York: Peter Lang, 1993), pp. 195–206.

the object of faith and our wisdom as the goal. "Christ is, then, our knowledge; the same Christ is our wisdom. He implanted in us faith that concerns temporal things; he himself reveals to us the truth that concerns eternal things." Hence, "it is by him that we go to him," for he is both the way and the truth, both our knowledge and our wisdom.[84]

I have tried to express what Augustine of Hippo held to be the ultimate reality and the source of meaning. I have argued that it is the omnipresent, immutable, and eternal God, who is the author of our being, the light of our minds, and the source of our happiness. I have tried to show that this framework within which Augustine articulated his understanding of the Christian faith was deeply influenced and clearly shaped by the Neoplatonism that he discovered in the Church of Milan, although what he accepted from Platonism and what he rejected was always determined by the rule of faith. I have tried to show that Plotinus and the Platonists remained his intellectual guides throughout his life. Plotinus remained such, in fact, even as the bishop of Hippo faced the approach of death. Possidius, his first biographer, tells us that in 430, the year of his death at the age of 75, as Hippo was threatened by the invading Vandals, Augustine "was comforted by the saying of a certain wise man: 'He is no great man who thinks it a great thing that sticks and stones should fall and that men, who must die, should die.'"[85] The saying is taken from *Ennead* I, 4, 7. Peter Brown adds in comment, "Augustine, the Catholic bishop, will retire to his deathbed with these words of a proud pagan sage"—surely not because Plotinus was a proud man, if indeed he was, but because he was one of those few wise men who saw that which is, albeit from afar.

---

84 *The Trinity* XIII, xix, 24.

85 Brown, *Augustine of Hippo: A Biography* (Berkeley: University of California Press, 1969), p. 425.

AUGUSTINE, FLEW, AND THE FREE WILL DEFENSE

In his recent book, *The Presumption of Atheism and Other Essays*, Antony Flew has an essay entitled, "The Free Will Defence."[1] I read this essay while I was teaching a graduate course on St. Augustine and was dealing with his struggles with the problem of evil in *De libero arbitrio*.[2] I had also been reading at roughly the same time the statements in the last two General Congregations regarding our mission to struggle against atheism.[3] Since Flew's essay presents a clear and strong argument that a set of claims that theists make about God and evil is inconsistent, a paper examining his argument seemed a suitable piece of work to present to Jesuit philosophers. Flew's essay is directed against the version of the free will defense that Alvin Plantinga has developed in his book, *God and Other Minds*.[4] I became convinced that there is a version of the free will defense present in St. Augustine that escapes some, if not all, of the difficulties that Flew finds in Plantinga's version of the argument.

In this paper I shall sketch briefly the version of the free will defense that Flew presents and attacks. Then I shall outline the version of the free will defense that Augustine develops in Book Two of *De libero arbitrio*. Finally, I shall turn to what are, I believe, the crucial points of difference between the two versions and shall try to indicate why the Augustinian version of the argument seems sound. Though I have

---

1 Antony Flew, *The Presumption of Atheism and Other Essays* (New York: Barnes and Noble, 1976), pp. 81–99.

2 Saint Augustine, *On the Free Choice of the Will*, translated by Anna S. Benjamin and L.H. Hackstaff, with an introduction by L.H. Hackstaff (Indianapolis: Bobbs-Merrill, 1964). All subsequent quotations from *De libero arbitrio* will be from this translation, but will indicate the book, chapter, and paragraph numbers from the *Patrologia Latina* text.

3 *Documents of the 31st and 32nd General Congregations of the Society of Jesus*, ed. John W. Padberg, SJ (Saint Louis: The Institute of Jesuit Sources, 1977), pp. 76–80 and 416–417.

4 Alvin Plantinga, *God and Other Minds* (Ithaca: Cornell University Press, 1967), pp. 131–155.

named Augustine in the title of the paper since I started out with his work, I shall also appeal to St. Thomas in the body of the paper, especially where St. Augustine needs further clarification or lacks precision.

I. FLEW'S VERSION OF THE FREE WILL DEFENSE

According to Flew, the free will defense is an attempt to answer the problem of evil; it attempts to show that it can be consistent to maintain that there is a God, that this God is omnipotent, omniscient, and perfectly good, and that there is much evil in his creation. Flew says that, though one usually views this as a problem of reconciling the God hypothesis with recalcitrant external facts, it can also be seen "as one of overcoming an apparent internal inconsistency within the system itself."[5] The first move in the argument is to insist that divine omnipotence does not mean that God can do what is logically impossible.[6] The next step is to claim that "the capacity to choose is a logically necessary precondition of the realization of various high values. ..."[7]

The third step is to claim that God does give at least to men this capacity to choose. The argument then claims that the gift of free will necessarily implies the possibility of choosing what is bad as well as the possibility of choosing what is good, that some or even most human creatures do choose through their own fault what is wrong, and that "all the evil of and consequent upon these wrong choices is ultimately more than offset by the actually achieved sum of these higher goods of which the capacity to choose is the logically necessary condition."[8] The capacity to choose does not entail that any wrong choices are made; yet many wrong choices have been, are being, and will be made. They will be used as the logically necessary foundations of such goods as acts of fortitude or forgiveness which will count as items in the sum of alleged higher values that is supposed to offset the sum of actual evils in the world. The defense is then extended to cover all evils by claiming that all evils in the world directly or indirectly stem from wrong choices. Furthermore, one should also argue that the evils resulting from wrong choices are not unjustly distributed and that the sum of

---

5 Flew, *Presumption*, p. 81.
6 Ibid. Flew here cites St. Thomas, *Summa Theologiae* I, q. 25, a. 4.
7 Ibid.
8 Ibid.

goods outweighs the sum of evils. As Flew sees it, the key to the argument is the claim that "there is a contradiction in the suggestion that God could create a world in which men are able to do either right or what is wrong, but in fact always choose to do what is right."[9]

Flew then turns to the question of compatibilism versus incompatibilism. The basic question regarding free will is not: free will or determinism, but free will and determinism or free will and indeterminism. A compatibilist holds both free will and determinism; an incompatibilist holds either free will or determinism. Flew attacks Plantinga's libertarian incompatibilist position and argues that one cannot be a traditional theist who holds that God creates, conserves, and cooperates with every act of his creatures and also be an incompatibilist who holds that free acts are uncaused. On the other hand, one cannot be a compatibilist and maintain that God is not responsible for the evil choices and their consequences.[10] Hence, Flew conlcudes that, if "the Compatibilist is ultimately right; then the Free Will Defence offers no hope whatsoever of justifying the ways of God to man."[11] If, however, the incompatibilist is correct— and Flew argues that he is not—then the problem is to square libertarian free will with the essentials of theism. For, if we really had libertarian free will, "we should all possess a premise from which we should have to deduce ... that such a Creator does not exist."[12] Thus Flew presents the theist with a dilemma: either compatibilism is true, or incompatibilism is true. If incompatibilism is true, then God escapes the blame for the evil in the world, but cannot be the creator he was thought to be. If compatibilism is true, then God is guilty as charged of all the evil in the world. In any case, God cannot be both perfectly good and creator; hence, the upshot of Flew's examination of the free will defense is the necessary non-existence of the alleged defendant.

---

9 Ibid.

10 Ibid., p. 93. Flew here cites St. Thomas, *Summa contra Gentiles*, III, 67, where Aquinas says, "Every operation ... of anything is traced back to him as its cause." Flew goes on to cite Luther (p. 94) and concludes that both Aquinas and Luther were compatibilists and that "the nightmare of the Great Manipulator is not ... the peculiarity of Calvin and Calvinism; but a necessary and immediate consequence of the essential theist doctrine of Divine creation" (p. 96).

11 Ibid.

12 Ibid.

Before turning to Augustine's version of the free will defense, some preliminary remarks on Flew's argument are in order. First of all, I agree with Flew that to extend the argument to cover all evils in the world involves some bold factual postulations. I do not know how one might plausibly argue that all the admitted evils in the world are directly or indirectly the results of wrong choices made by creatures. Secondly, even in cases where certain evils can be shown to be directly or indirectly consequences of the wrong choices of creatures, I do not know how one might argue that all the resultant evils are justly distributed. Thirdly, it follows that the free will defense, as far as I can see, cannot be a complete answer to the problem of evil. If the free will defense is going to be to any extent a correct answer to the problem of evil, it will be at most a partial answer.

Furthermore, if libertarian free will means that the act that is said to be free is an uncaused act, then Flew is, I believe, correct in maintaining that libertarian free will is incompatible with an essential tenet of theism. Within the context of traditional theism, to say that God is not the cause of human freedom or human free acts is to say that human freedom or human free acts do not exist.[13] For theism clearly maintains that God creates and conserves all that exists apart from himself and that he cooperates with every action of every creature.[14] To say that a free act is an uncaused act, as Hume has pointed out, leaves no one responsible for the act—neither a human nor a divine cause or agent.[15] Moreover, if the free act is uncaused and yet the cause of other events, it is an uncaused cause that would provide the premise from which one would have to deduce that such a creator as theists claim to exist does not exist.[16] This move, of course, sharpens the problem that a theist must face: If God is the cause of all that exists apart from himself, then how can one maintain that he is not the cause of sin and other evils within his creation?

---

13 Gerard Smith, SJ, *Freedom in Molina* (Chicago: Loyola University Press, 1966), p. 225. "And to say that God does not cause freedom or that there is no freedom is to say pretty much the same thing."

14 Aside from the texts to which Flew refers, namely, SCG III, 67 and 88–89, see also S.T. I, q. 104, a. 2 and q.105, a. 4 and a. 5.

15 David Hume, *An Enquiry concerning Human Understanding*, ed. L. A. Selby-Bigge, 2nd ed. (Oxford: Clarendon Press, 1902), Section VIII, Part II, pp. 98–99.

16 Flew, *Presumption*, p. 99.

And this is the question that Evodius raises for Augustine at the beginning of Book One of *De libero arbitrio*: "Tell me, please, whether God is not the cause of evil?"[17]

II. AUGUSTINE'S VERSION OF THE FREE WILL DEFENSE

At the beginning of Book One of *De libero arbitrio*, Augustine distinguishes two senses of evil. We speak of someone doing evil and of someone suffering evil. The Augustinian version of the free will defense is directly concerned only with doing evil, though we do sometimes suffer evil as a result of having done evil.[18] By the end of Book One Augustine has settled for himself that "we commit evil through the free choice of the will"[19] He has given a preliminary definition of what it is to do evil, namely, to neglect eternal things and to follow temporal things. "All sins are included under this one class: when someone is turned away from divine things that are truly everlasting, toward things that change and are uncertain."[20] Furthermore, nothing lies more within the power of the will than the will itself.[21] A good will, i.e., "a will by which we seek to live rightly and honorably and to come to the highest wisdom," lies in the power of our will.[22] Furthermore, a good will is something "more excellent than all the goods not in our power ...."[23] One who is a lover of his own good will possesses the four virtues of prudence, fortitude, temperance, and justice and will enjoy the happy life.[24] There remains, however, at the end of Book

---

17 Augustine, *De libero arbitrio* I, 1, 1.

18 Ibid. Thus Augustine will say that we suffer unhappiness as a result of doing evil. See *Confessions* VII, 3, 5. Similarly Aquinas distinguishes *malum culpae* and *malum poenae* in relation to the will; see S.T. I, q. 48, a. 5.

19 *De libero arbitrio* I, 16, 35.

20 Ibid.

21 Ibid. I, 12, 26.

22 Ibid. I, 12, 25 and 26.

23 Ibid. I, 12, 26. Augustine's claim about the excellence of a good will recalls Kant's similar claim. See Immanuel Kant, *Fundamental Principles of the Metaphysic of Morals*, 11.

24 *De libero arbitrio* I, 13, 20. The happiness of which Augustine speaks is something that is attained in this life. Indeed, in the earlier *De ordine* II, 9, 26, he spoke of an intellectual contemplation of God that is attainable by

One the question "whether free will ... ought to have been given to us by him who made us."[25] Since the possession of free will is a necessary condition for our being able to do evil or to sin, why is God not the cause of our doing evil?

At the beginning of Book Two, Evodius asks "why God gave man free choice of the will, since if he had not received it he would not be able to sin."[26] If God has given man free will for acting rightly, then man should not be able to use it to sin.[27] Hence, there is the prior question: Is free will a good gift or is it a gift from God?[28] Though Evodius believes that God gave us free will and that it is therefore a good gift, Augustine insists that "we want to know and understand what we believe."[29] Hence, he sets out to prove that God exists, that all things insofar as they are good are from God, and that free will is a good.[30]

Augustine's argument for the existence of God is long and technical as well as beyond the scope of this paper. It is, however, important for this paper to see that Augustine insisted on establishing by reason the existence of God as the source of every good before tackling the question of why God is not the cause of our doing evil. For, once he has proved that God exists, he has a fixed point of reference and is not dealing merely with the internal consistency of a set of statements.[31] Moreover, through his own intellectual struggle with the question of evil, Augustine found that before one can answer the question, whence

---

those who have undergone the proper philosophical *disciplina* and cannot be surpassed even after this life.

25 *De libero arbitrio* I, 16, 35.

26 Ibid. II, 1, 1.

27 Ibid. II, 2, 4.

28 Ibid.

29 Ibid. II, 2, 6.

30 Ibid. II, 3, 7.

31 This point is, I believe, extremely important. For, first of all, if one is dealing with a set of claims that seem inconsistent, one can alleviate the inconsistency by rejecting any one of the claims. If one is not committed to the theistic claims about God, it will seem easiest to reject some or all of those claims. But what is more important is that the view that evil is a privation of good seems to be a direct consequence of the theistic view of God as infinite creator of all else. Hence, if Augustine establishes that God exists and is the source of all else, then evil cannot be something positive.

is evil, one must answer the prior question, what is evil.[32] And the prior question was one that he could not answer until he was able to conceive of God as an infinite, immutable spiritual substance.[33] It was only after he came to the concept of God as spiritual substance that he could see that evil is not a substance, but a privation of good.[34] Hence, the concept of God as immutable truth and wisdom that can be shared in common by all rational beings without becoming proper to any rational being and without being changed by the rational beings that share it is crucial to the answer to the problem of evil.[35] For, once God is conceived as an infinite spiritual substance and creator, it follows that evil cannot be a positive reality.

Of almost equal importance to Augustine's version of the free will defense is his view of the created world as hierarchical. There are within the world things that merely exist, but do not live or understand, and there are things that exist and live, but do not understand. Finally, there are things that exist, live, and understand, such as, the soul of man. The latter sort of things that exist, live, and understand are more perfect than things that lack either understanding or life.[36] There is also a hierarchy within man of cognitive activities. The common or interior sense is superior to the five bodily senses, and reason or un-

---

32 *De libero arbitrio* I, 3, 6. See also *De natura boni* 4: "Proinde cum quaeritur unde sit malum, prius quaerendum est quid sit malum." So too when Augustine says that he sought in an evil way the answer to the question, whence is evil, the *male quaerebam* would seem to refer to his asking the wrong question first. *Confessions* VII, 5, 7.

33 In *Confessions* V, 10, 19–20, Augustine says, "I thought that anything not a body was nothing whatsoever. This was the greatest and almost the sole cause of my inevitable error." He then adds: "As a result, I believed that evil is some such substance. ..."

34 "For if I were only able to conceive a spiritual substance, then forthwith all those stratagems [of the Manichees] would be foiled and cast out of my mind. But this I was unable to do" (*Confessions* V, 14, 25).

35 The concept of God as a spiritual substance developed in Book Two of *De libero arbitrio* is equally as important to Augustine's aim as is the proof that God exists. Augustine never doubted the existence of God; his problems stemmed rather from his inability to conceive of a spiritual substance. For Augustine's dependence upon Plotinus in this crucial section of Book Two see: Robert J. O'Connell, SJ, *Augustine's Early Theory of Man, A.D. 386–391* (Cambridge: Harvard University Press, 1968), pp. 52–57.

36 *De libero arbitio* II, 3, 7.

derstanding is superior to the inner sense. Reason, the "head or eye of the soul," is the most noble part of man.[37] Augustine then argues that, if we can find something that not only exists, but is superior to our reason, that will be God. Though Evodius objects that God is "rather that to whom nothing is superior," Augustine replies that "if you find that there is nothing superior to our reason except what is eternal and immutable," then either that will be God or, if there is any-thing superior, it will be God.[38] Thus, the Augustinian God is immutable truth and wisdom in accord with which we judge, but about which we do not judge. All creatures are mutable, though there is no creature superior in nature to the rational soul of man.

Just as there is a hierarchy of beings in the Augustinian world and a hierarchy in human knowing, so there is within man another hierarchy of goods. There are the least goods or bodily goods without which man can live rightly. For example, one can still live rightly without eyes or without a limb, though the absence of eyes or of a limb in man is obviously a great evil. There are also within man the great goods by which man cannot live wrongly. These great goods are the virtues. For example, through justice one cannot live wrongly; such goods cannot be used wrongly precisely because "the very action of a virtue is the good use of those things we can also use for evil."[39] However, there are also intermediate goods without which one cannot live rightly, though, like the least goods, they can be used wrongly. Among these intermediate goods is free choice of the will. Thus, though free choice of the will is a necessary condition for doing evil or sinning, it is also a necessary condition for acting rightly.[40] Hence, free will is a good and is a greater good than those goods without which a man can live rightly, though it is a lesser good than the great goods by which a man cannot live wrongly.

When the will clings to the immutable good that is common to all, i.e., to God who is the highest good, then man lives a happy life. For happiness is "that disposition of the spirit which clings to the im-

---

37 Ibid. II, 6, 13.

38 Ibid. II, 6, 14.

39 Ibid. II, 19, 50; also II, 18, 48–50.

40 What is significant in Augustine's argument is that acting rightly or acting wrongly is a matter of acts of the will, not external actions. The goodness or evil of external actions derives from the goodness or evil of the will.

mutable goods" and "is man's proper and primary good."[41] Each man's happiness is his own good, but is attained only through clinging to the highest good common to all. In happiness lie all the virtues that man cannot use wrongly and that are the great goods proper to each man. Thus, the will, an intermediate good, obtains the first good and the great goods proper to each man, i.e., happiness and the virtues, by clinging to the common and immutable goods, truth and wisdom. Hence, free choice of the will is a necessary condition of man's attaining his proper and primary good and the great goods, the virtues.[42] Thus Augustine argues that the gift of free will is a necessary condition for the realization of other goods of great value.

On the other hand, by turning from immutable and common goods to its own private good or to some external goods or to some good lower than itself, the will sins. The will turns to its own private good when it desires to be its own master; it turns to external goods when it busies itself with the private affairs of others or with whatever is of no concern to it; it turns to goods lower than itself when it loves bodily pleasures. Thus Augustine's revised definition of sin includes pride, curiosity, and lust.[43] But what the will turns toward when it sins, namely, its own private good, the goods of others, or lower goods, are nonetheless all goods. So too the will itself is a good, though an intermediate good. "Evil is a turning away from immutable goods and a turning toward changeable goods. This turning away (*aversio*) and turning toward (*conversio*) result in the just punishment of unhappiness, because they are committed, not under compulsion, but voluntarily."[44]

Though the free will itself is a good and though what the sinner turns toward are goods, yet the movement of the will from an immutable good to a changeable one, i.e., the movement of the will away from God, is a sin and is evil. Since God cannot be the cause of sin, what is the origin of this movement?[45] Augustine says that, if he answers that he does not know, Evodius may be disappointed. "Yet that

---

41 *De libero arbitio* II, 19, 52.

42 Ibid.

43 Ibid. II, 19, 53.

44 Ibid.

45 Ibid. II, 20, 54.

would be the truth, for that which is nothing cannot be known."[46] The movement of the will away from God is a defective movement, and every defect comes from nothing.[47] Yet the defect is voluntary and, hence, lies within our power.[48]

The turning of the will from God to some lesser good is a defective or disordered movement; as the willing of a good, it is good, but as deficient and disordered, it is evil, The deficiency and disorder is a privation of direction and order that should be there. Once the evil that we do is seen to be rooted in a deficient or disordered willing, the origin of sinful willing does not require a positive evil cause.[49]

Hence, Augustine's version of the free will defense deals with the evil that we do. The evil that we do is voluntary. Sin lies in the movement of the will away from God toward lesser goods. However, free will is itself a good, though an intermediate good. Though it is a necessary condition of our doing evil, it is also a necessary condition of our living rightly, of clinging to God, the highest and common good of man, and of obtaining happiness, man's highest proper good, as well as the great goods, the virtues. Consequently, in giving us free choice of the will, God has given us a good gift. The evil of sin, of a movement of the will away from God, is a defective movement which, though voluntary, has no positive cause of its defectiveness or disorderedness. Hence, God cannot be its cause. Therefore, though without free will we would not be able to sin, God is not to be blamed for giving us free will.

At the beginning of this paper, I said that I would focus upon what I believe are the crucial points of difference between the two versions of the free will defense after I had indicated the main outlines of the two versions. What I see as the crucial points of difference can perhaps best be dealt with under three headings: divine goodness, moral goodness and evil, and free choice and causes.

---

46 Ibid.

47 Ibid.

48 Ibid.

49 For an exposition of Aguinas' further development and clarification of Augustine's doctrine, see Jacques Maritain, *St. Thomas and the Problem of Evil* (Milwaukee: Marquette University Press, 1942), pp. 22ff.

III. DIVINE GOODNESS

One of the main points of difference between the two versions of the free will defense lies in the different views of divine goodness. As we have seen, Augustine's argument intends to show that the gift of free-will is a good. Though it is not the greatest good of man, free will is a necessary condition of obtaining man's greatest good. Though it is through free will that we sin, our willing is within our power so that we can will rightly or wrongly. If willing rightly or wrongly is within our power, then it is we who are to blame if we will wrongly. Whether God could have given us a better sort of freedom by which we would as a matter of fact always will rightly is a question that Augustine does not raise within the context of the free will defense. Yet within the version of the free will defense that Flew uses, there is implicit the claim that, if God is to be all good, then he ought to have made man so that he always chooses to do what is right, unless, of course, it is logically impossible for God to have done so. More simply put, the version of the free will defense that Flew examines claims that God's goodness entails that the goodness of God's creation be limited only by logical impossibility, that the world be the best that is possible. Augustine, on the other hand, is content to have argued that creation is good and that free will is a good.

The key to the version of the free will defense that Flew uses is that "there is a contradiction in the suggestion that God could create a world in which men are able to do either what is right or what is wrong, but in fact always choose to do what is right."[50] That is, it is supposed to be logically impossible for God to create free creatures who always choose to do what is right, i.e., who freely, but always choose not to sin. The reasoning behind this position would seem to be that God can do whatever is not logically impossible if he is omnipotent and that a world in which creatures freely, but always choose to do what is right is a better world than a world in which creatures sometimes choose to do what is wrong. Therefore, in creating the latter sort of world, God would have chosen a world less good than is consistent with his being all good, unless the former sort of world were an impossible one. But to fail to choose to create the best sort of world, when one can, is a failure in goodness. Hence, to maintain both that God is omnipotent and that he is all good, one has to maintain that a world in which men

---

50 Flew, *Presumption*, p. 82.

freely and always choose what is right is not logically possible. If such a world is not logically possible, then God can be both omnipotent and all good.

In his recent book, *The God of the Philosophers*, Anthony Kenny, in a chapter entitled, "Omnipotence and Goodness," suggests that "the dispute between those, who like Abelard and Leibniz, think that God must have chosen the best world, and those who, like Aquinas, think that God must have chosen a good world but could have chosen other better ones" reflects a dispute in ethics between "partisans of the right and partisans of the good."[51] He argues that those who maintain that an all-good God must have chosen the best possible world are operating with a criterion of morality that claims that in any given situation there is only one right choice, usually, the choice that produces the optimal results or most felicific consequences. Within such a view a choice of a lesser good is a failure in goodness. However, in other moral perspectives, for example, in a morality of law, one is obligated to avoid evil and to choose a good, and in most situations there are more good choices than one available. Thus he argues that "the morality by which Abelard and Leibniz judge the divinity is a morality of rightness, not of goodness."[52] And a morality of rightness goes hand in hand with some form of consequentialism, which has an easier time justifying evil as a means toward good.[53] Now it seems to me that the version of the free will defense that Flew employs does involve the view that God must choose the one right course of action, namely, the action that produces the best possible world. So too, it seems that in Flew's version moral evil is justified by the larger resultant sum of higher goods.[54] Within a law-like morality, which is much more typical of the Christian tradition, moral goodness entails that one choose one among the (usually) many good actions available. However, such a morality cannot justify evil means by good ends.[55] Kenny leaves the resolution of the theologi-

---

51 Anthony Kenny, *The God of the Philosophers* (Oxford: Clarendon Press, 1979), p. 115.

52 Ibid., p. 116.

53 Ibid.

54 Flew, *Presumption*, p. 82.

55 Kenny, *God*, pp. 115–116.

cal dispute to moral philosophers for its resolution.[56] Though his brief history of the dispute about divine benevolence and its relation to different views of morality is illuminating, it does not settle the issue, and it does not get to the root of the matter.

To the best of my knowledge Augustine never argued that this world was the best possible world or that the goodness of God required that he create the best possible world. Augustine did argue that this world was good, that each nature was good, that there is a hierarchy of goods in this world, and that the totality was very good.[57] Aquinas clearly thought that this world is not the best possible and that God could have made another world better than this one.[58] He argues that the goodness of anything is twofold. There is, first, its essential goodness. In this sense, to be rational is of the essence of man. With respect to this sort of goodness, God cannot make something better than it is, though he could make something else better than it.[59] There is another goodness that lies outside of the essence of a thing. In this sense, to be virtuous or to be wise is a good of man. With respect to such a good, God can make things he has made better than he has made them.[60] If one dispenses with this distinction, one can simply say that God can make another thing better than anything that he has made. Yet God cannot create in a better way than he has, since he creates with his infinite goodness and wisdom, though he can create better things than he does.[61] This universe, given the beings that it contains, could not be better, though God could make other beings or add more beings to those he has made so that there would be another and better universe.[62] In answering an objection that, if God could make better things than he made and did not will to do so, he was mean (*invidus*), Aquinas simply answers that it does not belong to any creature to have

---

56 Ibid., p. 117. "... so here we may leave the theological problem to wait on the progress of moral philosophy."
57 *Confessions* VII, 12, 18.
58 S.T. I, q. 25, a. 6 ad 3um.
59 Ibid., corpus.
60 Ibid.
61 Ibid., ad 1um.
62 Ibid., ad 3um.

been made better than God has made it.[63] Hence, in Aquinas' view God could have made a better world than he has made; he could have made men wiser and more virtuous than they are. He could have made men at least less sinful, if not sinless.[64] However, what God has made is good, and the fact that sin and other evils exist is not seen by Aquinas as inconsistent with God's goodness or benevolence, even though God could have created another and better world.

If God had to create the best possible world if he created a world at all, then God is free in the sense that he could create or not create, but he is not free in the sense of being able to create this or that world. Aquinas held that God is not necessitated in creating, for any creature is a finite good and, as such, cannot necessitate God's will. "Since God's goodness is perfect and can exist without other things, since no perfection is added to him from other things, it follows that it is not absolutely necessary that he will things other than himself."[65] And Aquinas adds, "With respect to those things which he does not will necessarily, he has free choice."[66] God necessarily wills, according to Aquinas, his own infinite goodness; however, no finite good is able to necessitate God's will. However, if God had to create the best possible world, he would have only the freedom to will or not to will that world; he would not have freedom of choice to will this world or that world. If he is to create a world, he would be necessitated to create that one world that is the best possible world. It would follow that, given God's decision to create, the only world he could create is that world which is the best. That world then would impose some necessity upon God. He would be determined by the goodness of the world that is the best possible so that he could create no other. Hence, this position would seem to make God dependent upon something other than himself and would remove freedom of choice from God. If God is dependent upon something other than himself, then he cannot be the infinitely perfect God of theism. And if God does not have freedom

---

63 Ibid., ad 2um: "non est autem de ratione creaturae alicuius, quod sit melior quam a Deo facta est."

64 Indeed faith tells us of at least one human person who did not sin, though that person did not lose her free will. What God did in one case is certainly not logically impossible in that case or in others.

65 S.T. I, q. 19, a. 3.

66 S.T. I, q. 19, a. 10.

of choice, then he would lack a perfection that human persons have. Or it would seem that human freedom would not involve freedom of choice.[67] For it would not seem that God could give to his creatures a perfection that he himself lacked.

IV. MORAL GOODNESS AND MORAL EVIL

The different views of divine goodness operative in the two versions of the free will defense are reflected in their views of moral goodness and moral evil in human actions. According to Plantinga, moral evil is "the evil that results from human choice or volition," and physical evil is "that which does not."[68] Thus, "suffering resulting from human cruelty would be moral evil," but "suffering due to an earthquake ... would be physical evil."[69] For Plantinga and Flew moral evil, it would seem, lies primarily in the results of choices and volitions, i.e., it lies in the actions chosen and the consequences of those actions. There are at least three elements present: 1) the choice and/or volition, 2) the action resulting from the choice and/or volition, and 3) the results of the action. Though Plantinga seems to speak of moral evil as the result of choice and volition, Flew speaks of the evil of choices and the actions resulting from choices.[70] However, moral evil in their version of the free will defense seems to lie primarily in the action and its results; whereas, for Augustine and Aquinas moral evil lies primarily in the act of the will.[71] To avoid the confusion of speaking of two senses of moral evil, I shall use 'sin' to refer to moral evil in the Augustinian and Thomistic sense.

---

67 If God does not have free choice, then either his creatures cannot have it or it is not a perfection, but a limitation. Descartes, for example, regarded liberty of indifference as an imperfect form of freedom; hence, God would not have such freedom. See Descartes, *Meditations* IV; HR I, 175. However, if one regards freedom of choice as a perfection, then an all perfect God must have it and, as creator, could give it to some of his creatures.

68 Plantinga, *God*, pp. 131–132.

69 Ibid., p. 132.

70 Flew, *Presumption*, p. 82.

71 "At every point in the discussion he insists on the fact that it is not the external action of the body which is essentially sinful, but the inner intention of the will." Vernon J. Bourke, *Augustine's Quest for Wisdom* (Milwaukee: Bruce, 1945), p. 93. See also, S.T. I-II, q. 20, a. 1.

Hence, in Flew's version of the free will defense the aim is to defend the goodness and omnipotence of God, given a world in which moral evil lies primarily in the results of human choices. Hence, it is essential to such a version of the free will defense to show not merely that God could not have made men who were free and who did not do evil, but also that the evil resulting from wrong choices is outweighed by the sum of higher goods. Just as in assessing the divine goodness a consequentialist ethical norm was used, so too in assessing human choices it is the consequences that count. On the other hand, for Augustine and Aquinas moral goodness or sin lies primarily in the act of the will, and the goodness or evil of the external action is derivative from the act of the will. The Augustinian version of the free will defense attempts to show that God's gift of free will is a good gift even though it is through free will that we are able to sin. The evil that humans suffer requires another sort of argument.

However, this fact does not lessen the problem for Augustine. Sin, like any evil, is a privation of a good. However, a privation always is in a subject that is good. Evil as a privation is parasitic upon a good, and the degree of evil corresponds to the degree of good in which the evil exists. As Maritain has said,

> The more powerful this good is, the more powerful evil will be—not by virtue of itself, but by virtue of this good. That is why no evil is more powerful than that of the fallen angel. If evil appears so powerful in the world of today, this is because the good it preys upon is the very spirit of man.[72]

The evil of sin that lies in the free will of man is consequently the greatest. As the rational soul of man for Augustine is next to God in ontological perfection, so the evil of man's will is the greatest of evils. On the other hand, the goodness of a good will that clings to God and contains all the virtues is the greatest of created goods. Thus for Augustine the free will defense does not involve a calculus of consequences in accord with which the sum of higher goods must outweigh the sum of evils. Without free choice of the will there would not be the good will that clings to God, and that will is man's greatest proper good, even though it is through free will that man can turn away from God through sin—the greatest of evils.

---

72 Maritain, *Problem*, pp. 2–3.

So too Aquinas sees the evil of sin (*malum culpae*) as depriving the will of order toward the divine goodness. For that reason God does not will the evil of sin.[73] Indeed, it is impossible for God to will the evil of sin, for he necessarily wills his own goodness and to sin is to turn away from that goodness.[74] Thus sin for Aquinas is directly opposed to the uncreated goodness that is God and not merely to some created good.[75] Though God can will natural evils and the evil of punishment insofar as they are connected with the good of the order of the universe or with justice, God cannot will at all the evil of sin. He does not will the evil of sin in itself, for that would mean that God sins, which is logically impossible. He does not will the evil of sin *per accidens*, because, as directly opposed to the divine goodness, sin cannot be a means to a greater good. Nor is there some good that God wills that necessarily entails that sin occur. To say that God does not will sin in itself or *per accidens* and that he does not will that sin not occur is to say that he permits that sin occur.

Perhaps it sounds old-fashioned to try to maintain that the greatest of evils is sin or the perversity of a will turned away from God and that the greatest of goods is a will clinging to God in love. However, within a hierarchical universe and within a world created by a God who is wisdom and truth and love, it can hardly be otherwise.

V. FREE WILL AND CAUSES

Flew holds a compatibilist position and claims that most classical philosophers and theologians did so as well.[76] That is, he holds both determinism and free will. If determinism means that choices and actions are caused, then it is true that Augustine and Aquinas are determinists. If libertarian free will is taken to mean that a free choice or volition is an uncaused cause, then Aquinas at least would not share the libertarian position. Flew is, I believe, quite correct in maintaining

---

73 S.T. I, q. 19, a. 9.

74 S.T. I, q. 19, a. 10 ad 2um.

75 S.T. I, q. 48, a. 6: "Malum vero culpae opponitur proprie ipsi bono increato: contrariatur enim impletioni divinae voluntatis, et divino amori quo bonum divimun in seipso amatur: et non solum secundum quod participatur a creatura."

76 Flew, *Presumption*, p. 96.

that a theist ought to maintain, if he is consistent, that free human choices and volitions are caused by God.

Flew distinguished between what he calls motions and movings, i.e., between cases where my arm is moved, though I do not move it—a motion, and cases where I move my arm—a moving. "All movings are actions or parts of actions; all action involves moving or abstentions from moving; while choice too surely has to be understood by reference to actions or possibilities of actions."[77] Given this distinction, one can furthermore maintain that "people could usually—indeed, if we take the word 'do' strictly, could always—do other than they do do."[78] He further insists that, if someone claims that one of the social sciences has shown that no one ever can do other than he does, then either he has misread his source or the discipline in question is in error.[79]

Plantinga, on the other hand, defines determinism so that the possibility of alternative action is precluded. "To say of Jones' action A that it is *causally determined* is to say that the action is question has causes and that given these causes, Jones could not have refrained from doing A."[80] The sense of 'cause' that Plantinga employs makes the action inevitable given the causes. Flew regards this as the normal sense of cause when one is speaking of causing inanimate objects and some brutes. However, when we are speaking of causing someone to do something, we do not mean that the action we cause another person to perform is one that he could not have helped performing. In the second sense of 'cause' what "is caused is the free and deliberate act of a conscious and responsible agent, and 'causing him to do it' means affording him a motive for doing it."[81] In this sense, we cause students to do assignments and at least sometimes to turn them in on time. But when we cause someone to do something by giving him a motive for acting, we do not deprive him of the ability to do otherwise. Indeed, our presenting him with a motive presupposes that he can do otherwise, even though some motives are such that he might say, "I had no choice." Yet even in such a case where the caused agent might claim that he had no choice,

---

77 Ibid.

78 Ibid.

79 Ibid.

80 Plantinga, *God*, p. 133.

81 R. G. Collingwood, *An Essay on Metaphysics* (Oxford: Clarendon Press,1940), p. 285, quoted from Flew, *Presumption*, p. 98.

in a fundamental sense he did have a choice though the alternative might not have been what a reasonable person would have chosen.

When Flew turns to the question of how God causes our choices and actions, he finds that the first sense of 'cause' is inapplicable, for a cause in that sense would deny the obvious realities of choice and action. The second sense of 'cause' will, however, not do either, for causing in the second sense is immediately discernible by the motivated agent. Hence, Flew looks for a third sense of 'cause.' He suggests that "by direct physiological manipulation" God might "ensure that someone performs whatever actions ... [He] determines."[82] The actions of this creature would still be genuine actions so that the manipulated person could in a fundamental sense have done otherwise.[83] But God would be the Great Manipulator who by means of physiological changes causes all human choices and actions. However, if God causes all human choices and actions in this fashion, he is surely the one to be blamed for any wrong choices and actions. And the morality of the situation is even more grotesque since he is also judge, jury, and executioner.[84]

Flew's argument, of course, fails if there is another sense of 'cause,' besides the three senses that he has examined. However, before turning to another sense of 'cause,' let us see whether the third sense will do. Even though the manipulated agent would not be conscious of the divine causality that causes his choices and actions, it would seem that such physiological changes would render the choices and actions inevitable. If through such physiological manipulations God is going to ensure that certain choices and actions take place, then, given the changes effected by divine manipulation, the choices and actions are inevitable. Indeed, there would seem to be no difference between the first sense of 'cause' that Flew rejects because it runs against the known facts of human choices and actions and the third sense of 'cause.' For, given the effects of the divine manipulation upon the agent, he could not choose or do otherwise than he does. Certainly, our will would not be in our power, as Augustine claims, nor would we be masters of our

---

82 Flew, *Presumption*, p. 99.

83 Ibid. As I understand this claim, the agent could have done otherwise if he had chosen to do otherwise, and he could have chosen to do otherwise if he had been otherwise manipulated.

84 Ibid., pp. 96 and 99.

actions, in Aquinas' terms. And with advances in physiology we might well count on evidence that our actions are inevitable to be forthcoming.

Flew understands choices by reference to actions and possibilities of actions. With Aquinas it seems that just the opposite is true. Actions are understood as free or not with reference to choice. Furthermore, for Aquinas human choices have causes. The will is necessarily inclined toward the good and with necessity tends toward happiness which consists in the possession of God.[85] However, precisely because the will is necessitated toward the good in general or toward God, it is not necessitated with respect to any finite good. With respect to means toward an end, the will is free; yet there have to be finite goods perceived as means to an end grasped as unconditionally good before the will can after rational deliberation choose one of the finite goods. As in cases where we cause someone to do something by presenting him with a motive, so in other cases a human agent can motivate himself through the discovery of alternative means to a good that for him is perceived as unqualifiedly good. Just as the motives we present to others do not ensure that the others will choose and act accordingly, so not every motive or finite good that an agent discovers for himself ensures his choice of that good. Since free choices are not uncaused insofar as there must be motives for a rational choice, a free choice is not an uncaused act. And if libertarian free will means that the free act is uncaused, then Aquinas did not hold libertarian free will. On the other hand, if to be caused means to be rendered inevitable, given certain prior events or changes, then he denied that the will is caused in that sense. A necessary condition for a free act of the will is that there be no temporally prior event or set of events that render the act inevitable.[86] In other words, for Aquinas, the question regarding free choices is not whether or not they are caused, but how they are caused. A free choice is not merely unconstrained, but not necessitated. Some contemporary philosophers have admitted that there is such a third

---

85 S.T. I, q. 82 a. 1 and a. 2.

86 See my article, "Omniscience, Omnipotence, and Divine Transcendence," *The New Scholasticism* LIII (1979): 283–294, here 286.

view of human freedom and have referred to it as the theory of self-determination.[87]

Earlier in this paper I granted that Flew is correct in claiming that, if libertarian free will means that free acts are uncaused, then libertarian free will is incompatible with theism. Flew is also correct in claiming that, if God causes human choices by physiological manipulations, he—and not human agents—is responsible for whatever good or evil actions men do. He is also correct in claiming that God in the role of the Great Manipulator could cause human choices and actions so that men freely, i.e., without constraint, always choose to do what is right. However, by such physiological manipulations God could not cause human choices and actions that are free in the sense of self-determination so that the human agent is responsible for his good and evil choices and actions. Through physiological manipulations God as the Great Manipulator would remove the possibility of human morally good and morally evil acts in the Augustinian and Thomistic sense. However, human choices that are free in the sense of self-determination are not uncaused, though they are not necessitated.

For the purposes of this paper it is not necessary to establish that free choices in this sense do occur. Flew is claiming that a set of statements that theists make about God and evil is inconsistent. He has shown that, if God's causing human choices and actions is conceived as achieved through physiological manipulation and if human choices and actions are free in the sense of unconstrained, then God is responsible for the evil men do. However, that men are free in the sense of self-determination does not mean that human choices are uncaused. That men are free in this sense is at least logically possible, and that men are free in this sense is what theists, such as, Augustine and Aquinas, claim. Can the God of theism cause such free human acts to occur?

Flew appeals to Aquinas' claim that omnipotence does not mean that God can do what is logically impossible. However, omnipotence does mean that God can do whatever is logically possible. Flew is correct in claiming that a theist must, if he is consistent, maintain that God causes human free choices, if human free choices occur. However,

---

87 For example, see William K. Frankena, *Ethics* (Englewood Cliffs: Prentice-Hall, 1973), 2nd ed., p. 76. For a presentation of Aquinas' view of freedom as self-determination, see Vincent C. Punzo, *Reflective Naturalism* (New York: Macmillan, 1969), pp. 25ff.

even God cannot cause a human free choice that is not free. I have in a previous paper attempted to state Aquinas' solution to the question of how divine causality does not destroy human free acts.[88] The solution there is worked out in terms of an implicit definition of divine transcendence. If God knows, wills, and causes this free act to occur, then this free act occurs. However, it is a free act that occurs, and it occurs with conditional necessity which does not destroy freedom.

VI. CONCLUSION

In this paper I have tried to argue that there is present in Augustine a version of the free will defense that is significantly different from that which Flew attacks. In the version that Flew employs God's goodness is taken to mean that he would create the best world that he could. Thus God cannot have freedom of choice, but is necessitated to create the best possible world. In the Augustinian version God's goodness means that he created a good world, but he could have chosen a better world. Thus God has freedom of choice in creating. In the Flewian version moral goodness and moral evil are seen to lie primarily in actions and their results; in Augustine's version moral good and moral evil lie primarily in the acts of the will either clinging to God or turning away from God. Finally, I have tried to argue that Flew's presented alternatives between libertarian (uncaused) free choice and unconstrained (caused) free choice do not suffice. For Aquinas at least a free choice is caused and unconstrained, but not necessitated. Furthermore, if free choices are possible in that sense, then a God who is omnipotent is able to cause such free choices, though he does not and cannot will the evil of sin.

---

88 See my article "Omniscience," pp. 283–294. This article is a presentation of Fr. Bernard Lonergan's position, which in turn is developed out of Aquinas.

PLATONIC REMINISCENCE AND MEMORY OF THE PRESENT IN ST. AUGUSTINE

In *The Christian Philosophy of Saint Augustine* Etienne Gilson acknowledges that Augustine in his earlier writings used the language of Platonic reminiscence and was at one point even inclined to accept the doctrine of the pre-existence of the soul.[1] Gilson claims, however, that Augustine's doctrine of divine illumination "implies not Platonic memory of the past, but Augustinian memory of the present, and this is something altogether different."[2] He tells us that Augustine continues to use the language of 'remembrance' and 'reminiscence,' but he uses these terms in a non-Platonic sense. "The Platonic recollection of the past gives way to that Augustinian memory of the present whose role becomes more and more important."[3]

Subsequent commentators on Augustine seem to have agreed with Gilson and to have found his statement to be quite apt. For example, in the introduction to the Bibliothèque Augustinienne edition of the *Retractions*, Gustave Bardy says,

> As soon as one substitutes the memory of the present for the memory of the past, everything becomes clear; the soul does not remember what it has seen in the course of a previous existence. It rediscovers or recognizes what it has seen, what it does not cease to see in God.[4]

So too in his edition of the *De Trinitate*, P. Agaësse says,

---

1 Etienne Gilson, *The Christian Philosophy of Saint Augustine* (London: Victor Gollanz, Ltd., 1961), pp. 82, 71–72. This translation by L. E. M. Lynch is of the second French edition of *Introduction à l'étude de saint Augustin* (Paris: Vrin, 1943); the first edition appeared in 1929.

2 Gilson, p. 82.

3 Gilson, p. 75. I have not been able to find any such claim by any commentator on Augustine or any reference to such a claim prior to the date of the first edition of Gilson's work.

4 Saint Augustine, *Les Révisions. Bibliothèque Augustinienne* series of *Oeuvres de Saint Augustin*, vol. 12. (Paris: Desclée, De Brouwer et Cie, 1950), p. 147.

In brief, for a memory of the past, Saint Augustine is led to substitute a memory of the present, that is, the theory of reminiscence is replaced by the theory of illumination, already present in the *Soliloquies* (I, 8, 15).[5]

Le Blond goes even further to suggest that for Augustine memory is primarily a faculty of the present, not of the past.[6] And in a passing comment Vladimir Lossky refers to the "Augustinian noetic of the 'memory of the present'" as "the Christianisation of Platonic reminiscence."[7] So too Ronald Nash says of Augustine's mature position, "Augustine's theory of recollection, then, is not a remembering of the past. It is, on the contrary, a remembering of the present."[8]

In view of the importance attributed to Augustine's doctrine of 'memory of the present,' one would expect that the textual evidence for this doctrine would be both unambiguous and abundant. Such, however, is not the case. In fact, there seem to be but two texts that formally speak of remembering the present or of memory of the present. Moreover, it is disconcerting to find that the first of these texts, namely, *Letter* VII, does not substitute 'Augustinian memory of the present' for Platonic reminiscence. Rather in that text Augustine attributes memory of the present to Plato. Furthermore, the second text, *De Trinitate*

---

5 Saint Augustine, *La Trinité. Deuxième Partie: Les Images*. Bibliothèque Augustinienne series of Oeuvres de Saint Augustin, vol. 16. Translation by P. Agaësse, notes by P. Agaësse and J. Moingt. (Paris: Desclée, De Brouwer et Cie, 1955), p. 624.

6 J. M. Le Blond, *Les Conversions de s. Augustin* (Paris: Aubier, 1950), p. 16.

7 Vladimir Lossky, "Éléments de 'Théologie Négative' chez Saint Augustin," *Augustinus Magister*, I, 577.

8 Ronald H. Nash, *The Light of the Mind: St. Augustine's Theory of Knowledge* (Lexington: University of Kentucky Press, 1969), p. 83. Nash claims that in the *Retractationes* Augustine still maintains "the thesis that learning is a kind of remembering" (p. 83). He argues that this sort of remembering must be different from the Platonic view which requires the pre-existence of the soul—a doctrine that Augustine had by then rejected. He then finds in *De Trinitate* XII, 15, 24 grounds to conclude that Augustine holds "a remembering of the present." He bolsters this conclusion with a further quotation from *Retractationes* I, 4. Finally, he says, "Augustine can speak of recollection as a remembering of the present because truth is always available to us in the sense that Christ will make it available if we are attentive to it" (p. 84). However, that Augustine speaks of such a remembering of the present is not at all clear.

XIV, 10, 13–11, 14, seems to be limited to mind's memory of itself. And, hence, it would not seem to be able to be applied to all intelligible objects. The purpose of this paper, therefore, will be to re-examine the Gilsonian claim that Augustine replaced Platonic memory of the past with his own doctrine of memory of the present.[9]

Before we turn to an examination of the texts, it will be helpful to distinguish at least two senses in which 'memory of the present' is used. In one sense, 'memory of the present' is used to refer to recalling to mind objects that have been experienced in the past, but that have not ceased to exist and are, therefore, presently existing. For example, when I recall Chicago, I recall something that I have seen in the past and that has not ceased to exist, but exists at the present. My memory, however, of a building that has burned down is a recollection of an object that I experienced in the past and that has ceased to exist. Such a memory, then, is a memory of the past, i.e., of an object that is past. So too my recollection of the class that I taught yesterday is memory of the past, but my recollection of myself or of God is a memory of realities that are present and have not ceased to exist, even if I have experienced or known them in the past. There does not seem to be anything particularly problematic about 'memory of the present' in this sense, for, though one recalls an object that is presently existing, his experience of that object is past. Because one's experience of the object occurred in the past, he can now remember that object in the straightforward sense. However, the prior experience of the object

---

9 In examining the references to Augustine given by Gilson and others who place considerable importance upon 'Augustinian memory of the present,' one finds a wide selection of texts to which appeal is made. Gilson rejects *Letter* VII as containing memory of the present in the Augustinian sense; he appeals to a variety of texts from which he argues to a memory of the present stripped of any association with the past, such as, *De Trinitate* XV, 21, 40; XIV, 6, 8–7, 10; X, 3, 5; *Confessions* X, 25, 36; *Retractationes* I, 8, 2 and I, 4, 4, and *De Trinitate* XIV, 11, 14. It is not at all clear that "memoriae tribuimus omne quod scimus" (*De Trinitate* XV, 21, 40) entails 'Augustinian memory of the present.'

Bardy refers only to *Retractationes* I, 8, 2, upon which he is commenting. Agaësse's note on the rejection of Platonic reminiscence refers to *De Trinitate* XII, 15, 24. R. A. Markus refers to *Letter* VII, *De Trinitate* XII, 14, 23; *Confessions* X, 8, 12–27, 38; *De Trinitate* XV, 21, 40 and XIV, 11, 14. V. Lossky refers to *De Trinitate* X, 1, 1–2, 4 and XIV, 21, 40-41. Nash refers to *De Trinitate* XII, 15, 24 and *Retractationes* I, 4, 4.

seems to be a necessary condition of one's being able to remember that object now.

The Augustinian doctrine of 'memory of the present,' however, if it is to replace Platonic reminiscence that involves recollection of past experience and pre-existence, must not merely claim that the object remembered is presently existing, but must also make the further claim that the object was not first experienced in the past, then retained in memory, and finally recalled. In other words, for the the present, of which Gilson speaks, the pastness has to be eliminated. Here is the point of Gilson's claim that "Thinking, learning, and remembering are all one to the soul."[10] That is, if 'Augustinian memory of the present' is to replace Platonic reminiscence, then the Augustinian memory must be freed from reference to the past. R. A. Markus, for example, says that Augustine

> extends its [memory's] scope step by step until it includes everything that the mind is capable of knowing or thinking about, whether it is actually thought about or not. This is why the mind can be said to 'remember' objects such as God, the eternal truths, or the mind itself, none of which are 'remembered' from previous experiences. ...[11]

Augustine's memory of the present can replace Platonic reminiscence with its implication of a previous experience and pre-existence only if 'memory of the present' means not merely that the object remembered is present or presently existing, but that—to use Augustine's words— it is not the case that "retention in memory is earlier in time than the

---

10 Gilson, p. 75. After mentioning the role of the inner-teacher and divine illumination, Gilson says, "Consequently, association with the past ceases to be an essential characteristic of the memory. Since the soul remembers everything present to it even though unaware of it, we can say that there is a memory of the present which is even far more vast than the memory of the past" (p. 102). Here Gilson appeals to *De Trinitate* XIV, 11, 14 and XV, 21, 40.

11 R. A. Markus, "Augustine," in *The Cambridge History of Later Greek and Medieval Philosophy*, ed. A. H. Armstrong (Cambridge: Cambridge University Press, 1967), p. 371. "Augustine's conception [of memory] has two roots: the ordinary common-sense conception of memory as the mind's ability to preserve and recall past experience, and the Platonic conception as revised by him to free it from reference to the past" (p. 370).

vision in recollection"—as, he says, in the case of mind's memory of itself.[12]

I. LETTER VII AND MEMORY OF THE PRESENT

As early as 389 Augustine was encountering some difficulty in finding acceptance for the idea that we can remember not only things that are past, but also things that are present. He begins *Letter* VII by telling Nebridius that there can be memory without images or phantasms.

> First of all, one must see that we do not always remember perishing things, but frequently things that remain. Hence, though memory claims for itself a hold on past time, it is nonetheless partly of things that have left us behind and partly of things that we have left behind.[13]

Thus, in remembering his father who has died, Augustine recalls what has left him and does not now exist. But when he remembers Carthage, he remembers what he has left and what still exists.

> However, in each of these two kinds of things, memory retains past time. For I remember both that man and that city from having seen them and not from now seeing them.

Thus Augustine distinguishes the presentness or pastness of the object remembered and the presentness of the act of remembering from the pastness of the act of having seen his father or Carthage. Though the object remembered may still exist, memory depends upon the pastness of having seen the object, not upon a present act of seeing it. The example of remembering Carthage shows that 'memory' can be used of things that have not ceased to exist. He then tells Nebridius,

---

12 *De Trinitate* XIV, 10, 13.

13 *Letter* VII, 1, 1–2. The translation of the texts from Augustine here and elsewhere in this article is my own unless otherwise noted. The translation in the Fathers of the Church series seems to me to have completely missed the sense of the passage. Marcus Dods' translation is much clearer, though "we have, in the stream of mental activity, left these behind" as a translation of "a quibus ... defluximus" removes the clear allusion to the fall of the soul from the intelligibles. *The Works of Aurelius Augustine, Bishop of Hippo.* Trans. by Marcus Dods. Volume VI. *The Letters of Saint Augustine* (Edinburgh: T. and T. Clark, 1872), p. 14.

> Some unjustly attack Socrates' famous discovery in which it is asserted that things which we learn are not presented to us as something new, but are recalled to mind by recollection.

Their claim is that

> memory is only of past things, but that the things we learn by our intellect, on the authority of Plato himself, remain always, cannot be destroyed and, therefore, cannot become past.

These critics, Augustine points out,

> do not attend to the fact that that vision by which we formerly saw these things with our mind is past.

Nor do they attend to the fact that

> because we have flowed down from those things and have begun to see other things in another way, we see the former things again by recalling them, i.e., through memory.

With regard to this passage R. A. Markus has claimed that the knowledge recalled "is not really derived from past experience" and that "memoria does not necessarily refer to the past. ..."[14] Robert O'Connell, however, has correctly, I believe, interpreted *Letter* VII as claiming that "it is on the basis of the pastness of our having glimpsed them [the eternal truths] that we can now remember them."[15]

In *Letter* VII Augustine clearly maintains a doctrine of memory of the present. The intelligible objects, from which we souls have flowed down, are ever-present; however, our seeing them with the mind was in the past, presumably "before the soul used the body and the senses" (*Letter* VII, 3, 7). Now we have begun to see other things, i.e., sensible things, in another way, i.e., with the eyes of the body, and we recall the ever-present intelligible objects through memory. Yet what Augustine says here is not sufficient for what Gilson calls 'Augustinian memory of the present.' He says regarding *Letter* VII,

---

14 Markus, p. 370.

15 Robert J. O'Connell, SJ, *St. Augustine's Confessions: The Odyssey of Soul* (Cambridge: Harvard University Press, 1969), p. 130, n. 4. O'Connell says of *De Trinitate* XII, 21 and 24, "There, it would appear, Augustine is striving to liberate his conception of 'memory' (now become an acknowledgement of God as present, rather than God as present-but-object-of-a-past-vision) from the implications of Platonic reminiscence and pre-existence."

PLATONIC REMINISCENCE AND MEMORY OF THE PRESENT 67

> If his [Augustine's] mind had been settled on the point, this would have been an excellent opportunity to substitute the Augustinian memory of the present for Platonic recollection of the past, but Augustine does not do so. ...[16]

Yet there is clear mention of a memory of present intelligible realities on the basis of a past vision. For Gilson 'Augustinian memory of the present' means not merely that what is remembered is present, but that there is no past experience on the basis of which we now recall those realities. Nonetheless, *Letter* VII is one of the two texts—to the best of my knowledge—in which there is formal mention of a memory of the present.

II. DE TRINITATE XIV AND MEMORY OF THE PRESENT

The other text in which there is explicit discussion of 'memory of the present' is *De Trinitate* XIV, 10, 13–11, 14. In the latter section Augustine is dealing with the image of the Trinity found in memory, understanding, and love. He raises an objection, "But someone will say that it is not memory by which the mind, which is always present to itself, is said to remember itself." In support of this objection Augustine points out that in dealing with the virtue of prudence, Cicero divided it "into memory, understanding, and foresight and assigned memory to past things, understanding to present things, and foresight to future things." Augustine notes that certain foresight is beyond human ability unless it is God-given as it was in the case of the prophets. On the other hand, memory of past things and understanding of present things are certain, though understanding is of present incorporeal things, not of corporeal things that are present to the eyes of the body. To show that it is legitimate to speak of memory of something present, Augustine appeals to the authority of Vergil who said that Ulysses "did not forget himself" (*Aeneid*, III, 629).

> For, when Vergil said that Ulysses did not forget himself, what else did he wish to be understood than that he remembered himself? Therefore, since he was present to himself, he could not remember himself unless memory pertained to present realities.

And so Augustine concludes that

---

16 Gilson, p. 284, n. 11. Gilson admits that Augustine was inclined toward holding the doctrine of the soul's pre-existence at this period.

as in past things that is called memory by which it happens that they can be recalled and remembered, so in the case of a present reality—as the mind is to itself—that should without absurdity be called memory by which the mind is present to itself so that it can be understood by its thought and so that both can be joined by their love.

In this passage Augustine clearly argues that memory can legitimately refer to something present; he uses the mind which is present to itself as an example. There is, however, no indication that this memory of the present is intended to replace Platonic reminiscence. As a matter of fact, this passage seems to do no more than urge the legitimacy of speaking of a memory of a present object—precisely the Platonic doctrine that Augustine was explaining to Nebridius in *Letter* VII.

However, the preceding section in *De Trinitate* XIV marks a departure from the earlier view and throws a different light on the section we have just seen. In the earlier section Augustine, in speaking of knowledge of temporal things, says,

> Some knowable things temporally precede knowledge of them. Such are those sensibles that were already in things before they were known; such too are all those things which are known through history. On the other hand, some knowable things begin to be at the same time as knowledge of them. Thus, if something visible, which previously did not exist, arises before our eyes, it certainly does not precede our knowledge of it.

Augustine provided a further example of an object of knowledge and knowledge of it being simultaneous, namely, a sound and the hearing of the sound.

> Nonetheless, whether they precede in time or begin to be at the same time as knowledge of them, the knowable things generate the knowledge of them. But once knowledge has been acquired, when those things which we know are reconsidered by recollection, after they have been stored in memory, who does not see that retention in memory is prior in time to vision in recollection and the union of both of these by the will as a third element?

Thus far what Augustine has said seems unproblematic. First we know things, then store them in memory, and later recall them. In the case of knowledge of temporal things, the knowable things generate knowledge of them, and such things are retained in memory before they are seen in recollection.

"But in the case of mind, however, it is not so." Augustine claims that in the case of mind there are three points of difference. First, mind is not adventitious to itself.[17] Thus mind does not come to mind from somewhere else. Second, mind does not come to be in mind as faith comes to be in mind. Faith, which was not, comes to be in a mind that already existed. Mind cannot so come to be in itself already existing. However, the third point of difference is the one most relevant to our topic.

> After knowledge of itself mind does not by recollection see itself as stored in its memory as if it were not there before it knew itself. For from the moment it began to be, mind never ceased to remember itself, to understand itself, and to love itself.[18]

The three claims that Augustine makes, namely, that mind does not come to mind from someplace else, that mind does not come to be in itself as a virtue comes to be in a mind, and that mind does not first know itself, then store itself in memory, and later remember itself in recollection, are obviously claims about mind. However, there is nothing in these texts that indicates that in the case of any other intelligible object such as God, the retention in memory is not prior to vision in recollection. Indeed Augustine's argument for each of these claims seems to rest upon the unique relation that mind bears to itself such that it cannot come to itself from elsewhere, cannot come to be in itself already existing, and cannot store itself in memory as if it were not in itself before it knew itself.

There are, of course, other texts in Augustine in which there is talk of memory of realities that are present. In the straight-forward sense of 'memory of the present' all talk of memory of God, for example, is concerned with memory of a reality that can never be past, but is

---

17 It is interesting to find that Augustine uses "*adventitia*"—the same word that Descartes was to use in *Meditation* III in speaking of the kinds of ideas.

18 In the beginning of *De Trinitate* X Augustine argues that the mind is always present to itself and that the mind, therefore, always knows itself, even if it does not always think of itself. Lossky's appeal to this text as a justification for memory of the present is puzzling.

ever-present.[19] However, for what Gilson calls 'Augustinian memory of the present' more than the presentness of the object is required; the more that is required is the elimination of previous experience of such a reality as a condition of the possibility our remembering it.[20]

An examination of the texts from *Letter* VII and from *De Trinitate* XIV have not offered much support to Gilson's claim that Augustinian memory of the present replaces Platonic recollection of the past. Perhaps an examination of Augustine's rejection of Platonic reminiscence will provide evidence for the alleged important role for memory of the present.

III. AUGUSTINE'S REJECTION OF PLATONIC REMINISCENCE

In the well-known passage in *De Trinitate* XII, 15, 24, Augustine explains his rejection of Plato's doctrine of reminiscence and the pre-existence of the soul. Plato tried to persuade us, Augustine claims, that

> the souls of men lived here even before they governed these bodies and that, hence, it is that those things which are learned are rather remembered from being previously known than known for the first time.

Augustine reports the evidence from the *Meno* of the slave boy who was questioned on geometry. He argues that

> if this were recollection of things previously known, all people or almost all people would not be able to respond in this way when questioned. For, not all were geometers in a previous life, since geometers are so rare in the human race that hardly one can be found.

Augustine offers as a more credible explanation of the nearly universal ability to respond correctly to such question that

> the nature of the intellectual mind was so made that, subjected to intelligible things by the ordering of its Creator, it sees them in a

---

19 For example, *De Trinitate* XIV, 15, 21 speaks of God as being always. "He neither once was and now is not, nor is now and once was not, but as he will never not be, so he never was not." The ever presentness of Augustine's God certainly allows one to speak of memory of God as memory of the present. However, it is not clear that all memory of God is stripped of reference to the past.

20 Gilson, p. 102.

certain light of its own kind, just as the eye of the flesh sees what lies before it in this corporeal light—a light of which it was created capable and to which it is suited.

Augustine also points out that the fact that we distinguish black from white without a teacher does not imply our having known them prior to being in this flesh. Furthermore, he asks why we can only so respond to questions with regard to intelligible things and cannot do so with regard to sensible things unless we have seen them while in this body or believe others about them. He simply rejects the claim of Pythagoras of Samos to have remembered such things from a previous incarnation and likens such supposed memories to the sort of false memories that occur in dreams. He attributed the doctrine of repeated incarnations to evil spirits and claims that, if we all passed from life to death and from death to life again and again, we would all remember what we saw in other bodies. Clearly Augustine does not find Plato's claim that learning is remembering from a previous existence to be the correct explanation of our being able to respond correctly to questions about geometry and such intellectual disciplines.[21] He clearly attributes such an ability to our natural order under the intelligible realities and to the illumination by the incorporeal light.[22]

---

21 Besides *De Trinitate* XII, 15, 24 there are two other texts dealing with Augustine's rejection of Platonic reminiscence and the pre-existence of the soul, namely, *Retractationes* I, 4, 4 and I, 8, 2. In the latter text Augustine is commenting on his statement in *De quantitate animae*, 20, 34, that he believes "the soul brought with it all the arts and that what is called learning is nothing but remembering and recalling." He tells us that this statement should not be taken "as approving that the soul once lived either here in another body or elsewhere either in a body or out of a body or that the soul learned in another life what it answers to questions since it did not learn it here." He finds it more credible that the soul can respond correctly to questions because of its intelligible nature and its connection with intelligible and immutable things. He adds that in any case the soul does not bring with it all the arts since some of them pertain to the senses of the body. "But what the understanding alone grasps, when the soul is well questioned by itself or another, the soul answers having remembered." The "*recordata respondet*" of this text provides about the best evidence I have found for 'Augustinian memory of the present,' i.e., for remembering what one did not previously know.

22 The expression, "*luce sui generis,*" is ambiguous. It might mean that the light is of the same nature as the mind, or it might be interpreted to mean that

He clearly rejects all memories of sensible things from a previous incarnation and rejects the view that we are repeatedly incarnated. For one like Augustine who regarded life in the body as "living death or deathly life" (*Confessions* I, 6, 7), the doctrine of repeated incarnations was a ghastly idea.[23]

Though Augustine here clearly states that divine illumination provides a more plausible explanation for the correct responses regarding geometry by a person uneducated in such matters, he does not appeal to 'memory of the present' as replacing Platonic memory of the past. Indeed in the immediately preceding paragraph Augustine seems to speak of learning, forgetting, and remembering the intelligible and incorporeal reasons of things in the straightforward sense. What triggers the explanation of his rejection of Platonic reminiscence is the fact that what our mind has grasped and stored in our memory may be completely forgotten. In such a case, under the guidance of teaching, we will come back to what had completely slipped our mind and will discover it as it was.[24]

However, what Augustine seems to have held in the *Confessions* and even up to the time of *Letter* CLXVI (415 A.D.) is that the soul pre-existed its incarnation and brought with it into this life a memory of its former happiness and of its God.[25] Augustine's rejection of repeated incarnations of the soul, of the soul's remembering all the arts or at least the intellectual disciplines, and of the soul's remembering sensible things from a previous incarnation is not incompatible with

---

the nature of the light is of a particular kind. See Gilson's long note, pp. 289–290, n. 46.

23 "One bout with mortal misery is quite enough—an endless repetition of falls is what he finds 'horrible,' whether Origen, Plato, or Plotinus proposes it" (Robert J. O'Connell, SJ, "Augustine's Rejection of the Fall of the Soul," *Augustinian Studies*, IV (1973), p. 30.

24 *De Trinitate* XII, 14, 23. The implication here seems to be that, though completely forgotten, the truths remain or still exist so that they can be rediscovered under the guidance of teaching.

25 Besides O'Connell's book on the *Confessions* and his article on Augustine's rejection of the fall of the soul (see notes 15 and 23 above), see his *St. Augustine's Early Theory of Man, 386–391 A.D* (Cambridge: Harvard University Press, 1968).

his maintaining that the soul has a memory of its happiness and of God from prior to its embodiment.[26]

Another text, namely, *De Trinitate* XIV, 15, 21, deals with precisely the memory of the soul's happiness and the memory of its God. There Augustine rejects a memory of a former state of happiness, though he still speaks of a memory of God.

> When it [the soul], however, correctly remembers its Lord, after having received his Spirit, it is fully aware—because it learns this by interior instruction—that it cannot rise up except by the gratuitous love of God and that it could not have fallen except by its own voluntary failure. It does not, of course, recall its own happiness; that was and is no more, and the soul has completely forgotten it. And, therefore, it cannot be made to remember it.[27]

What is striking about this text is that Augustine does not say—as one would expect—that the soul does not remember its happiness because it never was happy. Rather he says that the soul's happiness is a thing of the past; it is no more. The soul has completely forgotten it and, therefore, cannot be made to remember it.[28] What seems to have gone unnoticed is that Augustine explicitly states that the happiness of the soul was once and is no more. Furthermore, what has been completely forgotten so that one cannot be made to remember it must have once been known. There is simply no way that one can completely forget what he never knew. These claims do deny any remembrance of the soul's happiness such as Augustine seems to have held in the *Confessions*. That happiness has been completely forgotten; its having been completely forgotten, however, requires that it did once exist.

Though the soul cannot remember its happiness, it does believe concerning it the Scriptures of its God, which are worthy of belief and

---

26 See *Retractationes* I, 8, 2, for Augustine's rejection of his earlier belief that the soul brought with it into the body all the arts. See *Retractationes* I, 4, 4, for his rejection of his early claim in *Soliloquies* II; 20, 35 that "those learned in the liberal disciplines uncover such knowledge buried in themselves when they learn and they in some way dig it out."

27 *La Trinité* II, 637. The note on "*commemoratus*" argues that it should be translated as passive, not as a deponent verb.

28 "Non sane reminiscitur beatitudinis suae: fuit quippe illa et non est, ejusque ista penitus oblita est; et ideoque nec commemorari potest" (*De Trinitate* XIV, 15, 21). The Latin could scarcely be more clear that that happiness once did exist, has been completely forgotten, cannot be remembered.

have been written by his prophet. Augustine, of course, is referring to the Genesis narrative of paradise and man's fall. Consequently, the previous state of happiness that has been completely forgotten is that happiness that the soul enjoyed in Adam in paradise.[29]

In contrast, however, to its happiness which the soul has completely forgotten, the soul does remember the Lord its God.

> For he always is; he neither once was and now is not, nor is now and once was not, but as he will never not be, so he never was not. And he is whole everywhere, and on account of that the soul lives and moves and is in him, and therefore it is able to remember him.

Augustine immediately goes on to say that the soul's ability to remember its God does not rest upon some knowledge of God that the soul had in Adam or somewhere before being in this body or when it was first made.

> Not that it recalls this, because it had known him in Adam or somewhere or other before the life of this body or when it was first made in order to be inserted in this body. None of these things does it remember at all; whatever of these things there is has been wiped out by forgetfulness.

Once again it is clear that the soul, when it remembers its Lord, does not remember what it knew in Adam or what it knew prior to its incarnation in this body or what it knew when it was first created. Augustine does not say that all of these have been wiped out by forgetfulness, but that whichever of these there is has been forgotten. To say that whichever of these is the case has been forgotten implies, of course, that one of these was the case. The expression, "quidquid horum est," avoids the implicit affirmation that the soul knew its Lord in Adam or before its incarnation or when it was first made. On the other hand, Augustine does not say: "If one of these is the case, it is completely forgotten." He says, "Whichever of these is the case it has been completely forgotten." Thus he implies that one of the three hypotheses mentioned is correct, even though any such previous knowledge of God has been completely forgotten and does not account for our being able to remember

---

29 *De Trinitate* XIV, 15, 21. Since the soul has completely forgotten the happiness it had in Adam so that it cannot be made to remember it, that happiness is with respect to its forgottenness on a par with the state of infancy which none of us remembers and about which we must believe others. See *Confessions* I, 6, 10.

God now. Have we then in such remembrance of God an instance of 'Augustinian memory of the present' in which all reference to the past has been removed? Here it is not only that which is remembered that is present, but there is no past vision of God, it seems, as the basis of the soul's being able to remember God.

Yet all reference to the past is not removed. Though the soul does not remember God on the basis of a knowledge that it had in Adam or before its embodiment, the soul was touched by God's light in the past when it was turned away from its God.

> But the soul is made to remember [its Lord] in order that it may be turned toward the Lord as toward that light by which it was being touched (*tangebatur*) in some way, even when it was turned away from him.

Because God always is—"as he will never not be, so he never was not"—and because he is whole everywhere, the soul not merely now lives, moves, and is in him, but always has lived, moved, and existed in him since it began to be. Augustine says that the soul is able to remember its God because of God's eternity and omnipresence, but that does not exclude any reference to the past. In fact, it would seem to imply a reference to the past. Furthermore, he says that the soul was being touched by God's light even when it was turned away from God, and there a reference to the past is explicit.

In *De Trinitate* XIV, 15, 21, Augustine clearly rejects a remembering of the soul's happiness or of God from some previous existence prior to embodiment. However, his grounds for the rejection of such memories are not that we never enjoyed such happiness or such knowledge of God. Rather his grounds for rejecting such memories are that the soul has completely forgotten such happiness and such knowledge of God. Whereas in the *Confessions* the memory of happiness and of God seemed to be the grounds for affirming the soul's pre-existence, by the time of *De Trinitate*—some twenty years later—the soul's enjoyment of happiness and knowledge of God prior to its embodiment is regarded as completely forgotten. But Augustine still holds that we were once happy and once knew God. Thus pre-existence remains in some form, even though its Platonic grounds have been removed.

IV. CONCLUSIONS

Of the two texts I have been able to find in which St. Augustine formally mentions a memory of the present, the first text, *Letter* VII, attributes the doctrine to Plato and insists upon a past vision of the objects remembered even if the objects are not past, but present. Gilson himself discounts this text as representing 'Augustinian memory of the present.' The second text, *De Trinitate* XIV, 10, 13–11, 14, does maintain a memory of the present in which there is no association with the past or in which reference to the past is eliminated. However, that text deals with mind's remembering itself, and it offers no justification for extending to other objects the claims made for mind's memory of itself. Furthermore, there are no grounds in the later text for claiming that Augustine either intended or saw such a memory of the present as replacing Platonic memory of the past.

In examining Augustine's rejection of Platonic reminiscence, we found that Augustine does regard divine illumination as a more plausible explanation of the *Meno* phenomenon. However, he makes no mention of a memory of the present as replacing Platonic memory of the past. Furthermore, the treatment of the soul's memory of its happiness and of God in *De Trinitate* XII—the very points to which as late as the *Confessions* Augustine appealed as evidence for holding the soul's pre-existence—offers no support for Gilson's claim. Though the soul does not, according to *De Trinitate* XII, remember its happiness, that state did exist and has been completely forgotten. The soul does remember its God, not because it recalls some knowledge it had of God in Adam or before its embodiment, but because the soul lives, moves, and exists in God who is eternal and whole everywhere, and has lived, moved, and existed in him and has been touched by his light even when it was turned away from him. Hence, I conclude that 'Augustinian memory of the present'—in the sense in which Gilson speaks of it—is neither found in St. Augustine nor used to replace Platonic memory of the past.

AUGUSTINE OF HIPPO ON SEEING WITH THE EYES OF THE MIND

A dozen years back, when I was asked to give the St. Augustine Lecture at Villanova University, my first choice of a topic was what Augustine understood by intellectual knowing, that is, by "*intelligere*," but I soon realized that the topic was beyond what I could handle at that time. I am not sure that I can deal with the topic even now in a satisfactory manner, but I cannot think of a better topic, nor am I likely to have a better occasion. The topic of intellectual knowing in Augustine is central to much of his thought, but what he says about intellectual knowing is not, in my judgment, always consistent with instances of such knowledge that we find in his writings. My thesis is that there is an official account of what he meant by intellectual knowing, that is, the sort of account that he did give of what it is to know intellectually, and that there are serious problems with that account of knowing, problems that are not found at least in some instances in which we can observe Augustine's activity in knowing intellectually or in bringing someone else to some instance of intellectual knowledge. If my thesis is correct, the conclusion will throw some light on several problems or debates that have occupied some contemporary Augustine scholars. I mean, for example, how we are to understand those passages in Book Seven of the *Confessions* that Pierre Courcelle described as vain Plotinan attempts at ecstasy or failed attempts to ascend to the vision of God. Hence, this lecture will have three parts and a conclusion: 1) Augustine's official account of intellectual knowing, 2) some difficulties with that account, 3) some actual instances of intellectual knowing, and 4) some concluding reflections.

I. THE OFFICIAL ACCOUNT

Augustine's account of intellectual knowing is highly Platonic. When, for example, St. Thomas speaks of intellectual knowing in his *Summa of Theology* I, qu. 84, a. 6, he contrasts the positions of Democritus and Plato with that of Aristotle. While Democritus held that all of our knowledge was sensory and that what we know are only bodily things, Plato distinguished the intellect from the senses and held that the intellect was an immaterial power that did not use a bodily organ and that the intellect knew immaterial forms separated from bodies. Aristotle, on the other hand, distinguished the intellect from the senses and maintained that the intellect, which is an immaterial power, is also a power of a soul that is the form of a body and that the intellect understands intelligible forms that it abstracts from material things by the agent intellect. Augustine's view comes very close to that of Plato, as St. Thomas well knew.

Augustine understands intellectual knowing by analogy with seeing with the eyes of the body. He develops this account of the two forms of seeing and points to the many parallels between them. He says that "to understand is to the mind what to see is for the senses."[1] Hence, Augustine identifies seeing God with understanding God.[2] So too, we have eyes of the mind just as we have eyes of the body.[3] And we see with the mind as opposed to seeing with the body.[4] But in order to see something with the eyes of the body, it is not enough to have eyes. Our eyes must also be open and healthy, and they must look in the right direction. There must also be something there to see, that is, a object that can be seen. So too, there must also be light to make the object visible. Similarly, the eyes of our mind must be open and healthy. In Book Seven of The *Confessions*, for example, Augustine describes how his face was so swollen with pride that the eyes of his mind could not see God.[5] In the *Soliloquies* he says that the eyes of the mind are healed by faith, hope, and love.[6] With the eyes of the body it is one thing to

---

1 *De ordine* II, 3, 10: "Menti hoc est intelligere, quod sensui videre."

2 *Soliloquia* I, 6, 12: "Sine tribus istis igitur anima nulla sanatur, ut possit Deum suum videre, id est intelligere," and *Soliloquia* I, 7, 14: "Ergo cum animae Deum videre, hoc est Deum intelligere contigerit, videamus utrum adhuc ei tria illa sint necessaria."

3 *De vera religione* 19, 37: "Hinc jam cui oculi mentis patent, nec pernicioso studio vanae victoriae caligant atque turbantur, facile intelligit, omnia quae vitiantur et moriuntur, bona esse, quanquam ipsum vitium, et ipsa mors, malum sit."

4 *Epistula* 7.

5 *Confessions* VII, 7, 11: "Et haec de vulnere meo creverant, quia humiliasti tanquam vulneratum, superbum; et tumore meo separabar abs te, et nimis inflata facies claudebat oculos meos."

6 *Soliloquia* I, 6, 12.

look and another to see; so it is with the mind.[7] The mind's gaze or look is reason, and reasoning is the movement of the mind over things that the mind gazes upon.[8]

Furthermore, just as for the eyes of the body to see anything, there must be some visible object present, so for the eyes of the mind to see anything there must be an intelligible object present. Augustine tells us in *Answer to the Academics*, one of his first extant works, where he presents a summation of the history of philosophy, that Plato's great achievement was the realization that there are two worlds. "After all," he says, "it is enough for what I want that Plato held that there are two worlds, one an intelligible world, where the truth itself dwells, and this sensible one, which we obviously perceive by sight and touch."[9] In another early dialogue, *On Order*, Augustine has the chutzpah to instruct his saintly mother, Monica, in the rudiments of philosophy and to claim that Christ himself taught that there were these two worlds. "Christ himself," Augustine said, "indicated well enough that there is another world far removed from these eyes, which the intellect of a few healthy human beings sees. For Christ did not say: 'My kingdom is not of the world,' but: *My kingdom is not of this world*" (Jn 17:36).[10] And Augustine, of course, located the intelligible world in the mind of God. After some speculation about whether Plato was the first to maintain that there were the Ideas or Forms, Augustine located them in the divine intelligence. "For," he says, "the principal ideas are certain forms or stable and immutable patterns of things, which are not themselves formed and are, for this reason, eternal and always existing in the same way and which are contained in the divine intelligence."[11] They are principal ideas, I think, in the sense that they are principles

---

7 *Soliloquia* I, 6, 12: "Non enim hoc est habere oculos quod aspicere; aut idem hoc est aspicere quod videre."

8 *De quantitate animi* 27, 53: "Ut ratio sit quidam mentis aspectus, ratiocinatio autem rationis inquisitio, id est, aspectus illius, per ea quae aspicienda sunt, motio."

9 *Contra Academicos* III, 17, 37.

10 *De ordine* I, 11, 32: "Esse autem alium mundum ab istis oculis remotissimum, quem paucorum sanorum intellectus intuetur, satis ipse Christus significat, qui non dicit, Regnum meum non est de mundo; sed, Regnum meum non est de hoc mundo."

11 *De diversis quaestionibus octaginta tribus*, qu. 46, 2: "Sunt namque ideae principales formae quaedam, vel rationes rerum stabiles atque incommuta-

or ἀρχαί of things in this sensible world. "Only a rational soul," Augustine tells us, "is permitted to gaze upon them by that part of itself by which it is excellent, that is, by the mind and reason, as if by its face or by its interior and intelligible eye."[12] Not every rational soul is suited for that vision, but only one that is holy and pure, "that is, one that has its eye, which sees these ideas, healthy, pure, calm, and like these things that it strives to see."[13] Furthermore, Augustine concedes that there are good and religious persons who cannot, nonetheless, gaze upon these ideas. He, however, claims that believers must maintain that there are such ideas in the mind of God if they are to hold that God knew what he was doing when he created the world and that he governs it providentially.[14]

Bodily eyes that are open, healthy, and looking in the right direction still do not see a object that is present unless there is light that makes the object visible. So too, the eyes of the mind need an intelligible light, and for Augustine God is that light of our minds. He says, "There is a certain ineffable and incomprehensible light of minds. Let this ordinary light teach us as much as it can how that light acts."[15] For some people have such healthy and strong eyes that they merely have to open them to see the sunlight, while others have to be gradually brought to see things the sunlight illumines until they are strong enough to look upon the sunlight itself. The light of minds is the Wisdom of God,[16] the true light that enlightens every human being who comes into this

---

biles, quae ipsae formatae non sunt, ac per hoc aeternae ac semper eodem modo sese habentes, quae in divina intelligentia continentur."

12 Ibid.: "Anima vero negatur eas intueri posse, nisi rationalis, ea sui parte qua excellit, id est ipsa mente atque ratione, quasi quadam facie vel oculo suo interiore atque intelligibili."

13 Ibid.: "Et ea quidem ipsa rationalis anima non omnis et quaelibet, sed quae sancta et pura fuerit, haec asseritur illi visioni esse idonea: id est, quae illum ipsum oculum quo videntur ista, sanum, et sincerum, et serenum, et similem his rebus quas videre intendit, habuerit."

14 Ibid.

15 *Soliloquia* I, 13, 23: "Lux est quaedam ineffabilis et incomprehensibilis mentium. Lux ista vulgaris nos doceat quantum potest, quomodo se illud habeat."

16 *Confessions* XI, 11, 13: "O Sapientia Dei, lux mentium."

world, as St. John said.[17] Just as the light of the sun makes other things visible by its light and is itself visible, so the intelligible light makes other things intelligible and is itself intelligible. "And so," Augustine says, "as in this sun we can observe three things: that it is, that is bright, and that it illumines, so in that most hidden God whom you want to understand, there are three things: that he is, that he is understood, and that he makes other things to be understood."[18] In prayer Augustine addresses God: "O God, the intelligible light in whom and by whom and through whom all things are intelligibly bright that are intelligibly bright."[19]

Contemporary scholars are more in agreement about what this divine illumination cannot mean than they are about what does mean. Scholars universally agree that Augustine's theory of divine illumination does not mean that God produces concepts or knowledge in our minds in the way the Avicennian agent intelligence caused human knowledge by producing ideas in our minds as it also produced forms in things in this sublunar world. So too, scholars are almost universally agreed that in Augustine God does not act like the Thomistic agent intellect, which abstracts universals from sensible things. For Augustine has no doctrine of universal ideas or abstraction. Some scholars claim—quite anachronistically—that Augustine held a version of ontologism, somewhat like Père Malebranche in the seventeenth century and like various nineteenth-century Catholic thinkers, such as the Italian Antonio Rosmini-Serbati and the Belgian Gerhard Ubaghs of Louvain. At least one prominent scholar held that it was before their embodiment that human souls were enlightened and that they now vaguely remember what they saw then. But there is, as I said, little

---

17 *In Joannis evangelium tractatus*, tr. 12, 5: "Quia ergo non videbatur lux hominum, id est lux mentium, opus erat ut homo diceret de luce testimonium, non quidem tenebrosus, sed jam illuminatus. Nec tamen quia illuminatus, ideo ipsa lux; sed ut testimonium perhiberet de lumine. Nam non erat ille lux. Et quae erat lux? Erat lux vera, quae illuminat omnem hominem venientem in hunc mundum."

18 *Soliloquia* I, 8, 15: "Ergo quomodo in hoc sole tria quaedam licet animadvertere; quod est, quod fulget, quod illuminat: ita in illo secretissimo Deo quem vis intelligere, tria quaedam sunt; quod est, quod intelligitur, et quod caetera facit intelligi."

19 *Soliloquia* I, 1, 3: "Deus intelligibilis lux, in quo et a quo et per quem intelligibiliter lucent, quae intelligibiliter lucent omnia."

agreement about what Augustine saw as the real role of divine illumination. There are certainly texts in which Augustine seems to say quite clearly that at least some human beings in this life can see and have seen the very substance by which God is what he is. Though he explicitly ascribes such a vision only to Moses and Paul, he perhaps extends it to the great Neoplatonists as well.[20] He certainly says that the great philosophers "saw that which is, but saw it from afar."[21] They saw the fatherland where we are to go, but in their pride they refused the way to it, namely, the Word become flesh.

There are other texts in which he says that we can and do see with the mind the eternal patterns or ideas in the mind of God. Etienne Gilson, the great historian of medieval philosophy, whose *The Christian Philosophy of Saint Augustine* written in the 1920s still continues to be a valuable source, classified those texts in which Augustine spoke of a vision of God or of things in God as mystical and classified all the other, less problematic texts, as ones referring to our natural knowledge.

There is one final point of similarity between seeing with the eyes of the body and seeing with the mind that I want to mention. At times things interfere with our bodily vision. For example, clouds or fog can prevent us from seeing even the sun, and gnats can get into our eyes. So too, phantasms, that is, images of bodily things, can like clouds or fog or gnats prevent our seeing with the eyes of the mind. Images rush into our minds like clouds or fog and have to be brushed away like a swarm of desert gnats. Hence, Augustine prays in *The True Religion* for someone who can think without imagining sensible objects.[22]

Thus far I have tried to illustrate Augustine's "official" account of what it is to understand in which he compares the mind's knowing with the eyes' seeing. Bernard Lonergan describes Augustine's theory of understanding as empiricism's most sublime form, but faults the bishop of Hippo for supposing that, because seeing is obviously knowing, seeing is obviously what knowing is.[23] Next, I want to turn to and

---

20 See "Augustine on the Vision of God," in *Augustine: Mystic and Mystagogue* (New York: Peter Lang, 1994), pp. 287–308.

21 *In Joannis evangelium tractatus* tr. 2, 4: "Illud potuerunt uidere quod est, sed uiderunt de longe."

22 *De vera religione* 64: "Date mihi qui videat sine ulla imaginatione visorum carnalium."

23 See Bernard Lonergan, *Insight: A Study of Human Understanding* (New York: Philosophical Library, 1957), p. 412.

emphasize some of the problems with the "official" account of what it is to know.

II. PROBLEMS WITH THE OFFICIAL VERSION

If to know with the mind is analogous to seeing with the eyes, there, of course, have to be intelligible objects that the mind sees. We have seen that Augustine considered Plato's discovery of the intelligible world and the Ideas as one of his great contributions to philosophy and as something that a Christian has to believe in, even if we do not ourselves see that world and those Ideas. Furthermore, Augustine located the Ideas in the mind of God. For, as St. Thomas wisely noted, Augustine saw that it was against the faith to leave such creative substances outside of God and, for this reason, placed them in the mind of God.[24] If we listen to Augustine's official version of what it is to know intellectually, it seems to follow inevitably that he held that we know intelligible objects and truths in knowing the divine ideas—and not merely in the way that we see visible things in the light of the sun, but by seeing the divine ideas themselves.

Let me illustrate this point from Augustine's argument for the existence of God, which he presents in Book Two of *Free Choice of the Will*. The basic structure of the argument is a hypothetic syllogism. Augustine gets his partner in the dialogue, Evodius, the future bishop of Uzalis, to agree that, if there is anything higher than the human mind, at least, if that something is eternal and immutable, that something is God, or God exists. Hence, Augustine has to show that there is above the human mind something that is eternal and immutable, and he does this by showing Evodius that there are truths of mathematics and of wisdom that are eternal and immutable. Augustine says to Evodius: "If without the use of any instrument of the body, neither of touch, nor of taste, nor of smell, nor by the ears, nor by the eyes, but by itself, reason sees something eternal and immutable, it must at the same time admit that it is inferior and that that being is its God."[25] Unlike the conclusion of one of the Five Ways of St. Thomas,

---

24 See Thomas Aquinas, *Summa theologiae* I, qu. 84, a. 5 cor.

25 *De libero arbitrio* II, 6, 14: "Quae si nullo adhibito corporis instrumento, neque per tactum, neque per gustatum, neque per olfactum, neque per aures, neque per oculos, neque per ullum sensum se inferiorem, sed per seipsam cernit aeternum aliquid et incommutabile, simul et seipsam inferiorem, et illum oportet Deum suum esse fateatur."

the term of Augustine's argument is reason's act of seeing something eternal and immutable, which is reason's God.

Before turning to the truths of mathematics and of wisdom, Augustine spends a number of paragraphs in an *exercitatio animi*, an exercising of the mind, in which he compares the act of seeing with the acts of the other external senses. His aim is to convince Evodius and us that what we see with our eyes can be something common and public for many or all of us to see, while what we taste or smell cannot be common and public in the same way. For, in tasting and smelling something, we change what we taste and smell so that it is something private and proper to each of us. Hence, he concludes, "We must understand by 'proper' and 'private' that which each of us alone possesses, which each senses in himself, and which properly belongs to his nature. But that is 'common' and 'public' which is perceived by all who sense it without any destruction or change of that object."[26]

Then Augustine says to Evodius, "Come on now, pay attention, and tell me whether something is found that all who reason see in common, each with his own reason and mind, though what is seen is available to all and is not changed for the use of those to whom it is available, like food or drink, but remains incorrupt and whole, whether they see it or not."[27] Evodius mentions "the nature and truth of number,"[28] which is available to all who reason and which every one who calculates tries to grasp by his own reason and intelligence. At this point Augustine has to face the objection "that these numbers are impressed on our mind, not from some nature of their own, but from those things that we at-

---

26 *De libero arbitrio* II, 7, 19: "Proprium ergo et quasi privatam intelligendum est, quod unicuique nostrum soli est, et quod in se solus sentit, quod ad suam naturam proprie pertinet: commune autem et quasi publicum, quod ab omnibus sentientibus nulla sui corruptione atque commutatione sentitur."

27 *De libero arbitrio* II, 8, 20: "Age, nunc attende, et dic mihi utrum inveniatur aliquid quod omnes ratiocinantes sua quisque ratione atque mente communiter videant, cum illud quod videtur praesto sit omnibus, nec in usum eorum quibus praesto est commutetur, quasi cibus aut potio, sed incorruptum integrumque permaneat, sive illi videant, sive non videant."

28 *De libero arbitrio* II, 8, 20: "Ratio et veritas numeri omnibus ratiocinantibus praesto est. . . ."

tain by the senses of the body, like certain images of visible things."[29] Evodius claims that, even if we perceive numbers by the senses of the body, we do not grasp in that way the laws of addition and subtraction, and he points to the incorruptible truth that seven plus three equals ten. Augustine, nonetheless, proceeds to show that numbers themselves cannot be derived from the senses of the body. He points out that each number is a multiple of one and argues that one cannot be attained by the bodily senses because everything we perceive by those senses is many. Any body we perceive has many parts, such as a right side and a left, a top and a bottom, a front and a back. Hence, he concludes, "And for this reason we grant that no body is purely one, though we could not count so many parts in it unless they were distinguished by a knowledge of one."[30] Augustine is claiming that a knowledge of one is a condition of the possibility of counting the many parts we find in any body. He says that he does not find one in any body and asks, "When, therefore, I know that a body is not one, I know what one is. For, if I did not know one, I could not count many parts in a body."[31]

Having established that a knowledge of one is the condition of the possibility of knowing the multiplicity in any body, Augustine turns to some simple rules of number, such as the double of any number "x" follows "x" numbers after "x." In any case, like "seven plus three equals ten," these truths about number are eternal and immutably true.

So too, Augustine gets Evodius to admit that there are truths of wisdom that are immutable and eternal, such as, that we should live justly, that we should subordinate the worse to the better, that we should treat equals as equal, and that we should give each what is his own, and he insists that these truths are available to all who see them.[32]

---

29 *De libero arbitrio* II, 8, 21: "Tamen, si tibi aliquis diceret numeros istos non ex aliqua sua natura, sed ex iis rebus quas sensu corporis attingimus, impressos esse animo nostro quasi quasdam imagines quocumque visibilium, quid responderes?"

30 *De libero arbitrio* II, 8, 22: "Propterea nullum corpus vere pureque unum esse concedimus, in quo tamen non possent tam multa numerari nisi illius unius cognitione discreta."

31 *De libero arbitirio* II, 8, 22: "Ubi ergo novi quod non est corpus unum, quid sit unum novi: unum enim si non nossem, multa in corpore numerare non possem."

32 *De libero arbitrio* III, 10, 28: "Item, juste esse vivendum, deteriora melioribus esse subdenda, et paria paribus comparanda, et propria suis quibusque

And after exploring the relation between number and wisdom, Augustine says to Evodius, "Hence, you will by no means deny that immutable truth exists and contains all these immutable truths. You cannot say that it is yours or mine or any human being's, but is available to and offers itself, like a light hidden and yet public in marvelous ways, to all who see the immutable truths."[33] Augustine still has to argue that the immutable truth is superior to our mind in order to come to the conclusion that God exists and truly exists. But in the passage just quoted there is also the problem that we see many immutable truths (*incommutabilia vera*) of number and wisdom. These truths are contained in the immutable truth, and the immutable truth is God.

What, then, is the relationship between the many immutable truths that we see and the immutable truth that contains them? The relation between *veritas* and *vera*, between the truth and objects that are true, would seem, in so Platonic a context, to be participation. For example, Augustine says in an earlier commentary on Genesis, "But chastity is chaste by participation in nothing; rather, by participation in it whatever is chaste is chaste. That chastity is, of course, in God where there is that wisdom that is not wise by participation, but by participation in which every wise soul is wise."[34] The relation between the immutable truth and those things that are immutably true cannot, however, be the same as the relation between wisdom and wise souls or between chastity and chaste souls. A soul that is wise or chaste by participation can, after all, cease to be wise or chaste; it is not immutably wise or chaste. But the truths of mathematics and of wisdom that are immutably and eternally true. They are, furthermore, things that are common and public and that are available to all who use their reason to see

---

tribuenda, nonne fateberis esse verissimum, et tam mihi quam tibi atque omnibus id videntibus praesto esse communiter?"

33 *De libero arbitrio* II, 12, 33: "Quapropter nullo modo negaveris esse incommutabilem veritatem, haec omnia quae incommutabiliter vera sunt continentem; quam non possis dicere tuam vel meam vel cujusquam hominis, sed omnibus incommutabilia vera cernentibus, tanquam miris modis secretum et publicum lumen, praesto esse ac se praebere communiter."

34 *De Genesi ad litteram liber imperfectus* 16, 57: "Castitas autem nullius participatione casta est, sed ejus participatione sunt casta quaecumque casta sunt. Quae utique in Deo est, ubi est etiam illa sapientia, quae non participando sapiens est, sed cujus participatione sapiens est anima quaecumque sapiens est."

them. Hence, I am convinced that participation will not work here to account for the relation between the *vera* and *veritas*, between those truths and the truth.[35]

Augustine says that the immutable truth *contains* the many immutable truths. I suggest that the immutable truth contains the many immutable truths in the way in which a mind contains the many truths it knows. But that leaves us with the problem that our minds or the minds of those whose eyes are open, healthy, gazing in the right direction, etc., literally see those immutable truths in the mind of God, who is the Truth. Now, to say the very least, it is a strange proof for the existence of God that moves from seeing the divine ideas in the mind of God to the existence of God.[36]

By way of confirmation of this, we find in Book Three that Augustine argues that, though there can exist in the world something that we do not think of by our reason, there cannot fail to exist what we think of with a true reason.[37] "Nor can you, after all, think of something better in creation that will have escaped the author of creation. The human soul, in fact, is naturally connected to the divine ideas (*divinis rationibus*), upon which it depends, when it says, 'This would be better than that.' And if it speaks the truth and sees what it says, it sees it

---

35 In BA 6 (Paris, 1952), p. 525, F. J. Thonnard appeals to the principle of participation. He distinguishes "deux modes d'être des vérités éternelles: l'un *participé*, en notre esprit, où elles vivent sous la forme multiple des règles des nombres et de la sagesse; l'autre *absolu*, dans la source du Verbe, où elles vivent sous la forme parfaite de l'infinie simplicité de la Vérité divine; et des unes à l'autre, des participations à la Source, il faut s'élever au moyen du principe de causalité ou de raison suffisante, qui est, sous sa forme augustinienne, le principe de participation."

36 I have argued that what we have in *De libero arbitrio* is not so much a proof that there is a God as an argument that God is truly, that is, that he is immutable and non-bodily. See my "The Aim of Augustine's Proof that God Truly Is," *International Philosophical Quarterly* XXVI (1986), 253–268, as well as "The *De Libero Arbitrio* Proof for the Existence of God," *Proceedings of the Jesuit Philosophical Association* (1987): 15–47; in revised form in *Philosophy and Theology* 2 (1987): 124–142.

37 *De libero arbitrio* III, 5, 13: "Potest ergo esse aliquid in rerum natura, quod tua ratione non cogitas. Non esse autem quod vera ratione cogitas, non potest. Neque enim tu potes aliquid melius in creatura cogitare, quod creaturae artificem fugerit."

in those ideas to which it is connected."[38] With an almost Leibnizian optimism Augustine says that, if with true reason we know that God ought to have made something, even if we do not see that thing with our eyes, we should believe that God did make it.[39] And the reason he gives is that "one would not see in thought that it ought to have been made except in those ideas by which all things have been made. What is not there, no one can see with true thought, and it is not true."[40]

Even in later works Augustine says quite clearly that the mind at least of a few human beings attains the intelligible forms in the mind of God. In Book Twelve of *The Trinity*, for example, Augustine distinguishes wisdom and knowledge and tells us that to wisdom there pertain the eternal intelligible and incorporeal patterns (*rationes*) of things. "They, however, remain, not fixed as if in places like bodies, but in their incorporeal nature they are, like intelligible things, available to the gazes of the mind, just as these visible or tangible things in places are available to the senses of the body."[41] He adds, "To attain to these patterns is the privilege of a few, and when one attains them, to the extent it is possible, the person who attains them does not remain in them, but is driven back, as if his eyes have been stuck, and there is produced the passing thought of a reality that does not pass."[42] Given Augustine's official view of intellectual knowing, we are faced with the problem that the mind of a few is able to attain in this life a vision of

---

38 *De libero arbitrio* III, 5, 13: "Humana quippe anima naturaliter divinis ex quibus pendet connexa rationibus, cum dicit, Melius hoc fieret quam illud; si verum dicit, et videt quod dicit, in illis quibus connexa est rationibus videt."

39 *De libero arbitrio* III, 5, 13: "Credat ergo Deum fecisse quod vera ratione ab eo faciendum fuisse cognovit, etiamsi hoc in rebus factis non videt."

40 *De libero arbitrio* III, 5, 13: "Non enim cogitatione videret fuisse faciendum, nisi in iis rationibus quibus facta sunt omnia. Quod autem ibi non est, tam nemo potest veraci cogitatione videre, quam non est verum."

41 *De trinitate* XII, 14, 23: "Manent autem, non tanquam in spatiis locorum fixa veluti corpora: sed in natura incorporali sic intelligibilia praesto sunt mentis aspectibus, sicut ista in locis visibilia vel contrectabilia corporis sensibus."

42 *De trinitate* XII, 14, 23: "Ad quas mentis acie pervenire paucorum est; et cum pervenitur, quantum fieri potest, non in eis manet ipse perventor, sed veluti acie ipsa reverberata repellitur, et fit rei non transitoriae transitoria cogitatio."

the divine ideas, at least momentarily. For those eternal, intelligible, incorporeal patterns or ideas are available to the gazes of the mind, just as visible and tangible things offer themselves to the bodily sight and touch.

III. AUGUSTINE'S UNOFFICIAL VERSION OF WHAT KNOWING IS

We have seen what I have called Augustine's official version of what intellectual knowing is, namely, that to understand is to see an intelligible reality with the eyes of the mind. We have seen that there are problems with his account of knowing as a seeing. The principal problem is, in my opinion, that the official version entails that, in knowing intellectually, we see the divine ideas in the mind of God. The official version, therefore, makes his argument for the existence of God at best a sort of intuition and at worst question-begging. Furthermore, the role of divine illumination seems to remain an unexplained and perhaps an inexplicable metaphor.

With reference to the various senses of scripture, scholars have often pointed out that it is necessary to look at what Augustine does rather than merely at what he says. I suggest that with reference to intellectual knowing, we should also look at what Augustine does rather than merely at what he says. Hence, I will examine two instances in which we can see how Augustine tries to bring others to an intellectual knowledge of something. First with:

(A) JEROME AND THE INCORPOREALITY OF THE SOUL

In 415 Augustine wrote to Jerome in Bethlehem, a holy, but cantankerous priest with whom he has earlier quarreled. Augustine asked Jerome for help with the question of the origin of the soul, that is, with the question of how post-Adamic human souls come to be in bodies, a problem that Augustine was never able to resolve to his own satisfaction. In the letter Augustine wanted to show Jerome that he knew something about the soul, and one of those things that he claimed to know was that the soul was incorporeal. In order to avoid a merely verbal dispute, he first of all clarifies what he means by a body and says that, if every substance is a body, then the soul too is a body. Similarly, if someone wants to maintain that only an absolutely immutable and omnipresent substance is non-bodily, then the soul is a body. "But if only that is a body that stands or moves with some length, breadth, and depth through some area of place, so that it occupies a larger place with a larger part of itself and a smaller place with a smaller part of itself and is smaller in a part than in the whole, the soul is not a body."[43] In order to show that the soul is not a body in this sense, Augustine appeals to the evidence from sensation that the soul is stretched out through the whole body, not by a local diffusion, but by a vital attention. He produces an argument that "the whole soul is simultaneously present through all the parts of the body, not smaller in smaller parts and larger in larger parts, but more intensely in one place and less intensely in another, whole in all the parts and whole in each part."[44] I do not want to examine the argument here in detail, but to focus on what Augustine does to prove to Jerome that he knows that the soul is not a body. He first makes it clear what he means by a body and defines something incorporeal by contrary properties. He appeals to our awareness of ourselves in sensation and claims that the whole soul could not be aware of something that happens in only a part of the body, unless the whole soul were present in each part of the body. For, when I feel a pain in my toe that I stub, my whole soul is aware of the pain in one small part of my body, though the soul continues to animate the rest of my body. And, if I manage to burn my finger while my toe is still hurting, my whole soul also becomes aware of the pain in my finger. Hence, the whole soul is present in the whole body which it animates, but the whole soul is also present in each of the parts, as is shown by my awareness of the pains in my toe and in my finger. He concludes, "Hence, whether it should be called a body or non-bodily, the soul is understood to have a certain nature of its own, created with a substance more excellent than all these elements with a worldly mass, and it cannot accurately (*veraciter*) be thought of in some picturing of bodily images, which we perceive through the senses of the flesh. Rather, it is understood by the mind and sensed by

---

43 *Epistula* 166, 2, 4: "Porro si corpus non est, nisi quod per loci spatium aliqua longitudine, latitudine, altitudine ita sistitur vel movetur, ut majore sui parte majorem locum occupet, et breviore breviorem, minusque sit in parte quam in toto, non est corpus anima."

44 Ibid.: "Nam per omnes ejus particulas tota simul adest, nec minor in minoribus, et in majoribus major; sed alicubi intentius, alicubi remissius, et in omnibus tota, et in singulis tota est."

life."⁴⁵ That is, the incorporeal nature of the soul cannot correctly be thought of (*cogitari*) by means of any bodily images, but is understood (*intelligi*) by the mind. When he says that it is "sensed by life (*vita sentiri*)," I think that he means that the soul's sensory awareness provides the evidence of the soul's presence as a whole in the whole body and in each of its parts. That the soul is incorporeal in that sense cannot, however, be imagined, but can only be understood by the mind.

This sort of intellectual knowing is hardly a seeing of an intelligible object in an intelligible world. It is rather an insight into the sort of reality the soul must be if we are to account for the evidence provided by sensory awareness, an insight that transcends anything that we can picture and is expressed in a definition of the soul's incorporeality. Second with:

(B) CONSENTIUS' AND KNOWLEDGE OF GOD

In 410 a young theologian from the Balearic Isles by the name of Consentius wrote to Augustine, asking for help in how to think about God. Consentius tells Augustine that he is convinced that the truth about God should be sought from faith rather than reason. Otherwise, he fears that "no one except philosophers and professors will attain happiness."⁴⁶ He is, moreover, convinced that heresies all stem from neglecting the authority of scripture and indulging in rational arguments. Like almost everyone in the Latin West prior to Augustine, Consentius was a man who pictured God to himself as a huge sort of body. He tells Augustine that he believes "that God is an infinite magnitude of a certain inestimable light and that the human mind, though it thinks lofty thoughts, is not sufficient to judge its quality nor measure its quantity nor imagine its beauty."⁴⁷ God, according to Consentius, is something that "has an incomparable form and inestimable beauty, which at least Christ could see even with the eyes of the

---

45 Ibid.: "Unde intelligitur anima, sive corpus, sive incorporea dicenda sit, propriam quamdam habere naturam, omnibus his mundanae molis elementis excellentiore substantia creatam, quae veraciter non possit in aliqua phantasia corporalium imaginum, quas per carnis sensus percipimus, cogitari, sed mente intelligi, vitaque sentiri."

46 *Epistula* 119, 1: "si enim fides sanctae Ecclesiae ex disputationis ratione, non ex credulitatis pietate apprehenderetur, nemo praeter philosophos atque oratores beatitudinem possideret."

47 *Epistula* 119, 3.

flesh."[48] He quotes from one of his writings where he had said, "God is one, and the persons are three. God is undivided; the persons are divided. God is within all things; he is beyond all things. He includes the last things, fills the middle things, and transcends the highest. He is poured out beyond all things and through all things. But the persons subsisting in themselves are distinguished by their proper character and are not mingled in confusion."[49] He adds, "God, therefore, is one and is everywhere, because there is no other besides him and there is no empty space where another could be. All things are filled with God, and apart from God there is nothing."[50]

Consentius clearly thought of God in terms of a Stoic corporealism of the sort that Augustine himself described as his own view early in Book Seven of the *Confessions*, where he says that he had thought that God was "a great corporeal substance, existent everywhere throughout infinite space, which penetrates the whole world-mass, and spreads beyond it on every side through immense, limitless space."[51] Or, to use the image he employs a few paragraphs later, the whole of creation is like a huge, but finite sponge in the infinite sea of God, who fills every part of the sponge and stretches endlessly beyond it.

Consentius is well aware that Augustine says "that God should not be thought of as some body," not even as "a light a thousand times more bright and more intense than this sun."[52] But Consentius thinks that to think of God as non-bodily means to think of him like righteousness or piety. For he concedes that we cannot think of righteousness or piety as bodily, unless we imagine some female figures, as the pagans

---

48 Ibid.

49 Ibid.: "Deus, inquam, unus est, et personae tres sunt. Deus indiscretus est, personae discretae sunt. Deus intra omnia, trans omnia est, ultima includit, media implet, summa transcendit, ultra universa et per universa diffunditur: personae autem sibi constantes, proprietate secernuntur, non confusione miscentur."

50 *Epistula* 119, 4: "Deus ergo unus est, et ubique est; quia et alius praeter illum non est, et locus non est vacuus ubi esse alius possit. Plena sunt Deo omnia, et praeter Deum nihil est."

51 *Confessions* VII, 1, 2.

52 *Epistula* 119, 5: "Ais non tanquam aliquod corpus debere cogitari Deum. Nam etiamsi quispiam animo lucem millies quam hujus solis clariorem intensioremque confingat, nullam illic Dei similitudinem comprehendi posse."

do, but he adds that he "still cannot think of God, that is, of a living nature, as being like righteousness, because righteousness is not living in itself, but in us."[53] That is, if he thinks of God as righteousness or piety, which he admits are not bodily, he finds that he cannot regard such abstractions as living in themselves, but only as living in righteous human beings.

Augustine replied to Consentius in Letter 120. He tells Consentius that he should hold that correct faith about the one God and the three persons, even if he cannot understand it, but he also urges Consentius to love understanding very much.[54] He tries to bring Consentius to understand that God is incorporeal. He warns him, "When you think of these things, drive away, deny, reject, cast aside, flee from whatever comes to mind with the likeness of a body."[55] One of the ways in which Augustine tries to get Consentius to transcend imagination or picture-thinking and to understand God involves the technique that he learned from Plotinus of bringing together images that clash with each other and force one beyond images.[56] Augustine takes the verse from Isaiah where it says, "The heaven is my throne, but the earth is my footstool" (Is 66:1). He says, "Even if we understand this in a carnal sense, we ought to believe that he is there in heaven and here on earth, though the whole of him is not there because his feet are here and the whole of him is not here because the upper parts of his body are there."[57] Another passage of scripture, he tells us, "can shake off for us this carnal thought." For Isaiah also said, "He measured the heaven

---

53 Ibid.

54 *Epistula* 120, 3, 13: "Intellectum vero valde ama."

55 *Epistula* 120, 3, 13: "Et quidquid tibi, cum ista cogitas, corporeae similitudinis occurrerit, abige, abnue, nega, respue, abjice, fuge."

56 I pointed out another example of this move in "Heresy and Imagination in St Augustine," *Studia Patristica*, Vol. XXVII, ed. E. A. Livingstone (Leuven: Peeters Press, 1993), pp. 400-404. See also Robert J. O'Connell, *St. Augustine's Early Theory of Man, A.D. 386–391* (Cambridge, MA: Belknap Press, 1968), pp. 58–60.

57 *Epistula* 120, 3, 14 : "Nam etsi carnaliter acceperimus quod scriptum est, Coelum mihi sedes est, terra autem scabellum pedum meorum; et ibi et hic cum esse credere debemus: quamvis non totum ibi, quia hic essent pedes; nec totum hic, quia ibi essent superiores corporis partes.

with the palm of his hand and the earth with his fist" (Is 40:12).[58] If one brings the two sets of images together, they clash and shatter each other so that we are forced to transcend them. Augustine says, "Who can sit in the space of the palm of his hand or can put his feet in a space as small as his fist can grasp? Unless perhaps the vanity of the flesh goes so far that it is not enough to attribute human members to the substance of God if it does not also make them monstrous so that the palm of his hand is wider than his hips and his fist is wider than both palms joined together."[59] Augustine explains that he says this "in order that, when those things that we hear in a carnal fashion conflict with one another, we may be admonished by them and think of spiritual realities in a way that is ineffable."[60]

Thus Augustine tries to bring Consentius to an intellectual grasp of the incorporeal nature of God by shattering one image against the other so that he is forced to transcend the imagination to a grasp of a reality that cannot be pictured or imagined, but can only be understood. This sort of intellectual knowing is, in my opinion, a seeing or insight into the nature of God that is much more plebeian than the seeing of the official version, which seems closer to an account of a mystical experience or of the vision of God by the blessed than of a philosophical insight.

IV. CONCLUDING REFLECTIONS

There are instances of knowing in Augustine's works that are closer to the official version than to the unofficial version that I have tried to illustrate. I think, however, that it is important to see that not every instance of intellectual knowing in Augustine involves a vision of intelligible things in the divine ideas or a vision of God himself. Furthermore, Augustine's official version of what it is to know intellectually

---

58 *Epistula* 120, 3, 14: "Quam cogitationem carnalem, rursum illud nobis excutere, quod de illo scriptum est, potest: Qui coelum mensus est palmo, et terram pugillo."

59 *Epistula* 120, 3, 14: "Quis enim sedeat in spatio palmi sui, aut in tanto loco pedes ponat, quantum ejus pugnus apprehendit? Nisi forte in tantum caro vana progreditur, ut ei parum sit humana membra substantiae Dei tribuere, si ea non etiam monstruosa confingat, ubi palmus lumbis, et pugillus ambabus palmis conjunctis sit latior."

60 *Epistula* 120, 3, 14: "Sed haec dicuntur, ut cum sibi non conveniunt quae carnaliter audimus, eis ipsis admoniti, ineffabiliter spiritualia cogitemus."

can be misleading and has, I think, misled some students of Augustine. Let me offer an example of this. In Book Seven of his *Confessions* Augustine speaks several times of his coming to a vision of God. He tells us that he was admonished by the books of the Platonists to return into himself and that he entered into his inmost self under God's guidance. He says, "I entered and saw with a certain eye of my soul above the same eye of my soul, above my mind, the immutable light, not this common light visible to all flesh, nor was it a greater light of the same kind.... Nor was it above my mind like oil above water nor like the heaven above the earth, but it was higher because it made me and I was lower because I was made by it."[61] Later he speaks of his having imagined God as extended over infinite stretches of space, but God, he says, soothed his head and closed his eyes so that he would not see vanity. He continues, "I withdrew from myself a little, and my insanity subsided. And I woke up in you, and I saw that you are infinite in another way, and this vision was not drawn from the flesh."[62]

If one understands these instances of seeing in terms of the official version, these passages from Book Seven are records of momentary mystical visions that Augustine enjoyed at Cassiciacum in the months before his baptism. If, however, one understands those instances of seeing in terms of philosophical insights, one can understand Augustine's "I saw" in a non-mystical sense, and one can, furthermore, view the later part of Book Seven subsequent to his encounter with the books of the Platonists, not as presenting a series of historical events that occurred over a relatively short period of time, but as presenting a set of philosophical or theological insights that sum up his newly found understanding of the Christian faith in the light of what he learned from Plotinus, an understanding that he need not have acquired over a few weeks or months, but that he more likely came to over a number of years of philosophical and theological reflection. The latter I suggest is a more plausible reading of these texts, which have troubled students of Augustine for decades. I have not, of course, settled the question of how to interpret what Pierre Courcelle called vain Plotinian attempts at ecstasy, but I have at least shown that one need not interpret Augustine's words as claims of having seen as a momentary, ecstatic visions of God.

---

61 *Confessions* VII, 10, 16.
62 Ibid. VII, 14, 20.

AUGUSTINE'S EPISTULA X: ANOTHER LOOK AT "DEIFICARI IN OTIO"

In 1962 Georges Folliet published a provocative article dealing with the meaning and source of Augustine's phrase in his letter to his friend, Nebridius: *"deificari in otio."*[1] Folliet points to previous works by Thimme, Bardy and Stoop[2] and states that all three say that the phrase should be understood "in a philosophical sense, as describing the blessed repose of the philosopher, the wise man, in whom the love of the world has died." He adds, "Undoubtedly, the word *deificari* cannot be understood here of the elevation to the supernatural order by grace, in view of the reflexive sense of the verb in the phrase and the complement *in otio* added to it."[3] On the basis of the supposedly reflexive sense of the verb, F. Van der Meer says of the phrase, "To be free from business and so be made like unto God—that was the thing for which they now had time, Augustine wrote quite simply to his intimate friend Nebridius, without ever guessing how selfish and presumptuous were those words."[4]

On the other hand, André Mandouze finds in the *otium* of Thagaste a considerable advance over the leisured life in philosophy that was the goal of Cassiciacum and finds in the common life of Thagaste the be-

---

1 "Deificari in otio". Augustin, Epistula X, 13," *Recherches Augustiniennes* 2 (1962): 225–236.

2 W. Thimme, *Augustins geistige Entwicklung in den ersten Jahren nach seiner "Bekehrung"* (386–391) (Berlin, 1908), p. 29, n. 1; G. Bardy, "Divinisation," in *Dictionnaire de spiritualité* III, c. 1390–1391; J. A. A. Stoop, *Die deificatio hominis in die Sermones en Epistulae van Augustinus* (Leiden, 1952), p. 48.

3 Folliet (my translation), p. 266: "[T]ous trois se contentent de dire qu'elle doit être comprise dans un sens philosophique, comme décrivant le repos bienheureux du philosophe, du sage, chez qui l'amour du siècle est mort. ... Nul doute que le mot *deificari* ne peut s'entendre ici de l'élévation à l'ordre surnaturel par la grâce, vu le sens réfléchi qu'a ce verbe dans la phrase et le complément 'in otio' qui lui est adjoint."

4 F. Van der Meer, *Augustine the Bishop: Church and Society at the Dawn of the Middle Ages* (New York: Harper, 1965), p. 209.

ginnings of Western monasticism. He claims that certain experts have failed to see this advance and have thought they were justified in denouncing the selfish and presumptuous character of this undertaking.[5] Similarly, George Lawless points out that the *otium* of Thagaste "is a far cry from the leisure of the philosophers" and finds in it "the seeds of the future bishop's mature thoughts on contemplation."[6] Hence, *Epistula* X and the phrase *"deificari in otio"* merit another look.

I. EPISTULA X: ITS CONTEXT AND CONTENT

Between 387 and 389 Augustine carried on with his friend, Nebridius, a fairly extensive correspondence of which we have twelve letters, nine from Augustine and three from Nebridius.[7] Augustine begins *Epistula* X, addressing the claim of Nebridius that Augustine has neglected the plans for their living together.[8] Augustine points out that reason seems

---

5 "Il est vraiment étrange que, sur le caractère de l'*otium* partagé à Thagaste, certains spécialistes aient pu se méprendre: au lieu de considerer le progrès que représente ici, par rapport au simple *otiose uiuere* du rêve milanais, la formule du *deificari in otio*, ils ont cru pouvoir dénoncer le caractère égoiste et présomptueux de ce propos'"(*Saint Augustin: L'aventure de la raison et de la grâce* [Paris: Etudes Augustiniennes, 1968], pp. 206–207. Mandouze here refers to and cites Van der Meer; see the previous note. He concludes, "Aussi, sans rénier l'*otium* envisagé á Milan, l'*otium* réalisé à Thagaste représente avant tout le cadre obligatoire d'une vie religieuse oú le partage des biens figure et, en même temps, rend possible l'assistance fraternelle et la communion spirituelle" (*Saint Augustin: L'aventure de la raison et de la grâce* [Paris: Etudes Augustiniennes, 1968], p. 209.

6 G. Lawless, *Augustine of Hippo and his Monastic Rule* (Oxford: Clarendon, 1987), p. 51.

7 Nebridius died shortly thereafter, probably in 390. In the *Confessions* Augustine speaks of Nebridius as a chaste youth and good friend who had no use for divination (IV, iii, 6); he left his home and mother in Carthage to be with Augustine in Milan (VI, x, 17) and debated the problem of evil with Augustine and Alypius (VI, xvi, 26). Nebridius provided Augustine with the decisive dilemma against the Manichees (VII, ii, 3) and tried to get Augustine to give up his interest in horoscopes (VII, vi, 8). Nebridus became a teacher in Milan and was absent when Ponticianus visited Augustine and Alypius (VIII, vi, 13-14). Nebridius had held that Christ's flesh was a mere phantasm, but later became a Christian and died soon after his return to Africa (IX, iii, 6).

8 The letter in which Nebridius made this claim does not seem to have survived, though Nebridius raises the question in *Epistula* V and Augustine

to indicate that Augustine and his companions most probably could better live as they proposed in Thagaste rather than in Carthage or in the country.[9] What then about Nebridius? Augustine suggests various means by which Nebridius might come to them, but the mother of Nebridius will not tolerate his absence, especially given the weakened state of his health. Augustine could go to Nebridius.

> But there are present here men who cannot come with me, and I regard it as unthinkable (*nefas*) to abandon them. You are able to be comfortably at home in your mind; effort is needed that these men can do the same thing.[10]

Augustine rules out traveling back and forth, for the distance is long, and undertaking such a trip again and again means not attaining the leisure he has desired. Furthermore, Augustine's bodily health sets a limit on what he can do.

Augustine begins the crucial paragraph with the statement:

> To have in mind through the whole of life journeys that can never be restful and easy is not the mark of a man who bears in mind that one last journey which is called death and which alone, as you know, one should truly keep in mind.[11]

Augustine points out that "God has granted to certain men whom he chose to be governors of churches that they not only bravely look forward to death, but eagerly desire it and undertake the toils of overseeing the churches without any anxiety."[12] There are others "who are

---

touched upon this topic in the beginning of *Epistula* IX.

9 *Epistula* X, 1: CSEL 34, 23: "sed cum perprobabilis ratio demonstare uideatur hic nos potius quam Carthagini uel etiam in rure ex sententia posse degere, quid tecum agam, mi Nebridi, prorsus incertus sum."

10 Ibid: "at hic sunt, qui neque uenire mecum queant et quos deserere nefas putem. tu enim potes et apud tuam mentem suauiter habitare; hi uero ut idem possint, satagitur." Compare with this passage Augustine's advice to Nebridus in *Epistula* IX, 1: CSEL 34, 20: "confer te ad animum tuum et illum in deum leua, quantum potes."

11 *Epistula* X, 2: CSEL 34, 23: "Profectiones ergo, quas quietas et faciles habere nequeas, per totam cogitare uitam non est hominis de illa una ultima, quae mors uocatur, cogitantis, de qua uel sola intellegis uere esse cogitandum."

12 Ibid: "dedit quidem deus paucis quibusdam, quos ecclesiarum gubernatores esse uoluit, ut et illam non solum expectarent fortiter, sed alacriter

brought to such works of administration by the love of temporal honor" and still others "who, as ordinary citizens, desire the busy life."[13] To neither of these latter groups is granted "this great good," namely, that they become familiar with death "amid noisy and restless comings and goings." But "both of them could become God-like in leisure."[14]

Augustine adds that, if this is not true, then he is, if not the most foolish, certainly the laziest of men, because without carefree leisure "I cannot taste and love that pure good."[15] Augustine adds that one must withdraw "from the tumult of perishing things" if one is to be free from all fear, "not out of insensitivity, nor out of recklessness, nor out of the desire of empty glory, nor out of superstitious belief." From such a freedom from fear there arises "that solid joy that should be compared to no delights in any way at all."[16]

If such a life free from fear is not the lot of humans, why, Augustine asks, do we at times attain such a freedom from cares (*securitas*)? And why we do attain it the more frequently we "adore God in the inmost temple of our mind?"[17] Why does it continue when we move to action from that shrine? We do not fear death when we speak of it and desire it when we do not. Augustine knows well the ascents upwards (*itinera in superna*) of Nebridius and his frequent experiences of the sweetness of the mind's dying to the bodily love. Hence, Nebridius will not deny that a man's whole life can become free of fear so that he is truly

    etiam desiderarent et harum obeundarum labores sine ulto angore susciperent. ..."

13 *Epistula* X, 2: CSEL 34, 23-24: "qui ad huius modi administrationes temporalis honoris amore raptantur... qui cum sunt priuati, negotiosam uitam appetunt. ..."

14 Ibid: "sed neque his... neque rursum his ... hoc tantum bonum concedi arbitror, ut inter strepitus inquietos conuentus atque discursus cum morte familiaritatem, quam quaerimus, faciant; deificari enim utrisque in otio licebat."

15 *Epistula* X, 2: CSEL 34, 24: "aut si hoc falsum est, ego sum omnium ne dicam stultissimus, certe ignauissimus, cui nisi proueniat quaedam secura cessatio, sincerum illud bonum gustare et amare non possum."

16 Ibid.: "magna secesssione a tumultu rerum labentium, mihi crede, opus est, ut non duritia, non audacia, non cupiditate inanis gloriae, non superstitiosa credulitate fiat in homine nihil timere. hinc enim fit illud etiam solidum gaudium nullis omnino laetitiis ulla ex particula conferendum."

17 *Epistula* X, 3: CSEL 34, 24: "in mentis penetralibus adorat deum?"

called a wise man. Nebridius will not dare to claim that this state ever comes about except when he is living among his friends. Hence, one course of action remains for Nebridius: that he too plan for the common good of their living together. Augustine closes with the suggestion that Nebridius' brother will certainly not abandon their mother and the promise that he will write more later.[18]

Apart from the reference to those who are specially gifted so that they become familiar with death while governing churches, there is nothing specifically Christian in the language of the letter. Stoic and Neoplatonic themes, such as the attainment of a state of freedom from fear and cares, of withdrawal from the body and bodily loves, of entering into one's mind, of the contemplation and desire of death, and of worshipping God in the recesses of the mind, dominate the letter. The life which Augustine and his friends have determined to live together in Thagaste and to which Augustine invites Nebridius indicate a commitment to common life that, on the basis of other sources, one can recognize as the beginnings of monastic life.[19] But apart from such other sources, one would not, on the basis of *Epistula* X alone, find much reason to suppose that Augustine is speaking of a specifically Christian way of life, much less of a form of Christian monasticism.

II. THE MEANING OF "DEIFICARI"

Neither the adjective "*deificus*" nor the verb "*deificare*" occur with any great frequency in Augustine's works.[20] The adjective "*deificus*" is found there seven times; in each case the term seems synonymous with "divine."[21] In every case, save one, the term is used by a Manichee or a

---

18 *Epistula* X, 3: CSEL 34, 24–25.

19 See Mandouze, p. 209.

20 L. Cilleruelo notes that the term "*deificare*" has a "carácter mistérico y neoplatónico" and suggests the "unión tranformante" of Neoplatonism so that "Agustín no volvió a utilizarlo" (*Obras completas de San Agustín* VIII [Madrid: Biblioteca de Autores Cristianos, 1986], p. 59, n. 1.

21 Three times it qualifies the Scriptures; see *Contra Felicem* I, 13: CSEL 25/2, 815; *Contra Crescentium* III, 70: CSEL 52, 485. *De baptismo* VI, 15: CSEL 51, 313. Twice it qualifies the message (*sermo*) of Christ; see *Contra Faustum* XXXII, 7 and 19: CSEL 25/1, 766 and 780. Once it modifies sacred vessels (*instrumentorum*); see *Contra Crescentium* III, 70: CSEL 52, 485. Once it qualifies the virtue of patience; see *De patientia* XVII, 14: CSEL 41, 679.

Donatist;[22] only once is it found in the words of Augustine.[23] There, in contrast with a false patience which he calls *diabolica*, he speaks of true patience as *deifica*.[24]

Aside from *Epistula* X, Augustine uses forms of the verb "*deificare*" seven times, including instances of the perfect passive participle. In commenting on Psalm 49 he uses the verb three times:

> It is clear, then, that he called men gods who were made gods by grace, not born from his substance. For he who is just through himself and not from another makes men just, and he who is God through himself and not by participating in another makes men gods. He who makes them just makes them gods, because by making them just, he makes them sons of God.[25]

Augustine uses the verb "*deificare*" once in commenting on Ps 117:16.

> The right hand of the Lord has acted with power." What power? "The right hand," he says, "of the Lord has raised me up." It takes great power to raise up the lowly, to make a mortal a god, to draw perfection from weakness, glory from subjection, victory from suffering, to provide help from tribulation. ...[26]

Twice Augustine uses the passive participle "*deificatus*." In *Sermo CXXVI* he contrasts human eyes which saw Christ in the form of the ser-

---

22 The term was also used by previous Christian authors though there is no reason to suppose Augustine knew this. The fact that he found it in the works of the Manichees may partially explain his not using the term more frequently.

23 *De patientia* XVII, 14: CSEL 41, 679.

24 Though the context would certainly admit the sense that true patience renders one godlike, the parallel with "*diabolica*" indicates that it should be translated simply as "divine."

25 *Enarratio in Psalmum* XLIX, 2: CCL XXXVIII, 575–576: "Manifestum est ergo, quia homines dixit deos, ex gratia deificatos, non de substantia sua natos. Ille enim iustificat, qui per semetipsum non ex alio iustus est; et ille deificat, qui per seipsum non alterius participatione Deus est. Qui autem iustificat, ipse deificat, quia iustificando, filios Dei facit."

26 *Enarratio in Psalmum* CXVII, 11: CCL XL, 1661: *Dextra Domini fecit uirtutem. Quam uirtutem? Dextra*, inquit, *Domini exaltauit me. Magna uirtus exaltare humilem, deificare mortalem, praebere de infirmitate perfectionem, de subiectione gloriam, de passione uictoriam, dare auxilium de tribulatione....*"

vant with the divinised eyes which will see him in the form of God.[27] In *Sermo CLXVI* Augustine speaks of the state of man after resurrection, "when the whole man, having been divinised, will cling to the everlasting and immutable truth."[28]

Augustine once uses the verb "*deificare*," while quoting from Porphyry.

> God, who is the father of all, has need of no one. But we are well off, when we worship him through justice and chastity and the other virtues, making our life a prayer to him by imitating and seeking him. For seeking purifies us, he says; imitation divinises us, by producing love for him.[29]

Every instance in which Augustine himself uses the verb "*deificare*," apart from *Epistula X*, clearly refers to the change that God produces in human beings by the justifying them and making them children of God or by transforming their mortal bodies into risen bodies. The philosophical tenor of *Epistula X* with its treatment of the double theme of the soul's withdrawal from the world and purification through the virtues leads Folliet to see Neoplatonism, especially that of Porphyry, in the background of the letter.[30] Folliet concludes, "Augustine's saying, *deficari in otio*, seems to me to take on its full meaning once it is situated in this [Porphyrian] context. It is the Platonic *omoiôsis theô* that Augustin found in Porphyry who is not content to repeat the words of Plotinus, but makes this ideal into a mysticism."[31] He suggests that

---

27 *Sermo* CXXVI, 14: RB 69 (1959), 190: "Et ille stans ante oculos serui, in forma serui, seruans oculis deificatis formam dei, ait illi: *Tantum tempore uobiscum sum, et non cognouistis me? Qui me uidet, uidet et patrem*" (Jn 14:9).

28 *Sermo* CLXVI, 4: SPM 62–63: "*Deponentes ergo mendacium, loquimini ueritatem* (Eph 4:25), ut et caro ista mortalis quam adhuc habetis de Adam, praecedente nouitate spiritus, mereatur et ipsa innouationem et commutationem tempore resurrectionis suae: ac sic totus homo deificatus inhaereat perpetuae ac incommutabili ueritatae."

29 *De civitate dei* XIX, 23: CCL XLVIII, 693: "Nam Deus quidem, utpote omnium pater, nullius indiget; sed nobis est bene, cum eum per iustitiam et castitatem aliasque uirtutes adoramus, ipsam uitam precem ad ipsum facientes per imitationem et inquisitionem de ipso. Inquisitio enim purgat, inquit; imitatio deificat affectionem ad ipsum operando."

30 Folliet, pp. 229–231.

31 Folliet, p. 234.

Augustine derived the word "*deificari*" from the Latin translations of Porphyry and argues that in the last clause of text from *De civitate dei* we find the specific sense of the word *deificari*: "It is by his actions, by the exercise of the virtues that the wise man makes himself like God. That is the sense that Augustine gives to *deficari in otio*."[32]

Folliet claims that at the time of *Epistula* X, "Augustine has not yet discovered the richness of the grace of Christ; purification, assimilation to God by the virtues, without the help of grace, are something possible in his eyes."[33] A. Mandouze, on the other hand, has pointed to the tenuous character of Folliet's inference tying *Epistula* X to Porphyry.[34]

Furthermore, in the citation from Porphyry in *De civitate dei*, our becoming gods results from our love for God—a view that Augustine learned early and never gave up. Nor need that view imply that we make ourselves gods. Even before his ordination Augustine wrote, "Since that which is loved necessarily transforms its lover out of itself, it happens that when what we love is eternal, it makes the soul eternal."[35] And much later he wrote in commenting on the Letter of John,

> Each one is the sort of person that his love is. Do you love the earth? You will be earth. Do you love God? What shall I say? You will be a god? I do not dare to say it on my own. Let us listen to the Scriptures: "I said, you are gods and children of the Most High. ..."[36]

Hence, even if there is the Porphyrian influence for which Folliet argues, there is no need to take Augustine's use of Porphyry as denying the influence of and the need for grace.

Regardless of whether or not Porphyry was the source behind Augustine's phrase "*deificari in otio*," there does not seem to be any grounds

---

32 Folliet, p. 235.

33 Folliet, pp. 235–236.

34 See Mandouze, p. 208, note 1.

35 *De diuersis quaestionibus octoginta tribus* XXXV, 2: CCL XLIV/A, 52: "Et quoniam id quod amatur afficiat ex se amantem necesse est, fit ut sic amatum quod aeternum est aeternitate animum afficiat."

36 *In epistolam Ioannis ad Parthos* II, 14: PL XXXV, 1997: "quia talis est quisque qualis eius dilectio est. Terram diligis? terra eris. Deum diligis? quid dicam? deus eris? Non audeo dicere ex me, Scripturas audiamus: 'Ego dixi, Dii estis, et filii Altissimi'. ..."

for interpreting the verb as reflexive, e.g., to make onself divine" or "to make oneself like God" ("se diviniser" or "se rendre sembable á Dieu").[37] The Latin verb is passive and might better be translated "to be made a god" or "to be made godlike." Like the passive infinitive, *concedi*, found shortly before it, *deificari* can surely be taken as a "theological passive." Augustine has stated that "God has given (*dedit quidem Deus*)" to some the ability to govern churches while meditating on and desiring death. He goes on to say that he thinks "this great good is granted" to neither of the other two classes of men when they are lacking leisure. Surely, then, if this great good is granted them in leisure, it is God who grants it; similarly, it is God who makes them divine or godlike in leisure. The other occurrences of "*deificare*" found in Augustine surely provide reason to question Folliet's claim that the phrase in *Epistula* X "cannot be understood here of the elevation to the supernatural order by grace."[38] In fact, *Epistula* X would be the only instance in which Augustine himself used the verb and did not refer to God's justification and divinisation of human beings. On the other hand, the language of *Epistula* X is philosophical and lacking in specifically Christian elements. How then can one determine the specific sense of "*deificari*" in *Epistula* X?

III. "IN OTIO": THE LEISURE OF THAGASTE

Perhaps the answer can be found in what Augustine understood by leisure or repose (*otium*) during the time he spent at Thagaste. George Lawless has pointed to *De vera religione*, which was written during this period, as indicating "the profoundly contemplative and decidedly Christian character" of the *otium* desired—an *otium* which "is a far cry from the leisure of the philosophers."[39] The passage in *De vera religione* XXXV, 65 not merely throws light upon the *otium* of Thagaste, but on the sense of *deificari*. There Augustine urges one who sees the true light to be still and to struggle only with the habit of bodies. "Con-

---

37 Mandouze has pointed out (p. 208) that there is no reason to take *deificari* in the letter to Nebridius as reflexive: "se diviniser." Folliet's claim that the verb is reflexive seems to be the basis for Van der Meer's charge that Augustine's enterprise at Thagaste is selfish and presumptuous.

38 See Folliet, p. 226.

39 Lawless, p. 51.

quer that, and everything will be conquered."[40] Our quest is for the One, than which nothing is more simple. In the simplicity of our heart, then, let us seek Him. He quotes the Psalmist, "Be still (*agite otium*), and you will recognize that I am the Lord" (Ps 45:11). He urges us to be still, not with a stillness of inactivity (*otium desidiae*), but with a stillness of thought (*otium cogitationis*), so that we might be free from times and places. "The phantasms of swollen and fleeting things do not allow one to see the unity that abides. Places present something to love; times snatch away what we love. ..."[41] Such phantasms rouse desires, and the soul becomes restless. We are called to leisure, that is, we are called not to love those things which cannot be loved without toil.[42] If one does not love such things, he will hold them subject and not be held subject to them. Christ's yoke is light; one who is subject to it holds all else subject and will not have to labor, because what is subject will not resist. The lovers of this world fear to be separated from the love of these things, but they will become masters of this world if they are willing to become children of God, for "he has given them the power to become children of God" (Jn 1:12).

Here Augustine links becoming children of God with being subject to the yoke of Christ and holding all other things subject to oneself by not loving bodily and temporal things, which the lovers of this world fear to lose. We see the themes of withdrawal from the world and from worldy fears linked with becoming children of God, just as in *Epistula* X they were linked with becoming godlike. Here the same themes are developed in a conscious dependence upon the Scriptures, while in *Epistula* X such biblical allusions are absent. Instead of supposing that the goal of becoming godlike in leisure that Augustine desired at Thagaste was philosophical, merely natural, and even selfish and pre-

---

40 *De Vera Religione* XXXV, 65: CCL XXXII, 229: "Ipsam uincite, uicta erunt omnia."

41 Ibid., 230: "Haec enim phantasmata tumoris et uolubilitatis constantem unitatem uidere non sinunt. Loca offerunt quod amemus, tempora surripiunt quod amamus. ..."

42 Lawless (p. 51) says that "Augustine defines [*otium*] as 'love for those realities which can only be loved with toil'"—a translation which simply reverses the sense of the Latin: "Vocatur ergo ad otium, id est ut ista non diligat, quae diligi sine labore non possunt" (*De uera religione* XXXV, 65: CCL XXXII, 230). That is, "otium" involves *not* loving the sort of thing that can only be loved with toil, but loving eternal things.

sumptuous, one would surely do better to read *Epistula* X in the light of the clearly Christian ideal of becoming children of God in leisure (*otium*), as it is found in the contemporary text, *De vera religione*.

IV. CONCLUDING REFLECTIONS

G. Folliet characterized Augustine's ideal at Thagaste of *deificari in otio* as purely philosophical, as a goal that is natural and attainable without grace.[43] In this paper I have shown that such a conclusion is reasonable if one looks only at the text of *Epistula* X. However, every other time Augustine uses the verb "*deificare*" in his own person, he uses it to speak of God's justification and divinisation of human beings. Hence, to interpret "*deificari*" in *Epistula* X exclusively in the sense of the citation of Porphyry in *De civitate dei*—and in the sense in which Porphyry might have meant it—seems unwarranted. Others have pointed to the difference between the philosophical *otium* of Cassiciacum and the Christian *otium* of Thagaste.[44] The comparison of *Epistula* X with the contemporary *De vera religione* reveals not merely a different sort of leisure, but shows that Augustine linked the "philosophical" themes of withdrawal from the world and its fears with explicitly Scriptural themes and with our becoming sons of God in the sense of Jn 1:12. Hence, there is very good reason to interpret not merely the *otium*, but the *deificari* of *Epistula* X as thoroughly Christian and as referring to what later theologians would call elevation to the supernatural order.

Why, then, one might ask is the tenor of *Epistula* X so "philosophical"? Two answers suggest themselves. One, a personal letter, unlike a treatise such as *De vera religione*, is naturally tailored to the mind and heart of the addressee. From the rest of the correspondence with Nebridius one can see that Nebridius' interests leaned to what we would call more philosophical rather than theological questions. Two, where we see a sharp difference between philosophy and Christianity, Augustine and Nebridius—at least at this point—saw continuity. Thus, Augustine could maintain in *De vera religione* that "we believe and teach as an essential point of human salvation that philosophy, that is, the pursuit of wisdom, is not one thing and religion another. ..."[45] So too,

---

43 Folliet, p. 226.

44 See Lawless, p. 51 and Mandouze, pp. 207–208.

45 *De Vera Religione* V, 9: CCL XXXII, 193: "Sic enim creditur et docetur, quod est humanae salutis caput, non aliam esse philosophiam, id est sapi-

Nebridius, filled with delight over Augustine's letters, could say, "For me your letters resound with Christ, with Plato, with Plotinus."[46]

---

entiae studium, et aliam religionem...."
46 *Epistula* IX, 1: CSEL 34, 12: "illae mihi Christum, illae Platonem, illae Plotinum sonabunt."

AUGUSTINE AS EXEGETE

AUGUSTINE, THE MANICHEES, AND THE BIBLE

Augustine engaged in polemics with many heretical groups, such as the Donatists, the Pelagians, and the Arians, but his confrontation with the Manichees is unique in so far as he himself had been a member of that sect for some nine years as a "hearer," or layman, as opposed to one of the "elect," or priestly class.[1] This essay will deal with the role the Bible played in Augustine's conversion to Manichaeism, with the Bible that he knew as a Manichee, and with his use of the Bible against the Manichees after his baptism.

I. THE BIBLE AND AUGUSTINE'S CONVERSION TO MANICHAEISM

In his nineteenth year Augustine read the *Hortensius* of Cicero, a work now lost save for some fragments. This work contained an exhortation to the life of philosophy and set the young Augustine aflame with the love for wisdom.[2] One thing, he tells us, held him back: "the name of Christ was absent and whatever was without that name, no matter how literary and polished and true, could not completely carry me off."[3] Hence, Augustine turned to a study of the Scriptures, but he found them unworthy of comparison with the lofty style of Cicero. The style of the Old Latin version was indeed barbarous, but Augustine found the content objectionable as well.[4] For this reason Augustine fell in with the Manichees, from whose lips the names of the Father and of the Lord, Jesus Christ, and of the Paraclete, our comforter, the Holy Spirit, were never absent.[5] The *Hortensius* set Augustine aflame with

---

1 See *Contra Faustum* XXX,1: CSEL 25/1,748, where Faustus speaks of the Elect as a sacerdotal rank as opposed to the Hearers; see also XXX,5: CSEL 25/1,753.

2 See *Confessions* III, iv, 7–8: CCL XXVII, 29–30

3 *Confessions* III, iv, 8: CCL XXVII, 30.

4 See H. Chadwick, *Augustine* (Oxford and New York: Oxford University Press, 1986), p. 11.

5 See *Confessions* III, vi, 10: CCL XXVII,31.

the love of truth, and the Manichees unceasingly spoke of the Truth which they promised to teach without first imposing the burden of believing. In *The Usefulness of Believing* Augustine writes to his friend, Honoratus, whom he had converted to Manichaeism and would now draw back to Catholicism, that

> we fell in with such men for no other reason than that they kept saying that, apart from the terror of authority, they would, by pure and simple reason, lead to God and free from all error those who were willing to be their hearers.[6]

The African church seems to have preserved the anti-intellectual spirit of Tertullian famous for his claim to believe precisely because it is absurd.[7] Reflections of such anti-intellectualism are found in Augustine's warning that there were within the Church bishops and priests who, "content with simple faith, have no concern for a deeper knowledge."[8] Similarly, Augustine mentions, in dealing with the Manichaean question about what God was doing before he created the world, that he will not give the answer that some give, namely, that God was preparing hell for those who ask such profound questions.[9]

The heart of Augustine's intellectual problems centered, as he later realized, around his inability to conceive of God and the soul as incor-

---

6 De utilitate credendi I, 2: CSEL 25/1, 4.

7 Tertullian asked, in *De praescriptione haereticorum* VII, 9: CCL I, 193, what Athens has to do with Jerusalem and what the Academy has to do with the Church. In *De carne Christi* V, 4: CCL II, 881, he stated that he believed in the death of the Son of God because it is absurd (*ineptum*) and in his resurrection because it is impossible.

8 *De moribus ecclesiae catholicae et de moribus Manichaeorum* I, 1, 1: PL XXXII,1311; see also the Manichaean claim that Catholics say that "one should not inquire into anything with curiosity, because Christian belief is simple and absolute" (*Contra Faustum* XII, 1: CSEL 25/1,329), which echoes Tertullian's claim that "we have no need for curiosity after Christ Jesus, or of inquiry after the Gospel" (*De praescriptione haereticorum* VII,12: CCL II,193.

9 See *Confessiones* IX, xii, 14: CC XXVII, 201. See also E. Peters, "What was God doing before He created the Heavens and the Earth?" *Augustiniana* 34 (1984): 53–74; Peters traces the question back to the Epicureans, who suggested that the gods were sleeping, and to the Gnostics who gave the question the above formulation.

poreal.[10] Like the rest of the Western world apart from a few Neoplatonists, Augustine shared the implicit corporealist metaphysics typified by Tertullian's insistence that, if it is not a body, it is not real.[11] Such a corporealism resulted in serious metaphysical problems.[12] But such a corporealism also resulted in serious problems for a literal interpretation of the Bible. For example, given such a corporealism, God and the soul must be bodily, and the Manichees, themselves corporealists in this sense, could use the claim in Genesis that man was made in God's image to argue that the Catholics thought of God as having human form and bodily parts.[13] If, after all, God is bodily, as humans obviously are, then human beings can hardly be the image of God unless God has a human body with hair and nails. In *On Genesis against the Manichees* Augustine points out that it was this question in particular that the Manichees used to raise against us

> because we believe that man was made to the image and likeness of God. For they attend to the shape of our body and ask in their unfortunate way whether God has a nose, teeth, a beard, interior organs and the other things we need.[14]

Another serious problem with the Old Testament for the young Augustine of 373 was the immoral lives of the Patriarchs. Augustine

---

10 See *Confessions* V, x, 19–20: CCL XXVII, 68.

11 For example, in *De carne Christi* XI, 4: CCL II, 895, he says, "Omne, quod est, corpus est sui generis. Nihil incorporale nisi quod non est," and in *De anima* VII, 3: CCL II, 790, he says, "Nihil enim, si non corpus." On the Stoic position that whatever is is a body, see E. Weil, "Remarques sur le 'materialisme' des Stoiciens," in *Melanges Alexandre Koyre*. II. L'aventure de l'esprit (Paris: Hermann, 1964), pp. 556-572. See Confessions V, x, 19: CCL XXVII, 68-69: "cogitare nisi moles corporum non noveram—neque enim uidebatur mihi esse quicquam quod tale non esset."

12 For some of the metaphysical implications, see my "The Aim of Augustine's Proof that God Truly Is," *International Philosophical Quarterly* 26 (1986): 253–268.

13 See *Confessions* III, vii, 12: CCL XXVII, 33.

14 See *Confessiones* V, x, 19 and VI, xi, 18: CC XXVII, 68–69 and 86, where Augustine obviously finds such an anthropomorphic view of God quite disgusting. He had, nonetheless, been convinced that the Catholic Church held such a view. See *Confessions* VI, iv, 5 and VI, xi, 18: CCL XXVII, 76–77 and 86, for his joy at finding that the spiritual believers in the Catholic Church did not hold such a view.

has preserved for us the objections raised by Faustus, the Manichaean bishop. Faustus accuses Abraham of "burning with an insane desire for offspring, not believing God who had promised him a child from Sarah, and having intercourse with a servant with—what is more shameful—his wife's knowledge." He accuses Abraham of lying to Abimelech and Pharaoh, claiming that Sarah was his sister and selling her into concubinage. He mentions Lot's incest with his daughters. And he becomes most indignant over Jacob's bigamous marriages to Rachel and Lia along with his relations with two servants, claiming that, "as the husband of four wives, he wandered among them like a goat," while they fought over who would have him each day as he returned from the field.[15] Secundinus, the Manichee, in writing to Augustine and inviting him to return to Manichaeism, lists such contents of the Old Testament and adds, "I know you always hated these things; I know you always loved great things that would leave the earth behind and seek the heavens, that would put the body to death and bring life to souls."[16] Even Gospels presented serious problems. For example, the genealogies of Christ in Matthew and Luke seem to contradict each other. Hence, both cannot be true. In fact, Augustine suggests that it was precisely the contradictions between the two genealogies that led him to abandon the Catholics for the Manichees.[17]

II. THE BIBLE AUGUSTI KNEW AS A MANICHEE

The Manichees not merely claimed to be Christian, but regarded the Catholics as only semi-Christian, largely because the Catholics retained the Jewish Scriptures.[18] In becoming a Manichee, Augustine would not have thought of himself as abandoning Christianity, but as becoming a member of Christianity's intellectual elite. Peter Brown compares Manichaeism to British Communism during the 30s and claims that the Manichaeism of Augustine was that "of the cultivated intelligentsia."[19] Though we now think of Manichaeism as a distinct

---

15 See *Contra Faustum* XXII, 5: CSEL 25/1, 594.

16 *Secundini Manichaei ad sanctum Augustinum epistula* 3: CSEL 25/2, 897.

17 See *Sermo* LI, 6: PL XXXVIII, 336–337.

18 *Contra Faustum* I, 2: CSEL25/1, 251.

19 Peter Brown, *Augustine of Hippo: A Biography* (Berkeley: University of California Press, 1969), p. 54.

world religion, like Islam, Augustine viewed it, after his baptism in the Catholic Church, as a Christian heresy.[20] But as a Manichee, Augustine would have thought of Manichaeism as the true and full Christianity, and he would have read or heard the Gospels and St. Paul.[21] Johannes Van Oort claims that "Manichaeism was so much imbued with Christianity and specifically with Pauline teachings that O'Meara could write ...: "In a sense it might seem that to become a Manichee was to depart little, if at all, from being a Christian.""[22] Within the Manichaean community the New Testament held a place roughly analogous to that of the Old Testament within the Catholic Church, while the Manichaean scriptures held a position like that of the New Testament in the Catholic community.[23] The Manichees rejected the Old Testament almost in its entirety, but they certainly were familiar with it and used it to undermine the faith of the uneducated Catholics and to lure them into their communion.[24]

F. Decret has summed up the Manichaean arguments against the Old Testament under three headings: 1) The Manichees argue that the Old Testament is its own undoing, since its prophecies have not been fulfilled, its Law is immoral and grotesque, and its principal personages led immoral and disgusting lives; 2) They argue that Christ himself rejected the Old Testament, and 3) They argue that in the

---

20 See *De haeresibus* XLVI, 1–19: CCL XLVI, 312–320.

21 See P. Brown, *Augustine of Hippo*, pp. 370–371, where he discusses the "Letter to Menoch," attributed to Mani by some scholars, which contains a fragment of a Manichaean commentary on Paul.

22 J. Van Oort, *Jerusalem and Babylon. A Study of St. Augustine's City of God and the Sources of His Doctrine of the Two Cities* (Leiden: E. J. Brill, 1991), p. 208. Van Oort cites J. J. O'Meara' *The Young Augustine. The Growth of St. Augustine's Mind up to his Conversion* (New York: Longmans, 1954), p. 79, where O'Meara is speaking specifically of one becoming a Hearer.

23 Van Oort and other recent scholars argue that the Christian elements in Manichaeism were present from the beginning and not simply syncretistic additions to African Manichaeism, as had previously been thought. See Van Oort, *Jerusalem and Babylon*, pp. 229–231. See also F. Decret, *Aspects du Manicheisme dans l'Afrique romaine* (Paris: Etudes Augustiniennes, 1970), pp. 11–12.

24 See *De Genesi contra Manichaeos* I, I, 2: PL XXXIV, 173. Van Oort claims that Manichees did not reject the Old Testament completely, since there is some good mixed with the bad; see *Jerusalem and Babylon*, p. 35, n. 104.

name of the New Testament, Christians reject the Law, and they point out that even the Catholics, who claim to retain the Old Testament, do not observe its Law.[25]

Moreover, the Manichees rejected from the New Testament the Acts of the Apostles. In fact, they were reluctant even to mention it, because this book reported the coming of the Paraclete, whom the Manicheans held to be Mani himself.[26] They even rejected parts of the Gospels and of the Letters of Paul, claiming that they had been interpolated by someone else who introduced Jewish elements into the Christian Bible. Hence, for all practical purposes the Bible for the Manichees was the Gospel and the Apostle, though without the passages they rejected as interpolations.[27]

For the Manichees the Gospel meant in essence the moral teaching of Christ. When asked whether he accepts the Gospel, Faustus replies that he certainly does, but insists that "the Gospel began to be and received its name from the preaching of Christ."[28] Faustus thus excludes the genealogies and infancy narratives from the Gospel, rejecting the claim that Christ was the son of David and born of a human mother. "The Gospel is not genealogy," he tells us; it is rather "the preaching of Christ" or "of the Son of God."[29] Again, asked whether he accepts the Gospel, Faustus insists that he does accept it, namely, "the preaching and command of Christ."[30] He points to the life of the beatitudes he himself is living and to the fact that Christ promised the kingdom of heaven to those who do his Father's will and who keep his commands. He adds, "Nowhere did he say, 'Blessed are those who confess that I

---

25 See F. Decret, *Aspects du Manicheisme*, pp. 146–149.

26 For the rejection of Acts, see *Contra Adimantum* XVII, 5, CSEL 25/1, 169–170; *Contra epistulam quam vocant Fundamenti* 5: CSEL 25/1, 198–199; *De utilitate credendi* III, 7: CSEL 25/1, 9–10; *Contra Faustum* XIX, 31 and XXXII, 15: CSEL 25/1, 534–535 and 774–775.

27 F. Decret's study of Augustine's works, *Contra Fortunatum*, *Contra Faustum*, and *Contra Felicem*, has shown that these Manichees referred most frequently to Matthew (58 references to 42 passages). Next came John's Gospel with 30 references to 23 passages, followed by the Pauline Letters. See F. Decret, *Aspects du Manicheisme*, pp. 169–173.

28 *Contra Faustum* 11, 1: CSEL 25/1, 253.

29 See *Contra Faustum* 11, 1: CSEL 25/1, 254.

30 *Contra Faustum* V, l: CSEL 25/1, 271.

was born."³¹ Given their rejection of the genealogies and the birth of Christ from Mary, the Manichees had to deny the reality of Christ's death and his resurrection. The wounds he showed to the doubting Thomas had, accordingly, to be merely simulated.³²

Even in the Letters of Paul there are passages that Faustus has to reject as falsified, for example, that "the Son of God was born according to the flesh of the seed of David" (Rm 1:3). He claims this reflects "an old and former opinion of Paul concerning Jesus, when he considered him the son of David, as the rest did." As proof of his claim, he invokes the text, "If we once knew Christ according to the flesh, we do not now know him" (2 Cor 5:16), to show that Paul later corrected his earlier belief.³³ On the other hand, the Manichees accepted various apocryphal books, such as The Acts of Thomas, as well as those of Peter, John, Andrew and those written by a certain Leutius.³⁴

Augustine later recounts how he used to enjoy his victories over the uneducated Catholics, which suggests that he had once used against them some of the same arguments from the Old Testament that he later answered in his writings against the Manichees.³⁵ Moreover, he mentions that the Manichaeans praised Mani, especially because "he spoke the bare and proper truth with all the wrappings of figures removed."³⁶ Later Augustine would hold them in turn to a literal interpretation of one of their own writings that described God as "a scepter-bearing king crowned with garlands of flowers."³⁷ But the fact that the Manichees boasted that their books presented the bare and proper truth without figures also indicates the typically Manichaean demand for the literal interpretation of the Catholic Scriptures. Au-

---

31 *Contra Faustum* V, 3: CSEL 25/1, 273.

32 See *Contra Faustum* XV, 10 and XVI, 11: CSEL 25/1, 437 and 450, where Augustine accuses Faustus of preaching a Christ with false or pretended wounds.

33 *Contra Faustum* XI, 1: CSEL 25/1, 313.

34 See *Contra Adimantum* XVII, 2 and 5: CSEL 25/1, 166 and 170; *Contra Faustum* XXII, 79 and XXX, 4: CSEL 25/1, 681 and 751–752; and *Contra Felicem* 11, 6: CSEL 25/2, 833.

35 See *De duabus animabus* XI: CSEL 25/1, 65–66.

36 *Contra Faustum* XV, 5: CSEL 25/1, 425.

37 *Contra Faustum* XV, 5–6: CSEL 25/1, 425–426.

gustine would come to learn that such a literal interpretation was fatal: "The letter kills" (2 Cor 3:6).

III. THE USE OF THE BIBLE AGAINST THE MANICHEES

Augustine's use of the Bible in controversy with the Manichees can be conveniently examined under three headings: one, the canon of the Scriptures, two, the proper approach to the Bible, and three, the interpretation of the biblical text.

(A) THE CANONICAL SCRIPTURES

The Manichees, as we have seen, rejected the Old Testament, as well as the Acts of the Apostles and various passages from the Gospels and Paul which they claimed had been added later. Augustine, on the other hand, insisted upon the canonical Scriptures, appealing to the authority of those books.[38] Thus Augustine holds the authority of those Scriptures are preeminent,

> which from the time of Christ's presence have come down to our times, preserved, recommended and rendered illustrious in the whole world through the ministry of the Apostles and the certain succession of bishops in their sees.[39]

Similarly, he tells the Manichees "that the authority of our books, strengthened by the assent of so many nations through the successions of apostles, bishops, and councils, is against you."[40] The credibility even of the Gospel rests upon the authority of the Church. In his *Reply to the Letter called "The Foundation,"* Augustine states, "I would not believe the Gospel, if the authority of the Catholic Church did not move me."[41]

Against the Manichaean claims that the New Testament contains passages added by later writers who interjected elements from the

---

38 One must bear in mind that there was not at this time an official Catholic canon of Scripture and that Augustine himself contributed to its formation at the first Council of Hippo in 393. See *Breviarium Hipponense* 36: CCL CXLIX, 43.

39 *Contra Faustum* XXXIII, 9: CSEL 25/1, 796.

40 *Contra Faustum* XIII, 5: CSEL 25/1, 382.

41 *Contra epistulam quam vocant Fundamenti* 5: CSEL 25/1, 197.

Jewish Scriptures, Augustine insists upon the integrity of the Scriptures handed down in the Church. He mentions that, even while he was a Manichee, he had regarded as feeble the Manichaean claim "that the New Testament writings were falsified by some unknown persons who wished to implant the law of the Jews in the Christian faith."[42]

Augustine points out that, though the Manichees accept the authority of Paul's Letters as the work of a holy man who speaks the truth, they claim that certain passages are not his. When challenged, they cannot produce better exemplars from more manuscripts or more ancient ones or from those in the original language. Rather they accept one passage as Paul's because it supports them and reject another because it is against them. To this Augustine retorts, "Are you then the standard of truth (*regula ueritatis*)?"[43] The Manichaean selectivity amounts to the destruction of all the authority of Scripture and makes each one his own authority.[44] But this means that the Manichee "is not subject to the authority of the Scriptures in faith, but subjects the Scriptures to himself ... so that he views something in Scripture as correct, because he finds it congenial."[45] Hence, Augustine insists upon the canonical Scriptures handed down in the Church from apostolic times and insists that whatever is stated in the Bible is true, though one may very well not understand how it is true.

(B) HUMBLE BELIEF BEFORE UNDERSTANDING

In approaching the Bible Augustine insists, first of all, that one accept as true what is stated there. It is this humble act of believing before understanding that is the key to the Catholic Augustine's approach to the Bible. Whereas the Manichees constantly repeated Mt 7:7: "Ask and you shall receive, seek and you shall find, knock and it will be opened," and Mt 10:26, "There is nothing hidden that will not

---

42 *Confessions* V, xi, 21:CCL XXVII, 69; see also *De utilitate credendi* 111, 7: CSEL 25/1, 9–10.

43 *Contra Faustum* XI, 2: CSEL 25/1, 315.

44 See *Contra Faustum* XXXII, 19: CSEL 25/1, 780: "You see, then, that your action removes all authority and each mind becomes an authority unto itself for what it approves or disapproves in any Scripture." So too, he claims, "You who believe what you will and do not believe what you will in the Gospel believe yourselves rather than the Gospel" (*Contra Faustum* XVII, 3: CSEL 25/1, 486).

45 *Contra Faustum* XXXII, 19: CSEL 25/1, 780.

be revealed," they refused to believe, that is, to accept as true, any passage of the Bible before they understood it.[46] From Is 7:9, which in Augustine's Old Latin read, "Unless you believe, you will not understand," Augustine argued for the need for humble intellectual submission to the word of God as the first step toward understanding. He tells Faustus, "The Catholic discipline teaches that the Christian mind should first be nourished by simple faith so that such faith may render it able to understand lofty and eternal things."[47] Thus when confronted with the apparent contradiction between the two genealogies, one must read the Gospels with piety and investigate diligently rather than condemn them rashly.[48] In preaching to his own flock Augustine presented the Manichaean argument and insisted upon the need for "simple and certain faith" until the Lord grants understanding.[49] When Augustine first confronted the difficulties with the Bible that lead him into the company of the Manichees, he had, he later reports, "disdained to be a little beginner. Puffed up with pride" he considered himself "a mature adult." He had not realized that "the Bible was composed in such a way that as beginners mature, its meaning grows with them."[50]

(c) THE INTERPRETATION OF SCRIPTURE

It is sometimes assumed that Augustine set aside the Bible in 373 when he became a Manichee and did not return to it until after his ordination in 391 when he asked his bishop, Valerius, for time to study

---

46 See *De moribus ecclesiae cathollcae et de moribus Manichaeorum* I, xvii, 31: PL XXXII, 1324.
47 *Contra Faustum* XII,46: CSEL 25/1,374–375.
48 *Contra Faustum* III,2: CSEL 25/1, 262.
49 See Sermo LI, 5: PL XXXVIII, 336. In *Contra Faustum* III, 3: CSEL 25/1, 263, Augustine argues that the two fathers of Joseph can be readily explained by one being his natural father and the other his father by adoption.
50 *Confessiones* III, v, 9: CCL XXVII, 31. I have here followed H. Chadwick's new translation (Oxford: Oxford University Press, 1991). For the role of the little ones or beginners as opposed to the adults or spirituals, see my "A Decisive Admonition for Augustine," *Augustinian Studies* 19 (1988): 85–92.

the Scriptures.[51] Augustine did ask Valerius for time to study the Scriptures.[52] But it was not that Augustine was unfamiliar with the Bible; he had, after all, been acquainted with the Gospel and the Apostle during his Manichaean years. He certainly knew the Manichaean complaints about the Old Testament. Indeed, he had already written his first commentary on the Bible, *On Genesis against the Manichees*, in 388-389

At this point Augustine accepted the whole of the canonical Scriptures. He needed time, not for a better acquaintance with the Bible, but for the diligent and pious study that would lead to a Catholic understanding of what he now believed to be true. In other words, having come to a Manichaean understanding of the Bible during his nine years as a "hearer," Augustine now needed time to come to a new understanding of the Bible in accord with the rule of faith in the Catholic Church.

Well before his baptism Augustine was influenced by the preaching of Ambrose who interpreted the Bible spiritually. As a result of first hearing Ambrose preach, probably late in 384, Augustine began to think that the Catholic faith could be defended against the Manichaean attacks, "especially after I had often heard [Ambrose] resolve one or another puzzle (*aenigmate*) from the Old Testament, where I was being killed, when I understood it literally."[53] Ambrose gave a spiritual interpretation of many passages from those books, and Augustine came to see that the Law and the Prophets could be defended. The *Confessions* record a second influence of Ambrose's preaching, which probably dates from late in 385. At this point Augustine discovered that the spiritual sons of God did not interpret man's being made in God's image and likeness so that it implied that God himself had the shape and members of a human body, though Augustine still had no idea of what a spiritual substance was. In his sermons Ambrose taught that "'the letter kills, but that the spirit gives life,' when he removed the

---

51 See V. Bourke, *Augustine's Quest for Wisdom. Life and Philosophy of the Bishop of Hippo* (Milwaukee: Bruce, 1944), p. 125, where Bourke says that "he simply had not had time since his conversion to become well acquainted with the Bible."

52 Epistula XXI 3-4 (ad Valerium): CSEL XXXIV, 49-54.

53 *Confessiones* V, xiv, 24: CCL XXVII, 71.

mystical veil and uncovered the spiritual sense of those things which in their literal meaning seemed to contain a perverse doctrine.[54]

Augustine was then no longer offended by what Ambrose said, but he still did not know whether what he said was true. What Augustine still needed was the philosophical concept of a non-bodily or spiritual substance which he was to get from "the books of the Platonists," which he read in late spring or summer of 386.[55] Ambrose himself was a student of Neoplatonic thought, along with a group of Milanese intellectuals, so that the sermons of Ambrose that Augustine heard were deeply imbued with Neoplatonic spiritualism.[56] As long as Augustine was unable to conceive of an incorporeal substance, he was unable to interpret the anthropomorphic descriptions of God in the Bible as metaphors for a spiritual reality. That is, what Augustine needed was precisely the philosophical concept of a non-bodily reality, and that he got from the books of the Platonists.[57]

Thus in *On Genesis against the Manichees*, Augustine's first attempt at biblical interpretation, he speaks of literal interpretation as taking the text "just as the letter sounds."[58] On the other hand, "all those who understand the Scriptures spiritually have learned to understand by those terms [God's eyes, ears, feet, and other parts] not as bodily members, but as spiritual powers. ..."[59] Thus "spiritual interpretation"

---

54 *Confessions* VI, iv, 6: CCL XXVII, 77.

55 See *Confessions* VII, ix, 13: CCL XXVII, 101. The Platonists in question were certainly Plotinus and possibly Porphyry, Plotinus's student and editor. Precisely which of Plotinus's *Enneads* and which works of Porphyry Augustine read is debated. As an example of this debate, see the articles by Frederick Van Fleteren and Robert O'Connell in *Augustinian Studies* 21 (1990): 83–152.

56 See the studies by Courcelle, which have shown that Augustine's conversion to Neoplatonism was not a conversion to a non-Christian philosophy. Rather he learned his Platonism within the Church of Milan; see P. Courcelle's *Recherches sur les Confessions de saint Augustin* (Paris: de Boccard, 1950), especially chapter III.

57 See my "Spirituals and Spiritual Interpretation in Augustine," *Augustinian Studies* 15 (1984): 65–81.

58 *De Genesi contra Manichaeos* II, ii, 3. Here literal interpretation excludes even such common figures of speech as metaphor and metonymy; it is not coincident with what the human author intended.

59 *De Genesi contra Manichaeos* I, xvii, 27: PL XXXIV, 186.

presupposes some grasp of a spiritualist metaphysics, for unless one can conceive of incorporeal realities, one cannot interpret a text that uses bodily images as referring to non-bodily realities.

In two of his early attempts at biblical exegesis, Augustine mentions four ways of interpreting the Old Testament for those who diligently desire to know it: as history, as etiology, as analogy, and as allegory.[60] In *The Usefulness of Believing*, Augustine explains that a text is presented "as history, when it teaches what was written or what was done, or what was not done, but is only written as if it were done." Thus something is presented as history as long as it is in narrative form, whether the events occurred or not. The text is presented "as etiology, when we are shown the reason why something was said or done," and the text is presented "as analogy, when it is shown that the two Testaments, the New and the Old, are not opposed to each other." Finally, the text is presented "as allegory, when one is taught that certain things which are written there are not to be interpreted literally, but should be understood as figurative."[61] Augustine shows that Christ and the Apostles used these ways of understanding the Law and the Prophets. For example, Jesus recalled as history how David and his men had eaten loaves from the Temple (Mt 12:3–4) and explained as etiology why Moses had permitted divorce (Mt 19:8).[62] Augustine does not here give a concrete example of understanding the text by analogy, but Augustine's work, *Against Adminantus*, written in 33 or 394 against a disciple of Mani, a man regarded as a great teacher in that sect and as second in learning only to Mani himself, provides twenty nine cases of alleged conflict between the two Testaments and Augustine's replies.[63] With regard to allegory Augustine points out that "our liberator" used it in appealing to the sign of Jonah (Mt 12:39–40) and that Paul used it in 1 Cor 10:1–10, where Paul says, "These things were figures of us," and, "All these thing happened to [the fathers in the desert] in figures."

---

60 See *De utilitate credendi* 111, 5: CSEL 25/1, 7–8 and *De Genesi ad litteram liber imperfectus* 11, 5: CSEL 28/1, 461.

61 *De utilitate credendi* 111, 6: CSEL 25/1, 8.

62 *De utilitate credendi* 111, 6: CSEL 25/1, 8.

63 On Adimantus, see *Contra Faustum* 1, 2: CSEL 25/1, 252 and *Contra Adimantum* xii, 2: CSEL 25/1, 139.

So too, he appeals to Gal 4:22–26, where Paul, speaking of the two sons of Abraham, says, "These things were said in allegory."[64]

The thirty three books of Augustine's *Contra Faustum* provide a wealth of examples of Augustine's interpretation of Scripture in controversy with the Manichees. Augustine states several general principles that he invokes in answering Faustus. For instance, when Faustus is asked whether he accepts the Old Testament, he answers, "How can I, when I do not observe its commandments?" and adds, "I don't think you do either."[65] He is referring to the Sabbath, circumcision, the sacrifices, abstinence from pork, and the observances of feasts, for he regards the moral precepts of the Decalogue as the law of the nations.[66] Augustine distinguishes between "commandments for living life" and "commandments for signifying life" and claims that "You shall not covet" is a commandment for living life, while the commandment to circumcise the male child is a commandment signifying life. The Manichees, he argues, fail to see that the practice of latter commandments were signs or shadows of what was to come about and that, once the reality foreshadowed has come about, the signs signifying its coming need no longer be observed.[67] The Catholics observe everything in the Old Testament, "not now in figures, but in the reality which those figures foretold by what they signified."[68] Thus Augustine can maintain that the Catholics hold that "everything written in the Old Testament is true and commanded by God and adapted to those times."[69] The teaching of both Testaments is found in both the Old and the New, "there in figures, here revealed, there in prophecy, here rendered present.[70]

Secondly, the Manichees denied that the Old Testament spoke of Christ at all, whether by foreshadowing him or by prophesying about

---

64 *De utilitate credendi* 111, 6-8: CSEL 25/1, 10-12.

65 *Contra Faustum* VI, 1: CSEL 25/1, 284.

66 In *Contra Faustum* XIX, 2: CSEL 25/1, 497, Faustus distinguished "three kinds of law: one is that of the Hebrews which Paul calls the law of sin and death, the second is that of the nations, which he calls natural ... and third kind of law is the truth. ..."

67 *Contra Faustum* VI, 2: CSEL 25/1, 285--286.

68 *Contra Faustum* XVI, 32: CSEL 25/1, 481.

69 *Contra Faustum* X, 3: CSEL 25/1, 311.

70 *Contra Faustum* XVI, 32: CSEL 25/1, 481.

him. Augustine, on the other hand, makes the rather bold claim that "everything that Moses wrote is about Christ, that is, pertains to Christ completely, either because it foretells him by figures of things done or said, or because it recommends his grace and glory."[71] Or, still more generally, he says, "The Old Testament is for those who understand correctly a prophecy of the New Testament."[72] Speaking of the Prophets, Augustine says "everything contained in those books was said about [Christ] or on account of him. But in order to incite the seeker and to delight the finder, many more things are taught there in allegories and enigmas, in part by words alone, in part by the narration of events."[73] Hence, Augustine charges the Manichees with abusing the marvelous work of the Holy Spirit in those books, in which

> many things are stated simply and in a way suited to those souls that creep on the ground so that they may rise up through human things to things divine, and many things are stated there in figures so that the studious mind may be more profitably exercised in its inquiries and may rejoice more richly in its discoveries.[74]

---

71 *Contra Faustum* XVI, 9: CSEL 25/1, 447.

72 *Contra Faustum* XV, 2: CSEL 25/1, 419.

73 Contra Faustum XII, 7: CSEL 25/1, 335--336.

74 *De moribus ecclesiae catholicae et de moribus Manichaeorum* I, xvii, 30: PL XXXII, 1324.

CRITERIA FOR FIGURATIVE INTERPRETATION IN ST. AUGUSTINE

I. THE DIFFERENT CRITERIA

When making a translation of *De Genesi contra Manichaeos*, I had to deal with Augustine's exegetical principles as they were embodied in that work, his first written attempt at Scriptural interpretation.[1] Augustine wrote this work in 388 or 389, soon after his conversion and his return to Africa from Italy, but prior to his ordination.[2] His principal audiences were the Manichees, especially those whom he himself had led into that sect, such as Honoratus and Romanianus, and the uneducated, "little ones" of the *Catholica* who were easy prey for the Manichean objections to the Old Testament.[3] Especially in the second book, the work presents a highly figurative interpretation of the Genesis narrative—so much so that Agaësse and Solignac suggest that in this earliest commentary on Genesis Augustine regarded the Paradise story as a parable without historical basis or as allegory in the modern sense, which denies or excludes rather than presupposes a literal and historical sense.[4] Nonetheless, the reasons that Augustine gives for providing a figurative interpretation of the text in this work always center around the impossibility of taking the text in its proper sense and, at the same time, avoiding blasphemy, impiety or absurdity in speaking about God. That is, his stated reasons for having recourse to a figurative interpretation of the text were those

---

1 See *Saint Augustine on Genesis: Two Books on Genesis against the Manichees and On the Literal Interpretation of Genesis: An Unfinished Book*. Translated by Roland J. Teske. Washington, D.C.: Catholic University of America Press, 1991.

2 See *De Genesi ad litteram* VIII, ii, 5: BA 49, 14, and *Retractationes* I, x, 1: CCL LVII, 29.

3 See *Saint Augustine on Genesis*, pp. 6–15.

4 See their introduction to *De Genesi ad litteram* in BA 48, pp. 33–34 and 38.

which Jean Pépin pointed out in his article, "A propos de l'histoire de l'exégèse allégorique: l'absurdité, signe de l'allégorie."[5]

Pépin found that among Christians of the first centuries, such as Origen and Augustine that "the principal indication that a biblical text had been written with an allegorical intent and ought to be understood as such is the absurdity of the text as long as one sticks to the literal sense."[6] He maintains that this absurdity criterion is the same one that found among pagan authors in their interpretation of classical literature.

Given the sober reasonableness of this criterion, which is the one Augustine claims to use in the *De Genesi contra Manichaeos*, I was quite startled to find that Augustine stated in the later *De doctrina christiana* another criterion for figurative interpretation that clearly goes far beyond this early and more sober one. There he writes, "You should know that whatever in the word of God cannot in the proper sense be referred to the goodness of morals or the truth of the faith is figurative."[7]

Henri-Irenée Marrou refers to this rule as Augustine's fundamental law of spiritual interpretation: "We find the theory formulated in the *De doctrina christiana*: it is summed up in a fundamental law: everything in Scripture that does not directly refer to faith and morals must be regarded as figurative."[8] Marrou asks his readers to weigh the import of this fundamental law and points out that "Saint Augustine does not merely say that we must take as figurative everything in Scripture that is contrary to faith and morals, but also everything that

---

5 *Studia Patristica* in *Texte and Untersuchungen* 63 (1955): 395–413.

6 "La réponse des chrétiens des premiers siècles est claire: le principal indice qu'un texte biblique a été écrit dans un dessein allégorique et doit être entendu comme tel, c'est son absurdité aussi longtemps que l'on s'en tient au sens littéral" (Pepin, p. 397).

7 *De doctrina christiana* III, x, 14: CCL XXXII, 86; see the following note for the Latin.

8 "Nous en trouvons la théorie formulée dans le *de doctrina christiana*: elle se résume en une loi fondamentale: tout ce qui dans l'Ecriture ne se rapporte pas directement à la foi et aux moeurs doit être tenu pour figuré, *quidquid in sermone divino neque ad morum honestatem, neque ad fidei veritatem proprie referri potest, figuratum est cognoscas*" (*Saint Augustin et la fin de la culture antique* [Paris: de Boccard, 1938], p. 478).

is not directly related to them."[9] Obviously, this fundamental law maximizes the amount of Scripture that has a figurative sense, for there is a vast amount of Scripture that does not in its proper or literal sense deal directly with matters of faith or of moral conduct. One need only think of Augustine's treatment the miraculous catch of fish in John 21, where he finds a figurative meaning in the number of disciples engaged in the fishing expedition, in the 153 fishes that were caught, in the lowering of the nets on the right side of the boat, in the fact that Jesus was standing on the shore, in the fact that the nets did not break, etc.[10] That is, given this fundamental law none of these things could have been mentioned pointlessly. Since in their proper sense such a passage does not present us with things we are to believe or with moral precepts, it must be taken as figurative of something else or of many other things.

Thus, while the criterion for figurative interpretation that Augustine claimed to be using in *De Genesi contra Manichaeos* is that comparatively sober and limited one which I have, following Pépin's lead, suggested, the criterion stated less than ten years later in *De doctrina christiana* is anything but sober and limited.[11] I began this paper convinced that there were in Augustine these two, quite different criteria for figurative interpretation, and the question I set out to answer was this: Why did Augustine move from the sober and reasonable criterion that Pépin pointed out to that criterion found in the *De doctrina christiana* which maximized the amount of the text that is taken as figurative? The conclusion I have come to is that my initial conviction was mistaken and my question misguided. The remainder of this paper will explain what had led me to my original hypothesis and why I now believe it to have been incorrect.[12]

---

9 "Saint Augustin ne dit pas seulement qu'il faut dans l'Écriture prendre au figuré tout ce qui est contre la foi et les moeurs, mais bien tout ce qui ne s'y rapporte pas directement" (Ibid, p. 479).

10 See *In Ioannis euangelium* CXXII,5–9: CCL XXXVI, 670–675.

11 Though Augustine completed the third book and added the fourth at the time of his writing the *Retractationes*, he completed the third book up to the point at which he broke off writing, i.e., at III, xxv, 35, ll. 9–11, no earlier than the end of 397. See the preface to CCL XXXII, vii–xi.

12 Apart from Marrou I have not found anyone else who has discussed these two criteria or who has dealt with the relations between them. In her *Saint Augustin exégète du quatrième évangile* (Paris: Beauchesne, 1930), M.

II. THE CASE FOR THE ABSURDITY CRITERION

It is well known that Augustine found serious difficulties with the Scriptures that contributed to his leaving the faith of Monica and becoming a Manichee.[13] It is also well known that it was the preaching of Ambrose that led him to see, first, that the Catholic faith could be defended and, later, that the spiritual men of the *Catholica* did not believe the "infantile nonsense" that he had thought they did.[14] Hence, it is reasonable to suppose that Augustine's account of the influence of Ambrose will throw light upon the criterion for figurative interpretation that played a decisive role in his own return to the faith of the Catholic Church and that he used in his first venture at Scriptural interpretation.

In the *Confessions* Augustine reports two occasions on which Ambrose's preaching had significantly influenced his understanding of the Scriptures. In the first passage, which marks an early contact with Ambrose probably dating from late 384, Augustine tells us that he began to think that the Catholic faith could be defended against the attacks of the Manichees,

> especially after having often heard [Ambrose] resolve one or more of the enigmas from the Old Testament, where I was being killed,

Comeau, for example, simply passes over my concern. Madeleine Moreau, in her "Lecture du *De doctrina christiana*" in *Saint Augustin et la Bible*, ed. Anne-Marie La Bonnardière (Paris: Beauchesne, 1986), pp. 253–285, simply notes, "Il importe tout d'abord d'éviter absolument tant la confusion entre valeur métaphorique et valeur propre d'une expression que la confusion inverse. Le critère à appliquer relève de la foi et des moeurs: tout ce qui, dans le texte biblique, est, dans sa littéralité, étranger à la morale ou à la vérité de la foi requiert une interprétation figurée" (p. 267). Marrou speaks of the twofold function of recourse to a mystical sense: "le recours au sens mystique a chez lui, comme première fonction, celle qu'il avait deja chez Origène: c'est un moyen d'expliquer tous les passages choquants de l'Ancien Testament, anthropomorphisme divin, immoralité de certaines prescriptions ou de certain récits, contradictions entre l'ancienne et la nouvelle loi" (Marrou, p. 478). But then he points out that the fundamental law goes way beyond this function in terms of what I have called the maximizing criterion.

13 See *Confessions* III, v, 9: BA 13, 376, and III, vii, 12–x, 18: BA 13, 384–398.

14 *Confessions* VI, iv, 5: BA 13, 526: "ecclesia unica ... non saperet infantiles nugas. ..."

when I understood it according to the letter. When he had spiritually explained many passages from those books, I blamed that despair of mine, at least insofar as I believed that the Law and the Prophets could in no way stand up against those who hated and mocked them.[15]

As a result of this first influence of Ambrose Augustine came to see that the Catholic way was undefeated, but not so undefeated that it had won the victory.[16]

Augustine later mentions the second influence of Ambrose's preaching, which probably dates from late in 385. At that point, he tells us, he was overjoyed to discover that the spiritual sons of God did not hold that man's being made to God's image and likeness entailed that God himself was confined to the shape of the human body. Even though Augustine himself still had no suspicion of what a spiritual substance was, he rejoiced that he had so long been opposed, not to the Catholic faith, but to the figments of a carnal imagination.[17] Augustine tells us that, in his sermons to the people, Ambrose taught that

> "the letter kills, but that the spirit gives life," when he removed the mystical veil and uncovered the spiritual sense of those things that in their literal meaning seemed to contain a perverse doctrine. He did not say anything that offended me, though I still did not know whether what he said was true.[18]

Given the importance of Ambrose's spiritual interpretation of the Old Testament for Augustine's subsequent conversion, it is not surprising

---

15 *Confessions* V, xiv, 24: BA 13, 508–510: "maxime audito uno atque altero et saepius aenigmate soluto de scriptis ueteribus, ubi, cum ad litteram acciperem occidebar, spiritaliter itaque plerisque illorum librorum locis expositis iam reprehenderam desperationem meam illam dumtaxat, qua credideram legem et prophetas destestantibus atque irridentibus resisti omnino non posse."

16 Ibid.: BA 13, 510: "ita enim catholica non mihi uicta uidebatur, ut nondum etiam uictrix appareret."

17 In *De beata vita* I, 4: CCL XXIX, 67, Augustine describes hearing Ambrose and Theodorus speak as though one should not think of a body, when one thinks of God or the soul.

18 *Confessions* VI, iv, 6: BA 13, 528: "'littera occidit, spiritus autem uiuificat,' cum ea, quae ad litteram peruersitatem docere uidebantur, remoto mystico velamento spiritaliter aperiret, non dicens quod me offenderet, quamvis ea diceret, quae utrum uera essent adhuc ignorarem."

to find that in his first attempt at scriptural exegesis he has recourse to the criterion for figurative and spiritual interpretation that he had found most helpful in the sermons of the bishop of Milan.[19]

If we turn to *De Genesi contra Manichaeos*, we find that he explicitly appeals to the absurdity criterion. In *De Genesi contra Manichaeos* II, i, 1, Augustine announces that in Genesis 2 "the whole narrative unfolds not openly, but in figures, in order to exercise the minds of those seeking the truth and to call them away from carnal concerns to a spiritual concern."[20] Then after presenting the account of the creation and sin in Genesis 2 and 3 and after admonishing the Manichees that they should rather seek to understand the secrets of the text rather than find fault with it, he proposes to examine the whole account first as history and then as prophecy, that is, first as narrating the facts and then as foretelling the future. Then he says,

> Of course, if anyone wanted to take everything that was said according to the letter, that is, to understand it exactly as the letter sounds, and could avoid blasphemies and explain everything in harmony with the Catholic faith, we should not only not envy him, but regard him as a leading and highly praiseworthy interpreter. But if there is no way in which we can understand what has been written in a manner that is pious and worthy of God without believing that these things have been set before us in figures and enigmas, we have the apostolic authority by which so many enigmas from the books of the Old Testament are solved.[21]

---

19 I stress Augustine's recourse to the criterion for figurative interpretation he found most helpful, since Ambrose's use of figurative interpretation certainly tends to be far less restrained than Augustine's. That is, there is good reason to suppose that Augustine also derived from Ambrose's preaching the grounds for maximizing the figurative interpretation.

20 *De Genesi contra Manichaeos* II, i, 1: PL XXXIV, 195: "Quae omnis narratio non aperte, sed figurate explicatur, ut exerceat mentes quaerentium veritatem, et spiritali negotio a negotiis carnalibus avocet."

21 Ibid. II, ii, 3: PL XXXIV, 197: "Sane quisquis voluerit omnia quae dicta sunt, secundum litteram accipere, id est non aliter intelligere quam littera sonat, et potuerit evitare blasphemias, et omnia congruentia fidei catholicae praedicare, non solum ei non est invidendum, sed praecipuus multumque laudabilis intellector habendus est. Si autem nullus exitus datur, ut pie et digne Deo quae scripta sunt intelligantur, nisi figurate et in aenigmatibus proposita ista credamus; habentes auctoritatem apostolicam a quibus tam multa de libris Veteris Testamenti solvuntur aenigmata. ..."

That is, Augustine admits that he himself cannot interpret the text of Genesis 2 and 3 "exactly as the letter sounds," but that he would welcome the interpretation of someone else who could do so. The grounds for resorting to figurative interpretation lie in his inability to "avoid blasphemies and explain everything in harmony with the Catholic faith." He cannot understand the text "in a manner that is pious and worthy of God" unless he believes that Genesis presents us with events "in figures and enigmas." That is, the only reason for believing that the text contains figures and enigmas is that such a belief provides the only escape (*exitus*) from understanding the text in a manner that is blasphemous, lacking in piety, and unworthy of God.

Much later in *De Genesi ad litteram*, Augustine reports that, when he came to deal in his first commentary on Genesis with the narrative of chapters 2 and 3:

> It did not then occur to me how I could interpret everything in the proper sense, and I thought that everything could not, or was hardly able, or was able only with difficulty to be so interpreted. Hence, in order to avoid delay, I explained as briefly and as clearly as possible the figurative meaning of those things for which I could not find a literal interpretation. ..."[22]

That is, Augustine reports that he had recourse to a figurative interpretation of the text only because of his inability or great difficulty in interpreting everything in the text in its proper sense. But he went on to tell us that in the later work he "thought that it could be shown even by him that these things [i.e., the creation narrative in Genesis 2 and 3] were written in a proper, not in anallegorical mode of expression."...[23]

---

22 *De Genesi ad litteram* VIII, ii, 5: BA 49, 14: "Et quia non mihi tunc occurrebant omnia quemadmodum proprie possent accipi magisque non posse uidebantur aut uix posse atque difficile, ne retardarer, quid figurate significarent, ea quae ad litteram inuenire non potui, quanta ualui breuitate ac perspicuitate explicaui."

23 Ibid. IX, ii, 5: BA 49, 16: "extimarem etiam per me posse secundum propriam, non secundum allegoricam locutionem haec scripta esse monstrari. ..." In the intervening years Augustine had attempted another literal interpretation of Genesis, namely, *De Genesi ad litteram liber imperfectus*. Of this work he tells us, "in scripturis exponendis tirocinium meum sub tanta sarcinae mole succubuit, et nondum perfecto uno libro ab eo quem sustinere non poteram labore conquieui" (*Retractationes* I, xviii: CCL LVII, 54).

The criterion for a figurative interpretation of a Scriptural text that, according to the *Confessions*, Augustine learned from Ambrose's preaching and that played a decisive role in his conversion was the more limited and sober one. In *De Genesi contra Manichaeos* he explicitly tells us that he used this criterion in his first venture at an interpretation of the opening chapters of Genesis. Furthermore, in retrospect he tells us in *De Genesi ad litteram* that he had recourse to figurative interpretation in *De Genesi contra Manichaeos*, only because he could not then interpret the text in its proper sense. Hence, I said of Augustine's practice in *De Genesi contra Manichaeos* that "he almost always resorts to regarding the text as figurative only if he cannot take it literally without blasphemy or having it say something unworthy of God."[24]

There is, however, at least one passage in *De Genesi contra Manichaeos* where Augustine's theory of figurative interpretation goes beyond the absurdity criterion. In speaking of Eve's being made from Adam's rib, Augustine explicitly distinguishes between a proper and a figurative expression. He says,

> For a proper expression is one thing; quite another is a figurative expression, such as we are dealing with here. Hence, even if in terms of history a visible woman was first made from the body of the man by the Lord God, she was certainly not made in this way without a reason, but to convey some secret.[25]

Augustine points out that there was plenty of mud available for God to make the woman as he had made the man and that he could have taken the rib from the man painlessly while he was awake.

> Whether, then, these things were said figuratively, or whether they were also done figuratively, they were not said or done in this way to no point. Rather they are clearly mysteries and sacraments, whether they are to be interpreted and understood in the way our modest

---

24 *Saint Augustine on Genesis*, p. 27, n. 54.

25 *De Genesi contra Manichaeos* II, xii, 17: PL XXXIV, 205: "Aliud est quippe propria locutio, aliud figurata, qualis ista est quam tractamus modo. Quapropter etsi visibilis femina secundum historiam de corpore viri primo facta est a Domino Deo, non utique sine causa ita facta est, nisi ut aliquod secretum imtimaret."

talent is trying or in some better way, though in accord with sound faith.[26]

In this one passage in *De Genesi contra Manichaeos*, Augustine offers a criterion for figurative interpretation that goes beyond his more modest criterion, namely, that the impossibility of taking the text in the proper sense without absurdity or impiety. Here he claims that the making of Eve could not be done or described as it was to no point (*frustra*) and that the events reported are mysteries and sacraments. However, there is on the basis of this text no reason to suppose that all the events reported in Genesis are mysteries and sacraments or that all the events reported either teach matters of faith and morals or are figurative of something else.

It is important to see what Augustine means by the text being figurative. He speaks of "figures of speech" and "figures of things."[27] By "figures of speech" he means such figures as metonymy, amphiboly, and metaphor.[28] By "figures of things" he means something that either symbolizes or prefigures something else. Thus, days of the Genesis narrative prefigure the six ages in the history of salvation and and the six stages in the life of every person.[29] As a narrative of past events Genesis is history; as prefiguring what is to come it is prophecy. Augustine treats the text of Genesis in each book of *De Genesi contra Manichaeos* first as history and then as prophecy. But "figures of things" not merely prefigure what is to come; they also symbolize or are signs of other things, often of spiritual or incorporeal things.[30] Thus in Genesis 2 where we are told that everything unfolds in figures, Augustine understands by "the green of the field" an invisible creature such as the soul, and by

---

26 Ibid. : PL XXXIV, 205–206: "Sive ergo ista figurate dicta sint, sive etiam figurate facta sint, non frustra hoc modo dicta vel facta sunt; sed sunt plane mysteria et sacramenta, sive hoc modo quo tenuitas nostra conatur, sive aliquo alio meliore, secundum sanam tamen fidem sunt interpretanda et intellegenda."

27 See *De Genesi contra Manichaeos* I, xxii, 34: PL XXXIV, 189, and II, ii, 3: PL XXXIV, 197.

28 See *Augustine on Genesis*, pp. 21–24

29 See *De Genesi contra Manichaeos* I, xxiii, 35–xxv,43: PL XXXIV, 190–194.

30 See *De Genesi ad litteram* VIII, i, 4: BA 49, 14. Augustine speaks of what the text teaches "figurata significatione ... sive ipsarum spiritalium naturarum vel affectionum sive rerum etiam futurarum."

the spring that watered the whole earth he understands the fountain of truth from which souls drank before the fall. So too by the tunics of skin he understands the mortal bodies the first couple received after their sin. Clearly in these cases the text contains figures that are enigmas or allegories.[31] When Augustine says of Genesis 2 and 3 that "the whole narrative unfolds in figures," he is primarily speaking of the text as history, for even Genesis 1 prefigures the future ages of each person and of human history. That is, he is stating that the whole narrative is expressed by words not used in their proper sense, but in a transferred or figurative sense. And his reason for recourse to such a figurative sense lies, he claims, with the absurdity criterion.

III. THE DE DOCTRINA CHRISTIANA CRITERION

The fundamental law for figurative interpretation from *De doctrina christiana* is precisely a criterion for distinguishing between cases when terms used in their proper sense and cases in which they are used in a transferred or figurative sense. At the beginning of Book Three of *De doctrina christiana*, Augustine points out that the ambiguity of Scripture lies in words used either properly or metaphorically.[32] Earlier he distinguished proper and metaphorical signs:

> [Signs] are called proper when they are used to signify these things on account of which they were instituted, just as we say "ox" when we understand the animal that all who speak the Latin language call by this name along with us. They are metaphorical, when the things themselves to which we refer by the proper terms, are used to refer to something else, just as we say "ox" and by that one syllable understand the animal that is usually called by this name, but again by it we understand an evangelist to whom Scripture referred, as the Apostle has shown, "You shall not muzzle the ox that treads the grain."[33]

---

31 In *De Genesi ad litteram liber imperfectus* II, 5: CSEL XXVIII, 461, Augustine says that to understand a text as allegory is to understand it as presenting something in figures. An enigma simply means a riddle or puzzle. In *De Genesi contra Manichaeos* Augustine seems to use "allegory" as synonymous with "enigma."

32 *De doctrina christiana* III, i, 1: CCL XXXII, 77: "sciat ambiguitatem scripturae aut in uerbis propriis aut in translatis. ..."

33 Ibid. II, x, 15: CCL XXXII, 41: "Propria dicuntur, cum his rebus significandis adhibentur, propter quas sunt instituta, sicut dicimus bouem,

Augustine first deals with ambiguity in words used in their proper sense, pointing out that here ambiguity may arise from dividing a sentence incorrectly, from mispronouncing a word, or from the similarity of the forms for different Latin cases.[34] But ambiguities of terms used in their proper senses rarely present problems that cannot readily be solved.

Ambiguities in metaphorical terms, on the other hand, demand considerable care and hard work. One must, first of all, avoid taking a figurative expression literally. Augustine points out that the Apostle's words, "The letter kills, but the spirit gives life" (2 Cor 3:6), are pertinent here.

> For when one takes what was said figuratively as if it were said in the proper sense, one thinks in carnal terms. For one who follows the letter regards metaphorical terms as proper and does not refer that which is signified by the proper sense of the word to another signification.[35]

As examples of such carnal thinking, Augustine points to understanding of Sabbath as merely referring to one of the seven days of the week or understanding sacrifice as only referring to the sacrifices of animals

---

cum intellegimus pecus, quod omnes nobiscum latinae linguae homines hoc nomine uocant. Translata sunt, cum et ipsae res, quas propriis uerbis significamus, ad aliquid aliud significandum usurpantur, sicut dicimus bouem et per has duas syllabas intellegimus pecus, quod isto nomine appellari solet, sed rursus per illud pecus intellegimus euangelistam, quem significauit scriptura interpretante apostolo dicens: 'bouem triturantem non infrenabis.'"

34 As an example of the first, Augustine gives the Arian division of Jn 1:1: "In principio erat uerbum et uerbum erat apud deum et deus erat; uerbum hoc erat in principio apud deum" (*De doctrina christiana* III, ii, 3: CCL XXXII, 78). As an example of the second he uses "*os*" which can mean either mouth or bone, depending upon whether the vowel long or short. As an example of an ambiguity of the Latin case, he cites 1 Thes 3:7, where "*fratres*" might be either accusative or vocative. See *De doctrina christiana* III, iii, 7–iv,8: CCL XXXII, 81–82.

35 *De doctrina christiana* III, v, 9: CCL XXXII, 82–83: "Cum enim figurate dictum sic accipitur, tamquam proprie dictum sit, carnaliter sapitur. ... Qui enim sequitur litteram, translata uerba sicut propria tenet neque illud, quod proprio uerbo significatur, refert ad aliam significationem. ..."

or of the fruits of the earth. Such understanding mistakes signs for things, and that is "a wretched slavery of the mind."[36]

Augustine also warns against a second danger, namely, of taking a proper expression as if it were figurative.[37] Obviously there is need of a way to discover whether an expression is proper or figurative. He then states the general criterion by which one can determine this. And in general the method is that you should know that whatever in the word of God cannot in the proper sense be referred to goodness of morals or to the truth of the faith is figurative.[38]

Augustine explains that goodness of conduct has to do with loving God and the neighbor, while the truth of faith has to do with knowing God and the neighbor. But, if that is the case, then any passage of Scripture that cannot in its proper sense be understood as either a matter of faith or of morals is to be understood as figurative. Here we have what I have referred to as Augustine's maximizing rule for figurative interpretation.

IV. THE DIFFERENT CRITERIA REEXAMINED

Up to this point I have indicated the two criteria that Augustine articulated for having recourse to a figurative interpretation of Scripture. In his earliest commentary on Genesis Augustine both articulates and employs the absurdity criterion. According to the *Confessions* it was this same criterion that Augustine learned from the preaching of Ambrose and found most helpful toward his own conversion. The second criterion articulated in *De doctrina christiana* and used in much of Augustine's Scriptural exegesis goes far beyond the absurdity criterion and claims that whatever is not related to faith and morals is figurative. I mentioned earlier that I now regard my initial question, namely, why Augustine moved from the absurdity criterion to the maximizing criterion of *De doctrina christiana*, as mistaken. Let me sketch my reasons for changing my initial hypothesis.

When writing the introduction to the translation of *De Genesi contra Manichaeos*, I focused too much upon what Augustine said was the

---

36 Ibid.: CCL XXXII, 83: "miserabilis animi seruitus. ..."

37 Ibid. III, x, 14: CCL XXXII, 86.

38 Ibid.: "Et iste omnino modus est, ut quidquid in sermone diuino neque ad morum honestatem neque ad fidei ueritatem proprie referri potest, figuratum esse cognoscas."

criterion for figurative interpretation rather than the interpretation that Augustine actually gave of the text. Years ago Henri de Lubac said that "it is of prime importance to observe Origen at work rather than to stick to some abstract explanation of his method,[39] even though the abstract explanation was given by Origen himself. Similarly, it is of prime importance to observe Augustine at work rather than to take at face value his stated criteria for figurative interpretation. In focusing upon the criterion that Augustine stated in De Genesi contra Manichaeos, I overlooked the criterion that he actually used, which in fact goes far beyond the absurdity criterion. Hence, I do not now believe that Augustine moved from the absurdity criterion to the maximizing criterion of De doctrina christiana.

The criterion of De doctrina christiana does, nonetheless, represent an advance over that found in Augustine's earlier works, but it represents not so much an advance in practice as in the articulation of Augustine's exegetical principles. The difference in the articulation of the criteria for recourse to figurative interpretation should not come as a surpise. For De Genesi contra Manichaeos is, after all, directed to the Manichees, and in justifying his use of figurative interpretation Augustine makes explicit appeal to the criterion that he found most helpful in his own conversion and that he might reasonably hope would be most of help to his readers, especially his Manichean friends and "the little ones" of the Catholica. The criterion articulated in De doctrina christiana, on the other hand, was intended for believers who were ready, able, and eager to understand the hidden richness of the word of God. One should not after all attempt to teach the deeper and figurative meaining to those unwilling to learn.[40]

Furthermore, it may well be that the sharpness of the distinction I drew between the criteria should be blurred or that one would speak

---

39 "[I]l importe avant tout de voir Origène à l'oeuvre plutôt que de se tenir à quelque exposé méthodique abstrait ..." (H. de Lubac, Histoire et esprit. L'intelligence de l'Ecriture d'apres Origène. Theologie 16 (Paris: Aubier, 1950), p. 34.

40 For example, in the late work, Contra adversarium legis et prophetarum I, xvi, 31: CCL XLIX, 59, Augustine says, "Verum quid opus est de mysticis significationibus sacrificiorum uestisque nuptialis inconuenientem carnalibus sensibus uelle inculcare sermonem?" That is, it is pointless to teach to carnal minds mystical meanings. So too, it was pointless to disclose the richness of the word of God to the Manichees.

more correctly of a single criterion with two functions or emphases. For example, Marrou ties the criterion found in *De doctrina christiana* with another that Augustine states in *De Genesi ad litteram* IX, xii, 22.[41] Augustine there says that he undertook the exposition of Genesis with two goals in mind, first, "to show that what some superficial or unbelieving readers might think impossible or contrary to the authority of Holy Scripture ... was neither impossible nor contrary to it." Secondly, he would show

> that what appears possible and has no semblance of contradictoriness, but could seem to certain people to be either superfluous or lacking sense, was not something produced in the natural or ordinary course of events. Thus we might believe that it has a mystical meaning, since nothing can be found there that is lacking sense."[42]

That is, though it was not Augustine's aim in that work to examine the hidden prophetic meaning (*prophetica aenigmata perscrutari*), he still would show that things that might seem superfluous or pointless were not simply natural events, but ones that we should believe have a mystical or hidden meaning.[43] The sense of the passage will depend upon

---

41 H.-I. Marrou, p. 479.

42 *De Genesi ad litteram* IX, xii, 22: BA 49, 120–122: "ut quod impossibile uideri uanis atque incredulis potest aut ipsi auctoritati sanctae scripturae uelut testificatione contraria repugnare ... demonstrem neque inpossibile esse neque contrarium; quod autem possible quidem adparet nec habet ullam speciem repugnantiae, sed tamen quasi superfluum uel etiam stultum quibusdam uideri potest, hoc ipsum disputando demonstrem, quod ideo non tamquam rerum gestarum naturali uel usitato ordine factum est, ut ... quia stultum esse non potest, mysticum esse credatur. ..."

43 Marrou also points to the Preface to *Speculum*, where Augustine says that in the Scriptures "quaedam sic esse posita, ut tantum scirentur et crederentur ... et quaedam facta divina vel humana tantummodo cognoscenda narrantur: quaedam vero sic esse jussa, ut observarentur et fierent, vel prohibita, ne fierent. ... Horum autem quae jubendo et vetando scripta sunt, alia sunt sacramentorum velata mysteriis, quae multa Veteris Testamenti populo illa facienda mandata sunt, neque a populo christiano nunc fiunt. ... sed aliquid significare intelliguntur. Alia vero etiam nunc facienda sunt ..." (*Speculum*, praef.: PL XXXIV, 887–889). This position does not have the force of the criterion in *De doctrina christiana* since it admits reports of human and divine actions as matters merely to be known and since it seems to limit figurative interpretations to the area of Old Testament commands and prohibitions.

the force one gives to *superfluum* and *stultum*. For if one takes *stultum* as "foolish" or "fatuous," one comes close to the "absurdity" criterion for taking a text as figurative. Much the same thing occurs, if one takes *superfluum* in the sense of *otiosum* (see Mt 12:36).[44] This passage from *De Genesi ad litteram* is, in any case, merely a generalization of the criterion we saw in *De Genesi contra Manichaeos* for interpreting the creation of Eve as figurative.

Marrou suggests two reasons for Augustine's having adopted what I have called his maximizing criterion for figurative interpretation. One, he suggests that Augustine took very literally the text from Timothy: "*omnis scriptura divinitus inspirata utilis est.*" Given those words, Augustine said, "We have then to seek a hidden meaning for all those passages whose usefulness is not apparent in the literal sense."[45] Marrou points to the fundamental idea underlying this position: "Nothing in the Bible is useless, not even less useful; it is in its entirety inspired, and the inspiration is equally portioned out, and has everywhere the same density."[46]

Marrou's second reason for Augustine's having adopted this maximizing criterion is that his training in rhetoric taught him to study a text verse by verse and word by word rather than sentence by sentence. "The tendency is reenforced by the habit inherited from the profane grammarian that consists in reading the text verse by verse, in commenting on it word by word, in breaking it down into isolated fragments which are examined each separately in the utmost detail."[47] Similarly, Joseph Lienhard has said quite well, "The ancients' first unit

---

44 In his *De trinitate*, c. 19, when arguing that the Father could only speak one Word, William of Auvergne argues that he who has forbidden that we speak an idle word, would certainly not do so himself. So too, one might argue that God could hardly have uttered an idle word in Scripture.

45 "Or saint Paul nous dit (2 Tim. 3, 16) que toute l'Ecriture est divinement inspirée et utile. ... Il faut donc chercher un sens caché à tous les passages dont l'utilité n'apparait pas au sens litteral" (Marrou, p. 479).

46 "[R]ien dans la Bible n'est inutile, ni même moins utile; elle est tout entière inspirée, et l'inspiration y est également repartie, à partout la même densité" (Marrou, p. 480).

47 "Tendance que renforce l'habitude, heritée du grammairien profane, qui consiste à lire le texte verset par verset, à le commenter mot par mot, à le décomposer en fragments isolés qu'on examine chacun séparément avec la plus stricte minutie" (Marrou, p.480).

of understanding was not the pericope, or the sentence, but the single word. The word as a the starting point for understanding was an assumption of ancient education in poetics and rhetoric."[48] Coupled with Marrou's first reason, this second reason means that divine inspiration bears upon individual words and phrases rather than upon larger units of meaning.

Another reason for Augustine's having recourse to the more ample criterion for figurative interpretation is tied to his conviction that Scripture contains only a few truths to be believed and a few moral precepts to be followed. After stating his fundamental law, he points out that "good moral conduct has to do with loving God and the neighbor, and the truth of the faith has to do with knowing God and the neighbor."[49] Furthermore, our hope lies in our consciousness of progressing in the knowledge and love of God.[50] The truths to be believed and the moral precepts to be followed are comparatively few in number. Scripture "merely states the Catholic faith in things past, present and future ... but all of these serve to nourish and strengthen charity and to conquer and extinguish cupidity."[51] The whole of Christian morality is summed up in fostering charity and conquering its opposite, cupidity.[52] Then Augustine makes the startling claim: "One supported by faith, hope and charity and firmly holding unto them has no need of the Scriptures save for teaching others."[53] And he appeals to the example of Christian hermits who have lived without

---

48 J. Lienhard, "'The Glue Itself is Charity': Ps 62:9 in Augustine's Thought," in *Collectanea Augustiniana: Presbuter Factus Summa*, ed. by J. Lienhard, E. Muller, and R. Teske (New York: Peter Lang, 1993), pp. 375–384.

49 *De doctrina christiana* III, x, 14: CCL XXXII, 86: "Morum honestas ad diligendum deum et proximum, fidei ueritas ad cognoscendum deum et proximum pertinet."

50 Ibid.

51 Ibid. III, x, 15: CCL XXXII, 87: "Non autem adserit nisi catholicam fidem rebus praeteritis et futuris et praesentibus. ... sed omnia haec ad eandem caritatem nutriendam atque roborandam et cupiditatem uincendam atque exstinguendam ualent."

52 Ibid.: "Non autem praecipit scriptura nisi caritatem nec culpat nisi cupiditatem et eo modo informat mores hominum."

53 Ibid. I, xxxiv, 43: CCL XXXII, 31: "Homo itaque fide et spe et caritate subnixus eaque inconcusse retinens non indiget scripturis nisi ad alios instruendos."

the Scriptures.[54] Given Augustine's view that the essence of Scripture is contained in the Creed and the commandments to love God and neighbor, the vast majority of the Bible would be *"superfluum"* and *"stultum"* unless it contained hidden meanings, *enigmata* and figures to be understood by those who would seek to understand the word of God. Hence, most of the Bible would be pointless and senseless if we were not to take it as figurative.

One final thought: In *De doctrina christiana* Augustine says that Scripture teaches us the historical events in which we must believe and that the purpose of this faith is to nourish and strengthen charity. Had I not earlier read *De Genesi contra Manichaeos* with almost exclusive attention to the absurdity criterion, I might have noticed that the Cherubim and the flaming sword set to guard Paradise were interpreted by Augustine as signifying that we can return to the tree of life only through the flaming sword, i.e., through tribulations, and through the Cherubim, i.e., the fullness of knowledge, as he assures us the term means in Hebrew. But the fullness of knowledge is the fullness of the Law, that is, the full content of Scripture. And Paul has assured us that the fullness of the Law is charity (Rom 13:10). Hence, with a bit of Augustinian exegesis of Augustine, one might argue that the core of the *De doctrina christiana* criterion was already present in his earliest work on Genesis, where "the whole narrative unfolds, not openly, but in figures, to exercise the minds of those seeking the truth."[55]

---

54 Ibid.
55 *De Genesi contra Manichaeos* II, i, 1: PL XXXIV, 195.

ST. AUGUSTINE AND THE VISION OF GOD

In his classic study of western mysticism, Dom Cuthbert Butler says of Augustine of Hippo:

> Augustine is for me the Prince of Mystics, uniting in himself, in a manner I do not find in any other, the two elements of mystical experience, viz. the most penetrating intellectual vision into things divine, and a love of God that was a consuming passion.[1]

This paper will deal with the first of the two elements of mystical experience in St. Augustine, namely, the "intellectual vision into things divine." Butler sums up Augustine's teaching on the nature of such intellectual vision or contemplation in two theses: one, "[t]he Contemplation of God is the lot of the Blessed in heaven; in it consists their eternal happiness," and, two, "[t]hough Contemplation really belongs to the next life, in this life some beginnings of it are possible, some passing glimpses or intuitions of divine things."[2] That is, contemplation or intellectual vision of God, though properly the reward of the saints in heaven, is anticipated to some degree by some persons in this life. This paper will deal with some of the things that Augustine has to say about the second thesis, that is, about the intellectual vision of God attained by some in this life. Butler refers to such a vision of God as "the fundamental Postulate of Mysticism: that it is possible in this life to see somewhat of God—to have an experimental perception of him."[3]

One might approach this topic through an examination of texts in which Augustine describes a contemplation that he himself attained.[4]

---

1 Cuthbert Butler, *Western Mysticism: The Teaching of Augustine, Gregory and Bernard on Contemplation and the Contemplative Life*. 2nd ed., with Afterthoughts (New York: Harper and Row, 1966), p.20.

2 Ibid., pp. 26 and 27.

3 Ibid., p. 25.

4 That is, one might deal with the ascents to God in *Confessions* VII, x, 16–xi,17 BA 13, 614-618), VII, xvii, 23 (BA 13, 626–630), and VII, xx, 26 (BA 13, 634), as well as with the vision at Ostia in *Confessions* IX, x, 23–26 (BA 14, 114–120). See F. Van Fleteren, "The Early Works of Augustine and his Ascents at Milan," *Studies in Medieval Culture* X, ed. John R. Som-

However, one can also approach the topic through an examination of texts that describe mystical experience of God in an objective rather than an autobiographical mode. Among the latter sort of texts there are, in the works of St. Augustine, at least two that have been regarded as treatises on mystical theology. Butler says that *De quantitate animae* XXX,73–76 is, among all of Augustine's utterances, "the nearest approach to a formulation of Mystical Theology."[5] And Matthias Korger calls *De Genesi ad litteram* XII, in which Augustine deals with Paul's being taken up to the third heaven (2 Cor 12:2-4), "the first systematic writing on mysticism."[6] This paper, then, will examine what Augustine says about the possibility of an intellectual vision of God in this life by studying these two basic texts on Augustinian mysticism, along with *Epistola* CXLVII, *De videndo Deo liber*, which is closely related to the *De Genesi ad litteram* text and clarifies some points key to this topic.

I. DE QUANTITATE ANIMAE XXX,70–76.

In *De quantitate animae* XXX, 70 Augustine begins to speak of the power of the human soul and describes seven steps or levels in the soul's ascent toward God. At the first level the soul vivifies, unifies and preserves the body—all those functions that we have in common with plants. At the second level there is the life of sensation, which we have in common with the other animals. The third level is proper to mankind and involves all those things we owe to reason. Here we have great human achievements, but no differentiation between the learned and unlearned or between morally good and evil souls.[7]

---

merfelt and Thomas Seiler (Kalamazoo: The Medieval Institute, 1977), pp. 19–23, as well as his "Augustine's Ascent of the Soul in Book VII of the Confessions: A Reconsideration," *Augustinian Studies* 5 (1974): 29–72, for such an approach.

5 Ibid., p. 48.

6 "So wird der Paulustext zum Auggangspunkt jener grundsetzlichen Besinnung über das Wesen mystischer Phänomene überhaupt, die man mit Recht die erste systematische Schrift über Mystik nennen konnte" (Matthias E. Korger, "Grundprobleme der augustinischen Erkenntnislehre Erläutert am beispiel von *de genesi ad litteram* XII," *Recherches Augustiniennes* 2 [1962]: 33–57, here 34).

7 "Magna haec et omnino humana. Sed est adhuc ista partim doctis atque indoctis, partim bonis ac malis animis copia communis" (*De quantitate animae* XXX, 72; CSEL LXXXIX, 220).

At the fourth level we have the beginning of moral goodness; here the soul dares to assert its superiority not only to its own body, but to the whole corporeal universe.[8] At this level the soul takes up the task of its purification amid the fear of death, but at the fifth stage the soul emerges free from all impurity. "Then it possesses itself most happily in itself and does not fear anything for itself or suffer anything on its own account."[9] Augustine adds,

> At this level the soul grasps every sort of greatness it has, and when it has grasped this, it then advances with a great and incredibile trust toward God, that is, toward the contemplation of the truth and that most high and most hidden reward on account of which it has toiled so much.[10]

Augustine's sixth step, then, involves the movement "toward God, that is, toward the contemplation of the truth." The soul's action by which it seeks to know those things that exist truly and in the highest manner is the highest gaze of the soul; it has none more perfect, better or more correct.[11] While the fourth step involves cleansing the soul's eye so that it does not look in vain or rashly and see poorly and the fifth step involves protecting and preserving its healthy condition, the sixth step involves "directing the calm and correct gaze toward what is to be seen (*iam serenum atque rectum aspectum in id quod videndum est, dirigere*)."[12]

---

8 *De quantitate animae* XXX, 73; CSEL LXXXIX, 220–221.

9 "Tum se denique in seipsa laetissime tenet nec omnino aliquid metuit sibi aut ulla sua causa quidquam angitur" (*De quantitate animae* XXX, 74; CSEL LXXXIX, 222). The translations of Augustine are my own.

10 "In hoc gradu omnifariam concipit, quanta sit: quod cum conceperit, tunc vero ingenti quadam et incredibili fiducia pergit in Deum, id est in ipsam contemplationem veritatis, et illud, propter quod tantum laboratum est, altissimum et secretissimum praemium" (*De quantitate animae* XXX, 74; CSEL LXXXIX, 222).

11 See *De quantitate animae* XXX, 75; CSEL LXXXIX, 222.

12 *De quantitate animae* XXX, 75; CSEL LXXXIX, 223. Butler (p.26) takes this phrase as a definition of contemplation, but directing one's gaze toward what is to be seen is not the same thing as seeing. See *Soliloquia* I, vi, 13; CSEL LXXXIX, 21. At this sixth level there is "actio, id est, appetitio, intelligendi ea quae vere summeque sunt" (*De quantitate animae* XXX, 75; CSEL LXXXIX, 222). Contemplation, that is, the vision of the truth is the seventh and last step of the soul, not the sixth.

The seventh step is not so much a step (*gradus*) as an abode (*mansio*) at which one arrives by these steps. Augustine finds it difficult to express "the joys, the fruition of the highest and true good, and the breathe of peacefulness and of eternity" found at this level.[13] But he adds, "We believe that certain great and peerless souls have also seen and do see these things, and they have expressed these things to the extent that they judged that they should be expressed."[14] The identity of these souls is left unspecified, though the evidence indicates that Augustine meant to include among them Plato, some Neoplatonists and, possibly, St. Paul.[15] In any case Augustine says,

> This I venture to tell you quite plainly: if we follow the course that God commands us and we have undertaken to follow, we shall arrive by the power and wisdom of God at that highest cause, or highest author, or highest principle of all things, or whatever other name is more suitable for so great a reality.[16]

---

13 "Quae sint gaudia, quae perfruitio summi et veri boni, cuius serenitatis atque aeternitatis adflatus" (*De quantitate animae* XXX, 76; CSEL LXXXIX, 223).

14 "Dixerunt haec, quantum dicenda esse iudicaverunt, magnae quaedam et incomparabiles animae, quas etiam vidisse ac videre ista credimus" (*De quantitate animae* XXX, 76; CSEL LXXXIX, 223).

15 See J. Maréchal, SJ, "La vision de Dieu au sommet de la contemplation d'après saint Augustin," *Nouvelle Revue Théologique* 58 (1930): 89–109 and 191–214, here 97. Maréchal bases this identification on a comparison with *De ordine* II, x, 28 (CCL XXIX, 123), where Augustine refers to the works of the Neoplatonists as "magnorum hominum et paene diuinorum libri plenissimi," as well as on "le chevauchement qui règne encore, dans cet ouvrage, entre le plan de la foi et celui de la philosophie" (p. 97). See also Butler's statement: "The reference to the experience of 'certain great and incomparable souls' is without doubt to the ecstasies of Plotinus and Porphyry" (p. 43). Butler cites in an appendix (pp. 232–236) the relevant texts from Plotinus and appeals to *De quantitate animae* 33, 76 as evidence that "St Augustine accepted them as fully religious mystical experiences" (p. 236). Even Charles Boyer, in *L'idee de vérité dans la philosophie de saint Augustin* (Paris: Beauchesne, 1940), p. 215, who sees here a reference to St. Paul "entre autres," admits that Plato and Plotinus have employed the same language and that the whole purpose of the *Enneads* "est de révéler les étapes par lesquelles on arrive progressivement à la contemplation de l'Intelligence et à la fusion avec l'Un" (p. 217).

16 "Illud plane nunc ego audeo tibi dicere, nos si cursum, quem nobis deus imperat et quem tenendum suscepimus, constantissime tenuerimus, per-

That is, Augustine is at this point confident that he and his friends will attain in this life to the vision of God that the great and peerless souls he has mentioned have described, provided that they persevere in the path they have taken. Though it is not clear from this passage that the vision that was attained by these souls and that Augustine hopes to attain with his friends is the sort of vision of God that the blessed souls will enjoy in heaven, other texts from this early period do make that clear.

Perhaps the clearest indication that Augustine did hold that such a vision of God was attainable in this life is found in the second book of *De ordine*, where Augustine begins to set forth the program of studies for those resolved to seek God with all their strength.[17] He points out that we are led to learn in two ways: by authority and by reason. While authority is temporally prior, reason is prior by its nature as the more valuable. Though authority is more beneficial for the unlearned multitude, reason is better suited to the learned. Yet, since we only become learned from a state in which we lack learning, we ought to present ourselves to our teachers as docile so that authority can open the door for us who desire to come to know the great and hidden goods. Once one has become docile through following the precepts of the best life,

> he will learn with what reason those precepts were endowed which he followed prior to reason. He will learn what reason itself is which he follows and comprehends, now strong and suited there to, after the cradle of authority. He will learn what the intellect is in which all things are—or rather it itself is all things—and what is the principle beyond all things.[18]

Thus one who begins in faith and follows the precepts of the best life and pursues the disciplines of the intellect comes to a knowledge of

---

venturos per virtutem dei atque sapientiam ad summam illam causam vel summum auctorem vel summum principium rerum omnium vel si quo alio modo res tanta congruentius adpellari potest." (*De quantitate animae* XXX,76; CSEL LXXXIX, 223–224).

17 *De ordine* II, ix, 26; CCL XXIX, 122.

18 "Discet et quanta ratione praedita sint ea ipsa, quae secutus est ante rationem, et quid sit ipsa ratio, quam post auctoritatis cunabula firmus et idoneus iam sequitur atque comprehendit, et quid intellectus, in quo uniuersa sunt—uel ipse potius uniuersa—et quid praeter uniuersa uniuersorum principium" (De ordine II, ix, 26; CCL XXIX, 122).

the Trinity: reason, intellect and principle.[19] Of such knowledge Augustine says,

> In this life a few arrive at this knowledge, but beyond this knowledge no one can advance even after this life. There are men content with authority alone, who devote themselves to fine conduct and correct desires, either contemning or refusing education in the finest and liberal disciplines. I do not know how I could call them happy as long as they live this human life; still I firmly believe that, as soon as they have left this body, they are set free with greater ease or difficulty in accord with whether they lived more or less well.[20]

Though the above passage from *De ordine* is perhaps the clearest statement that through intellectual training some few men can attain a knowledge in this life that cannot be surpassed even after this life, there are other texts that imply this same position. For example, in *De beata vita*, Augustine draws the conclusion,

> No one doubts that everyone in need is unhappy, and the bodily needs of wise men do not shake our position. For the mind itself, in which is found the happy life, does not need these things. The mind itself is perfect, and nothing perfect needs anything. It will take what seems necessary for the body if it is available, and if it is not, the lack of such things will not crush it.[21]

---

19 In Neoplatonic terms he comes to know *logos, nous* and *arche*; in Christian terms the Spirit, Word and Father. See Olivier du Roy, *L'intelligencede la foi en la trinité selon saint Augustin* (Paris: Etudes Augustiniennes, 1966), pp. 125–128. Du Roy notes the parallel between *De ordine* II, ix, 26 and *Enneads* I, 8, 2 and V, 3, 5.

20 "Ad quam cognitionemin hac uita peruenire pauci, ultra quam uero etiam post hanc uitam nemo progredi potest. Qui autem sola auctoritate contenti bonis tantum moribus rectisque uotis constanter operam dederint aut contemnentes aut non ualentes disciplinis liberalibus atque optimis erudiri, beatos eos quidem, cum inter homines uiuunt, nescio quo modo appellem, tamen inconcusse credo, mox ut hoc corpus reliquerint, eos, quo magis minusue uiuerunt, eo facilius aut difficilius liberari" (*De ordine* II, ix, 26: CCL XXIX, 122). See also *De moribus ecclesiae* I, I, l (PL XXXII, 1311), where Augustine speaks of bishops and priests "contenti simplici fide" and warns those desirous of knowledge of the truth not to despair of finding it in the Catholic Church because of them.

21 "Ergo, inquam, miserum esse omnem qui egeat, dubitat nemo nec nos terrent quaedam sapientium corpori necessaria. Non enim eis eget ipse animus, in quo posita est beata uita. Ipse enim perfectus est: nullus autem

Earlier Augustine had said in his dedication that Theodorus was already clinging to the happy life—perhaps a reason for his regretting his fulsome praise for Theodorus.[22] In any case, when reviewing his works, Augustine comments on this passage and says that he was displeased by his having said,

> that in this lifetime the happy life abides in the mind alone of the wise man, regardless of the condition of the body. For the Apostle hoped for the perfect knowledge of God in the life to come (1 Cor 13:12). A man cannot possess a greater knowledge than that, and we should speak of the happy life only when the incorruptible and immortal body will be subjected to the spirit without any difficulty or reluctance (1 Cor 15:44ff).[23]

Even in the *Retractationes* Augustine does not, one should note, deny to those in this life every sort of vision of God. What he explicitly rejects is the view that the happy life can in this life be found in the mind alone, and he claims that we will enjoy a perfect knowledge of God only when the immortal body is completely subject to the spirit.

In a similar vein, Augustine recalls, in the second book of *De libero arbitrio*, the text of Isaiah, "Unless you believe, you will not understand," and goes on to point out how the Lord exhorted those he called to salvation to believe first.[24]

> But afterwards when he spoke of the gift he would give to those who believe, he did not say, "This is eternal life that they believe," but "This is eternal life that they know you the only true God and him whom you sent, Jesus Christ" (Jn 17:3). Then he said to those who believe, "Seek and you shall find" (Mt 7:7). For what one believes without knowing cannot be said to have been found, nor does

---

perfectus aliquo eget et, quod uidetur corpori necessarium, sumet, si adfuerit, si non adfuerit, non eum istarum rerum franget inopia" (*De beata vita* IV, 25; CCL XXIX, 78).

22 See *De beata vita* I, 5 (CCL XXIX, 68) and *Retractationes* I, 2; (CCL LVII, 11).

23 "Quod tempore uitae huius in solo animo sapientis dixi habitare beatam uitam, quomodolibet se habeat corpus eius, cum perfectam cognitionem dei, hoc est qua homini maior esse non possit, in futura uita speret apostolus, quae sola beata uita dicenda est, ubi et corpus incorruptibile atque inmortale spiritui suo sine ulla molestia uel reluctatione subdetur" (*Retractationes* I, 2; CCL LVII, 11).

24 Isaiah 7:9 LXX.

anyone become fit to find God unless he first believes what he afterwards will know.[25]

Hence, we should seek with diligence. And what we seek with his encouragement, we will find under his instruction,

> to the extent that it can be found in this life and by such as we are. For we must believe that these things can be seen and possessed more clearly and more perfectly by better men even while they inhabit this earth and certainly by all good and pious men after this life. ...[26]

Even some eight years after his conversion, in *De duabus animabus*, while arguing against the Manichean defenders of a principle that is pure evil, Augustine asks whether the evil souls knew the good principle that they wanted to harm. For, if they knew it, their mind was a great good.

> Is there any other goal toward which good men direct their intention with great labor than the goal of understanding that highest and pure good? Will that unadulterated evil, then, have been able to attain, without the help of any good, what is granted now to only a few good men? If those souls governed bodies and saw that with their eyes, how many tongues and hearts and minds are enough to praise and extol those eyes, which the minds of the just can scarcely equal? What great goods we find in the highest evil! For, if to see God is bad, God is not the good. But God is the good. Hence, it is good to see God, and I know of no good that can be compared to this good.[27]

---

[25] "Sed postea cum de ipso dono loqueretur quod daturus credentibus non ait: 'Haec est autem uita aeterna ut credant,' sed: *Haec est*, inquit, *uita aeterna ut cognoscant te uerum deum et quem misisti Iesum Christum*. Denique iam credentibus dicit: *Quaerite et inuenietis*; nam neque inuentum dici potest quod incognitum creditur neque quisquam inueniendo deo fit idoneus, nisi ante crediderit quod postea cogniturus:" (*De libero arbitrio* II, ii, 6; CCL XXIX, 239).

[26] "Quantum in hac uita et a nobis talibus inueniri queunt. Nam et a melioribus, etiam dum has terras incolunt, et certe a bonis et piis omnibus post hanc uitam euidentius atque perfectius ista cerni obtinerique credendum est. ..." (*De libero arbitrio* II, ii, 6; CCL XXIX, 239).

[27] "An quicquam est aliud, quo magnis laboribus omnis bonorum porrigatur intentio, nisi ut summum illud et sincerum bonum intelligatur? quod ergo nunc uix paucis bonis iustisque conceditur, id tunc illud merum malum

Furthermore, the highest evil was, according to the Manichean myth, not merely something that can be made to see the divine substance, but was capable of this vision by itself from eternity. *"Difficile,"* Augustine notes ironically, *"hoc malo quicquam melius inuenitur."*[28] For our purposes it is crucial to note that Augustine clearly implies that in this life at least a few good men see the divine substance, the highest good.

So too, in *De moribus ecclesiae*, Augustine mentions the hermits who have withdrawn to the desert and live on bread and water, while "enjoying converse with God to whom they cling with pure minds, most happy in the contemplation of that beauty that can be perceived only by the intellect of the saints."[29] The apostles also attained such a vision of God. In his commentary on the Sermon on the Mount, Augustine explains each of the Beatitudes, including, "Blessed are the pure of heart, for they shall see God." Augustine says that the pure of heart will be given the ability to see God, like a clear eye to perceive eternal realities. But then he adds, "These things can be fully attained even in this life, as we believe the apostles fully attained them."[30] Much later Augustine warns that we should not understand this last statement to mean that the apostles experienced in this life no rebellion of the flesh against the spirit. He says,

> I did not say: "These things can be fully realized in this life, because the apostles fully attained them." I said, "As we believe that the apostles fully attained them," so that they are attained in that fullness with which the apostles attained them, that is, with the perfection that is possible in this life, not as they are to be attained in the per-

---

nullo bono adiuuante iam poterat? si autem illae animae corpora gerebant et id oculis uiderant, quot linguae, quot pectora, quae ingenia laudandis istis oculis praedicandisque sufficiunt, quibus uix possunt mentes iustorum adaequari? quanta bona inuenimus in summo malo? si enim uidere deum malum est, non est bonum deus; bonum est autem deus: bonum est igitur deum uidere et nescio quid huic bono conparari queat" (*De duabus animabus* 16; CSEL XXV, 72–73).

28 *De duabus animabus* 16; CSEL XXV, 73.

29 "Perfruentes colloquio Dei, cui puris mentibus inhaeserunt, et ejus pulchritudinis contemplatione beatissimi, quae nisi sanctorum intellectu percipi non potest" (*De moribus ecclesiae* I, xxxi, 66; PL XXXII, 1338).

30 "Et ista quidem in hac uita conpleri possunt, sicut conpleta esse in apostolis credimus" (*De sermone Domini in monte* I, iv, 12; CCL XXXV, 12).

fect peace we hope for, when we shall say, "Where, O death, is your sting?"[31]

That is, Augustine does come up with an ingenious interpretation of what he had said that "saves" the literal meaning of the words. But in the light of the other texts we have seen, it seems most likely that he thought at the time he wrote *De sermone Domini in monte* that holy souls could through intellectual training and moral purification come even in this life to the vision of God in which happiness consists.[32] The texts I cite do, I submit, make it very probable that Augustine thought, at least early in his career, that the wise man could attain a happiness in this life that could not be surpassed even hereafter. Furthermore, it is reasonably clear that he thought that among the great and incomparable souls who attained such a vision of God there were to be found Plato and some of the great Neoplatonists.[33] From the texts that we have seen so far it might seem that Augustine had in his early writings thought—perhaps under the influence of his discovery of the *libri*

---

31 "Non enim dictum est: ista in hac uita compleri possunt, nam completa esse in apostolis credimus, sed dictum est: *sicut conpleta esse in apostolis credimus*, ut ita compleantur sicut in illis completa sunt, id est quadam perfectione, cuius capax est ista uita, non sicut complenda sunt in illa quam speramus pace plenissima, quando dicetur: *Vbi est, mors, contentio tua?*" (*Retractationes* I, xix, 2; CCL LVII, 56).

32 Thus far I am in basic agreement with F. Van Fleteren's claim that "Augustine was firmly convinced in 386, the time of his conversion, and for at leat eight years thereafter, that man, with God's help, could attain the vision of God for a protracted period in this life" ("The Early Works," p. 19). Gilson, on the other hand, says, "we know of no single instance where Augustine ... believed that reason attained its goal before the sight of God in the kingdom of heaven" (*The Christian Philosophy of St. Augustine* [New York: Random House, 1960] p. 34.)

33 I do not mean to claim that Augustine did not hold an immediate vision of God in his later writings. Indeed, *De trinitate* VIII, iii, 4 (CCL L, 272), though hypothetically expressed, seem to presuppose that one can attain an intellectual vision of the Good itself that, when loved, is beatifying: "Cum itaque audis bonum hoc et bonum illud, quae possunt alias dici etiam non bona, si potueris sine illis quae participatione boni bona sunt, perspicere ipsum bonum cujus participatione bona sunt: simul enim et ipsum intelligis, cum audis hoc aut illud bonum: si ergo potueris illis detractis per se ipsum perspicere bonum, perspexeris Deum. Et si amore inhaeseris, continuo beatificaberis."

Platonicorum—that some great souls attained a beatifying vision of God in this life, but that in his later works he completely abandoned this view.[34] An examination of *De Genesi ad litteram* XII, however, will show that such is not a correct description how Augustine's thought changed on this point.

II. DE GENESI AD LITTERAM XII

In the final book of his twelve books on the literal interpretation of Genesis, Augustine turns to the topic of paradise and puzzles over the various references to paradise in the Scriptures—not merely the paradise in which Adam and Eve were placed, but the paradise promised to the good thief and the paradise to which Paul was snatched up. The central problem of the book arises from Paul's statement that he knew that he was taken up to the third heaven, but did not know whether or not he was in the body. In working out a solution to the problem posed by what Paul claimed to know and not to know, Augustine distinguishes three kinds of vision: corporeal, spiritual and intellectual. He illustrates the three by means of the commandment to love one's neighbor. There are three kinds of vision:

> one through the eyes by which the letters [of the written commandment] are seen, the second through the spirit of man by which we think of the neighbor, though he is absent, and the third through the intuition of the mind by which love itself is seen when it is known.[35]

---

34 Such seems to be Courcelle's view; he concludes regarding the ascents in *Confessions* VII, "Le rhéteur milanais, lorsque il lut avec enthousiasme et présomption les *libri Platonicorum*, se crut capable de parvenir à l'*henosis*, comme Plotin et Porphyre. Devant l'échec de cette expérience, il prit conscience de son impuissance, de son impureté, fut humilié, demoralisé. Il devait apprendre avant Ostie ... qu'un tel échec était le lot commun de bien des contemplatifs, mais que la jouissance de Dieu est promise par saint Paul aux chétiens ressuscités" (Pierre Courcelle, "La première experience augustinienne de l'extase," *Augustinus Magister* [Paris, 1954] I, 57).

35 "Unum per oculos, quibus ipsae litterae uidentur, alterum per spiritum hominis, quo proximus et absens cogitatur, tertium per contuitum mentis, quo ipsa dilectio intellecta conspicitur" (*De Genesi ad litteram* XII, vi, 15; BA 49, 348). I have used the text edited by J. Zycha in CSEL 28/1, pp. 1–435 as emended in *La Genèse au Sens Litteral*, BA 49 (Paris: Desclée de Brouwer, 1972), by P. Agaësse and A. Solignac, who have incorporated various corrections to the Zycha text, especially from J. H. Taylor ("The

The meanings of corporeal and spiritual vision are relatively unproblematic, but intellectual vision requires more explanation.[36] Spiritual vision in this text involves a special meaning for "spirit" and "spiritual."[37] After listing five meanings of "spirit" and "spiritual" that he found in the Scriptures, Augustine points to another meaning that is relevant here. He appeals to 1 Cor 14:14, where Paul says, "If I pray with the tongue, my spirit prays, but my mind draws no fruit."[38] In this passage "spirit" means "a certain power of the soul inferior to mind in which there are impressed likenesses of bodily things."[39] The vast majority of the twelfth book deals with this spiritual vision, which is distinct from corporeal vision and from intellectual vision.[40]

> This spiritual nature, then, in which there are impressed not bodies, but the likenesses of bodies, has visions of a kind inferior to that

---

Text of Augustine's *De Genesi ad litteram*," *Speculum* 25 [1950]: 87–93). I have also followed the numbering of BA edition which indicates book, chapter, and paragraph.

36 "In his tribus generibus illud primum manifestum est omnibus; ... Nec alterum, quo absentia corpora corporalia cogitantur, insinuare difficile est. ... Tertium uero illud, quo dilectio intellecta conspicitur, eas res continet, quae non habent imagines sui similes, quae non sunt quod ipsae" (*De Genesi ad litteram* XII, vi, 15; BA 49, 348).

37 *De Genesi ad litteram* XII, vii, 16; BA 49, 350.

38 The five uses of "spirit" and/or "spiritual" that Augustine points to are: (1) the spiritual body at the resurrection, (2) the wind or its blowing, (3) the soul of an animal or of man, (4) the rational mind, and (5) God. See *De Genesi ad litteram* XII, vii, 18; BA 49, 352–354.

39 "Vis animae quaedam mente inferior, ubi corporalium rerum similitudines exprimuntur" (*De Genesi ad litteram* XII, ix, 20; BA 49, 358).

40 A great deal has been written on this sense of "spiritual" which marks a departure from what Augustine usually means by the term, namely, what is neither bodily nor like a body, e.g., God and the soul. See the note, "'Spiritus' dans le livre XII du De Genesi," by P. Agaësse and A. Solignac, in BA 49, 559-566, for an ample survey of the literature. See also J. H. Taylor's annotated translation, *The Literal Meaning of Genesis*, ACW 41 and 42 (New York: Newman, 1982). Despite the interesting character of this spiritual vision, it is of concern to the thrust of this paper only insofar as one needs to be clear about the difference between spiritual vision of God and intellectual vision of God before one can understand what Augustine meant by the claim that at least some persons attain before death an intellectual vision of the divine substance.

light of the mind and the intelligence by which these inferior things are discerned and by which are seen those things which are not bodies and do not have forms like bodies, such as the mind itself and every good affection of the soul ... and God himself.[41]

There are then three kinds of vision in the soul, and they have an order of excellence. "For spiritual vision is more excellent than corporeal, and intellectual vision is more excellent than spiritual vision."[42]

Augustine finds in Scripture passages in which God is seen in all three kinds of vision. For example, he finds a corporeal vision of God in Exodus 19 when God came down upon Sinai in fire and the whole mountain was covered with smoke and in Exodus 33 when God appeared in a pillar of cloud. He speaks of such corporeal vision of God mainly by way of contrast with other visions. Thus he says that the third heaven to which St. Paul was taken up was

> not some corporeal sign like that shown to Moses who was so well aware of the difference between the very substance of God and the visible creature in which God made himself present to the corporeal senses that he said, "Show me yourself" (Ex 33:13 LXX).[43]

Later Augustine again speaks of this vision by way of contrast with an intellectual vision of God; unlike the vision at Sinai or in the tent the intellectual vision of God occurs "without assuming a corporeal creature which is presented to the senses of the mortal flesh."[44]

---

41 "Haec igitur natura spiritalis, in qua non corpora, sed corporum similitudines exprimuntur, inferioris generis uisiones habet quam illud mentis atque intellegentiae lumen, quo et ista inferiora diiudicantur et ea cernuntur, quae neque sunt corpora nec ullas gerunt formas similes corporum, velut ipsa mens et omnis animae adfectio bona ... et ipse Deus. ..." (*De Genesi ad litteram* XII, xxiv, 50; BA 49, 414).

42 "Praestantior est enim uisio spiritalis quam corporalis et rursus praestantior intellectualis quam spiritalis"(*De Genesi ad litteram* XII, xxiv, 51; BA 49, 414–416).

43 "Non signum aliquod corporale, quod cum ostenderetur Moysi, usque adeo sentiebat aliud esse ipsam Dei substantiam, aliud uisibilem creaturam, in qua se Deus humanis et corporalibus sensibus praesentabat, ut diceret: *ostende mihi temet ipsum*" (*De Genesi ad litteram* XII, iv, 9; BA 49, 338–340).

44 "Nulla assumpta corporali creatura, quae mortalis carnis sensibus praesentetur"(*De Genesi ad litteram* XII, xxvii, 55; BA 49, 424).

Augustine finds examples of spiritual vision of God in Isaiah 6:1–7 or in Revelation 1:13–20. There Isaiah saw God seated with the Seraphim as well as the altar and the coal that cleansed his lips, and John saw one like the Son of Man amid the seven lampstands.[45] In such cases of spiritual vision what Isaiah or John saw was not something presented to the senses of the body; what they saw "in the spirit" were likenesses of bodies or images of bodies though these visions were signs or figurative. Unlike what is seen by corporeal vision the objects of spiritual vision are not publicly visible by others who might be present.[46]

According to Augustine we have spiritual vision whenever we have images or likenesses of bodily things before our mind. We have such vision when we are awake and picture absent persons or things and when we are asleep and dream. Spiritual vision can involve having images of things we have previously had presented to our senses or images of things we have made up from what we have previously had presented to our senses.[47] Augustine speaks of sleep as involving an alienation from the senses insofar as, while asleep, we do not attend to what is presented to the senses, and during sleep we can have spiritual vision in dreams.[48]

Such cases of spiritual vision are, I suspect, fairly normal. But Augustine also allows for a spiritual vision in an ecstasy when one is awake. He reports that he knew a person who had, while awake, a spiritual vision of something not present to his senses that he claimed his soul saw.[49] In both dreams and ecstasy images of corporeal things are present to the mind, but one is not awake while dreaming and usually recognizes only upon awaking that he was seeing images and not real objects. But in ecstasy one is awake and knows that he is; he also knows that he sees something, though he does not see it by the eyes of the body. Moreover, in ecstacy he does not generally see things that are bodily present.[50] As Scriptural examples of such vision Augustine

---

45 *De Genesi ad litteram* XII, ii, 5; BA 49, 334.

46 *De Genesi ad litteram* XII, xxvii, 55; BA 49, 424.

47 *De Genesi ad litteram* XII, vi, 15; BA 49, 348.

48 See *De Genesi ad litteram* XII, xxvi, 53; BA 49, 420.

49 *De Genesi ad litteram* XII, ii, 4; BA 49, 334.

50 See *De Genesi ad litteram XII*, xii ,25; BA 49, 368. In *De Genesi ad litteram* XII, xxiii, 49; BA 49, 410–414, Augustine presents a summary of the vari-

gives Peter's vision of the vessel lowered from heaven (Acts 10:11), John's vision of the Son of Man (Rev 1:13-20), Ezechiel's vision of the plain covered with bones (Ezk 37:1–10), and Isaiah's vision of God (Is 6:1–7).[51]

At times what is seen in spiritual vision may be without any significance or meaning, but at other times what is seen in the spirit has significance or meaning.[52] One can, however, have a spiritual vision that has meaning without understanding what one sees. For example, Baltasar saw by corporeal vision the hand as it wrote on the wall; by spiritual vision he retained the image of the hand and the writing after the hand and the writing disappeared. He could not, however, understand what the writing signified until Daniel interpreted the dream (Dn 5:5–28).[53] So too Pharaoh saw by spiritual vision the cattle and ears of grain, but Joseph was able to interpret the significance of the vision (Gn 41:1-32). One is more a prophet, according to Augustine, if one can interpret the spiritual vision than if one merely has such a vision, and one is most a prophet if he both has the spiritual vision and can interpret its significance.[54]

When one has spiritual vision while awake or while asleep or even while in ecstasy, one's soul is still in the body, even if the mind is withdrawn or alienated from the senses of the body in sleep and, more so, in ecstasy.[55] But Augustine envisages the possibility not merely that the soul might have been alienated from the senses in ecstasy, but also that it has completely left the body so that the body is dead, even though the person comes back to life.[56]

Finally, there is intellectual vision of God. Just as one can be alienated from the senses of the body so that he sees likenesses of bodies in the spirit, one can also be removed from these likenesses of bodies

> so that he is also taken up from them and carried into that region, as it were, of intellectual or intelligible realities where the clear truth

---

ous sorts of spiritual vision discussed earlier in the book.

51 *De Genesi ad litteram* XII, ii, 5; BA 49, 334.

52 *De Genesi ad litteram* XII, xxii, 45; BA 49, 406.

53 *De Genesi ad litteram* XII, xi, 23; BA 49, 362–364.

54 *De Genesi ad litteram* XII, ix, 20; BA 49, 356–358.

55 See *De Genesi ad litteram* XII, xxvi, 53–54; BA 49, 420–422.

56 *De Genesi ad litteram* XII, v, 14; BA 49, 344–346.

is seen without any likeness of the body, where it is not obscured by any clouds of false opinions.[57]

When one reaches this point the life of virtue is no longer a matter of toil or effort.

> There the whole of virtue is to love what you see and the supreme happiness is to have what you love. For there the happy life is drunk at its source from which this human life is sprinkled so that we might live temperately, bravely, justly and prudently amid the temptations of this life.[58]

There we will have

> secure rest and the ineffable vision of the truth. There the brightness of the Lord is seen not by a vision in signs, whether bodily as it was seen on Mount Sinai, or spiritual as Isaiah saw it or John in Revelation saw it, but by sight, not in obscure images, insofar as the human mind can grasp it in accord with the grace of God raising one up so that God speaks to him whom he has made worthy of such converse, mouth to mouth, not the mouth of the body, but of the mind. ...[59]

---

[57] "Ita et ab ipsis rapiatur in illam quasi regionem intellectualium uel intellegibilium subuehatur, ubi sine ulla corporis similitudine perspicua ueritas cernitur, nullis opinionum falsarum nebulis obfuscatur" (*De Genesi ad litteram* XII, xxvi, 54; BA 49, 422).

[58] "Una ibi et tota uirtus est amare quod uideas et summa felicitas habere quod amas. ibi enim beata vita in fonte suo bibitur, unde aspergitur aliquid huic humanae uitae, ut in tentationibus huius saeculi temperanter, fortiter, iuste prudenterque uiuatur" (*De Genesi ad litteram* XII, xxvi, 54; BA 49, 422).

[59] "Secura quies ... et ineffabilis uisio ueritatis. Ibi uidetur claritas domini non per uisionem significantem siue corporalem, sicut uisa est in monte Sina, siue spiritalem, sicut uidet Esaias uel Iohannes in Apocalypsi, sed per speciem non per aenigmata, quantum eam capere humana mens potest, secundum assumentis Dei gratiam, ut os ad os loquatur Deus ei quem dignum tali conloquio fecerit, non os corporis, sed mentis ..." (*De Genesi ad litteram* XII, xxvi, 54; BA 49, 422–424). Butler says of this passage that "it is impossible to read the account of the highest intellectual vision ... without the conviction that it describes a personal experience, wherein Augustine believed had been seen the Brightness of the Lord by 'species', not by enigma, in the same manner as Moses had seen it" (p. 61).

Augustine adds that it is in this sense that we should understand what the Scripture says about Moses who desired to see God—not as he had seen him on Sinai and not as he saw him in the tent, but

> in that substance by which he is God, without assuming a corporeal creature which is presented to the senses of the mortal flesh, and not in the spirit by figurative likenesses of bodies, but by a vision of him to the extent that the rational and intellectual creature is able to attain it, once it is removed from every sense of the body, from every image of the spirit in signs.[60]

Augustine held that Moses desired to see the very substance of God in an intellectual vision apart from any bodily sense and from any imaginative vision in the spirit. And he argued that Moses did see God as he had desired to see him. For in Ex 11:17 we read, "God spoke to Moses face to face, as a friend speaks to a friend." Yet in Ex 33:13 LXX Moses pleaded with God, "If I have found favor in your eyes, show yourself clearly to me so that I can see you." Shortly thereafter God said to him, "You have found favor in my sight, and I know you in preference to all others" (Ex 33:17 LXX). And Moses said, "Show me your glory" (Ex 33:18). To this request, Augustine tells us, Moses received a figurative response which would require a lengthy interpretation.[61] The words of Ex 33:20, however, seem clear, "For a man will not see my face and live." However, despite this text Augustine maintains that Moses did merit to see the glory of God that he desired to see. He does so on the basis of Nm 12:6-8, where God says to Aaron and Miriam,

> Hear my words: If you have a prophet, I the Lord will make myself known to him in a vision, and I will speak to him in a dream. But not such is my servant, Moses, who is a faithful man in all my house. I will speak to him mouth to mouth by sight and not by obscure images, and he has seen the glory of the Lord.

---

60 "In ea substantia, qua Deus est, nulla adsumpta corporali creatura, quae mortalis carnis sensibus praesentetur, neque in spiritu figuratis similitudinibus corporum, sed per speciem suam, quantum eam capere creatura rationalis et intellectualis potest seuocata ab omni corporis sensu, ab omni significatiuo aenigmate spiritus" (*De Genesi ad litteram* XII, xxvii, 55; BA 49, 424).

61 Augustine interprets Ex 33:21–23 as referring to the Church since it is the place close to the Lord and built upon rock (*De Genesi ad litteram* XII, xxvii, 55; BA 49, 426).

Augustine argues that this vision of the Lord's glory was not a bodily vision of the sort Moses enjoyed when he asked to see the glory of the Lord. God then spoke to Moses by means of a bodily creature presented to the senses of the flesh.

> In this way, then, he speaks in that form by which he is God, ineffably, far more hidden and yet more present. No one sees this vision, when living this life by which we live subject to death in these senses of the body, but only one who dies to this life in a certain sense, either entirely leaving the body or so turned away and alienated from the carnal senses that he truly does not know, as the Apostle says, whether he is in the body or outside the body, when he is taken up and carried off to that vision.[62]

The vision, then, that Moses had of the glory of God was a vision of that form by which he is God. No one living in this life that we live subject to death in these bodily senses can attain such a vision, but Augustine allows for the possibility that one might undergo some sort of death (*quodammodo moriatur*), whether one's soul leaves his body or is simply so alienated from the bodily senses that one does not know whether one is in the body or not. That is, the soul might leave the body temporarily so that the resulting state differs from death only in being temporary, or the soul, while remaining in the body, might be alienated from the bodily senses in a manner similar to sleep or ecstasy, though more completely removed from the senses and also from spiritual vision. Augustine concludes that the Apostle called this third kind of vision the third heaven. In it the glory of God is seen by the clean of heart; he interprets the Beatitude to mean that the clean of heart will see God

> face to face, as was said of Moses, "mouth to mouth," namely, through that form (*speciem*) by which God is whatever he is, insofar as the mind, which is not what God is, even when cleansed from all

---

62 "Illo ergo modo in specie, qua Deus est, longe ineffabiliter secretius et praesentius loquitur locutione ineffabili, ubi eum nemo uiuens uidet uita ista, qua mortaliter uiuitur in istis sensibus corporis, sed nisi ab hac uita quisque quodammodo moriatur siue omnino exiens de corpore siue ita auersus et alienatus a carnalibus sensibus, ut merito nesciat, sicut apostolus ait, utrum in corpore an extra corpus sit, cum in illam rapitur et subuehitur uisionem" (*De Genesi ad litteram* XII, xxvii, 55; BA 49, 426–428).

earthly stain, can grasp it, when alienated and removed from every body and likeness of body.[63]

Lest there be any doubt about the fact that Augustine claimed that Moses saw God with the sort of face-to-face vision of his substance that will be the joy of eternal life, he adds the same sort of claim regarding Paul.

> Why should we not believe that God wanted to show to so great an apostle, the teacher of the nations, when he was taken up to this most excellent vision, the life in which we are to live eternally after this life?[64]

That is, both Moses and Paul saw God with an intellectual vision, a vision of the substance by which God is God, a vision which is the eternal life we are to live after this life.

In *Epistola* CXLVII, Augustine also argues that Moses and Paul were able to see the divine substance in this life, "only because the human mind can to be taken up by God from this life to the life of the angels, before it is freed from the flesh by this common death."[65] In Paul's rapture there is such an aversion of the mind's intention from the bodily senses that it is not clear "whether the bond of the body remains or it is completely resolved as happens in full death."[66] That is, Augustine believed that it was possible that such a vision was granted

---

63 "Facie ad faciem, quod de Moyse dictum est 'os ad os', per speciem scilicet, qua Deus est quidquid est, quantulumcumque eum mens quae non est quod ipse, etiam ab omni terrena labe mundata, ab omni corpore et similitudine corporeis alienata et abrepta capere potest" (*De Genesi ad litteram* XII, xxviii, 56; BA 49, 428).

64 "Cur autem non credamus, quod tanto apostolo gentium doctori rapto usque ad istam excellentissimam uisionem, uoluerit Deus demonstrare uitam, in qua post hanc uitam uiuendum est in aeternum" (*De Genesi ad litteram* XII, xxviii,56; BA 49, 428–430).

65 "Nisi quia potest humana mens diuinitus rapi ex hac uita ad angelicam uitam, antequam per istam communem mortem carne soluatur" (*Epistola* CXLVII, xiii, 31; CSEL XLIV, 305).

66 "Manente corporis uinculo, an omnino resolutio, facta fuerit qualis in plena morte" (*Epistola* CXLVII, xiii, 31; CSEL XLIV, 305).

to "some of the saints who were not dead in such a fashion that their corpses remained behind for burial."[67]

In *De Genesi ad litteram* XII and *Epistola* CXLVII, Augustine clearly claims that both Moses and Paul enjoyed prior to death, though in a state like death, a vision of the divine substance and of the glory of God. That such a vision was granted to two great leaders of the people of God in the Old and the New Testament is perhaps not surprising, since their important missions were fittingly accompanied by extraordinary graces.[68] Was such vision of God restricted to these two principal personages in salvation history, or did Augustine regard such vision as something shared more widely by other mystics? In the text we have just seen from *Epistola* CXLVII, Augustine seems to extend the possibility of such a vision of God to "certain of the saints," and he also points out that Ambrose, upon whose text he is commenting, did not say that the apostles did not see Christ, but that not all the apostles saw Christ.[69] Ambrose, he suggests, believed that "to certain of them the vision of the divinity of which he was speaking could also have been given even then" and that "perhaps some of them even at that time saw in accord with what I have said."[70] Certainly St. John would seem to be a plausible candidate for having received such vision.

---

67 "Quibusdam sanctis nondum ita defunctis, ut sepelienda cadavera remanerent" (*Epistola* CXLVII, xiii, 31; CSEL XLIV, 305).

68 In their note on "Les trois genres de visions" (BA 49, 575–585), Agaësse and Solignac agree with H. U. von Balthasar and M. E. Korger that for Augustine "la connaissance de Dieu n'a jamais pour fin l'illumination d'une âme individuelle, mais une *fonction charismatique* au service du peuple de Dieu; c'est pourquoi, d'après Augustin, les seuls bénéficiaires d'une vision plenière de Dieu, dans un état d'extase parfaite, ont été Moïse, le prophète de l'ancienne Alliance, et Paul, l'apôtre de la Nouvelle ... (p. 580). See also M. E. Korger, "Grundprobleme," pp. 50–51, and H. U. von Balthasar and M. E. Korger, *Aurelius Augustinus, Psychologie und Mystik. De Genesi ad litteram 12*, coll. Sigillum 18 (Einsiedeln: Johannes, 1960), pp. 13ff.

69 *Epistola* CXLVII, xiii, 31; CSEL XLIV, 305. The fact that Augustine uses Ambrose's *Expositio evangelii secundum Lucam* I, 24–27 (CSEL XXXII, 25–28) as an authoritative text for dealing with the question strikes me as quite unusual; it may be that he felt the need for such an authority in his corner on a question which he found highly problematic and on which he was being quite venturesome.

70 "Quibusdam eorum divinitatis quoque ipsius visionem de qua loquebatur, etiam tunc potuisse donari ... forte aliqui eorum etiam ipso tempore vid-

"There remains the eagle; he is John who preached things sublime and contemplated with steady eyes the internal and eternal truth."[71] Augustine's language is tentative and guarded with regard to the extension of such a vision of the divinity beyond Moses and Paul and some of the apostles. If one agrees, however, with Butler that it is impossible to read *De Genesi ad litteram* XII, xxvi, 54 without being convinced that it describes Augustine's personal experience, then one also has to grant that Augustine himself enjoyed such a vision of God.[72]

III. CONCLUSION

I began work on this paper because I had long found troubling some of the passages in the earlier writings in which Augustine spoke of certain men attaining in this life a vision of God beyond which we cannot go even in the hereafter. I had expected to find that such statements were the result of Augustine's early and excessive enthusiasm for Neoplatonism and that in his later writings he abandoned any claim to a vision of the divine substance in this life. An investigation, however, of the two texts that have been taken as the beginnings of mystical theology has shown that, far from abandoning the claim that some attain an intellectual vision of God in this life, in both *De Genesi ad litteram* XII and *Epistola* CXLVII Augustine has spelled out in greater clarity the psychology and theology of such a vision of the divine substance in itself. Even such a text as Ex 33:20, despite its seemingly clear exclusion in this life of a vision of God himself, is not taken as decisive against a vision of the divine substance. Rather Augustine explains it in terms of a temporary separation of the mind from the body that differs from death only insofar as it is temporary. No one can see God

---

erunt, secundum ista quae dixi" (*Epistola* CXLVII, xiii, 31 and xiv, 33; CSEL XLIV, 305 and 307).

71 "Restat aquila: ipse est Ioannes, sublimium praedicator, et lucis internae atque aeternae fixis oculis contemplator" (*In Ioannis evangelum tractatus* XXXVI, 5; CCL XXXVI, 327).

72 See Butler, pp. 59–60. Maréchal finds "raisons de convenance" to extend the privilege of such a vision of God to Mary, to founders of religious orders and other mystics (See Maréchal, p. 205). On the other hand, M. Comeau, in *S. Augustin exégète du quatrième évangile* (Paris: Beauchesne, 1930), p. 376, regards the passage from *De Genesi ad litteram* XII as an isolated text and insists that "rien n'autorise à étendre ... cette possibilité d'une vision de l'essence divine à d'autres personnes."

and live is interpreted to mean that one who sees God undergoes a temporary death.

There are, of course, clear differences between the *De quantitate animae* text and *De Genesi ad litteram* XII. In the earlier text the "*magnae et incomparabiles animae*" who attained the vision of God seem to be the Platonists rather than saintly men of the Scriptures, and in the earlier text the vision of God is seen more as the hoped for goal of a program of studies and a life of virtue than as the gracious act of God raising the mind up to a vision of himself. So too, in the earlier text there are comparatively few references to Scripture, while in the later text it is Scripture that poses the question and that sets the parameters of the solution. But in both *De quantitate animae* XXX and *De Genesi ad litteram* XII, Augustine held that the mind of at least a few men can come in this life to a vision of God, which is not merely a dim foreshadowing of the life of heaven, but a genuine anticipation of the eternal life of the saints. Far from abandoning in his later writings the position that the vision of God himself is attainable in this life at least by a few, Augustine has come to see the occurrence of such a vision as attested to in both the Old and New Testaments, as supported by writings of St. Ambrose, and as very probably grounded in his own experience of God.

ST. AUGUSTINE ON THE GOOD SAMARITAN

Over thirty-five years ago, Jean Daniélou complained that modern exegetes have all but unanimously interpreted the parable of the Good Samaritan as providing a concrete example of a moral lesson about the identity of our neighbor and the way we are to love that neighbor.[1] The consensus among contemporary exegetes is much the same. One highly respected work says of the parable, "The passage is two-pronged. While providing a powerful lesson about mercy toward those in need, it also proclaims that non-Jews can observe the law and thus enter into eternal life."[2] A recent annotated Bible states, "In response to a question from a Jewish legal expert about inheriting eternal life, Jesus illustrates the superiority of love over legalism through the story of the good Samaritan."[3] In the Anchor Bible, Joseph Fitzmyer states, "The point of the story is summed up in the lawyer's reaction, that a 'neighbor' is anyone in need with whom one comes into contact and to whom one can show pity and kindness, even beyond the bounds of one's own ethnic or religious group."[4] Fitzmyer mentions other quite different interpretations, for example, a Christological, an ecclesiological, a sacramental, or a so-

---

1 J. Daniélou cites the interpretation of M. Hermaniuck (in *La parabole évangélique* [Bruges and Paris; Desclée de Brouwer, 1947], p. 252) that the parable of the Samaritan is "une illustration par un exemple concrèt d'une vérité générale" and adds, "Cette interprétation est celle de la totalité des exégètes modernes, à la seule exception d'Edwyn Hoskyns" (J. Daniélou, "Le Bon Samaritan," in *Mélanges bibliques rédigés en honneur de André Robert* [Paris: Travaux de l'Institut Catholique, 1956], pp. 457–465, here 457; he refers to Hoskyns' *The Fourth Gospel* [London: Faber and Faber, 1947], p. 377).

2 *The New Jerome Biblical Commentary*, ed. R. E. Brown, J. A. Fitzmyer, and R. E. Murphy (Englewood Cliffs, NJ: Prentice-Hall, 1990), p. 702.

3 *The Catholic Study Bible*, ed. D. Senior et al. (New York: Oxford University Press, 1990), "The New Testament," p. 120.

4 *The Gospel according to Luke X-XXIV*. Introduction, translation and notes by J. A. Fitzmyer (New York: Doubleday, 1985), p. 884.

teriological interpretation. But he dismisses them as "allegorical and extrinsic" or "far-fetched."[5]

Augustine of Hippo, on the other hand, following Ambrose of Milan, Origen, and Irenaeus, most often interprets the Samaritan as Christ who in his mercy came down from heaven, became our neighbor, and healed the wounds of our race that were inflicted by sin.[6] Given this interpretation of the Samaritan, the parable becomes, as Dominique Sanchis has well put it, "une des plus admirables expressions de l'économie du salut, une révélation des secrets du Royaume."[7] Similarly, Henri de Lubac says of this interpretation of the parable that it "lends itself to a full statement of our collective history" and that "it presented an epitome of the whole mystery of our redemption."[8] Moreover, as de Lubac notes, the fact that Origen attributes this interpretation to one of the "elders" indicates that "it must have been current by the end of the second century."[9]

It has been some thirty years since Sanchis wrote his splendid study of St. Augustine's exegesis of the parable of the Good Samaritan. In a volume dedicated to the exegesis of the bishop of Hippo, it seems fitting to return to this parable in order to see whether Augustine cannot speak to us today and enrich our understanding of this passage of the Gospel of Luke.

I. THE "LITERAL" OR MORAL INTERPRETATION OF THE PARABLE

Though Augustine most frequently interprets the parable in a Christological sense, he also several times offers a purely moral interpre-

---

5 Ibid., p. 885. Fitzmyer here seems to equate "extrinsic" with "far-fetched," though he does at least acknowledge the existence of such modern interpretations of the parable.

6 For Irenaeus's, Origen's, and Ambrose's treatments of the parable, see *Adverus haereses* III, 17, 2: *Sources Chrétiennes* 34, 307–8, *Homilia in Lucam* XXXIV: *Sources Chrétiennes* 87, 400–411, and *Expositio evangelii secundum Lucam* VII, 71–84: CCL XIV, 237–241.

7 D. Sanchis, "Samaritanus ille: L'exégèse augustinienne de la parabole du bon Samaritain," *Recherches de science religieuse* 40 (1961): 406–425, here 406.

8 H. de Lubac, *Catholicism: Christ and the Common Destiny of Man*. Tr. by L. C. Shepherd and E. England (San Francisco: Ignatius Press, 1988), p. 204.

9 H. de Lubac, *Catholicism*, pp. 204–205.

tation of it that is quite in accord with what contemporary exegetes call the "literal" interpretation.[10] For example, in *Enarratio in Psalmum* CXVIII, Augustine appeals to the parable to show the universality of Christian love. He says that in comparision with knowledge of God, knowledge of the neighbor is easier. Augustine explains, "Every human being is a neighbor to every other human being. Nor should we suppose any distance in the human race, where there is a common nature." Then after appealing to the parable, Augustine concludes, "The man who asked the question judged that only the one who showed him mercy was a neighbor to him, and it was made clear that in doing acts of mercy no one is to be considered a stranger by one who loves the neighbor."[11]

Again, in *Sermo* CCXCIXD, Augustine, speaking of the man who asked who his neighbor was, said, "He thought that the Lord would say, 'Your father and your mother, your wife, your children, your brothers, your sisters.' This was not his answer; rather, he wanted to teach that every human being was a neighbor to every other human being and began a story." Then after a summary of the parable, he says,

> This man from Jerusalem considered the priests and Levites as neighbors and the Samaritans as strangers. His neighbors passed him by, and a stranger became his neighbor. Who then was neighbor to this man? ... What did he say? "I believe, the one who showed mercy." And the Lord said to him, "Go and do likewise."[12]

---

10 Contemporary exegetes understand by the "literal" sense of a passage the sense that was intended by the human author. When Augustine speaks of a "literal" interpretation of a text, he means something quite different, as becomes immediately apparent to anyone who reads his *De Genesi ad litteram*. Later in this paper, we will return to the question of the "literal" sense. Until then my use of quotation marks is meant to warn the reader that one should not assume that it should be taken in the contemporary sense.

11 *Enarratio in Psalmum* CXVIII, Sermo VIII, 2: CCL XL, 1686: "Omnis quippe homo est omni homini proximus, nec ulla cogitanda est longinquitas generis, ubi est natura communis. ... cui proximum non fuisse, nisi qui cum illo fecit misericordiam, ipse qui interrogauerat iudicauit; patuitque in facienda misericordia neminem alienum esse deputandum ab eo qui diligit proximum."

12 *Sermo* CCXCIXD 2: MA I, 76: "Et ille, qui hoc audivit, ait: Et quis est mihi proximus? Putabat dicturum dominum: Pater tuus et mater tua, coniux tua, filii tui, fratres tui, sorores tuae. Non hoc respondit, sed qui volebat commendare omnem hominem omni homini proximum, instituit

So too, in *Contra mendacium*, Augustine is commenting on St. Paul's command in Eph 4:25, "Put aside lying, and speak the truth, each of you, with your neighbor." He warns that this does not mean that we may lie to those who are not members of Christ's body.

> Rather, this was stated in that way, because each of us ought to regard persons as what we want them to become, even if they have not yet become such. So too, the Lord showed that the Samaritan foreigner was the neighbor of the one to whom he showed mercy. We should then regard as neighbors, not as strangers, those with whom we should act this way, lest they remain strangers.[13]

In one passage Augustine presents a "literal" interpretation, but points out that the text has a hidden meaning. Commenting on Ps 48:11, which states that the wicked die and leave their wealth to strangers, Augustine is faced with a puzzle, since many children of the wicked inherit from their parents. He asks,

> How are one's children strangers? The children of the wicked are strangers. We find that a certain foreigner became a neighbor, because he was the source of benefit. If your children are no benefit to you, they are strangers. Where do we find a foreigner who became a neighbor, because he was the source of benefit? In the Gospel. A certain man lay wounded on the road.[14]

---

    narrationem. ... Iste enim homo Hierosolymitanus proximos habebat sacerdotes et leuitas, samaritanos alienigenas. Transierunt proximi, et extraneus factus est proximus. Quis ergo erat huic homini proximus? ... Quid ergo ait? Credo, qui cum illo fecit misericordiam. et dominus ad illum: uade, et tu fac similiter."

13 *Contra mendacium* VI, 15: CSEL XLI, 486–487: "sed ideo dictum est, quia unusquisque nostrum hoc debet quemque deputare, quod eum uult fieri, etiam si nondum factus est. sicut dominus alienigenam Samaritanum proximum eius ostendit, cum quo misericordiam fecit. proximus ergo habendus est, non alienus, cum quo id agendum est, ne remaneat alienus. ..."

14 *Enarratio in Psalmum* XLVIII, Sermo I, 14: CCL XXXVIII, 561–562: "Sed tamen ait mihi aliquis: Ecce quos maledictos dixit scriptura, quos dixit perire et relinquere alienis diuitias suas. ... Quomodo alieni sunt filii? Iniquorum filii alieni sunt; nam inuenimus quemdam extraneum propinquum factum, quia profuit. Si quis tuorum tibi nihil prodest, alienus est. Ubi inuenimus nescio quem exterum propinquum factum, quia profuit? In euangelio. Iacebat quidam uulneratus a latronibus."

After a summary of the parable, Augustine concludes, "One to whom you show mercy is your neighbor. If then the foreign Samaritan became a neighbor by showing mercy and giving help, then those who cannot give you help in tribulation have become strangers to you."[15] Here those who cannot help one in tribulation are exemplified in the Lukan parable by the five brothers of the rich man who has died.[16] Despite this moral interpretation of the parable, Augustine, nonetheless, adds, as soon as he has finished recounting the facts of parable, "These things were stated as a mystery and seem too lengthy to be discussed at the moment."[17]

Similarly, in *De doctrina christiana*, Augustine appeals to the parable of the Samaritan when discussing whether a Christian's love should extend even to the angels. He states that it clearly excludes no human beings and argues that it also includes the angels.

> Both the Lord in the Gospel and the apostle Paul showed that he who commanded that we love the neighbor excluded no human being. For that man, to whom he had presented these two commandments and to whom he said that the whole law and the prophets depended upon them, asked, "Who is my neighbor?" The Lord told him of a certain man who went down from Jerusalem to Jericho. ... The Lord said to him, "Go and do likewise," obviously, so that we might understand that our neighbor is the person to whom we have the duty to show mercy, if there is need, or to whom we would have this duty, if there were need. From this it also follows that the person who in turn has this duty toward us is our neighbor. For

---

15 *Enarratio in Psalmum* XLVIII, Sermo I, 14: CCL XXXVIII, 562: "Cui misericordiam facis, proximus tibi est. Si ergo extraneus Samaritanus faciendo misericordiam et subueniendo proximus factus est; quicumque tibi in tribulatione subuenire non possunt, alieni a te facti sunt."

16 *Enarratio in Psalmum* XLVIII, Sermo I, 14: CCL XXXVIII, 562: "Sed forte non habuit qui illi succederent, et alieni possederunt diuitias ipsius? Inuenimus in ipso euangelio quia habuit; ait enim: Habeo quinque fratres. Fratres ipsius subuenire illi ardenti in flamma non potuerunt."

17 *Enarratio in Psalmum* XLVIII, Sermo I, 14: CCL XXXVIII, 562: "Quae in mysterio dicta sunt, et ad discutiendum nunc prolixiora uidentur. ..." For something to be stated "in mysterio" means that it was stated in a hidden manner, though it has been now revealed. Thus Augustine says in *In Iohannis Euangelium tractatus* XLIII, 2: CCL XXXVI, 374: "Denique ut plenius noueritis mysterium quare se Samaritanum negare non debuit, parabolam illam notissimam adtendite. ..."

the term "neighbor" is relative, and one can only be a neighbor to a neighbor. Who can fail to see that no one is excluded so as to be denied the duty of mercy, since it extends even to enemies? For the same Lord says, "Love your enemies; do good to those who hate you."[18]

Since the angels show mercy toward us, they are clearly included in the commandment enjoining love of the neighbor. But then Augustine adds, "For this reason even our God and Lord willed that he be called our neighbor. After all, the Lord Jesus Christ signified that it was he himself who had helped the man lying in the road attacked and left half-dead by robbers."[19]

Hence, we come to the more typically Augustinian interpretation of the parable in which the facts are reported *"in mysterio"* and in accord with which the Samaritan is Christ.

II. THE CHRISTOLOGICAL INTERPRETATION OF THE PARABLE

From his earliest commentary on Scripture, Augustine viewed the parable of the descent from Jerusalem to Jericho as requiring a spiritual interpretation. Though Jerusalem and Jericho are the names of real cities, "That man who went down from Jerusalem to Jericho, as the Lord says, and was wounded and left by robbers injured and half-dead on

---

18 *De doctrina christiana* I, xxx, 31: CCL XXXII, 24: "Nam quod nullum hominum exceperit, qui praecepit, ut proximum diligamus, et ipse in euangelio dominus ostendit et apostolus Paulus. Namque ille, cui duo ipsa praecepta protulerat atque in eis pendere totam legem prophetasque dixerat, cum interrogaret eum dicens: Et quis est mihi proximus? Hominem quendam proposuit descendentem ab Hierusalem ad Hierichum. ... Cui dominus ait: Vade et tu fac similiter, ut uidelicet esse eum proximum intellegamus, cui uel exhibendum est officium misericordiae, si indiget, uel exhibendum esset, si indigeret. Ex quo iam est consequens, ut etiam ille, a quo nobis hoc uicissim exhibendum est, proximus sit noster. Proximi enim nomen ad aliquid est nec quisquam esse proximus nisi proximo potest. Nullum autem exceptum esse, cui misericordiae denegetur officium, quis non uideat, quando usque ad inimicos etiam porrectum est, eodem domino dicente: Diligite inimicos uestros, benefacite eis, qui uos oderunt?"

19 *De doctrina christiana* I, xxx, 33: CCL XXXII, 25: "Ex quo et ipse deus et dominus noster proximum se nostrum dici uoluit. Nam et se ipsum significat dominus Iesus Christus opitulatum esse semiuiuo iacenti in uia afflicto et relicto a latronibus."

the road clearly demands that those places of the earth be understood spiritually. ..."[20] Immediately prior to this citation, Augustine explains that "in the allegories of Scripture" Jerusalem and Sion are often used to signify spiritual realities.[21] Here it is important to remember that *"allegoria"* in Augustine does not have its modern meaning of an extended metaphor; rather, it simply means that a term that signifies one thing in its proper sense is used to signify something else.[22] In the parable both "Jerusalem" and "Jericho," which are names of earthly cities, are used to signify something else. "Jerusalem is that heavenly city of peace from the beatitude of which [Adam] has fallen. Jericho means 'the moon' and signifies our mortality, because it is born, becomes larger, grows old, and dies."[23]

---

20 *De Genesi contra Manichaeos* II, x, 13: PL XXXIV, 203: "Et ille qui descendebat ab Jerusalem in Jericho, sicut Dominus dicit, et in via vulneratus, saucius et semivivus relictus est a latronibus, utique locos istos terrarum, quamvis secundum historiam in terra inveniantur, spiritualiter cogit intelligi."

21 *De Genesi contra Manichaeos* II, x, 13: PL XXXIV, 203: "Sicut Jerusalem quamvis sit visibilis et terrenus locus, significat tamen civitatem pacis spiritualiter: et Sion quamvis sit mons in terra, speculationem tamen significat; et hoc nomen in Scripturarum allegoriis ad spiritualia intelligenda saepe transfertur. ..."

22 See, for example, Quintillian, *Institutio oratoria* IX, 2, 92: "Totum allegoriae simile est aliud dicere, aliud intelligi velle." Augustine defines and provides examples of the trope in *EnaOrratio in Psalmum* CIII, Sermo I, 13: CCL XL, 1486: "allegoria dicitur, cum aliquid aliud uidetur sonare in uerbis, et aliud in intellectu significare. quomodo dicitur agnus christus: numquid pecus? leo christus: numquid bestia? petra christus: numquid duritia? mons christus: numquid tumor terrae? et sic multa aliud uidentur sonare, aliud significare; et uocatur allegoria. ... ergo quod dicimus allegoriam figuram esse, sacramentum figuratum allegoria est." For more on "allegoria" in Augustine, see *Augustinus-Lexikon*, ed. C. Mayer (Basel-Stuttgart: Schwabe, 1986) I, 1/2, pp. 234–239.

23 *Quaestiones euvangeliorum* II, xix: CCL XLIV/B, 62: "Ierusalem, ciuitas pacis illa coelestis, a cuius beatitudine lapsus est, Iericho, luna interpretatur, et significat mortalitatem nostram, propter quod nascitur, crescit, senescit, et occidit." See also *Enarratio in Psalmum* LXXXVIII, Sermo II, 5: CCL XXXIX, 1236: "Per lunam solent significare scripturae mortalitatem carnis huius, propter augmenta et decrementa, propter transitoriam speciem. Denique et Iericho luna interpretatur; et utique quidam qui descendebat ab Ierusalem in Iericho, incidit in latrones; descendebat

Augustine consistently identifies the Samaritan (*Samaritanus ille*) with Christ. He again and again appeals to an etymological interpretation of the term "Samaritan" as "guardian" or "protector" and interprets the guardian or protector as the Lord.[24] Given the etymological interpretation of "Samaritan" as "guardian" or "protector," Augustine uses Ps 120:4 to justify his identification of the Samaritan with the risen Christ. "But who is the guardian if not the Savior, our Lord Jesus Christ? Since he has risen from the dead and will die no more, 'he who guards Israel does not slumber nor will he fall asleep.'"[25] In fact, Au-

enim ab immortalitate ad mortalitatem. Similis est ergo caro ista lunae, quae omni tempore et omni mense patitur augmenta et decrementa; sed erit caro ista nostra in resurrectione perfecta; et testis in caelo fidelis." See also *Enarratio in Psalmum* CXXI, 7: CCL XL, 1807: "Quo adscenderunt tribus? In ciuitatem cuius participatio eius in idipsum. Ergo illuc adscenditur, in Ierusalem. Homo autem qui descendebat de Ierusalem in Iericho, incidit in latrones. Non descenderet, et non incideret in latrones. Quia uero descendendo incidit in latrones, adscendendo ueniat ad angelos." See also *Enarratio in Psalmum* CXVIII, Sermo XV, 6: CCL XL, 1713: "Ipsa est illa humilitas in loco mortalitatis peregrinantis hominis de paradiso et de illa superna ierusalem, unde quidam descendens in Iericho incidit in latrones; sed propter misericordiam quae per illum Samaritanum cum illo facta est, cantabiles illi erant iustificationes dei in loco peregrinationis suae. ..."

24 *Quaestiones euangeliorum* II, xix: CCL XLIV/B, 62–63: "Samaritanus custos interpretatur, et ideo ipse dominus significatur hoc nomine"; *Quaestiones euangeliorum* II, xl: CCL XLIV/B, 101: "iste uero qui erat Samaritanus, quod interpretatur custos. ..."; *In Iohannis Euangelium tractatus* XLIII, 2: CCL XXXVI, 374: "Samaritanus enim interpretatur custos"; *Sermo* CXXXI VI, 6: PL XXXVIII, 732: "in iumentum suum levavit eum transiens Samaritanus, quod interpretatur custos. ...; *Sermo* CLXXI II, 2: PL XXXVIII, 934: "In quo Samaritano se voluit intelligi Dominus Iesus Christus. Samaritanus enim Custos interpretatur"; *Enarratio in Psalmum* XXX, Enarratio II, Sermo I, 8: CCL XXXVIII, 197: "transiens Samaritanus misertus est, id est ipse Dominus. ... Samarites custos interpretatur"; *Enarratio in Psalmum* LXVIII, Sermo II, 11: CCL XXXIX,925: Samarites latine custos interpretatur; quis autem custos, nisi Saluator Dominus noster Iesus Christus?"; *Enarratio in Psalmum* CXXV, 15: CCL XL, 1855–56: "Transit Samaritanus quidem, id est Dominus noster Iesus Christus ... Samarites enim interpretatur, custos"; *Enarratio in Psalmum* CXXXVI, 7: CCL XL, 1968: "Hunc ille custos noster, id est Samaritanus (Samaritanus enim custos interpretatur). ..."

25 *Enarratio in Psalmum* LXVIII, Sermo II, 11: CCL XXXIX, 925–926: "quis autem custos, nisi Saluator Dominus noster Iesus Christus? Qui

gustine argues that Jesus implicitly claimed that he was a Samaritan. He says,

> Who will protect us if he abandons us? When the Jews accused him and said, "Do we not speak the truth that you are a Samaritan and have a devil?" he rightly rejected the one, but accepted the other. He said, "I do not have a devil." He did not say, "I am not a Samaritan." Thus he wanted us to understand that he is our guardian.[26]

After all, Augustine points out, "If he had said, 'I am not a Samaritan,' he would be saying, 'I am not a guardian.'"[27] But, according to Augustine, Jesus is not merely claiming to be a Samaritan; rather, he is claiming to be the Samaritan of the parable. Though the priest ignored the man wounded by robbers and the Levite too passed him by, "there came along a certain Samaritan; he is our guardian. He approached the

---

quoniam surrexit a mortuis iam non moriturus, non dormit neque obdormiet qui custodit israel." See also *Sermo* CLXXI II, 2: PL XXXVIII, 933: "Samaritanus enim Custos interpretatur. Ideo surgens a mortuis, iam non moritur, et mors ei ultra non dominabitur: quia non dormit, neque dormitat qui custodit Israel."

26 *Enarratio in Psalmum* XXX, Enarratio II, Sermo I, 8: CCL XXXVIII, 197: "Et quis nos custodit, si ille deserit? Merito, cum Iudaei conuiciantes dicerent: Nonne uerum dicimus, quia Samaritanus es, et daemonium habes, unum respuit, alterum amplexus est; Ego, inquit, daemonium non habeo; non dixit: Non sum samaritanus; sic intellegi uolens nostrum se esse custodem." See also *Enarratio in Psalmum* CXXXVI, 7: CCL XL, 1968: "Hunc ille custos noster, id est samaritanus ... cui obiectum est a iudaeis et dictum: nonne uerum dicimus quia samaritanus es, et daemonium habes?" See also *Sermo* CLXXI II, 2: PL XXXVIII, 934: "Denique quando conuiciis tantis blasphemabant Iudaei, dixerunt illi: Nonne verum dicimus, quia Samaritanus es, et daemonium habes? Cum ergo duo essent verba conuiciosa obiecta domino, dictumque illi esset, Nonne verum dicimus, quia Samaritanus es, et daemonium habes? poterat respondere: Nec samaritanus sum, nec daemonium habeo: respondit autem, Ego daemonium non habeo. Quod respondit, refutavit: quod tacuit, confirmavit. Negavit se habere daemonium, qui se noverat daemoniorum exclusorem: non se negauit infirmi custodem."

27 *Enarratio in Psalmum* CXXV, 15: CCL XL, 1856: "Si diceret: Non sum Samaritanus, diceret: Non sum custos."

wounded man; he showed mercy, and he offered himself as a neighbor to him whom he did not regard as a stranger."[28]

Once Augustine develops the idea of the Samaritan becoming our neighbor into a whole theology of incarnation and redemption. He begins with the Old Latin version of Phil 4:5: "*Dominus in proximo est*" and explains that the Lord is "near because he has come to be near."[29] He stresses the remoteness of God from human beings. "What is so distant, what is so remote, as God from human beings, the immortal from the mortal, the righteous from sinners? Not distant by reason of place, but by reason of unlikeness."[30] Augustine points out that we often speak of human beings as distant from one another because of their moral conduct, "even if they are standing next to each other, even if they live near each other, even if they are chained together."[31] The immortal and righteous God, then, came down to us mortal sinners in order to become near to us. "And what did he do? ... If he assumed both of our evil states, he would have become our equal and would have needed along with us someone to set him free. What then did he do in order to be someone near to us."[32] Augustine explains that our neighbor is not the same as we are, but close to us.

---

28 *In Iohannis Euangelium tractatus* XLIII, 2: CCL XXXVI, 374: "Transiit sacerdos, neglexit eum; transiit Leuites, et ipse praeteriit; transiit quidam Samaritanus, ipse est custos noster; ipse accessit ad saucium, ipse impendit misericordiam, eique se praestitit proximum, quem non deputauit alienum."

29 *Sermo* CLXXI II, 2: PL XXXVIII, 934: "Ergo Dominus in proximo est; quia Dominus nobis factus est in proximo." The Vulgate has: "Dominus prope est." Paul seems clearly to refer to the imminent coming of the Lord, but in the context of his comments on the parable of the Samaritan Augustine interprets the verse in terms of the incarnation.

30 *Sermo* CLXXI III, 3: PL XXXVIII, 934: "Quid tam longinquum, quid tam remotum, quam Deus ab hominibus, immortalis a mortalibus, iustus a peccatoribus? Non loco longe, sed dissimilitudine."

31 *Sermo* CLXXI III, 3: PL XXXVIII, 934: "Nam solemus etiam ita loqui, cum de duobus hominibus dicimus, quando diversi sunt mores: Iste longe est ab illo. Etiamsi iuxta steterint, etiamsi vicinius inhabitent, etiamsi una catena colligentur; longe est pius ab impio, longe est innocens a reo, longe est iustus ab iniusto."

32 *Sermo* CLXXI III, 3: PL XXXVIII, 934: " Et quid fecit? ... si utrumque malum nostrum suscepisset, par noster factus esset, et liberatore nobiscum opus haberet. Quid ergo fecit, ut esset proximus nobis?"

In order to become a neighbor, he assumed your punishment; he did not assume your sin, and if he did assume it, he assumed it to destroy it, not to commit it. As righteous and immortal, he was far from sinners who are not righteous. As a mortal sinner, you were far from the righteous and immortal one. He did not become a sinner like you, but became mortal like you. By assuming the punishment and not assuming the sin, he destroyed both the sin and the punishment.[33]

Given this basic identification of the Samaritan as Christ, the other elements of the parable do not constitute other distinct interpretations, but rather complement the Christological interpretation.[34] For instance, the man who went down from Jerusalem to Jericho is Adam. "A certain man went down from Jerusalem to Jericho; he is understood to be Adam in the human race."[35] But the Adam who went down from Jerusalem was not a single individual. "He who went down from Jerusalem to Jericho fell among robbers. ... It was Adam then who went down and fell among robbers, for we are all Adam."[36] Or, as Augustine puts it elsewhere, "The whole human race, after all, is that man who was lying in the road, left half-dead by robbers."[37] Again, Augustine says that Adam "received a deadly wound, and all the human race would have perished in him, if that Samaritan had not come down and

---

33 *Sermo* CLXXI III, 3: PL XXXVIII, 934: "Proximus non hoc quod nos, sed prope nos. ... Ille ut esset proximus, suscepit poenam tuam, non suscepit culpam tuam: et si suscepit, delendam suscepit, non faciendam. Iustus et immortalis, longe ab iniustis et mortalibus. Peccator mortalis, longe eras a iusto immortali. Non est factus ille peccator, quod tu: sed factus est mortalis, quod tu. Manens iustus, factus est mortalis. Suscipiendo poenam et non suscipiendo culpam, et culpam delevit et poenam."

34 Fitzmyer's claim that there have been soteriological, ecclesial, and sacramental interpretations besides the Christological interpretation makes these multiple interpretations seem much more far-fetched than they are in Augustine.

35 *Quaestiones euangeliorum* II, xix: CCL XLIV/B, 62: "Homo quidam descendebat ab Ierusalem in Iericho; ipse Adam intelligitur in genere humano."

36 *Enarratio in Psalmum* CXXV, 15: CCL XL, 1855: "qui descendebat ab Ierusalem in Iericho, incidit in latrones. ... iam ergo Adam descendit, et incidit in latrones; omnes enim nos Adam sumus."

37 *Sermo* CLXXI II, 2: PL XXXVIII, 933: "Totum enim genus humanum est homo ille qui jacebat in via semivivus a latronibus relictus."

healed its grievous wounds."[38] Accordingly, "the Samaritan passing by showed mercy, that is, the Lord himself who had mercy on the human race."[39] Augustine states that we or his congregation were the man left half-dead on the road. "Remember that, though you were weak and were lying half-dead in the road, you have been lifted upon the beast and brought into the inn."[40]

Augustine interprets the robbers as "the devil and his angels who stripped him of immortality and, by the blows they inflicted through persuading him to sin, left him half-dead."[41] So too, we have been redeemed by Christ from the devil. "Who has redeemed us? Christ. From whom has he redeemed us? From the devil. The devil and his angels, then, took us captive.... They are also the robbers who wounded that traveler who went down from Jerusalem to Jericho and left him wounded and half-dead on the road."[42] Once Augustine explains why the man was half-dead: "inasmuch as he can understand and know God, the man is living; inasmuch as he is wasting away and pressed down by sins, he is dead, and thus he is said to be half-dead."[43] The priest and the Levite who passed the wounded man by "signify the

38 *Contra Iulianum* I, iii, 10: PL XLIV, 646: "Et sic lethale vulnus accepit, in quo omne genus occidisset humanum, nisi Samaritanus ille descendens vulnera eius acerba curasset."

39 *Enarratio in Psalmum* XXX, Enarratio II, Sermo I, 8: CCL XXXVIII, 197: "Quem ... transiens Samaritanus miseratus est, id est ipse dominus, qui miseratus est genus humanum."

40 *Enarratio in Psalmum* XXXI, Enarratio II, 7: CCL XXXVIII, 230: "memento quia etsi languebas, et in uia semiuiuus iacebas, leuatus es in iumentum, et perductus in stabulum." See also *Enarratio in Psalmum* CXXV 15: CCL XL, 1856: "Transiens Samaritanus non nos contemsit: curauit nos. ..."

41 *Quaestiones euangeliorum* II, xix: CCL XLIV/B, 62: "Latrones, diabolus et angeli eius; qui eum spoliauerunt immortalitate: et plagis impositis, peccata suadendo: reliquerunt eum semiuiuum. ..."

42 *Enarratio in Psalmum* CXXXVI, 7: CCL XL, 1968: "Quis nos redemit? Christus. A quo nos redemit? A diabolo. Diabolus ergo et angeli eius captiuos nos duxerunt. ... Ipsi sunt etiam latrones uulnerantes illum uiatorem qui descendit ab ierusalem in iericho, quem sauciatum semiuiuum reliquerunt."

43 *Quaestiones euangeliorum* II, xix: CCL XLIV/B, 62: "quia ex parte qua potest intelligere et cognoscere Deum, uiuus est homo; ex parte quo peccatis contabescit et premitur, mortuus est, et ideo semiuiuus dicitur."

priesthood and ministry of the Old Testament, which was unable to restore him to health."[44] So too, the Samaritan's return on the next day signifies "after the resurrection of the Lord."[45]

The inn (*stabulum*) to which the Samaritan brings the wounded man is the Church. "The inn is the Church in which travelers are refreshed from the pilgrimage as they return to the eternal fatherland."[46] Thus Augustine can say to his own soul, "You recognize that you are certainly in that inn to which that Samaritan brought the man he found half-dead from the many wounds inflicted by robbers."[47] We who are wounded should beg the physician that we may be carried to the inn to be cared for.[48] Though human beings were originally created in sound health, without sin, and with free choice and the power to live lives of righteousness, "we are now," Augustine points out, "dealing with that man whom robbers left half-dead on the road. Injured and suffering from serious wounds, he cannot rise to the peak of righteousness, as he was able to come down from there. If he is now in the inn, he is

---

44 *Quaestiones euangeliorum* II, xix: CCL XLIV/B, 62: "Sacerdos autem et leuita qui eo uiso praeterierunt sacerdotium et ministerium ueteris testamenti significant, quod non poterat prodesse ad salutem." See *Enarratio in Psalmum* LXVIII, Sermo II, 11: CCL XXXIX, 925: "quem sacerdos et Leuites transeuntes inuenerant et contemserant a quibus curari non potuit. ..." and *Enarratio in Psalmum* CXXV, 15: CCL XL, 1855: "Sed transit sacerdos, et contempsit; transit Leuita, et contempsit, quia lex sanare non potuit."

45 *Quaestiones euangeliorum* II, xix: CCL XLIV/B, 63: "Altera dies est post resurrectionem Domini."

46 *Quaestiones euangeliorum* II, xix: CCL XLIV/B, 63: "Stabulum est ecclesia, ubi reficiantur viatores de peregrinatione in aeternam patriam redeuntes." See also *Sermo* CLXXI VI, 6: PL XXXVIII, 732: "Stabulum si agnoscitis, ecclesia est"; *In Iohannis Euangelium tractatus* XLI, 13: CCL XXXVI, 365: "Ergo, fratres, et ecclesia hoc tempore in qua saucius sanatur, stabulum est uiatoris; sed ipsi ecclesiae sursum est hereditas possessoris"; and *Enarratio in Psalmum* CXXV, 15: CCL XL, 1856: "perduxit ad stabulum, id est ad ecclesiam."

47 *De trinitate* XV, xxvii, 50: CCL L/A, 532: "Agnoscis te certe in illo esse stabulo quo Samaritanus ille perduxit eum quem reperit multis a latronibus inflictis uulneribus semiuium."

48 See *In Iohannis Euangelium tractatus* XLI, 13: CCL XXXVI, 365: "Precemur medicum saucii, portemur in stabulum curandi."

still being healed."[49] So too, Augustine argues that Pelagius must grant that human nature was corrupted in those who have not been baptized, "if, now as one of the baptized, that wounded man has emerged from the inn in good health or is in good health in the inn where the merciful Samaritan brought him to be healed."[50]

The beast of the Samaritan onto which he lifted the wounded man is the flesh of Christ. "As he passed by," Augustine says, "the Samaritan did not look upon us with contempt; he healed us, raised us up onto his beast, on his own flesh."[51] Augustine explains, "His beast is the flesh in which he deigned to come to us. To be placed upon his beast is to believe in the incarnation of Christ."[52] Again he says, "Robbers have left you half-dead in the road, but you have already been found lying there by the Samaritan who passed by and was merciful. ... You have been lifted upon his beast; you have believed that Christ has become incarnate."[53] Once Augustine comments on Christ's words, "I will show myself to him" (Jn 14:21).

---

49 *De natura et gratia* XLIII, 50: CSEL LX, 270: "Sed nunc de illo agitur, quem semiuiuum latrones in uia relinquerunt, qui grauibus saucius confossusque uulneribus non ita potest ad iustitiae culmen ascendere, sicut potuit inde descendere, qui etiam si iam in stabulo est adhuc curatur."

50 *De natura et gratia* LII, 60: CSEL LX, 277: "Certe uel in eis concedit esse uitiatam, si iam in baptizatis ille saucius sanus de stabulo egressus est, aut sanus in stabulo est, quo eum curandum misericors Samaritanus aduexit."

51 *Enarratio in Psalmum* CXXV, 15: CCL XL, 1856: "Transiens Samaritanus non nos contempsit: curauit nos, leuauit in iumentum, in carne sua. ..." See also Augustine's use of "iumentum," along with "vehiculum," "vestis," and "templum," for the body of Christ in *Sermo* CXIX VII, 7: PL XXXVIII, 675: "Ille carnem suam non solum tenuit, ut nasceretur, viveret, ageret; sed etiam mortuam suscitauit, et vehiculum quoddam in quo processit ad nos, ad patrem levavit. Vestem dicas carnem Christi, vehiculum dicas, et quomodo forte ipse significare dignatus est, iumentum ipsius dicas; quia in ipso iumento levauit eum qui fuerat a latronibus sauciatus: postremo, quod ipse apertius dixit, templum dicas. ..."

52 *Quaestiones euangeliorum* II, xix: CCL XLIV/B, 63: "Iumentum eius est caro in qua ad nos uenire dignatus est. Inponi iumento est in ipsam incarnationem Christi credere."

53 *Sermo* CLXXIXA, 7: PLS II, 714–715: "Semivivum te latrones in via dimiserunt, sed iam a transeunte et misericordii Samaritano iacens inuentus est; ... levatus es in iumentum eius, incarnatum Christum credidisti. ..."

He was present to those to whom he was speaking. They saw the form of the servant; they did not see the form of God. They were being brought by the beast to the inn in order to be healed, but once they have been made healthy, they will see.[54]

In one text Augustine offers two interpretations of the two denarii that the Samaritan gives to the innkeeper. They either signify the two commandments of love or the promises for the present life and the life to come.[55] In other texts he offers only the first interpretation: "He gave two denarii for his care, love of God and love of the neighbor, for on these two commandments depend the law and the prophets."[56]

The inn-keeper of the parable is the apostle.[57] Elsewhere Augustine tentatively identifies the apostle as Paul, "To which innkeeper? Perhaps to him who said, 'We serve as ambassadors of Christ'"[58] But the role of innkeeper is not exclusively Paul's. "I too do this," Augustine

---

54 *In Iohannis Euangelium tractatus* XIX, 18: CCL XXXVI, 201: "Quibus loquebatur, praesens eis erat; sed formam serui uidebant; formam autem dei non uidebant. Per iumentum ad stabulum ducebantur curandi, sed sanati uidebunt. ..."

55 *Quaestiones euangelium* II, xix: CCL XLIV/B, 63: "Duo denarii sunt uel duo praecepta charitatis, quam per spiritum sanctum acceperunt apostoli ad euangelizandum ceteris, uel promissio vitae praesentis et futurae, secundum enim duas promissiones dictum est: accipiet in hoc saeculo septies tantum, et in futuro saeculo uitam aeternam consequetur."

56 *Enarratio in Psalmum* CXXV, 15: CCL XL, 1856: "dedit duos denarios unde curaretur, caritatem dei et caritatem proximi: in his duobus enim praeceptis tota lex pendet et prophetae." See also *In Iohannis Euangelium tractatus* XLI, 13: CCL XXXVI, 365: "Dedit etiam duos nummos, qui impenderentur saucio curando; forte ipsa sunt duo praecepta, in quibus tota lex pendet et prophetae" and *In Iohannis Euangelium tractatus* XVII, 6: CCL XXXVI, 173: "In his duobus praeceptis tota lex pendet et prophetae. Merito et illa uidua omnes facultates suas, duo minuta misit in dono dei; merito et pro illo languido a latronibus sauciato, stabularius duos nummos accepit unde sanaretur. ..."

57 *Quaestiones euangeliorum* II, xix: CCL XLIV/B, 63: "Stabularius ergo est apostolus." See also *Enarratio in Psalmum* CXXV, 15: CCL XL, 1856: "commendauit stabulario, id est apostolo. ..."

58 *In Iohannis Euangelium tractatus* XLI, 13: CCL XXXVI, 365: "Cui stabulario? Forte illi qui dixit: Pro Christo legatione fungimur."

says; "we all do this; we serve in the role of the innkeeper."[59] Once Augustine identifies the preachers of the Gospel as "the physicians who heal the man wounded by robbers, but it was the Lord who brought him to the inn."[60]

Augustine explains binding of the wounds and the wine and oil which the Samaritan poured on the wounds of the man left on the road. "The binding of the wounds signifies the curtailing of sins; the oil is the consolation of good hope on account of the forgiveness received toward peaceful reconciliation; the wine is an exhortation to act with a fervent spirit."[61] Once he interprets the wine and the oil as "the sacrament of the Only-Begotten."[62] And once he explicitly identifies them as Baptism,

> All sins were wiped away by the sacrament of Baptism. ... But this is the wine and the oil that were administered on the road. Recall, my friends, how that man, wounded by robbers and half-dead on the road, was consoled, when he received wine and oil for his wounds. He has now been forgiven his error, and his weakness is still being healed in the inn.[63]

In a series of texts Augustine focuses upon the Samaritan's words to the innkeeper, "If you spend something more, I will repay you when I return" (Lk 10:35). He offers two explanations of the extra expenditure on the part of the innkeeper.

---

59 *Sermo* CLXXIXA, 8: PLS II, 715: "hoc etiam ego, hoc nos omnes agimus; stabularii fungimur munere."

60 *Enarratio in Psalmum* LXXXVII, 13: CCL XXXIX, 1218: "Ipsi sunt medici curantes a latronibus sauciatum; sed Dominus eum perduxit ad stabulum. ..."

61 *Quaestiones euangeliorum* II, xix: CCL XLIV/B, 63: "Alligatio uulnerum est cohibitio peccatorum; oleum consolatio spei bonae propter indulgentiam datam ad reconciliationem pacis; uinum est exhortatio ad operandum feruentissimo spiritu."

62 *Sermo* CLXXIXA, 7: PLS II, 715: "infusum est tibi uinum et oleum, sacramentum Unigeniti percepisti. ..."

63 *Sermo* CXXXI VI, 6: PL XXXVIII, 732: "Deleta sunt cuncta peccata in sacramento baptismatis. ... Sed hoc est quod infusum est in via, oleum et vinum. Retinetis, charissimi, semivivus ille in via a latronibus sauciatus, quomodo sit consolatus, accipiens oleum et vinum uulneribus suis. iam utique errori eius indultum fuit, et tamen sanatur languor in stabulo."

The extra money that he spent is either that counsel which [Paul] gives, "With regard to virgins I have no commandment from the Lord, but I offer a counsel" or the fact that he worked with his own hands so that he was not a burden to one of the weak when the Gospel was first preached, though he was permitted to live from the Gospel.[64]

In accord with the first interpretation, Augustine says that the extra expenditures of the innkeeper are matters that do not fall under the commandment of the law, but the counsel of love. "These are the further things which are given to the wounded man who was brought to the inn to be healed by the pity of that Samaritan. And thus they are not said to be commanded by the Lord, though we are advised to offer them to the Lord. ..."[65] In accord with the second interpretation, given the identification of the innkeeper as the apostle Paul, Augustine claims that he "spent something more who, as he himself testifies, served at his own expense."[66] Once, after stating that we all function as the innkeeper, he adds, "Would that we would at least spend what

---

64 *Quaestiones euangeliorum* II, xix: CCL XLIV/B, 63: "Quod supererogat aut illud consilium est quod ait: de uirginibus autem praeceptum domini non habeo, consilium autem do, aut quod etiam manibus suis operatus est, ne infirmorum aliquem in nouitate euangelii grauaret, cum ei liceret pasci ex euangelio." Here the verb "supererogat" replaces the "amplius erogat." which is found in the other citations of the parable in Augustine.

65 *De adulterinis coniugiis* I, xiv, 15: CSEL XLI, 364: "Ita ostendit ea quae licita sunt, id est nullo praecepto domini prohibentur, sicut expedit, potius esse tractanda non praescripto legis, sed consilio caritatis. Haec sunt, quae amplius erogantur saucio, qui curandus ad stabulum Samaritani illius miseratione perductus est. Et ideo dicuntur non a domino praecipi, quamuis domino moneantur offerri. ..."

66 *De opere monachorum* V, 6: CSEL XLI, 540: "Amplius ergo erogabat apostolus Paulus, qui suis, ut ipse testatur, stipendiis militabat." In the same vein, see *Enarratio in Psalmum* CXXV, 15: CCL XL, 1856: "Amplius erogauit apostolus; quia cum omnibus apostolis permissum esset ut acciperent tamquam milites christi stipendia a prouincialibus christi, ille manibus suis laborauit, et annonas suas prouincialibus donauit," and *Sermo* XLVI, 4: CCL XLI, 531: "et dicit alios coapostolos suos usos fuisse hac potestate non usurpata sed data. plus ille fecit ut nec quod debebatur acciperet. ipse ergo donauit et debitum, sed alius non exigit indebitum: ille plus fecit. fortassis enim ipsum significabat, qui aegrum cum adduceret ad stabulum dixit: si quid amplius erogaueris, in redeundo reddam tibi."

we have received! But whatever we spend, brothers, the money is the Lord's."[67]

Hence, Augustine presents a Christological interpretation of the parable whose central feature is the identification of Christ as the Good Samaritan. Can such a reading of the parable be regarded as viable and legitimate today? How might Augustine defend his interpretation of this parable of the Samaritan?

III. A VIABLE INTERPRETATION FOR TODAY?

If Augustine were to agree that the Christological interpretation was allegorical in the modern sense and was not the meaning of the parable that Luke intended, the question would be by and large settled, since such an allegorical interpretation can be dismissed as far-fetched and extrinsic. Augustine, however, makes it quite clear that he holds that Jesus himself taught in the Gospel of Luke that he was the Good Samaritan.[68] Hence, Augustine clearly held that the Christological sense of the parable is not merely one possible, albeit extrinsic and far-fetched, meaning of the parable, but the meaning which Christ himself intended.

If Augustine had the opportunity to confront modern exegetes and argue the point with them, what might he say in defense of his Christological interpretation of the parable? There are at least three lines of argument that might be drawn from his works, the first based on his confrontation with exegetes of his own day concerning the first verses of Genesis, the second based on some of the principles of exegesis that he stated, and the third based upon what he took to be the goal of scriptural exegesis.

In *Confessions* XII, first of all, Augustine describes how he would respond to some unnamed contemporaries who disagreed with him on the meaning of the beginning of the Book of Genesis. Augustine's interlocutors admitted the truth of what he says, but denied that what

---

67 *Sermo* CLXXIXA, 8: PLS II, 715: "Illi dictum: si quid amplius erogaveris, in redeundo reddam tibi. Utinam nos hoc saltem erogemus, quod accepimus! Sed quantumqueque erogemus, fratres, pecunia dominica est."

68 See *De doctrina christiana* I, xxx, 33: CCL XIV, 25: "Ex quo et ipse deus et dominus noster proximum se nostrum dici uoluit. Nam et se ipsum significat dominus Iesus Christus opitulatum esse semiuiuio iacenti in uia afflicto et relicto a latronibus." See also above note 26.

he says was the intention of the author of Genesis.[69] So too, contemporary exegetes grant that, in becoming man, Christ showed mercy to the whole human race that lay wounded by sins and brought at least many human beings into the Church where they can receive further healing from the wounds of sin. But while they grant that Augustinian interpretation of the parable is in full accord with the mission of Christ, they claim that Luke did not intend such a Christological sense in writing the parable.

Against the unnamed exegetes of Genesis, Augustine argues that no harm results, if, while trying to determine what the author of the Scripture intended, one does not arrive at that truth, but comes to some other truth that God, the light of our minds, shows to be true.[70] He points out that two sorts of disagreement can arise when truthful messengers report something through the use of signs. The dispute can be about the truth of what is reported, or the dispute can be about the intention of those who reported it.[71] For it is one thing to inquire into what is true about the creation of the world; it is something quite different to inquire into what Moses ... intended the reader and the hearer to understand by these words.[72]

---

69 See *Confessions* XII, xvi, 23–xvii, 24: CCL XXVII, 227–8: "Cum his enim uolo coram te aliquid conloqui, deus meus, qui haec omnia, quae intus in mente mea non tacet ueritas tua, uera esse concedunt. ... Dicunt enim: 'Quamuis uera sint haec, non ea tamen duo Moyses intuebatur, cum reuelante spiritu diceret: In principio fecit deus caelum et terram.'"

70 See *Confessions* XII, xviii, 27: CCL XXVII, 229–230: "Dum ergo quisque conatur id sentire in scripturis sanctis, quod in eis sensit ille qui scripsit, quid mali est, si hoc sentiat, quod tu, lux omnium ueridicarum mentium, ostendis uerum esse, etiamsi non hoc sensit ille, quem legit, cum et ille uerum nec tamen hoc senserit?"

71 See *Confessions* XII, xxiii, 32: CCL XXVII, 233: "duo uideo dissensionum genera oboriri posse, cum aliquid a nuntiis ueracibus per signa enuntiatur, unum si de ueritate rerum, alterum, si de ipsius qui enuntiat uoluntate dissensio est."

72 *Confessions* XII, xxiii, 32: CCL XXVII, 233: "Aliter enim quaerimus de creature conditione, quid uerum sit, aliter autem quid in his uerbis Moyses, egregius domesticus fidei tuae, intellegere lectorem auditoremque uoluerit." Here one should recall that for Augustine all human language and, therefore, the language of scripture is a matter of using signs—a mode of communication that was not needed in paradise and that depends upon divine illumination if our minds are to grasp the truth. See *De Genesi contra*

Augustine says that "many truths occur to those who investigate" the first verses of Genesis "as those words are understood in different senses."[73] His language reflects the loose connection between the words of the text and the truths that "occur" to its students as they understand those words in different senses. Augustine prays,

> May I be joined, O Lord, to them in you, and may I find delight in you with those who feed upon your truth in the love's broad scope. May we together approach the words of your book and search out in them your intention through the intention of your servant, by whose pen you have given them to us.[74]

But no one can be as confident of having grasped the meaning that the author had, or intended that we should understand, as one can be of having grasped a truth.[75] Indeed, "amid such an abundance of true opinions that can be drawn from these words" it is foolish "rashly to affirm which of these opinions Moses especially held. ..."[76] Moreover, Augustine claims that, if he were Moses and were given the task of writing the Book of Genesis, he would want to have such an ability to write that the less intelligent readers would not reject his words as beyond them and that the more intelligent "would not find in the few

---

Manichaeos II, iv, 5: PL XXXIV, 199, as well as my "St. Augustine's View of the Original Human Condition in *De Genesi contra Manichaeos*," AS 22 (1991): 141–155. In that sense Christ is the only teacher. As the Wisdom of God, he teaches, while as incarnate, he merely admonishes us by human words. See *De libero arbitrio* II, xiv, 38: CCL XXIX, 263: "foris admonet intus docet. ..."

73 *Confessions* XII, xxiv, 33: CCL XXVII, 233–234: "multa uera, quae in illis uerbis aliter atque aliter intellectis occurrunt quaerentibus. ..."

74 *Confessions* XII, xxiii, 32: CCL XXVII, 233: "Coniungar autem illis, domine, in te et delecter cum eis in te, qui ueritate tua pascuntur in latitudine caritatis, et accedamus simul ad uerba libri tui et quaeramus in eis uoluntatem tuam per uoluntatem famuli tui, cuius calamo dispensasti ea."

75 *Confessions* XII, xxiv, 33: CCL XXVII, 233–234: "Sed quis nostrum sic inuenit eam" [i.e., the intention of the author] "inter tam multa uera ... ut tam fidenter dicat hoc sensisse Moyen atque hoc in illa narratione uoluisse intelligi, quam fidenter dicit hoc uerum esse, siue ille hoc senserit siue aliud?"

76 *Confessions* XII, xxv, 35: CCL XXVII, 236: "Iam vide, quam stultum sit in tanta copia uerissimarum sentiarum, quae de illis uerbis erui possunt, temere adfirmare, quam earum Moyses potissimum senserit. ..."

words of your servant that any true opinion to which they had come by their own reflection had been omitted, and if someone else saw another truth in the light of the truth, it too could be understood from those words."[77] Hence, Augustine states that,

> if I were writing something with the highest authority, I would prefer to write so that whatever truth anyone might grasp in these matters would find their echo in my words rather than that I should state a single true view with greater clarity in such a way that I would exclude others that could not offend me by their falsity.[78]

Hence, along the lines of the argument in *Confessions* XII, Augustine might argue that the content of his interpretation of the parable is true, that what Luke intended is less certain than the truth of the Christological interpretation, that Luke surely would have intended us to be able to find in what he wrote other truths, even if he did not have them in mind, and that *"latitudo caritatis"* should be able to embrace all true interpretations.

Second, in several other works Augustine states more formally various principles of exegesis that might provide another line of argumentation in defense of his interpretation of the parable. Augustine, first of all, gives a special preference for the sense of a passage that the author certainly intended. At the end of the first book of *De Genesi ad litteram*, Augustine sets forth the ideal goal of the exegete.

> And when we read the divine books, amid such a great number of true interpretations that are drawn from a few words and are defended by the soundness of the Catholic faith, we should preferably choose that interpretation which it appears certain that the author we are reading held.[79]

---

77 *Confessions* XII, xxvi, 36: CCL XXVII, 236: "in quamlibet ueram sententiam cogitando uenissent, eam non praetermissam in paucis uerbis tui famuli reperirent, et si alius aliam uidisset in luce ueritatis, nec ipsa in eisdem uerbis intelligenda deesset."

78 *Confessions* XII, xxxi, 42: CCL XXVII, 240: "Ego certe ... si ad culmen auctoritatis aliquid scriberem, sic mallem scribere, ut, quod ueri quisque de his rebus capere posset, mea uerba resonarent, quam ut unam ueram sententiam ad hoc apertius ponerem, ut excluderem ceteras, quarum falsitas me non posset offendere."

79 *De Genesi ad litteram* I, xxi, 41: CSEL XXVIII, 31: "Et cum diuinos libros legimus in tanta multitudine uerorum intellectuum qui de paucis uerbis

However, the ideal is not always attainable. Hence, Augustine immediately adds the following:

> But if that interpretation remains hidden, we should certainly choose one that is not ruled out by the context of Scripture and that agrees with sound faith. If, however, the context of Scripture cannot be examined and discussed, we should at least choose only that interpretation which sound faith prescribes.[80]

Augustine could certainly maintain that his Christological interpretation of the parable agrees with sound faith and that the context of Scripture does not rule it out. He explains,

> It is, after all, one thing to fail to discern the interpretation that the author held in preference to all others; it is something else to depart from the rule of piety. If one avoids both of these, the reader has the full benefit, but even if the intention of author is uncertain, it is not without value to attain a view in accord with sound faith.[81]

But he is equally clear that there are, if not always, at least often, many true interpretations of a passage of Scripture.[82] Furthermore, even if the sense intended by the human author remains hidden, there need not be any danger, "provided that each of [these interpretations] can be shown from other passages of the holy Scriptures to be congruous with the truth."[83] The exegete should, nonetheless,

---

eruuntur et sanitate catholicae fidei muniuntur, id potissimum deligamus quod certum apparuerit eum sensisse quem legimus. ..."

80 *De Genesi ad litteram* I, xxi, 41: CSEL XXVIII, 31: "si autem hoc latet, id certe, quod circumstantia scripturae non inpedit et cum sana fide concordat; si autem et scripturae circumstantia pertractari ac discuti non potest, saltem id solum, quod fides sana praescibit."

81 *De Genesi ad litteram* I, xxi, 41: CSEL XXVIII, 31: "Aliud est enim, quid potissimum scriptor senserit, non dinoscere, aliud autem a regula pietatis errare. Si utrumque uitetur, perfecte se habet fructus legentis; si uero utrumque uitari non potest, etiam si uoluntas scriptoris incerta sit, sanae fidei congruam non inutile est eruisse sententiam."

82 See above notes 73 and 76.

83 *De doctrina christiana* III, xxvii, 38: CCL XXXII, 99–100: "Quando autem ex eisdem scripturae uerbis non unum aliquid, sed duo uel plura sentiuntur, etiam si latet, quid senserit ille, qui scripsit, nihil periculi est, si quodlibet eorum congruere ueritati ex aliis locis sanctarum scripturarum doceri potest. ..."

try to determine the intention of the author through whom the Holy Spirit produced the passage, whether he attains this or culls from those words some other meaning that is not opposed to the correct faith, by relying on testimony from some other passage of God's word.[84]

Augustine suggests that the human author of the passage may have seen that meaning. But he is, in any case, convinced that "the Spirit of God who produced the passage through him certainly foresaw that this meaning too would undoubtedly occur to the reader or hearer; indeed, he providentially arranged that it would occur, because it too rests upon the truth."[85] Indeed, the generosity and richness of divine providence in the divine Scriptures is shown by the fact that "the same passage is understood in many ways, and other passages, no less the word of God, lead us to give them our approval by reason of their support."[86]

Hence, Augustine would at very least argue that the Christological sense of the parable of the Good Samaritan was providentially intended by God under whose inspiration Luke wrote his Gospel. Moreover, he would argue that the content of the parable interpreted in the Christological sense is true, even if Luke did not intend that sense. In any case, Augustine is quite convinced that Jesus Christ taught us that he was that Samaritan. And if one takes the Good Samaritan as Christ and the wounded man as the human race, the punch line of the parable, "Go and do likewise" (Lk 10:37) is really equivalent to the words of Christ, "Love one another as I have loved you" (Jn 15:12). That is,

---

84 *De doctrina christiana* III, xxvii, 38: CCL XXXII, 100: "id tamen eo conante, qui diuina scrutatur eloquia, ut ad uoluntatem perueniatur auctoris, per quem scripturam illam sanctus operatus est spiritus; siue hoc assequatur siue aliam sententiam de illis uerbis, quae fidei rectae non refragatur, exsculpat, testimonium habens a quocumque alio loco diuinorum eloquiorum."

85 *De doctrina christiana* III, xxvii, 38: CCL XXXII, 100: "Ille quippe auctor in eisdem uerbis, quae intellegere uolumus, et ipsam sententiam forsitan uidit et certe dei spiritus, qui per eum haec operatus est, etiam ipsam occursuram lectori uel auditori sine dubitatione praeuidit, immo ut occurreret, quia et ipsa est ueritate subnixa, prouidit."

86 *De doctrina christiana* III, xxvii, 38: CCL XXXII, 100: "Nam quid in diuinis eloquiis largius et uberius potuit diuinitus prouideri, quam ut eadem uerba pluribus intellegantur modis, quos alia non minus diuina contestantia faciant adprobari?"

even if it is not what Luke intended, Augustine's Christological interpretation of the parable is in full accord with the Christian faith and also makes most effectively the point which John clearly taught in his Gospel. Hence, the Christological interpretation of the parable is at least a canonical interpretation.[87]

But for Augustine that Christological interpretation of the parable is considerably more than that, and this brings us to the third line of argumentation Augustine might take in defending his interpretation of the parable. It conforms to what he sees as the beginning and end of all exegesis. In *De doctrina christiana* Augustine makes the strong claim, in summing up what he has said in the first book: "The sum of all we have said ... comes to this: the fullness and the end of the law and of all the divine scriptures is the love of that Being whom we are to enjoy and of that being who can enjoy him along with us." So too, he says that at the level of knowledge,

> every student of the divine scriptures trains himself and will find in them nothing other than that we are to love God on account of God and the neighbor on account of God, and that we are to love God with our whole heart, our whole soul, and our whole mind and the neighbor as ourselves, that is, so that our whole love of the neighbor is referred to God.[88]

James J. O'Donnell has pointed out that for Augustine the beginning and end of all of exegesis is practical: the love of God and of neighbor. He has well put it,

> What is important, then, is that this deeper message be uncovered. This approach imputes a fundamentally instrumental quality to scriptural texts: God works on the individual soul through scripture, and however God works is good. Having a correct opinion about the meaning of an obscure word in scripture is a good thing,

---

87 I owe the expression "canonical interpretation" to my colleague, William Kurz, S.J., who has written extensively on Luke. See also Gerald T. Sheppard, "Canonical Criticism," in *The Anchor Bible Dictionary*, ed. David. N. Freedman. 6 vols (New York: Doubleday, 1992), I, 861–866.

88 *De doctrina christiana* II, vii, 10: CCL XXXII, 37: "Nam in eo se exercet omnis diuinarum scripturarum studiosus, nihil in eis aliud inuenturus quam diligendum esse deum propter deum et proximum propter deum, et illum quidem ex toto corde, ex tota anima, ex tota mente, proximum uero tamquam se ipsum, id est, ut tota proximi, sicut etiam nostri dilectio referatur in deum."

but ultimately irrelevant; but having a correct opinion about the need to love God and reform one's life is not only a good thing, but ultimately the only thing to be expected from scripture.[89]

The merely instrumental character of scripture for Augustine is perhaps most evident in his claim that "one who is supported by faith, hope, and charity and holds on to them firmly does not need the scriptures except for teaching others."[90] Hence, Augustine is convinced that anyone whose interpretation of scripture

> does not build up the this twofold love of God and neighbor has not yet understood them. But anyone who has drawn from them an interpretation that is useful for building up love, even though he does not say the same thing that the author he is reading is shown to have thought in that passage, is mistaken, but suffers no harm, and is guilt of no untruth.[91]

Since Augustine's Christological interpretation of the parable of the Good Samaritan certainly is useful for building up the love of God and of neighbor, and useful for this in a way that a merely moral interpretation of the parable is not, it conforms to what Augustine taught was the beginning and end of all exegesis. And, even if this interpretation does not represent what Luke thought, the mistake is not harmful, since

> if one errs with an interpretation that builds up charity, which is the goal of the commandment, one errs like one who leaves the road by mistake and crosses through the countryside to the very spot to which the road leads.[92]

---

89 James J. O'Donnell, *Augustine* (Boston: Twayne, 1985), p. 25. O'Donnell's discussion of Augustine's exegetical principles in *De doctrina christiana* is, I believe, a splendid introduction to the topic.

90 *De doctrina christiana* I, xxxix, 43: CCL XXXII, 31: "Homo itaque fide et spe et caritate subnixus eaque inconcusse retinens non indiget scripturis nisi ad alios instruendos."

91 *De doctrina christiana* I, xxxvi, 40: CCL XXXII, 29: "Quisquis igitur scripturas diuinas uel quamlibet earum partem intellexisse sibi uidetur, ita ut eo intellectu non aedificet istam geminam caritatem dei et proximi, nondum intellexit. Quisquis uero talem inde sententiam duxerit, ut huic aedificandae caritati sit utilis, nec tamen hoc dixerit, quod ille quem legit eo loco sensisse probabitur, non perniciose fallitur nec omnino mentitur."

92 *De doctriana christiana* I, xxxvi, 41: CCL XXXII, 30: "Sed quisquis in scripturis aliud sentit quam ille, qui scripsit, illis non mentientibus fallitur,

For such a person attains the ultimate goal of scriptural exegesis, even if he is mistaken about the sense intended by the human author.

Hence, I believe that Augustine himself provides us with good grounds for maintaining that the Christological and soteriological interpretation of the parable is not quite so far-fetched and extrinsic as most contemporary exegetes seem to hold. Just as we do not interpret the parable of the Good Shepherd as merely providing us with a moral example of what a good pastor ought to be, but as a revelation of Christ's love and concern for his people, so Augustine—along with Ambrose, Origen, and Irenaeus—would have us understand the parable of the Good Samaritan as revealing Christ's loving mercy toward our fallen race and as teaching us that his love for us provides the standard and model of how we should love one another.

---

sed tamen, ut dicere coeperam, si ea sententia fallitur, qua aedificet caritatem, quae finis praecepti est, ita fallitur, ac si quisquam errore deserens uiam eo tamen per agrum pergat, quo etiam uia illa perducit."

ST. AUGUSTINE'S USE OF "MANENS IN SE"

In the central seventh book of the *Confessions*, Augustine claims that he read in the *libri Platonicorum*

that the only-begotten Son of God remains unchangeably before and above all times and that souls receive from his fullness so that they might be happy and are renewed by sharing in the wisdom that remains in itself so that they might be wise.[1]

Augustine clearly alludes to Wis 7:27b: *in seipsa manens innouat omnia*, though his words are less than a quotation. A few chapters later in the seventh book, Augustine explicitly cites Wis 7:27b, when he says,

But it is good for me to cling to God, because, if I do not remain in him, I will not be able to remain in myself. He, while remaining in himself, renews all things, and you are my lord, because you have no need of my goods.[2]

The purpose of this paper is to examine Augustine's use of the phrase *"manens in se"* and its variations in order to discover what it is precisely that he means by the phrase.

In her study of Augustine's use of the Book of Wisdom, A.-M. La Bonnardière says with regard to Augustine's use of Wis 7:27b, "C'est le verset qui exprime le mieux l'immutabilité divine, qu'il s'agisse de l'éternité de Dieu ou de son être. Mais le verset s'applique surtout au Fils de Dieu, en tant qu'il est Verbe."[3] She has pointed out that Augus-

---

1 *Confessiones* VII, ix, 14: CCL XXVII, 102: "Quod enim ante omnia tempora et supra omnia tempora incommutabiliter manet unigenitus filius tuus coaeternus tibi et quia *de plenitudine eius* accipiunt animae, ut beatae sint, et quia participatione manentis in se sapientiae renouantur, ut sapientes sit, est ibi."

2 *Confessiones* VII, xi, 17: CCL XXVII, 104: "Mihi autem inhaerere deo bonum est, quia, si non manebo in illo, nec in me potero. Ille autem in se manens innouat omnia; et dominus meus es, quoniam bonorum meorum non eges."

3 See A.-M. La Bonnardière, *Le livre de la Sagesse*, pp. 157–158.

tine cited Wis 7:27b fifteen times.[4] The text is, however, also cited, at times with slight variations, in at least five other passages, e.g., in *Sermo* CXVII, II, 3: *"manens in se, innouans omnia,"* in *Sermo* CLXXXVII, II, 2: *"in se manens innouat omnia,"* in *Sermo* CCCLXI, XVI, 16: *"in se ipsa manens, innouans omnia,"* and *In Iohannis euangelium tractatus* XXXVIII, 11: *"in se manet, et innouat omnia."* Finally, *Sermo* LII, II, 2: *"diuinitatem apud se ipsam manentem, omnia innouantem,"* which is closer to being a citation than *Confessiones* I, iv, 4 or VII, ix, 14. There are, moreover, many other instances in which Augustine uses the phrase, *"manens in se,"* or a variation of it, particularly in regard to the immutable Word of God. Hence, there is reason to take another look at Augustine's use of the phrase *"manens in se."*

At least from the time of *De immortalitate animae*, written while he was still in Rome, Augustine was concerned with the problem of how something unchanging could, nonetheless, be the source of change in other things. It would, for example, seem that the doctrine of temporal creation implies a change in the Creator, and Augustine met such a challenge both from the Manichees and from philosophers.[5] Very ear-

---

4 Cf. A.-M. La Bonnardière, *Biblia Augustiniana. A.T. Le livre de la Sagesse* (Paris: Etudes Augustiniennes, 1970), pp. 157 and 283–284. The fifteen citations she points to are: *De libero arbitrio* II, 17, l. 15; *De fide et symbolo* III, 3; *Sermo* XII, 10; *Confessiones* I, iv, 4; VII, ix, 14; and VII, xi, 17; *De natura boni* XXIV, 24; *De trinitate* II, 8; *Enarrationes in Psalmos* CIX, 12; CXXXVI, 7; and CXXXVIII, 8; *Epistulae* CXLVII, 19 and CCXXX-VIII, 4; *Quaestiones euangeliorum* I, 28; and *De octo quaestionibus ex ueteri testamento* II. With regard to these, it should be noted that the text is cited twice in *De trinitate* II, 8 and twice in *Enarrationes in Psalmos* CIX, 12. On the other hand, *Confessiones* I, iv, 4 has only *"innouans omnia"* and VII, ix, 14 is an allusion rather than a citation, as we have seen. Other variations in the fifteen passages are slight, e.g., *"in se"* or *"in seipsa"* for *"in se ipsa."*

5 See T. J. Van Bavel, "The Creator and the Integrity of Creation in the Fathers of the Church especially in Saint Augustine," *Augustinian Studies* 21 (1990): 1–33, esp. pp. 5-6, where he points out that pagan authors found a god who acts at a certain moment ridiculous. In *Confessiones* XI, x, 12-xii, 14: CCL XXVII, 200-201, Augustine faced the Manichean question as to what God was doing before he created the world. In *De ciuitate Dei* XII, 18: CCL 373–374, he faces a similar objection from philosophers who claimed, "bonitas autem eius numquam uacua fuisse credenda est, ne sit temporalis eius operatio, cuius retro fuerit aeterna cessatio, quasi paenituerit eum prioris sine initio uacationis ac propterea sit operis adgressus initium. ..." In response to such a view, he says, "Nobis autem fas non est credere, aliter affici

ly in his works, Augustine argued against such a view, using an analogy with the will of a human artist,

> From this we conclude that there can exist something that is not changed when it moves changeable things. For there is no change in mover's intention of bringing the body he moves to the end he wants, while that body in which the change takes place is changed from moment to moment by the same motion, and it is clear that the intention of accomplishing this remains utterly unchanged, while it moves the limbs of the artist and the wood or stone subject to the artist. Who, then, has any doubt that the conclusion we stated follows?[6]

I. EARLY CITATIONS OF AN ALLUSIONS TO WIS 7:27B

As early as the Cassiciacum dialogues, Augustine uses the phrase "*apud eum ... manens*" to illustrate how divine law is unchanged, despite its being imprinted upon the souls of the wise. He says,

> This doctrine is the very law of God. While always remaining fixed and unshaken with him, it is, as it were, transcribed into wise souls so that they know that they live better and more sublimely to the extent that they contemplate it more perfectly with their intellect and keep it more diligently in their lives.[7]

Once Licentius uses "*in se manens*" of the wise man who embraces and enjoys God. "Though immoble and remaining in himself, the wise man

---

Deum cum uacat, aliter cum operatur; quia nec affici dicendus est, tamquam in eius natura fiat aliquid, quod ante non fuerit. ... Potest ad opus nouum non nouum, sed sempiternum adhibere consilium. ..."

6 *De immortalitate animae* III, 4: CSEL LXXXIX, 105: "Hinc iam colligimus, posse esse quiddam quod cum mouet mutabilia, non mutatur. Cum enim non mutetur mouentis intentio perducendi ad finem quem uolet corpus quod mouet, illudque corpus de quo aliquid fit eodem motu per momenta mutetur, atque illa intentio perficiendi quam immutatam manere manifestum est, et ipsa membra artificis, et lignum aut lapidem artifici subiectum moueat, quis dubitet consequens esse quod dictum est?"

7 *De ordine* II, viii, 25: CCL XXIX, 121: "Haec autem disciplina ipsa dei lex est, quae apud eum fixa et inconcussa semper manens in sapientes animas quasi transcribitur, ut tanto se sciant uiuere melius tantoque sublimius, quanto perfectius eam contemplantur intellegendo et uiuendo custodiunt diligentius."

cares for the private goods of his slave so that as a diligent servant he uses him as valuable and guards him with thriftiness."⁸

In *De moribus ecclesiae catholicae et Manichaeorum*, Augustine once speaks of the highest Good as that which is most truly; he adds in explanation of its meaning. "For it is that which is said to be most truly. After all, this word signifies a nature that remains in itself and exists immutably. We can call it nothing other than God. ..."⁹

Augustine alludes to Wis 7:27b once in *De musica* in an exercise in versification, where he again emphasizes that the truth remains unchanged though it is the source of change other things.

You see all things made by the truth are set in order,

The truth remains; making new, it moves what is renewed.¹⁰

The first citation of Wis 7:27b in Augustine's works is found in the second book of *De libero arbitrio*, where he speaks of the form by which bodies and souls are formed,

> To that Form Scripture says, "You will change them, and they will be changed, but you are the Selfsame, and your years will not fail" (Ps 101:27–28). The prophetic language uses "years without fail" in place of "eternity." Of this Form Scripture likewise says that, "while remaining in itself, it renews all things."¹¹

Earlier in the same book, Augustine contrasted our mutable minds with the immutable Truth: "At times our minds see it less, at times more, and by this very fact they acknowledge that they are mutable, while, remaining in itself, it neither increases when it is seen by us

---

8 *De ordine* II, ii, 6: CCL XXIX, 110: "Curat autem immobilis et in se manens serui sui quodam modo peculium, ut eo tamquam frugi et diligens famulus bene utatur parceque custodiat."

9 *De moribus ecclesiae catholicae et Manichaeorum* II, i, 1: PL XXXII, 1346: "Id enim est quod esse uerissime dicitur. Subest enim huic uerbo manentis in se atque incommutabiliter sese habentis naturae significatio. Hanc nihil aliud quam Deum possumus dicere. ..."

10 *De musica* IV, PL XXXII, 1132: "ueritate facta cuncta cernis ordinata, / ueritas manet, nouans mouet quod innouatur."

11 *De libero arbitrio* II, xvii, 45: CCL XXVII, 267: "Cui formae dictum est: *mutabis ea et mutabuntur; tu autem idem ipse es, et anni tui non deficient.* Annos sine defectu, pro aeternitate posuit prophetica locutio. De hac item forma dictum est, quod *in seipsa manens innouat omnia.*"

more, nor decreases when it is seen by us less."[12] Once Augustine alludes to the verse in *De uera religione* where he speaks of the incorruptible truths that reasoning does not produce, but discovers. "Therefore, before they are discovered, they remain in themselves, and when they are discovered, they renew us."[13]

In *De fide et symbolo*, Augustine contrasts the Word of God with our words which pass away. "After all, that Word remains immutably. For Scripture spoke of it, when it said of wisdom: 'While remaining in itself, it renews all things.'"[14] Similarly, the verse is cited in *De natura boni*, where Augustine applies the verse to God. "Thus Scripture says that God is immutable in the Psalms: 'You will change them, and they will be changed, but you are the Selfsame,' and in the Book of Wisdom it says of wisdom: 'While remaining in itself, it renews all things.'"[15]

II. WIS 7:27B IN DE TRINITATE

There are two citations of Wis 7:27b in *De trinitate*, as well as eight allusions to the phrase. Referring to the Arians, Augustine says, that he will pass over "those who have thought in an excessively carnal manner that the nature of the Word of God and the Wisdom, which, 'remaining in itself, renews all things,' whom we call the only Son of God, is not only subject to change, but also visible."[16] A few lines later, he explains that it is the immutability of the Word which is expressed in

---

12 *De libero arbitio* II, xii, 34: CCL XXVII, 260: "Mentes enim nostrae aliquando eam minus aliquando eam plus uident et ex hoc fatentur se esse mutabiles, cum illa in se manens nec proficiat cum plus a nobis uidetur nec deficiat cum minus. ..."

13 *De uera religione* XXXIX, 73: CCL XXXII, 235: "Ergo antequam inueniantur, in se manent, et cum inueniantur, nos innouant."

14 *De fide et symbolo* III, 3: CSEL XLI, 6–7: "Manet enim illud uerbum incommutabiliter. Nam de ipso dictum est, cum de sapientia diceretur: *in se ipsa manens innouat omnia.*"

15 *De natura boni* XXIV: CSEL XXV, 866: "Itaque Deum esse incommutabilem sic scriptum est in psalmis: *mutablis ea, et mutabuntur; tu autem idem ipse es;* et in libro sapientiae de ipsa sapientia: *in se ipsa manens innouat omnia.*"

16 *De trinitate* II, viii, 14: CCL L, 98: "Omittamus igitur eos qui nimis carnaliter naturam uerbi dei atque sapientiam quae *in se ipsa manens innouat omnia,* quem unicum filium dei dicimus, non solum mutabilem uerum etiam uisibilem esse putauerunt."

Wis 7:27b.[17] Later in the same book Augustine speaks of the Father as appearing to Adam and the Patriarchs through a visible creature, "though he remains in himself and in his substance by which he is immutable and invisible."[18] In the fourth book, speaking of the Platonists, Augustine says that

> they refused to consider how it could be that the Word of God, while remaining in himself and not subject to change through himself in any respect, was able to suffer something more lowly through the assumption of a lower nature— something that an unclean demon could not suffer, because it does not have an earthly body.[19]

Augustine alludes to Wis 7:27b twice in book five, while arguing that the Holy Spirit is a principle along with the Father and the Son.

> If whatever remains in itself and gives birth to something or produces something is a principle for that thing to which he gives birth or which it produces, we cannot deny that the Holy Spirit is rightly called a principle, since we cannot deprive him of the title of "creator." And Scripture says that he produces things, and he, of course, produces them, while remaining in himself. After all, he is not changed and transformed into any of those things which he produces.[20]

Here the Holy Spirit is said to remain in himself, precisely because he is a principle for creatures without himself being changed into that of which he is the principle.

In the seventh book Augustine again describes wisdom as remaining in itself, even though a soul which participates in wisdom loses its

---

17 *De trinitate* II, viii, 14: CCL L, 99: "Eadem quippe incommutabilitas eius commemorata est ut diceretur: *in se ipsa manens innouat omnia.*"

18 *De trinitate* II, x. 17: CCL L, 103: "cum ipse in se ipso atque in substantia sua qua est incommutabilis atque inuisibilis maneat."

19 *De trinitate* IV, xiii, 18: CCL L, 185: "Nec sic uolunt considerare quae fieri potuerit ut in se manens nec per se ipsum ex ulla parte mutabile uerbum dei per inferioris tamen naturae susceptionem aliquid inferius pati posset quod immundus daemon quia terrenum corpus non habet, pati non possit."

20 *De trinitate* V, xiii, 13: CCL L, 221: "Si autem quidquid in se manet et gignit aliquid uel operatur principium est ei rei quam gignit uel ei quem operatur, non possumus negare etiam spiritum sanctum recte dici principium quia non eum separamus ab appellatione creatoris. Et scriptum est de illo quod operetur, et utique in se manens operatur; non enim in aliquid eorum quae operatur ipse *mutatur et uertitur.*"

wisdom. "Wisdom remains in itself, nor is it changed when a soul has changed to folly."[21] Furthermore, Augustine points out that the case with wisdom is not like that of whiteness, since, when a white body has been changed to another color, the whiteness does not remain, but simply ceases to be.[22] Hence, wisdom remains in itself, because it is not dependent upon those things that participate in it, as an accidental form, such as whiteness, is dependent for its continued existence upon the subject which has it. In book eight, Augustine expresses much the same idea with regard to the Good which remains in itself, even though the soul, which is good by conversion toward it, loses its goodness by turning away.[23] Finally, in book ten Augustine says that "the immutably good Son of God, remaining in himself what he was and receiving on our behalf what he was not, without loss to his nature, deigned to share in ours. ..."[24]

III. WIS 7:27B IN THE HOMILIES AND SERMONS

There is one citation of Wis 7:27b in *In Iohannis euangelium tractatus*. When asked who he is, Jesus answers, "'The principle.' Behold, what it means to be. The principle cannot be changed; the principle remains in itself and renews all things; the principle is he to whom it was said, 'You are the Selfsame, and your years will not fail.'"[25] One other time, in speaking of the forms of the dove and of the fire in which the Holy

---

21 *De trinitate* VII, i, 2: CCL L, 248: "Et quoniam quaecumque anima participatione sapientiae fit sapiens, si rursus desipiat, manet tamen in se sapientia; nec cum fuerit anima in stultitiam commutata, illa mutatur."

22 *De trinitate* VII, i, 2: CCL L, 248: "Non ita est in eo qui ex ea fit sapiens quemadmodum candor in corpore quod ex illo candidum est; cum enim corpus in alium colorem fuerit commutatum, non manebit candor ille atque omnino esse desinet."

23 *De trinitate* VIII, iii, 4: CCL L, 273: "Unde se si rursus auertat fiatque non bonus, hoc ipso quod se auertit a bono, nisi maneat in se illud bonum unde se auertit, non est quo se iterum si uoluerit emendare conuertat."

24 *De trinitate* XIII, x, 13: CCL L/A, 400: "dei filius immutabiliter bonus in se manens quod erat et accipiens quod non erat praeter suae naturae detrimentum nostrae dignatus inire consortium. ..."

25 *In Iohannis euangelium tractatus* XXXVIII, 11: CCL XXXVI, 344: "Et ille: *Principium*. Ecce quod est esse. Principium mutari non potest; principium in se manet, et innouat omnia; principium est, cui dictum est: *Tu autem idem ipse es, et anni tui non deficient.*"

Spirit appeared, Augustine says that these forms "were made by God for a time from a creature in his service, not from that ruling nature which, while remaining in itself, moves what it wills and changes what it wills, while remaining immutable."[26]

Augustine cites Wis 7:27b for the first time in his *Sermones* in 394 or 395, arguing against the Manichees that the substance of the Lord underwent no change at the Incarnation. He points out that the Manichees do not want to read or understand Ps 101:27–28 and "what is written in the words of divine wisdom concerning wisdom: 'remaining in itself, it renews all things.'"[27] However, he alludes to Wis 7:27b in an earlier Sermon where he says of God,

> For he is not increased in time, or stretched out in place, or enclosed or bounded by some matter, but he remains with himself and in himself full and perfect eternity, which human thought cannot comprehend nor the human tongue express.[28]

In the years 410 to 412 Augustine cited Wis 7:27b once and alluded to it twice. In *Sermo* LII he speaks of "this ineffable divinity remaining with itself, while renewing all things, creating, recreating, sending, recalling, judging, setting free. ..."[29] In *Sermo* CCCLXI he poses the rhetorical question:

> Could there die even that divinity, the Word equal to the Father, the art of the omnipotent artist, through whom all things were made, the immutable wisdom, remaining in itself, renewing all things,

---

26 *In Iohannis euangelium tractatus* IC, 2: CCL XXXVI, 583: "Ista ... ad horam diuinitus facta sunt de creatura seruiente, non de ipsa dominante natura, quae in se manens quod uult movet, et quod uult immutabilis mutat."

27 *Sermo* XII, 10: CCL XLI, 172: "Et quod diuinae in sapientiae litteris de ipsa sapientia scriptum est: *in seipsa manens innouat omnia.*"

28 *Sermo* CCXV, 2: RB 68 (1958), 19: "Non enim tempore augetur, aut loco distenditur, aut aliqua materia concluditur aut terminatur: sed manet apud se et in se ipso plena et perfecta aeternitas, quae nec comprehendere humana cogitatio potest, nec lingua narrare."

29 *Sermo* LII II, 2: PL XXXVIII, 355: "hanc ineffabilem diuinitatem apud se ipsam manentem, omnia innouantem, creantem, recreantem, mittentem, reuocantem, iudicantem, liberantem. ..."

stretching from end to end with strength, arranging all things with gentleness?"[30]

In another text from this period, Augustine says of the Word by way of contrast with human words,

> How much the more could the Word of God, through which all things were made and which, while remaining in itself, renews all things, which is not enclosed in places, nor stretched out by times, nor changed by short or long pauses, nor formed by sounds, nor ended by silence—how much the more could this so great a Word make the womb of his mother fruitful when he assumed a body, without leaving the bosom of the Father?"[31]

Some years later, in 418, Augustine says of the incomprehensible Word, "the Word does not benefit or increase as a knower approaches, but it is whole if you remain, whole if you depart, whole when you return; remaining in itself and renewing all things. Hence, it is the form of all things, the form that is not made. ..."[32] In the undated *Sermo* CCCLXXVII Augustine expresses much the same idea: "He is not distended by places nor changed by times, nor does he have increase and decrease. Remaining in himself, as a whole he is everywhere. What spaces are there that are without the Omnipotent. ...?"[33] Finally, in contrast with us who fall if we do not remain in him, Christ is not home-

---

30 *Sermo* CCCLXI XVI, 16: PL XXXIX, 1607: "Illa etiam diuinitas uerbum aequale patri, ars omnipotentis artificis, per quem facta sunt omnia, incommutabilis sapientia, in se ipsa manens, innouans omnia, attingens a fine usque ad finem fortiter et disponens omnia suauiter, mori potuit?"

31 *Sermo* CLXXXVII II, 2: PL XXXVIII, 1001: "Quanto magis Verbum Dei, per quod facta sunt omnia, et quod in se manens innovat omnia; quod nec locis concluditur, nec temporibus tenditur, nec morulis brevibus longisque uariatur, nec vocibus texitur, nec silentio terminatur; quanto magis hoc tantum et tale uerbum potuit matris uterum assumpto corpore fecundare, et de sinu patris non emigrare."

32 *Sermo* CXVII II, 3: PL XXXVIII, 663: "Non enim Verbum proficit aut crescit accedente cognitore: sed integrum, si permanseris; integrum, si recesseris; integrum, cum redieris; manens in se, et innouvans omnia. Ergo est forma omnium rerum, forma infabricata. ..."

33 *Sermo* CCCLXXVII, 1: PL XXXIX, 1672: "Locis non distenditur, neque temporibus uariatur, neque habet accessus et recessus: in se manens, ubique circuit totus. quae sunt spatia quae non habent omnipotentem. ... ?"

less if he does not remain in us. "After all, he knows how to remain in himself, who has never abandoned himself."[34]

IV. WIS 7:27B IN ENARRATIONES IN PSALMOS

Augustine cites Wis 7:27b twice in the *Enarrationes*, once in *Enarratio in Psalmum CXXXVI*, where he says that "we do not now breathe the air of that liberty; we do not enjoy the purity of the truth and that wisdom, which, while remaining in itself, renews all things."[35] Again speaking of the immutable wisdom of God, in a passage where he makes the interesting distinction between immutability and immobility, Augustine says after citing Ps 101:27–28,

> And in another place when Scripture was speaking of wisdom, it says, "While remaining in itself, it renews all things." That wisdom, then, standing—if one should say "standing," for it is immutability, not immobility that is meant—and always existing in the same way, changed by no place, by no time, nowhere different whether here or there, never different whether now or before, is the very speech of God.[36]

He cites the verse with slight variations twice in *Enarratio in Psalmum CIX* 12. In comparison with the form of the servant, he says,

> The immutable Truth, which is the Word of God, God with God, through whom all things were made, while remaining in himself, renews all things. In order that we might see it, there is needed great and perfect purity of heart, which comes about through faith.[37]

---

34 *Sermo* CXXXIV, I, 1: PL XXXVIII, 743: "Nouit enim ille manere in se, qui nunquam deserit se."

35 *Enarratio in Psalmum* CXXXVI, 7: CCL XL, 1968: "Non enim respiramus iam in auras illius liberatits; non enim fruimur puritate ueritatis, et illa sapientia quae *in seipsa manens innouat omnia.*"

36 *Enarratio in Psalmum* CXXXVIII, 8: CCL XL, 1994–1995: "Et alio loco de sapientia cum scriptura diceret: *in seipsa manens,* ait, *innouat omnia.* Illa ergo sapientia stans (si dici debet vel stans: dicitur autem propter incommutabilitatem, non propter immobilitatem) et eodem modo se semper habens, nullo loco, nullo tempore uariata, nusquam aliter quam hic aut ibi, numquam aliter quam nunc aut antea, ipsa est locutio Dei."

37 *Enarratio in Psalmum* CIX, 12: CCL XL, 1612: "Veritas enim incommutabilis quod est Verbum Dei, Deus apud Deum, per quem facta sunt omnia, in se manens innouat omnia. hanc ut uideamus, magna et perfecta cordis munditia necessaria est, quae fit per fidem."

Later in the same paragraph he says, "The brightness of God is ineffable light, the source of light without any mutability, the truth without defect, wisdom remaining in itself, renewing all things; this is the substance of God."[38]

Augustine speaks of God as "remaining in himself" twice. Once, while warning against our thinking of God as in place, he says,

> Think nothing of the sort about God, who is contained by no place and who dwells in the mind of the pious. And God dwells in the hearts of men in such a way that, if man falls away from God, God remains in himself, not as if he would fall because he does not find a place to be.[39]

In a similar vein, he says that one should not think that one is a temple that supports God so that God would fall if one withdrew. "If God should withdraw, woe to that man, because it is he who falls, for God always remains in himself."[40] Three times Augustine speaks of the Word "remaining in himself" in contrast to what he has become for us. Having cited Jn 1:14, he says, "He has come down to you in such a way that he remains in himself: he came down to you to become your valley of tears; he remained in himself to be your mountain of ascent."[41] In the following paragraph he says that John speaks to spiritual persons on heights, but that he descends to speak to the carnal ones. "In order that you might know that, when he comes down, he speaks of him who came down, see, John speaks of him who remains in himself: 'In the beginning was the Word. ...'"[42] Again, after citing Jn 1:14, he says,

38 *Enarratio in Psalmum* CIX, 12: CCL XL, 1612: "Haec claritas Dei est ineffabilis lux, fons lucis sine commutabilitate, ueritas sine defectu, sapientia in seipsa manens, innouvans omnia: haec substantia Dei est."

39 *Enarratio in Psalmum* XLV 9: CCL XXXVIII, 523: "Nihil tale cogitetis de Deo, qui nullo capitur loco, cui sedes est conscientia piorum; et ita sedes Dei est in cordibus hominum, ut si homo cecederit a Deo, Deus in se manet, non quasi cadat, non inueniendo ubi sit."

40 *Enarratio in Psalmum* CXXII, 4: CCL XL, 1817: "Vae illi si se subtraxerit Deus, quia ipse cadit; nam Deus in se semper manet."

41 *Enarratio in Psalmum* CXIX, 1: CCL XL, 1777: "Sic descendit ad te, ut maneret in se: descendit ad te, ut fieret tibi conuallis plorationis; mansit in se, ut esset tibi mons adscensionis."

42 *Enarratio in Psalmum* CXIX, 2: CCL XL, 1778: "Nam ut sciatis quia dum descendit, de illo qui descendit loquitur; ecce Iohannes manentem in se

The Word remains in himself; that is, he is the truth to which we come and which sets us free. But that he is preached as the word of faith in which the Lord wants us to remain in order that we might know the truth; that means, "The Word was made flesh and dwelled among us."[43]

Once Augustine contrasted those who remain in temporal pleasure with "eternal life" which "remains in itself."[44]

V. WIS 7:27B IN THE LETTERS

Augustine cites and alludes to Wis 7:27b several times in *Epistula* CXLVII. First, in discussing the theophanies of the Old Testament, he speaks of the nature of God as "remaining immutable with itself," though some persons who are not clean of heart might see God in the form which his will produced.[45] Secondly, he points out that "God produces these [visions] for those to whom he appears as he wills, for whom he wills, when he wills, while his substance is hidden and remains immutably in itself."[46] Immediately thereafter he uses almost the same phrase with reference to the human will's ability to reveal itself to God through speech, "while remaining with itself and hidden without any change in itself." He goes on to ask,

> How much more easily can almighty God, while his nature is hidden and remains unchangeably, appear in whatever form he wills

---

loquitur: *in principio erat uerbum. ...*"

43 *Enarratio in Psalmum* CXXIII, 2: CCL XL, 1826: "Quod ergo manet Verbum in se, ueritas est ad quam uenimus, et quae nos liberat; quod autem praedicatur uerbum fidei, in quo nos uult Dominus permanere, ut cognoscamus ueritatem, hoc est: *Verbum caro factum est, et habitavit in nobis.*"

44 *Enarratio in Psalmum* CXXXVI, 15: CCL XL, 1974: "Vita enim aeterna manet in se; illi remanent in delectatione temporali."

45 *Epistula* CXLVII, XV, 37: CSEL XLIV, 310: "Verum tamen non esse mirandum, si aliqui etiam non mundi corde uident deum in specie, quam uoluntas eius fecerit, latente inuisibili et apud se incommutabili manente natura."

46 *Epistula* CXLVII, XIX, 47: CSEL XLIV, 322–323: "Facit enim istas [uisiones] deus, quibus, ut uult, cui uult, quando uult, appareat sua latente atque in se incommutabiliter manente substantia."

to whomever he wills, since he created all things from nothing and, while remaining in himself, he renews all things.[47]

In *Epistula* CLXX, he says of the Father that he "did not lessen himself in order that he might have the Son from himself, but he begot from himself an other than himself so that he might remain whole in himself and might be in the Son as great as he is alone."[48] In *Epistula* CLXXXVII, Augustine states that God, "while remaining in himself by his eternal stability, is able to be present whole to all things and whole to each of them, although those in whom he dwells have him, some more than others in accord with their different capacities. ..."[49] Finally, Augustine says against the Arians,

> If that wisdom of which Scripture said, "it reaches everywhere because of its purity" and "nothing impure enters it" and "while remaining in itself, it renews all things" ... is corruptible, I do not know what to say except that I grieve over man's presumption and that I am amazed at God's patience.[50]

VI. OTHER OCCURRENCES OF WIS 7:27B

Augustine alludes to Wis 7:27b three times in *De Genesi ad litteram*. He says that the intellectual creature is formed when it is converted to its principle, the light of wisdom.

---

47 *Epistula* CXLVII, XIX, 47: CSEL XLIV, 323: "Si enim uoluntas nostra apud se manens et latens sine ulla sui commutatione, per quas se utcumque ostendat, exprimit uoces, quanto facilius deus omnipotens sua latente et incommutabiliter manente natura, in qua uoluerit specie, potest, cui uoluerit, apparere, qui ex nihilo creauit omnia atque in se manens innouat omnia."

48 *Epistula* CLXX, 5: CSEL XLIV, 625: "Neque enim Pater, ut haberet filium de se ipso, minuit se ipsum, sed ita genuit de se alterum se, ut totus maneret in se et esset in filio tantus quantus est solus."

49 *Epistula* CLXXXVII, VI, 19: CSEL LVII, 98: "Sed aeterna stabilitate in se ipso manens totus adesse rebus omnibus potest et singulis totus, quamuis, in quibus habitat, habeant eum pro suae capacitatis diuersitate alii amplius alii minus. ..."

50 *Epistula* CCXXXVIII, IV, 23: CSEL LVII, 551–552: "Iam uero sapientia illa, de qua dictum est: *adtingit ubique propter munditiam* et: *nihil inquinatum in eam incurrit* et: *in se ipsa manens innouat omnia* ... si corruptibilis est, nescio quid dicam, nisi ut doleam praesumptionem humanam et mirer patientiam diuinam."

The principle of the intellectual creature is, of course, eternal wisdom, and that principle, remaining in itself immutably, never ceases to speak by the hidden inspiration of his call to that creature whose principle it is in order that it might be converted to that from which it has its being. Otherwise, it could not be formed and perfect.[51]

Once he says that the whole of creation "does not remain in itself, but in him of whom Scripture says, 'In him we live and move and have our being.'"[52] Augustine adds in explanation that, though each part of creation is in the whole, the whole exists only in him by whom it was created. Again in the context of the angelic creature's conversion to its God, Augustine says, "And thus, while [God] remains in himself, he turns back toward himself whatever has its origin from him so that every creature might have in him the limit of its nature where it is not what he is, but has that place of rest in where it preserves what it is."[53]

Once in *De ciuitate dei* Augustine uses the phrase "*in se incommutabiliter manens*" of the Son. "The grace of God could not be more graciously presented than that the only Son of God, while remaining in himself immutably, put on a man and gave the Spirit of his love to men by the mediation of a man. ..."[54] In *De diuersis quaestionibus octoginta tribus*, while commenting on the Pauline phrase "*et habitu inuentus ut homo*," Augustine explains his comparison of the assumed human nature to a garment. He points out that there are four kinds of "*habitus*." First, some things which come to us and produce a habit "are

51 *De Genesi ad litteram* I, v, 10: BA 48, 94: "Principium quippe creaturae intellectualis est aeterna sapientia: quod principium manens in se incommutabiliter nullo modo cessaret occulta inspiratione uocationis loqui ei creaturae, cui principium est, ut conuerteretur ad id, ex quo esset, quo aliter formata et perfecta esse non posset."

52 *De Genesi ad litteram* IV, xviii, 32: BA 48, 322: "Neque enim caelum et terra et omnia, quae in eis sunt, uniuersa scilicet spiritalis corporalisque creatura in se ipsa manet, sed utique in illo, de quo dictum est: *in illo enim uiuimus et mouemur et sumus*. ..."

53 *De Genesi ad litteram* IV, xviii, 34: BA 48, 326: "Et ideo, dum ipse manet in se, quidquid ex illo est retorquet ad se, ut omnis creatura in se habeat naturae suae terminum, quo non sit, quod ipse est, in illo autem quietis locum, quo servet, quod ipsa est."

54 *De ciuitate Dei* X, 29: CCL XLVII, 305: "Gratia Dei non potuit gratius commendari, quam ut ipse unicus Dei Filius in se incommutabiliter manens indueretur hominem et spiritum dilectionis suae daret hominibus homine medio. ..."

not changed by us, but change us into themselves, while they remain whole and unaffected, as wisdom itself is not changed when it comes to someone, but changes the person from foolish to wise."[55] Second, there are things which both change the things to which they come and are changed by them, such as the food we eat. Third, there are those things which are changed by the things to which they come, but do not change them. For example, a robe's shape is changed when we put it on or take it off, without our being changed. Fourth, some things neither change the things to which they come nor are changed by them, such as a ring put on a finger.[56] The "habit" in question is not one of the first kind, "for the nature of man, while remaining in itself, did not change the nature of God."[57] It is not one of the second kind, since the man did not change God, while being also changed by him. Nor is it an example of the fourth kind, since in that case the man would not have been assumed by the Word. Hence, the "habit" in question is the third sort. While the Word remains unchanged in himself, the human nature "is assumed so that it is changed for the better and is formed by [the Word] with inexpressably more excellence and greater unity than a garment when one puts it on."[58]

Augustine cites Wis 7:27b in *De octo quaestionibus ex ueteri testamento*, in explaining that all of creation eternally existed in the divine art, though it unfolds gradually through time.

> Thus every creature, even that man who was going to receive in an inexpressible manner and bear mystically the person of the same Wisdom, always existed in that wisdom as if in the eternal art of

---

55 *De diuersis quaestionibus octoginta tribus*, qu. 73, 1: CCL XLIV/A, 209–210: "Verumtamen hoc interest, quod quaedam eorum quae accidunt nobis ut habitum faciant non mutantur a nobis, sed ipsa nos mutant in se, ipsa integra et inconcussa manentia, sicuti sapientia cum accidit homini non ipsa mutatur, sed hominem mutat, quem de stulto sapientem facit."

56 Augustine confesses that this fourth kind really does not exist, if one looks at the matter with care.

57 *De diuersis quaestionibus octoginta tribus*, qu. 73, 2: CCL XLIV/A, 211: "Iste autem habitus non est ex primo genere, non enim manens in se natura hominis naturam dei commutauit."

58 *De diuersis quaestionibus octoginta tribus*, qu. 73, 2: CCL XLIV/A. 211: "sic enim assumtus est, ut commutaretur in melius, et ab eo formaretur ineffabiliter excellentius atque coniunctius quam uestis ab homine cum induitur."

God, though it brings about individual things in their own times. It stretches from end to end with power and arranges all things graciously; while remaining in itself, it renews all things.[59]

In *Contra Faustum* Augustine explains that, because the Manichees can only think with bodily images, they "do not at all grasp how the Word of God, the power and wisdom of God, while both remaining in himself and with the Father and ruling all of creation, stretches from end to end mightily and arranges all things graciously."[60]

In *De doctrina christiana* Augustine compares the vocal expression of our mental word to the incarnation of the Word of God.

> The word which we bear in the heart becomes a sound and is called speech, and yet our thought is not transformed into that sound. Rather, while remaining whole with itself, it assumes the form of the spoken word by which it is conveyed to our ears without any taint of change. So the Word of God, without being changed, nonetheless became flesh....[61]

Augustine cites Wis 7:27b once in *Quaestiones euangeliorum*. He contrasts the temporal economy with "the eternity of the Word, which, while remaining in itself, renews all things."[62] Once he says that, though numbers can vary due to the lack or presence of one, "the

---

59 *De octo quaestionibus ex ueteri testamento* I. 25: "Sic omnis creatura et ipse homo qui eiusdem sapientiae personam mystice et inenarrabili susceptione gestaturus erat, in ipsa sapientia tamquam dei arte sempiterna semper erat, quamuis suis quaeque temporibus efficiat, quae pertendit a fine usque ad finem fortiter et disponit omnia suauiter, quae in se manens innouat omnia."

60 *Contra Faustum* XXIII, 10: CSEL XXV/2, 716: "Ista omnino non capitis, quomodo dei uerbum, dei uirtus et sapientia et in se manens et apud patrem et uniuersam creaturam regens pertendat a fine usque ad finem fortiter et disponat omnia suauiter."

61 *De doctrina christiana* I, xiii, 12: CCL XXXII, 13: "fit sonus uerbum quod corde gestamus, et locutio uocatur, nec tamen in eundem sonum cogitatio nostra conuertitur, sed apud se manens integra, formam uocis qua se insinuet auribus, sine aliqua labe suae mutationis adsumit: ita uerbum dei non commutatum caro tamen factum est. ..."

62 *Quaestiones euangeliorum* I, 28: CCL XLIV/B, 23: "Non enim sicut illa dispensatio temporalis ita etiam uerbi aeternitas transit, quae in se ipsa manens innouat omnia."

One itself, remaining in itself without any variation, perfects, when it approaches."[63]

Augustine clearly makes use of the phrase *"manens in se"* in its various forms chiefly in reference to the Word of God, often under the title of Wisdom or Truth, though he also uses the phrase in reference to God or the divine nature and a few times in explicit reference to the Father or in reference to the Holy Spirit. There are several times that he uses the expression of the human mind which need not be changed, though it produces change. At least once the phrase is used of the human nature of Christ assumed in the incarnation. Nonetheless, Augustine uses the phrase most often in reference to God and especially in reference to the Word. Though the phrase connotes immutability—or at least the absence of change—in that of which it is predicated, it is almost always used in a context where absence of change is asserted, despite what might seem grounds for its subject being changed. Augustine, that is, tends to use the phrase, as well as the verse from the Book of Wisdom in which it occurs, in contexts where he not merely affirms the immutability of God or of the Word or lack of change in a creature, but does so *despite* the fact that God or the Word or the human mind is the source of change in other things.

VII. SOURCES OF THE PHRASE "MANENS IN SE"

The frequent citation of Wis 7:27b is strong evidence that the principal source of the expression *"manens in se"* is the Book of Wisdom. There is, however, Augustine's explicit statement in *Confessions* VII, ix, 14 that he found this doctrine in the *libri Platonicorum* that he read in those momentous months prior to his baptism at Easter in 387. In his recent commentary on this passage in the *Confessions*, James J. O'Donnell has pointed out that "[t]he text of Wisd. is similar to Plot. 6.5.10.1, μένει οὖν ἐν ἑαυτῷ σωφρονοῦν, a passage with numerous parallels to the part of *lib. arb.* just cited (i.e., II, xii, 24)."[64]

There are in fact a number of texts in Plotinus in which Augustine could have found this phrase and this idea. Scholars remain quite di-

---

63 *Quaestiones euuangeliorum* II, 32: CCL XLVI/B, 73: "ipsum uero unum sine uarietate in se manens cum accesserit perficit. ..."

64 J. J. O'Donnell, *Augustine: Confessions: Volume II: Commentary Books 1–7* (Oxford: Clarendon Press, 1992), p. 447, where he refers to R. J. O'Connell, "Ennead VI, 4-5 in the Works of St. Augustine," *Revue des études augustiniennes* 9 (1963), 22.

vided on the issue of which *Enneads* Augustine read and when he read them.⁶⁵ However, in *Ennead* I, 6 "On Beauty"—which is admitted to be one read by Augustine, even by those who would insist that Augustine read only "a very few books of Plotinus,"⁶⁶ Augustine certainly found a text similar to Wis 7:27b. There Plotinus says of absolute beauty, "If then one sees that which provides for all and, remaining by itself (ἐφ' ἑαυτοῦ δε μένον), gives to all but receives nothing into itself, if he abides in the contemplation of this kind of beauty and rejoices in being made like it, how can he need any other beauty?"⁶⁷ Similarly, in *Ennead* I, 8, which Augustine at least very probably read, Plotinus says of the Intellect that it "is the first act of the Good and the first being, while the Good remains in itself" (ἐκείνου μένοντος ἐν ἑαυτῷ).⁶⁸ So too, in *Ennead* VI, 9, Plotinus says of the One that "it is the source of the best things and the power generating beings, though

---

65 A. Solignac, for example, listed in his introduction to *Les Confessions*, BA 13, p. 110 the following *Enneads* as one that Augustine certainly read: I, 6 "On Beauty"; I, 8 "On the Origin of Evil"; V, 1, "The Three Principal Hypostases"; V, 2 "On the Origin and Order of Beings Following on the First"; and III, 2-3 "On Providence." He adds as ones which Augustine very probably read: V, 3 "On the Knowing Hypostases and the Transcendent"; VI, 6 "On Numbers"; VI, 9 "On the Good or the One" and IV, 7 "On the Immortality of the Soul." E. TeSelle adds to the list of those he believes that Augustine certainly read: IV, 3-4 "On the Soul" and VI, 4-5 "How That Which is One and the Same Can Be Everywhere," while dropping I, 8 to the second group and dropping V, 2 from his list entirely. To the second group TeSelle adds: I, 2 "On the Virtues"; I, 4 "On Happiness"; III, 7 "On Eternity and Time"; and V, 8 "On Intelligible Beauty" (E. Teselle, *Augustine the Theologian*, pp. 43–45). For the current state of the question, see the articles by R. J. O'Connell and F. Van Fleteren in *Augustinian Studies* 21 (1990).

66 *De beata uita* I, 4: CCL XXIX, 67: "Lectis autem Plotini paucissimis libris. ..." See also the reference to the Neoplatonist writings in *Contra academicos* II, ii, 5: CCL XXIX, 20 where Augustine speaks of *unguenti guttas paucissimas* that caused his love of philosophy to burst into flame.

67 *Ennead* I, 6, 7, ll. 25–28; the translation is mine and slightly modifies that of A. H. Armstrong in Plotinus, *Ennead* I (Cambridge: Harvard University Press, 1967), p. 255.

68 *Ennead* I, 8, 2, ll. 21–22; the translation is mine and slightly modifies that of A. H. Armstrong, *Plotinus* I, p. 281.

it remains in itself (μένουσαν ἐν ἑαυτῇ) and is not diminished."[69] Augustine could have or, in some cases, most probably did read in the Latin translations of the *Enneads* the phrase, *"manens in se."* Though Plotinus is speaking of the transcendant One, the Good, or absolute beauty, he uses the phrase in contexts where he stresses the immutable transcendence of the One, the Good, or absolute beauty, *despite* its bestowing beauty on all else or *despite* its generating beings or producing other good things which depend upon it. That is, the phrase occurs in Plotinus in contexts where he is teaching the undiminished sameness of the One, despite its activity in the world.

Hence, from a sampling of texts from the *Enneads* which Augustine certainly or at least very probably read, it is clear that Augustine could have found—or at least could have thought that he found—in the philosophy of Plotinus much the same idea that he found in his Bible in Wis 7:27b. One must, of course, admit that Augustine—or perhaps the translator of the *Enneads* into Latin—had seen in the One of Plotinus the God Who Is of Exodus. But given this very basic shift in metaphysical perspective, he could have seen in both Wis 7:27b and in Plotinus the same idea, an idea that might, in almost every case, be summed up as saying that a higher reality can act upon the lower, while the higher reality remains unchanged,[70] or that the immutable God can act in the world, while remaining in himself absolutely unchanged.

VIII. CONCLUSION

Any philosopher or theologian in the theistic tradition is faced with the problem of reconciling the theses that God is absolutely immutable and that he is, nonetheless, active in the world at particular places and times. For the Christian theologian the Incarnation of the Word poses this problem in its sharpest possible form, for it means that the absolutely immutable Word of God, without any change to the Word, assumed into union with his person a mutable human nature at a particular time and place in human history. As early as the *De immortalitate animae*, Augustine was grappling with the problem of

---

69 *Ennead* VI, 9, 5, ll. 36–37; my translation.

70 The one obvious exception to this is the passage in *De diuersis quaestionibus octoginta tribus*, qu. 73, 2 (see note 57), where Augustine speaks of the human nature of Christ remaining in itself.

the immutable God active in human history. His frequent allusions to and citations of Wis 7:27b, at least from the time of *De libero arbitrio*, indicate that he found in that text of Scripture grounds for believing that Wisdom could remain immutable in itself, while making all things new. In his writings Augustine used Wis 7:27b most frequently and fruitfully, though not exclusively, in thinking of the immutability of the Word despite the Word's entrance into human history. Augustine tells us in *Confessions* VII, ix, 14, that he found in the *libri Platonicorum* that the Son remains coeternal with the Father above all time, that souls receive of his fullness, and that they are renewed by participation in wisdom, but that he did not find there that the Word became flesh, suffered, and died. Though Augustine did not find in Wis 7:27b or in Plotinus that the Word personally entered human history, he did find there that, while remaining immutable, God could act in the world. It is perhaps not unreasonable to suppose that what he believed when he read Wis 7:27b, he came to understand when he encountered it in the philosophy of Plotinus and that he was able to extend the basic insight to his thinking of the Incarnation, the mystery of the eternal Word's entrance into human time and history, while remaining immutable in himself.

AUGUSTINE AS THEOLOGIAN

ST. AUGUSTINE ON THE HUMANITY OF CHRIST AND TEMPTATION

In the Aquinas Lecture for 1999 Marilyn McCord Adams addressed the question of what sort of human nature the Word of God assumed in the incarnation according to various medieval thinkers. Given the Chalcedonian definition, one might suppose that there would not be much difference among the views of subsequent orthodox Christian thinkers.[1] She, however, examined the understanding of Christ's human nature in six theologians of the Middle Ages, namely, Anselm, Peter Lombard, Bonaventure, Aquinas, Scotus, and Martin Luther, and showed that their conceptions of the human nature of Christ differed considerably and in interesting ways that had a significant impact on how they understood the role of Christ. This study will take Augustine of Hippo as example of another thinker with an interestingly different conception of the human nature assumed by Christ. Or, more precisely, this study will examine two aspects of Augustine's view of Christ's human nature, which, I believe, have interesting implications for our understanding of Christ's role in our redemption and salvation and as a model for our imitation, especially in enduring temptation.

No one who accepts the Gospels can deny that Christ was tempted. His fast for forty days and subsequent temptation by the devil are presented in all three of the synoptic Gospels, and Augustine clearly recognized this and held that Christ's temptations were meant to teach us how we are to respond to temptation. He said, for example, in a homily on the Gospel of John that "he was tempted, but not in danger, in order that he might teach you who are in danger how to reply to the tempter and how not to follow the tempter, but to escape from the

---

1 Marilyn McCord Adams, *What Sort of Human Nature? Medieval Philosophy and the Systematics of Christology*. The Aquinas Lecture, 1999 (Milwaukee: Marquette University Press, 1999). Adams briefly mentions Augustine's interpretation of the words of Psalm 21, which drew my attention to the topic of this paper.

danger of temptation."[2] But he also claimed that Christ would not have been tempted if he had not willed to be. "For," Augustine says, "he also deigned to be tempted by the devil, by whom he, of course, would not have been tempted if he did not will to be, just as, if he did not will it, he would not have suffered, and he replied to the devil what you ought to reply to him in temptations."[3] Augustine sees the triple temptation of Christ by the devil as exemplifying every sort of temptation that a human being can face. Speaking of the triple sin of 1 John, Augustine says, "These are three, and you find nothing by which human cupidity can be tempted except the desire of the flesh or the desire of the eyes or the ambition of the world. Through these three the Lord was tempted by the devil."[4] Similarly, in a homily on Psalm 30, Augustine interprets the Psalmist's words, "You will lead me out of the snare they have hidden for me," as referring to the suffering of Christ and to the snare that the devil lays for every human being. Of that snare he says that the devil "put in the snare error and terror: error by which he entices, terror by which breaks and snatches. Close the door of cupidity against error; close the door of fear against terror, and you will be led out of the snare. Your commander, who deigned even to be tempted on your account, revealed in himself an example of such a fight."[5] Clearly Augustine thought that Christ's temptations by the devil were meant to be a lesson for Christians in facing and overcoming temptation.

---

2 "Et ille quidem tentatus est, sed non periclitatus; ut doceret te in tentatione periclitantem tentatori respondere, et post tentatorem non ire, sed de periculo tentationis exire" (*In Iohannis evangelium tractatus* 52, 3: CCL 36, 447).

3 "Nam et tentari dignatus est a diabolo, a quo utique si nollet non tentaretur, quemadmodum si nollet non pateretur: et ea respondit diabolo, quae tu in tentationibus debeas respondere." (Ibid.)

4 "Tria sunt ista, et nihil invenis unde tentetur cupiditas humana, nisi aut desiderio carnis, aut desiderio oculorum, aut ambitione saeculi. Per ista tria tentatus est Dominus a diabolo" (*In Johannis epistulam* 2, 14: PL 36, 1996).

5 "Posuit in muscipula errorem et terrorem: errorem quo illiciat, terrorem quo frangat, et rapiat. Tu claude januam cupiditatis contra errorem; tu claude januam timoris contra terrorem, et educeris de muscipula. Hujusmodi pugnae exemplum ipse tibi Imperator tuus, qui propter te etiam tentari dignatus est, in se demonstravit" (*Enarrationes in Psalmum* XXX, Enarratio 2, Sermo 1, 10: CCL 38, 198).

There are, however, in Augustine limitations on the extent to which Christ was tempted. For example, the bishop of Hippo never directly cited Heb 4:15, which says, "For we do not have a high priest who is unable to sympathize with our weaknesses, but one tempted in everything like us, but without sin. With confidence, therefore, let us approach the throne of grace in order that we may obtain mercy and find grace in timely help." The author of the Letter to the Hebrews urges us to approach with confidence the throne of grace in order to obtain mercy and to find grace in opportune help, precisely because we have a high priest who can show compassion toward our weaknesses and who was tempted in all things like us, but was without sin. Augustine, however, alludes to this passage only five times, always while quoting Ambrose of Milan as an authority against the Pelagians in order to show that Ambrose held the doctrine of original sin.[6] Each time he quotes the late bishop of Milan's words from his no longer extant commentary on Isaiah. Ambrose had said: "And so as a man, he was tempted in all things, and in the likeness of human beings he endured all things, but as one born of the Spirit, he held back from sin. For 'every human being is a liar' (Ps 115:2), and no one is without sin except the one God. It remained true, then, that from a man and a woman, that is, through that union of bodies, no one is found to be free of sin. But he who is free of sin is also free from this sort of conception."[7] The allusion to Heb 4:15, while clear enough and noted by the editors of PL, is hardly the focal point of the quotation.

When, moreover, Augustine looks at certain specific instances in which Christ was, it would seem, tempted, he virtually removes him from any exposure to temptation. In the body of this paper I will look at two instances of this procedure, which throw interesting light upon

---

6 Augustine quotes Ambrose's *Expositio in Isaiam prophetam*, a work that is no longer extant, in *De gratia Christi et de peccato originali* II, 41, 47, in *De nuptiis et concupiscentia* I, 35, 40, and II, 5, 15, in *Contra Julianum* I, 4, 11, and in *Opus imperfectum contra Julianum* IV, 106, 3.

7 "Item idem ipse cum exponeret Isaiam prophetam loquens de Christo: 'Ideo,' inquit, 'et quasi homo per universa tentatus est, et in similitudine hominum cuncta sustinuit: sed quasi de Spiritu natus abstinuit a peccato. *Omnis enim homo mendax* (Ps 115:2); et nemo sine peccato, nisi unus Deus. Servatum est igitur, ut ex viro et muliere, id est, per illam corporum commixtionem, nemo videatur expers esse delicti. Qui autem expers est delicti, expers est etiam hujusmodi conceptionis" (*De peccato originali* II, 41, 47: PL 41, 410).

the sort of human nature that Christ assumed and, I believe, raise some questions about whether the bishop of Hippo accepted in its literal sense the claim that our high priest was tempted like us in all things, while remaining without sin.

I. THE TEMPTATION TO DESPAIR IN THE FACE OF DEATH

In speaking of the fear of death, Karl Rahner said that a Christian need not face death like a Stoic or like Socrates, but may "imitate Jesus in the Garden of Olives or pray as he did on the cross, 'God, my God, why have you abandoned me?' and then add, 'Into your hands I commend my spirit, O absolutely incomprehensible God.'"[8] That is, in the face of death a Christian might acknowledge a desperate fear and yet also confidently entrust himself to the hands of God, as Christ did in confronting his death. But if Christ on the cross is to be a model for Christians in the face of death, Christ had to say those words from Psalm 21 as an expression of his own fear and feeling of abandonment in the face of death. Augustine, however, claims that Christ's words on the cross, "My God, my God, why have you abandoned me?" (Mt 27:46) did not express Christ's own personal fear and feeling of abandonment by God. Rather, he claims that Christ spoke those words in the person of his body, the Church. In both his *Enarrationes in Psalmos* and *De gratia Novi Testamenti*, which are the only two of his writings in which he comments extensively on the Psalm, Augustine places Christ's expression of abandonment in the mouth of the Church.

In the *Enarrationes in Psalmos* he asks, "What did the Lord intend to say? After all, God had not abandoned him since he himself was God. Certainly, the Son of God is God; certainly, the Word of God is God."[9] In confirmation that he is God, Augustine appeals to the words of John's Prologue and says, "And since God, the Word, became flesh, he hung upon the cross and said, 'My God, my God, look at me. Why

---

8 Karl Rahner, *Karl Rahner in Dialogue: Conversations and Interviews 1965 – 1982*, ed. Paul Imhof and Hubert Biallowons, tr. Harvey Egan (New York: Crossroad, 1986), pp. 209–210.

9 "Quid voluit dicere Dominus? Non enim dereliquerat illum Deus, cum ipse esset Deus; utique Filius Dei Deus, utique Verbum Dei Deus" (*Enarrationes in Psalmos* XXI, enarratio 2, 3: CCL 38, 123).

have you abandoned me?'" (Ps 21:2)[10] But Augustine goes on to ask why he said this: "Why does he say this if not because we were there, if not because the Church is the body of Christ."[11] Why did he say this "if not somehow to make us attentive, saying: 'This Psalm was written about me.'"[12] Augustine seems not to think that the incarnate Word could have addressed the words of the Psalm to God the Father.

But the Psalm continues: "Far from my salvation are the words of my sins" (Ps 21:2). Augustine asks, "Which sins? For it was said of him, 'He did not commit sin, nor was deceit found in his mouth'" (1 Pt 2:22).[13] Hence, Augustine asks, "How could Christ have said, 'My sins,' except because he prays for our sins and made our sins his sins in order that he might make his righteousness our righteousness."[14] Since Christ himself had no sins, he must—at least on the assumption that the whole Psalm was about him—have said, "My sins," in the person of the Church. And in the same way, he said, "My God, my God, why have you abandoned me?" not in his own person, since he was God and could not abandon himself, but in the person of the Church. But in that case Christ the man on the cross was not tempted by thoughts of abandonment in the face of death, as other human beings might be tempted. That is, he is not himself someone who is able to sympathize with our weaknesses because he experienced them, although he was instructing us on how we might behave.

Augustine is simply applying to the words of Christ on the cross the first rule of Tyconius, "On the Lord and his Body," which the bishop had found in the Donatist exegete's *Liber Regularum*.[15] Augustine in-

---

10 "Et cum Verbum Deus factum esset caro, pendebat in cruce, et dicebat: Deus meus, Deus meus, respice me: quare me dereliquisti?" (Ibid.).

11 "Quare dicitur, nisi quia nos ibi eramus, nisi quia corpus Christi Ecclesia" (Ibid.).

12 "Utquid dixit, Deus meus, Deus meus, respice me: quare me dereliquisti? nisi quodammodo intentos nos faciens et dicens, Psalmus iste de me scriptus est?" (Ibid.).

13 "Quorum delictorum, de quo dictum est: Qui peccatum non fecit, nec inventus est dolus in ore ejus?" (Ibid.).

14 "Quomodo ergo dicit delictorum meorum; nisi quia pro delictis nostris ipse precatur, et delicta nostra sua delicta fecit, ut justitiam suam nostram justitiam faceret?" (Ibid.)

15 See *The Book of Rules of Tyconius*, ed. F. C. Burkitt (Cambridge: University Press, 1894; repr. Nendeln, Liechtenstein: Kraus, 1967).

corporated Tyconius' seven rules in his own work on biblical interpretation, *De doctrina Christiana* III, 30, 42–56, 134.[16] He illustrates the first rule with a verse from Isaiah: "He placed a crown on me as on a bridegroom and adorned me with jewels as a wife" (Is 61:10). Augustine says, "One person, after all, is speaking ... and yet it is of course necessary to understand which of these two statements belongs to the head and which to the body, that is, to Christ and to the Church."[17] Similarly Tyconius interprets the stone hewn from the mountain in Dan 2:24 as referring initially to Christ the head, but then to his body when it fills the whole world.

In Letter 140, which is also in the *Retractationes* called a work, namely, *De gratia Novi Testamenti*,[18] Augustine uses Psalm 21 as a framework for structuring his response to the five questions posed for him by his friend and former Manichee, Honoratus,[19] for whom he had earlier written *De utilitate credendi*. The first of Honoratus' five questions asked what the words of the Lord, "My God, my God, why have you abandoned me?" meant.[20] Turning to these words, Augustine says, "Hence, Christ the man and the same Christ God, by whose most merciful humanity and in whose form of a servant we ought to learn what we should scorn in this life and what we should hope for in the next, took up in his Passion ... the voice of our weakness ... said, 'God, my God, why have you abandoned me?' (Ps 22:2).[21] Since Honoratus had asked about the meaning of these words, Augustine begins an explanation of the whole Psalm in order to distinguish the grace of the New Testament from that of the Old.

---

16 See *Augustine: De Doctrina Christiana*, ed. with an introduction, translation, and notes by R. P. H. Green, Oxford Early Christian Texts (Oxford: Clarendon Press, 1995).

17 Augustine, *De doctrina Christiana* III, 31, 44: CCL 32, 104.

18 Augustine, *Retractationes* II, 36: CCL 57, 119–120.

19 In *Opus imperfectum contra Julianum* V, 26: PL 45, 1464, Julian seems to confirm that the Manichean Honoratus was the same person as the Honoratus with whom Augustine later corresponded.

20 See Augustine, *Epistula* 140, 1, 2: CSEL 44. 156.

21 "Proinde homo Christus idemque Deus Christus, cujus misericordissima humanitate, atque in cujus forma servili discere deberemus quid in hac vita contemnendum, et quid in alia sperandum esset, in ipsa passione ... suscepit vocem infirmitatis nostrae ... et dixit: Deus meus, Deus meus, ut quid me dereliquisti?' (*Epistula* 140, 5, 14: CSEL 44, 165).

Christ's words on the cross, Augustine explains, show that the Psalm was a prophecy about him so that we can understand "how the grace of the New Testament did not go unmentioned even at that time when it was veiled in the Old."²² Augustine says that the Psalm says "in the person of Christ what belongs to the form of the servant in which he bore our weakness."²³ Augustine's words need to be read with care for he distinguishes the person of Christ, the form of the servant, and our weakness. He says that Christ said the words of the Psalm "in the voice of our weakness," and adds that Paul also prayed with that voice when his prayer was not heard and he was in some sense abandoned. "In the voice of this weakness of ours, which our head transferred to himself, there is said in the Psalm, 'My God, my God, why have you abandoned me?' He is, of course, abandoned in prayer insofar as he is not heard."²⁴

Up to this point it is not perfectly clear whose voice it is that speaks these words. But Augustine continues, "Jesus transferred this voice to himself, namely, the voice of his body, that is, of his Church, which needs to be reformed from the old human being into the new, the voice, namely, of his human weakness, to which the goods of the Old Testament had to be denied in order that it would learn to desire and to hope for the goods of the New."²⁵ Among the goods of the old human being the continuation of the present life is chief. "But these words by which the human day and the length of this life are desired are words of sins and are far from that salvation of which we do not possess the reality, but for which we do already possess the hope."²⁶ Augustine

---

22 "Quemadmodum gratia Testamenti Novi nec eo tempore tacebatur, quando in Vetere velabatur" (*Epistula* 140, 6, 15: CSEL 44, 166).

23 "Dicitur enim ex persona Christi, quod ad formam servi attinet, in qua portabatur nostra infirmitas" (Ibid.).

24 "Ex voce ergo hujus infirmitatis nostrae, quam in se transfiguravit caput nostrum, dicitur in hoc psalmo, Deus meus, Deus meus, respice in me; quare me dereliquisti? In eo quippe derelinquitur deprecans, in quo non exauditur" (Ibid.).

25 "Hanc in se vocem transfiguravit Jesus, vocem scilicet corporis sui, hoc est Ecclesiae suae a vetere homine in novum reformandae; vocem scilicet infirmitatis suae humanae, cui deneganda fuerant bona Veteris Testamenti, ut bona Novi Testamenti optare atque sperare jam disceret" (Ibid.).

26 "Sed haec verba, quibus humanus dies et vitae hujus prolixitas concupiscitur, verba sunt delictorum, et longe sunt ab ea salute cujus nondum rem,

explains that immediately after the words, "My God, my God, why have you abandoned me?" the Psalm adds: "Far from my salvation are the words of my sins" (Ps 21:2). In one sense this can mean: "'These are words of my sins, and they are far from that salvation of mine.'"[27] But the words could also be grouped in another way so that they say: "'Why have you abandoned me far from my salvation?' as if to say: 'By abandoning me, that is, by not hearing me you have become far from my salvation, that is, from the present salvation of this life,' so that the other sense is: The words of my sins, that is, these words I spoke, are words of my sins because they are the words of carnal desires."[28]

At this point Augustine makes it clear that these are the words of the Church. "Christ says these words in the person of his body, which is the Church. He says these words in the person of the weakness of sinful flesh, which he transferred to that likeness of sinful flesh, which he assumed from the Virgin."[29] Here again it is important to see the distinction Augustine makes between sinful flesh, in the weakness of which Christ said these words, and the likeness of sinful flesh, which Christ assumed from the Virgin. He continues, "He speaks these words in the person of his spouse, because he has united her to himself in some way."[30] Augustine cites Is 61:10, which he had used in *De doctrina christiana* to exemplify Tyconius' first rule, and applies them to what Paul said about Christ and the Church in Eph 5:31–32. As if his readers might balk at this interpretation, Augustine asks, "Why, then, do we disdain to hear the voice of the body from the lips of the head? The Church suffered in him when he suffered for the Church,

---

sed jam spem gerimus" (Ibid.).

27 "Haec verba delictorum meorum sunt, et longe ab illa salute mea sunt" (*Epistula* 140, 6, 17: CSEL 44, 167).

28 "Quare me dereliquisti longe a salute mea? tanquam diceret, Relinquendo me, hoc est, non me exaudiendo, longe factus es a salute mea, praesenti scilicet salute hujus vitae: ut alius sensus sit, verba delictorum meorum, id est, ista quae dixi, verba sunt delictorum meorum, quia verba sunt carnalium desideriorum" (*Epistula* 140, 6, 17: CSEL 44, 166–167).

29 "Haec ex persona sui corporis Christus dicit, quod est Ecclesia. Haec ex persona dicit infirmitatis carnis peccati, quam transfiguravit in eam quam sumpsit ex Virgine, similitudinem carnis peccati" (*Epistula* 140, 6, 18: CSEL 44, 168).

30 "Haec Sponsus ex persona sponsae loquitur, quia univit eam sibi quodam modo" (Ibid.).

just as he suffered in the Church when the Church suffered for him. For, just as we heard the voice of the Church suffering in Christ: 'God, my God, look,' and so on, so we also heard the voice of Christ suffering in the Church: 'Saul, Saul, why are you persecuting me?'"[31] Augustine uses his doctrine of the whole Christ (*totus Christus*), both head and body, in order to remove the cry of abandonment on the cross from the person of Christ the head and to apply it to Christ the body, that is, the Church. Thus on the cross Christ himself did not experience any thoughts of abandonment by God, but simply applied to himself the words of his body, the Church.

II. CHRIST AND SEXUAL TEMPTATION

In the fourth book of Julian of Eclanum's *Ad Florum* Augustine read quite to his surprise that Julian had accused him of reviving the heresy of the Apollinarists.[32] Augustine had a right to be surprised since he was writing his reply to Julian's *Ad Florum*, the huge *Opus imperfectum contra Iulianum*, at the same time that he was writing for Quodvultdeus, a deacon and the future bishop of Carthage, *De haeresibus*, in which he, of course, dealt with Apollinarism, listing it as the fifty-fifth of the eighty-eight heresies that had arisen since the coming of Christ.[33] Augustine was well informed about what Apollinaris of Laodicea held according to the best sources available to him, namely, the *Anaceph-*

---

31 "Quid ergo dedignamur audire vocem corporis ex ore capitis? Ecclesia in illo patiebatur, quando pro Ecclesia patiebatur: sicut etiam in Ecclesia patiebatur ipse, quando pro illo Ecclesia patiebatur. Nam sicut audivimus Ecclesiae vocem in Christo patientis, Deus, Deus meus, respice, etc., sic etiam audivimus Christi vocem in Ecclesia patientis, Saule, Saule, quid me persequeris" (*Epistula* 140, 6, 18: CSEL 44, 169).

32 See *Opus imperfectum contra Iulianum* IV, 47: PL 45, 1365. Apollinaris of Laodicea was a prominent theologian, exegete, polemicist, and man of letters in the 4th century. He broke away from the Church in 375. See Augustine, *De haeresibus* 55: CCL 46, 325; for an English translation see *Heresies* in *Arianism and Other Heresies* (Hyde Park, NY: New City Press, 1995). Or see Charles Kannengieser, "Apollinaris of Laodicea, Apollinarism," in *The Encyclopedia of the Early Church*, 2 vols. (New York: Oxford University Press, 1992), I, 58-59.

33 See *Epistula* 224, 2: CSEL 57, 452, in which Augustine explains that he is writing his answer to Julian's *Ad Florum* and writing his *Retractationes*, but will, nonetheless, begin *De haeresibus* for Quodvultdeus.

alaiosis attributed to Epiphanius of Salamis and the *Diversarum haeresion liber* of Philaster of Brescia.[34]

The accusation that Julian brought against Augustine of reviving the heresy of the Apollinarists initially stunned Augustine, but the ensuing debate presents a key for opening up the two quite different views of the humanity assumed by the Word according to the two bishops, especially with relation to Christ's experiencing sexual temptation. Both of them held that Christ, the Son of God, assumed a true human nature, like ours in all things save sin. But the nature that Christ assumed according to Julian and the nature that Christ assumed according to Augustine seem quite different and have quite different implications, not merely for the masculinity of Jesus, but also for his ability to function as a model, especially for male chastity. Hence, the difference between Augustine's view of the human nature of Christ and that of Julian is not merely speculatively interesting, though somewhat indelicate in the discussion of the body of the savior to which it leads. It is also practically of interest in terms of Christ's being a model of chastity, because, if Augustine is correct, then Jesus never experienced the sort of sexual arousal and temptations that other men experience and with which they have to struggle if they are to remain chaste.

In the fourth book of *Ad Florum* Julian warns his reader against the teaching of Augustine.[35] He says to Augustine, "I warn the reader, then, to be fully alert at this point, for he will see that you revive the heresy of the Apollinarists with an addition from Mani,"[36] Julian goes on to explain what Apollinaris held, namely, that he "is said to have first introduced such an incarnation of Christ that he said that he as-

---

34 Epiphanius (315–403), bishop of Salamis on Cyprus, wrote a large work on heresies called *Panarion*, a "medicine chest" of antidotes for heresy. Augustine knew only the *Anacephalaiosis*, which he took to be a work of Epiphanius, though scholars now claim that the work was produced by someone else. Philaster of Brescia wrotes his *Diversarum heresion liber* between 380 and 390. For Philaster's work, see CCL 9, 207–324.

35 Julian's work is extant only in the *Opus imperfectum*, though because of the bitterness that had arisen over Augustine's having allegedly misquoted Julian in *De nuptiis et concupiscentia*, it seems certain that Augustine quoted the whole of the first six books of *Ad Florum*. The last two books of the work are lost, since Augustine died before responding to them.

36 "Hic igitur ut adsit toto animo lector, admoneo: videbit enim Apollinaristarum haeresim, sed cum Manichaei per te adjectione reparari" (*Op. imp.* IV, 49: PL 45, 1365).

sumed from the human substance only the body, while the deity itself took the place of the soul. Christ would seem to have assumed, not a man, but the cadaver of a man."[37] This first position of Apollinaris was, Julian notes, quickly and easily refuted by the words of the Lord: "I have it in my power to lay down my soul, and I have it in my power to take it up again" (Jn 10:18). But Apollinaris "thought up something else which might give birth to this heresy of his, which lasts up to the present, and he said that there was indeed a human soul in Christ, but that he did not have any senses of the body, and he declared that he was unable to suffer any sins."[38]

Augustine appeals to the book that Epiphanius of Cyprus wrote on heresies[39] and reports what the book contained, namely, that some Apollinarists held that Christ's "body was consubstantial with the divinity," while others "denied that he assumed a human soul," and still others taught that "he did not assume flesh from created flesh, that is, of Mary, but that the Word became flesh," and still later some claimed that "he did not assume a mind."[40] Augustine insists, "I have never read, except in your book, your claim that the Apollinarists held that

---

37 "Apollinaris quippe primo talem incarnationem Christi induxisse fertur, ut diceret solum corpus de humana substantia assumptum videri, pro anima vero ipsam fuisse deitatem; Christusque non hominem, sed cadaver videretur hominis suscepisse" (Ibid.).

38 "Excogitavit aliud unde ejus haeresis, quae perdurat hactenus, nasceretur; et dixit, animam quidem humanam in Christo fuisse, sed sensus in eo corporis non fuisse, atque impassibilem eum pronuntiavit universis exstitisse peccatis" (Ibid.).

39 For the *Anacephaiosis*, see *Epiphanius I: Panarion Haeres. 1–33*, ed. K. Holl (Leipzig: J.C. Hinrichs'she Buchhandlung, 1915), 234–237, *Epiphanius II: Panarion Haeres. 34–64*, ed. K. Holl and J. Dummer (Berlin: Akademie Verlag, 1980), 1-4, 211-214, and *Epiphanius III: Panarion Haeres. 65-80*, ed. K. Holl and J. Dummer (Berlin: Akademie Verlag, 1985), or see PG 42, 853–873.

40 "Epiphanius ... dixit Apollinaristarum quosdam in Domino Jesu Christo divinitati corpus consubstantiale dixisse; alios autem negasse quod animam sumpserit; alios ... contendisse non eum carnem sumpsisse de creata carne, id est, Mariae, sed Verbum carnem factum; postea vero ... dixisse quod non sumpserit mentem" (*Op. imp.* IV, 49: PL 45, 1365).

Christ did not have the senses of the body and was incapable of suffering, nor have I ever heard it from anyone."[41]

Nello Cipriani has in a recent study examined the character of the Apollinarism with which Julian charges Augustine and has pointed to its sources in the anti-Apollinarism of the writings of Theodore of Mopsuestia.[42] Cipriani argues that Apollinaris himself did not deny the senses to Christ's body, as Julian claimed that he did.

> Egli aveva semplicemente detto che i movimenti o affezioni (*pathemata*) della psiche animale e della carne, invece di essere guidati da un *nous* humano, erano guidati dal Verbo, perché questo era sufficiente a garantire la santità del Redentore. Erano stati i critici di Apollinare a dedurre dalla tesi della vivificazione della carne ad opera del Verbo, comme logica consequenza, negazione della sensibilità corporale e perfino il carattere fittizio del corpo di Christo."[43]

Cipriani also argues that it was Theodore of Mopsuestia who was the source of the Aristotelian elements that François Refoulé had pointed out in Julian's thought.[44]

The accusation that Augustine denied bodily sensibility or senses to Christ must have initially struck Augustine as outlandish, but Julian soon makes it clear what he has in mind. He claims that, according to Apollinaris and Augustine, "Christ did not avoid sins by virtue of his judgment, but that by the blessedness of a flesh, which was deprived of our senses, he could not experience the desire for sins."[45] Apollinaris, Julian claims, "deprived [Christ] of the fullness of our natural senses for fear that he would become lowered in dignity by sharing in our

---

41 "Quod ergo affirmas Apollinaristas asseverasse in Christo sensus corporis non fuisse, eumque illos pronuntiasse impassibilem; nec uspiam legi, nisi in hoc libro tuo, nec aliquando ab aliquo audivi" (Ibid.). See Augustine, *De haeresibus* 55,: CCL 46, 325 and *Anacephalaiosis* III, ii, 1: PG 42: 873.

42 See N. Cipriani, "Echi antipollinaristici e aristotelismo nella polemica di Giuliano d'Eclano," *Augustinianum* 21 (1981): 373–389.

43 Cipriani, "Echi antipollinaristici," p. 383. Cipriani cites a passage from a homily of Theodore of Mopsuestia in which he uses the same line of argument against Apollinarism.

44 See François Refoulé, "Julien d'Éclane, théologien et philosophe," *Recherche de science religieuse* 53 (1964): 42–84 and 233–247.

45 "Non qui virtute judicii delicta vitasset; sed qui felicitate carnis a nostris sensibus sequestratae, cupiditatem vitiorum sentire nequivisset"(*Op. imp.* IV, 48: PL 45, 1366).

flesh."[46] Julian points out that the Catholic opposition to Apollinaris was fierce "because in accord with such a faith the mysteries of Christ would suffer a greater loss than the members of Christ."[47] The Catholics argued, "For, if Christ ... was born a son of David ... in order that he might give us an example and that we might follow in the footsteps of him who committed no sin ... but did not, nonetheless, put on the characteristics of our substance in every respect, if he possessed either flesh without a soul or a human nature without the senses that nature gave us, we are shown that he could not have fulfilled the role of an example and of the law."[48] Julian runs through the temptations associated with the senses of sight, smell, taste, and hearing and claims that there would have been nothing praiseworthy in Christ's self-discipline if he did not have these senses. Finally, however, he asks, "But what is the glory of chastity if he lacked virility rather than had will power, and if what he was thought to accomplish by the strength of his mind came from the weakness of his members?"[49] Not merely would Christ have lost all merit for his actions and suffering, but his teaching would have been charged with fraud if he said to human beings: "By conquering the real impulses of your nature, imitate the chastity of him whose impotence made him appear chaste."[50] Then in a somewhat surprising turn, Julian acknowledges that Apollinaris did not say all these things, but he insists that they all follow from his one claim that "Christ the

---

46 "Ne carnis nostrae communione vilesceret, naturalium eum sensuum integritate fraudavit" (*Op. imp.* IV, 49: PL 45, 1367).

47 "Quia apud talem fidem majus damnum mysteria Christi, quam membra perferrent" (Ibid.).

48 "Si enim ... factus est Christus ex semine David ... ut nobis daret exemplum, et sequeremur vestigia ejus, qui peccatum non fecit, ... nec tamen per omnia substantiae nostrae induit proprietatem, si vel carnem sine anima, vel hominem sine sensibus, quibus nos imbuit natura, gestavit, exempli formam et legis non docetur implesse" (Ibid.).

49 "Quae autem gloria castitatis, si virilitas magis aberat quam voluntas, et quod putabatur fieri de vigore animi, veniebat de debilitate membrorum?" (Ibid.).

50 "Imitamini castitatem, certa naturae vestrae irritamenta vincentes, illius quem debilitas fecit pudicum videri" (*Op. imp.* IV, 50: PL 45, 1368).

man lacked those senses that are given by nature and that fall into sins, not by use, but by excess."[51]

Julian accuses Augustine of blaming "concupiscence of the flesh in accord with the statements of his teacher, Mani."[52] He continues, "You say that the concupiscence of the senses was not present in the body of Christ, either in accord with the Manichees or in accord with the Apollinarists."[53] Then in another odd twist Julian seems to concede that Augustine really was not an Apollinarist, but was a Manichee—something that is, of course, worse. At that point Julian demands the passage of scripture where Augustine "read that Christ was naturally a eunuch."[54] He insists that Christ "did not shun the male sex, but assumed its reality, in every respect whole in his organs, whole in his body, a true human, a complete man" and that "there was in him the concupiscence of the flesh mingled with the senses of the whole body and the reality and sound condition of his members."[55] Against the docetist views of Mani and Apollinaris, by whom he means, of course, Augustine, Julian insists, "Nothing in my Lord causes me shame. I maintain the reality of the members into which he entered on account of my salvation in order that I might receive the solid support of his example."[56] The holiness of Christ was, Julian insists, due to "the

---

51 "Et Apollinaris omnia ista non dixerat: per illud unum quod pronuntiarat, homini Christo defuisse eos sensus, qui a natura inditi, non usu, sed excessu ad vitia labuntur; haec omnia quae a Catholicis relata sunt, praejudicio opinionis suae mutus excepit." (Ibid.).

52 "Concupiscentiam carnis accusas, juxta praeceptoris tui dicta Manichaei" (Ibid.)

53 "Dicis concupiscentiam sensuum in Christi corpore non fuisse, vel secundum Manichaeos, vel secundum Apollinaristas" (Ibid.).

54 "Illud efflagito, ubi tu legeris Christum eunuchum fuisse naturaliter" (*Op. imp.* IV, 52: PL 45, 1369).

55 "Et tamen ita aversatus non est sexum virilem, ut ejus susciperet veritatem, integer per omnia viscerum, integer corporis, homo verus, vir perfectus ... concupiscentiam carnis totius corporis immixtam sensibus, et veritatem ac sanitatem conditionemque membrorum fuisse in eo" (*Op. imp.* IV, 52: PL 45, 1369–1370).

56 "Nihil ergo me pudet in Domino meo: in quae propter salutem meam venit, teneo veritatem membrorum, ut exempli ejus soliditatem arcemque suscipiam" (*Op. imp.* IV, 52: PL 45, 1370).

goodness of his mind," not to "a defect of his flesh."[57] He proclaims that "the faith of Christians is not embarrassed to say that Christ has sexual organs, even though we conceal these in our own case as modestly as possible."[58] Christ lacked "nothing belonging to nature," and his "chastity was lofty in its constant integrity and was not aroused by the longing of desire because it was the virgin spouse of his holy mind."[59] Julian argues that, even if Christ had not assumed concupiscence of the flesh—for once using Augustine's biblical terminology—he would not have condemned it by not assuming it, just as he did not condemn marriage by choosing the higher good of chastity. He "would not have condemned the sense of the genital flesh, even if he had chosen not to have the capacity for it in his substance."[60]

Augustine, on the other hand, insists that Christ did not have sinful flesh, but only the likeness of sinful flesh and that he, therefore, did not have concupiscence of the flesh that resists the spirit.[61] He accused Julian of not even sparing Christ's dreams. Augustine regularly personifies "concupiscence of the flesh" in arguing against Julian and speaks of it as Julian's "darling" or "favorite." He says, "We know that Christ did, of course, sleep, and if your darling ("*suscepta*") was present in him, she at times surely deluded his sleeping senses by such dreams that it seemed to him that he was even having intercourse, and so his flesh

---

57 "Praedico omnem in eo sanctitatem beneficio animi, non carnis stetisse praejudicio" (*Op. imp.* IV, 54: 1371).

58 "Non erubescit fides Christianorum, dicere Christum habuisse genitalia; cum tamen ea in nobis, quam honestissime possumus, occultamus" (Ibid.).

59 "Castitasque ejus continua integritate celsa, nullo permota libidinis appetitu, quae virgo sanctae mentis exstiterat (*Op. imp.* IV, 57: PL 45, 1373).

60 "Ita nec sensum carnis genitalis damnasset, si ejus possibilitatem nec in substantia sua habere voluisset" (*Op. imp.* IV, 58: PL 45, 1374).

61 On the distinction between "sinful flesh" (*caro peccati*) and "the likeness of sinful flesh" (*similitudo carnis peccati*), which is based on Rom 8:3, see Thomas Weinandy, *In the Likeness of Sinful Flesh: An Essay on the Humanity of Christ* (Edinburgh: T&T Clark, 1993). Weinandy argues strongly that Christ assumed "our own sinful humanity" although "he never sinned personally, or ... had an inner propensity to sin (concupiscence) ..." (p. 18).

aroused by the stimulus of this good of yours would make his genitals uselessly erect and pour forth useless seed."[62]

Again Julian argues that, even if Christ did not include in his own members "the sense of the sexual organs," he surely did not make something evil when he formed the members of the patriarchs and gave them "sex and its sense."[63] For Julian the body of the savior lacked nothing of the nature of human beings. Augustine, on the other hand, says to Julian, "You blaspheme enormously when you make the flesh of Christ equal to the flesh of other human beings. You do not see that he came, not in sinful flesh, but in the likeness of sinful flesh."[64] Augustine argues that "Christ abstained from sin in such a way that he abstained from every desire for sin, not so that he resisted a desire he had, but so that the desire never existed at all. It was not that he could not have had it, if he had willed to, but he would not have rightly willed to have what sinful flesh, which he did not have, would not have forced him to have even against his will."[65]

The two bishops used a different language in referring to what one says Christ had and the other says he did not have. For Julian it is a natural sense of the body; more specifically it is the sense of the sexual organs, which for Julian includes a natural concupiscence or desire. At times he calls it simply virility.[66] Julian almost always avoids using

[62] "Dormisse quippe novimus Christum, in quo si erat ista tua suscepta, profecto sopitos ejus sensus aliquando per talia somnia deludebat, ut sibi etiam concumbere videretur, atque ita caro ejus isto tuo bono stimulante commota, et in irritum extenderet genitalia et irrita effunderet semina. (Ibid.).

[63] "Fac ergo, quoniam Christus, cum sua membra formaret, noluerit eis sensum admiscere genitalium, quo usurus non erat: num ideo cum Isaac, Jacob, et omnium membra fingebat, eisque et sexum dabat et sensum, malum aliquid faciebat? (*Op. imp.* IV, 59: PL 45, 1375).

[64] "Immaniter, Juliane, blasphemas, coaequans carnem Christi caeterorum hominum carni; nec videns illum venisse non in carne peccati, sed in similitudine carnis peccati, quod nullo modo verum esset, nisi caeterorum esset caro peccati" (*Op. imp.* IV, 60: PL 45, 1375).

[65] "Christus abstinuit a peccato, ut abstineret etiam ab omni cupiditate peccati: non ut ei existenti resisteret, sed ut illa nunquam prorsus existeret; non quod eam non posset habere si vellet, sed non recte vellet, quod eum caro peccati quam non gerebat, etiam invitum habere non cogeret (*Op. imp.* IV, 58: PL 45, 1374).

[66] See above note 49.

the words "concupiscence of the flesh," by which Paul says the flesh lusts against the spirit (Gal 5:17) and which John says does not come from the Father (1 Jn 2:16). He prefers to speak of a "natural concupiscence," which he holds is not blameworthy in its genus, species, or moderate use, but only in its excess.[67] For Julian sexual desire is as natural and good as the desire for food and drink, provided, of course, it is not excessive. Without it Christ was, according to Julian, impotent, a eunuch, not a real man. As Julian sees the Augustine's position, Christ's discipline with regard to food, drink, and sex was due to a lack of human senses and their corresponding desires, not to the strength of his will. Just as he cannot serve as a model for temperance regarding food or drink, since he did not have the sense of taste and the desire for food and drink, so he cannot, in Julian's view, serve as a model of chastity, since he did not have any sensation in his sexual organs or any sexual desires. So too, for Julian his status as a teacher is undermined, since he could not know what he was talking about if he simply lacked the desires, urges, and longings of the rest of mankind.

For Augustine, on the other hand, what Christ lacked was not something natural, but a defect in human nature stemming from original sin and inclining one to sin. Christ had a human soul and a human, male body; what he lacked was "sinful flesh," the injured or damaged human nature the rest of us have inherited from Adam. He lacked the desire or longing of the flesh that rebels against the mind, but he had the full range of human senses and the male sexual organs, which he could have used if he had wanted to. What he lacked was any desire or longing that he had to fight against or resist in order to be temperate or chaste. For such a desire, which would have to be resisted, is for Augustine a sinful desire.

For Julian human nature is much closer to the sort of human nature of which Aristotle writes, namely, the specific essence as a source of activities, including natural desires. Refoulé argues that Julian derived his concept of nature along with numerous other features of his thought from the Aristotelian philosophy of the period.[68] In fact, he concludes, "Julien fut sans nul doute l'un des premiers à tenter une

---

67 "Clarebit ... concupiscentiae naturalis non genus, non speciem, non modum, sed excessum tantum in culpam venire" (*Op. imp.* IV, 25: PL 45, 1351.

68 Though others limit the influence of Aristotle to the categories and dialectic, Refoulé points to the Aristotelian influence on Julian's concepts of justice, of the virtues, and of nature. See Refoulé, pp. 233-244.

synthèse entre les principes de la philosophie aristotélicienne et les données de la Révélation."[69] He even likens Julian to Thomas Aquinas![70] Such an Aristotelian human nature contains only good characteristics, which for a Christian Aristotelian are God-given. For Augustine, on the other hand, "human nature," as it has existed, not as it will exist in the future life, means either that state in which Adam and Eve were created by God, a state in which there was nothing but good, or that state in which we humans are now born with the damage inherited from Adam's sin.[71] Sexual desire (*libido*) can be called natural, "because every human being is born with it,"[72] but in itself it is something evil. "It is not our nature, but a defect against which we must fight by means of virtue. For we do not conquer something good by a good, but something evil by a good"[73] For Augustine the human nature assumed by the Word is like the human nature with which Adam and Eve were created, not like the fallen human nature with which each of us is now born.[74] As Adam and Eve were not created with sinful flesh and its disorderly desires, so the human nature Christ assumed was not sinful flesh, but the likeness of sinful flesh, and had no such disorderly desires or concupiscence of the flesh.

Given Augustine's conviction rooted in the Letters of Paul and of John that concupiscence of the flesh is a disordered desire that is not

---

69 Refoulé, p. 245.

70 Refoulé, p. 44.

71 Augustine stated such a definition of "nature" in *De libero arbitrio* III, 19, 54: CCL 29, 307: "Sic etiam ipsam naturam aliter dicimus cum proprie loquimur naturam hominis in qua primum in suo genere inculpabilis factus est, aliter istam in qua ex illius damnati poena et mortales et ignari et carni subditi nascimur, iuxta quem modum dicit Apostolus: Fuimus enim et nos naturaliter filii irae sicut et ceteri."

72 "Quod autem nunc agitur, naturalem esse libidinem et ego dico, quia cum illa nascitur omnis homo ..." (*Contra Iulianum* V, 7, 27: PL 44, 801).

73 "Adhuc non euigilas, ut intelligas nostram naturam non esse, sed uitium, contra quod uirtute pugnamus? Neque enim bono bonum, sed bono utique malum uincimus" (*Contra Iulianum* V, 7, 28: PL 44, 801).

74 This is especially apparent from Augustine's claim in *De civitate Dei* XIV, 23 that, if Adam and Eve had not sinned, they would have given birth to children in paradise without an lust and that their sexual organs would have obeyed their will in the same way as our hands and feet now are moved in obedience to our will.

merely the result of Adam's sin, but also an evil in itself, though an evil of which one can make good use within marriage, it is understandable why he denies its presence in Christ. The human Christ could not, according to Augustine, be subject to such disordered longings and desires, sexual or otherwise. Christ's sexuality was completely under the control of his will so that he experienced no rebellion of the flesh; he had no sexual desire since he did not will to. Otherwise, he would have had sinful flesh like ours rather than the likeness of sinful flesh. On the other hand, Julian certainly seems to have a strong argument when he claims that the Augustinian Christ cannot be a credible teacher or model of chastity if he had none of the urges and inclinations of other males. Hence, Julian presents us with a Christ who is, in some ways, is a much more attractive teacher and example of the virtues, and especially of chastity, than the Christ of Augustine. The problem is a knotty one, and the heart of the problem lies in the different concepts of nature and their implications—an issue that will surface in different forms later in the history of theology at the time of Baius and Jansenius, especially in the latter's battle against the Jesuit defenders of the so-called "pure nature."[75] But that is another story for another time. For the present let it suffice that this paper has shown that the sort of human nature that Christ assumed according to Augustine, that is, the likeness of sinful flesh, is significantly different from the sort of human nature we have, that is, sinful flesh, so that the temptations that the Augustinian Christ faced seem quite different from the temptations that the rest of the human race encounters.

---

75 See my "Augustine, Jansenius, and the State of Pure Nature," in *Augustinus in der Neuzeit*, ed. Kurt Flasch and Dominique de Courcelles (Turnhout: Brepols, 1998), pp. 161–174.

AUGUSTINE, MAXIMINUS, AND IMAGINATION

In a paper presented at the 11th Oxford Patristics Conference, I pointed out that Augustine accuses all heretics of being carnal persons, that is, the sort of persons who can think of God only as in bodily terms.[1] I showed that Augustine specifically accuses the Arians of thinking of God in a carnal or bodily fashion and even claims that their heresy arises from an image-controlled interpretation of Jn 5:19, "The Son cannot do anything of himself, except what he sees the Father doing."[2] To illustrate his point, Augustine reconstructs the logic of the Arians in thinking about Jn 5:19 as follows:

> As far as I can see, you understand that the Father makes some things, but the Son watches how the Father makes them so that he too can make what he has seen the Father making. You have set up two carpenters, as it were, thinking of the Father and the Son like a master and his apprentice, in the way that fathers who are carpenters teach their sons their craft. See, I come down to your carnal mind; I think the same way you do. ...[3]

---

1 "Heresy and Imagination in St. Augustine," *Studia Patristica* 11. vol. 23, pp. 400– 404. For Augustine's understanding of the Pauline terms "carnal," "animal," and "spiritual," see my "Spirituals and Spiritual Sense in St. Augustine," *Augustinian Studies* 15 (1984): 65–81; "*Homo spiritalis* in St. Augustine's *De Genesi contra Manichaeos*," *Studia Patristica* 10, vol. 22, pp. 351–355; "A Decisive Admonition for St. Augustine?" *Augustinian Studies* 19 (1988): 85–92, and "*Homo spiritalis* in St. Augustine's *Confessions*," in *Augustine: From Rhetor to Theologian*, ed. Joanne McWilliam (Waterloo, Ont.: Wilfrid Laurier University Press, 1992), pp. 67–76.

2 See *Tractatus in Iohannis Euangelium* XVIII, 3: CCL XXXVI,181: "Ariani quidem haeretici ... capiunt ex his uerbis ansam calumniae. ..." See also *Sermo* CXXVI, 8: *RB* 69 (1959): 186-187: "Non potest filius a se facere quidquam, nisi quod uiderit patrem facientem (Io 5,19). Hic arrianorum error exsurgit. ..."

3 *Tractatus in Iohannis Euangelium* XVIII, 5: CCL XXXVI, 182: "sic, quantum opinor, intelligis, quoniam quaedam facit Pater, Filius autem attendit quemadmodum faciat Pater, ut possit et ipse ea facere quae uiderit Patrem facientem. Duos quasi fabros constituisti: ita Patrem et Filium, ut etiam

In this paper I shall first show that Augustine explicitly accuses the Arians in general and Maximinus in particular of thinking of God in a carnal or bodily fashion. Then I will try to determine from what Maximinus himself said in the debate with Augustine whether or not Augustine's accusations are justified.[4] In conclusion, I shall suggest some reflections on the charges that Augustine is guilty of Hellenizing the biblical doctrine of God.

I. THE ACCUSATION AGAINST THE ARIANS

Augustine's anti-Arian writings are relatively late and few in number. In 418 Augustine received a copy of an anonymous Arian tract, *Sermo Arianorum*, in response to which he wrote his Contra *sermonem Arianorum*.[5] There are also an number of anti-Arian passages in the *Tractatus in Iohannis Euangelium*, dating from the years 413–418, and in a number of Augustine's *Sermones*.[6] Finally, there is the *Collatio cum Maximino*, a verbatim record of the debate between Augustine and Maximinus held in Hippo in 427 or 428, and the two books of the *Contra Maximinum Arianum*, which Augustine wrote after the debate, because Maximinus's filibuster had deprived him of a chance to answer on the day of the debate.

---

magistrum et discipulum, quomodo solent patres fabri docere filios suos artem suam. Ecce descendo ad carnalem sensum tuum, ita interim cogito ut tu. ..." See also *Sermo* CXXVI, 9: *RB* 69 (1959): 187.

4 Augustine denounces the Arian use of image-thinking, but he himself frequently uses images to illustrate Trinitarian doctrine. See especially *Sermo* CXVII, VI, 10–IX,12: PL XXXVIII, 666–668, where he uses images of the brightness of light and of a reflection of a reed in water to illustrate how the Father is not temporally subsequent to the Son. The difference is that, while Augustine uses images to aid in understanding the rule of faith, the Arians allow images to determine what the rule of faith is.

5 See *Epistula* XXIII*A: CSEL LXXXVIII, 122, where Augustine says, "dictaui contra Arrianos ad illud quod Dionysius noster de Vico Iuliano miserat. ..."

6 Of the *Homilies on the Gospel of John*, the most important in terms of their anti-Arian doctrine are XVIII and XX, which date from 413, and XXVI and LXXI, which are dated after 418. The principal anti-Arian *Sermones* are *Sermo* CXVII [418], *Sermo* CXXXV [417], *Sermo* CXXXIX [416–418], *Sermo* CXL [427 or 428], *Sermo* XLXXXIII [after 416], *Sermo* CCXXVI [416-417], *Sermo* CCCXLI [418], *Sermo* CCCXXX [417], and *Sermo Guelferbytanus* XVII [421–423].

Maximinus, the Arian bishop, came to Africa in 427 or 428 with Count Sigisvult, a Goth, who was sent to suppress the rebellion of Bonafacius. The fact that he accompanied Sigisvult suggests that he was a Goth, though Meslin has argued that he was a Roman by birth.[7] In any case, Maximinus took as his rule of faith the Council of Ariminum (386) which espoused the Homoian Arianism of Ulfila, the apostle of the Goths.[8] Maximinus began the debate with Heraclius, the priest whom Augustine had appointed to take over the administration of his diocese, but when Heraclius found himself in trouble, Augustine was summoned to his aid.[9]

This paper will focus upon the accusations of carnal thinking that Augustine raised against the Arians first in his earlier *Contra sermonem Arianorum* and then in his writings against Maximinus.[10] In the third chapter of his *Contra sermonem Arianorum*, Augustine takes issue with the Arian claim that the Son created all things at the command of the Father. He asks, "What do they mean when they say that the Son created everything at the bidding of the Father, as if the Father did not create, but commanded that everything be created by the Son?"[11] Augustine suggests that such people "who are wise in a carnal manner should ask themselves by what other words the Father com-

---

7 See M. Meslin, *Les ariens d'Occident* (Paris: Editions du Seuil, 1967).

8 See R. Gryson, *Scolies ariennes sur le councile d'Aquilée*. Sources chrétiennes 167 (Paris: du Cerf, 1980), pp. 250–263, for the Creed of Ulfila and Maximinus' commentary on it. See R. P. C. Hanson, *The Search for the Christian Doctrine of God: The Arian Controversy 318–381* (Edinburgh: T. & T. Clark, 1988), pp. 557–597, for an account of the Homoian Arianism and its principal representatives. For an excellent account of the Homoian Arian theology, see R. Gryson, *Les scolies ariennes*, pp. 171–200.

9 From Possidius's *Vita Augustini* VIII, vi, 3: PL XXXII, 543–544, we learn that it was the same Heraclius who was administering the affairs of the diocese who initially debated Maximinus.

10 M. Simonetti has argued that the author of the anonymous *Sermo Arianorum* represents the same sort of Arianism as is found in the writings of Maximinus. See his "Agustin e gli Ariani," *Revue des études augustiniennes* 13 (1967): 55–84, here 72. Hence, what is said in *Sermo Arianorum* may be counted as evidence, if not explicitly against Maximinus, at least against the Homoian Arianism that he represented.

11 *Contra sermonem Arianorum* III, 4: PL XLII, 685: "quid est quod dicunt, jubente Patre creasse omnia Filium, tamquam Pater non creaverit, sed a Filio creari jusserit?"

manded the only Word."[12] Then, he explicitly accuses them of forming a phantasm, that is, a false image, in their heart of two people, the one commanding and the other obeying.

> They form for themselves in a phantasm of their heart two people, as it were, though next to each other, still set in their own places, the one commanding, the other obeying. Nor do they understand that the command of the Father that all things be made is none other than the Word of the Father by whom all things were made.[13]

In the *Contra sermonem Arianorum* XII, Augustine cites a text from the Arian sermon, "He heard from the Father, 'Sit at my right hand,' and thus he sat at the Father's right hand." He comments, "as if he did this at the Father's bidding, not by his own power as well."[14] Augustine says, "Unless this is interpreted spiritually, the Father will be on the Son's left."[15] He warns that one should not think of the hand of God "in terms of the dimensions of the body, which do not exist in God, but in terms of the power to act."[16] Augustine at least implies that the Arians interpret Christ's being seated at the right hand of the Father in a bodily manner.

---

12 *Contra sermonem Arianorum* III,4: PL XLII, 685: "Cogitent qui carnaliter sapiunt, quibus aliis verbis jusserit Pater unico Verbo."

13 *Contra sermonem Arianorum* III,4: PL XLII, 685: "Formant enim sibi in phantasmate cordis sui quasi duos aliquos, etsi juxta invicem, in suis tamen locis constitutos, unum jubentem, alteram obtemperantem. Nec intelligunt ipsam jussionem Patris ut fierent omnia, non esse nisi Verbum Patris per quod facta sunt omnia." Here Augustine explicitly points out that the Arians think in phantasms and do not understand (*intelligunt*) the Father's command.

14 *Contra sermonem Arianorum* XII: PL XLII, 692: "Audivit, inquiunt, a Patre, 'Sede ad dexteram meam,' et ideo sedit ad dexteram Patris, tanquam paterna jussione, non etiam sua id fecerit potestate." See *Sermo Arianorum* 9: PL XLII, 680: "Is qui voluntate Patris descendit et ascendit, voluntate et praecepto Patris sedet ad dexteram ejus, audiens Patrem sibi dicentem: 'Sede ad dexteram meam, donec ponam inimicos tuos scabellum pedum tuorum'" (Ps 109:1).

15 *Contra sermonem Arianorum* XII: PL XLII, 692: "Hoc quidem nisi spiritualiter acceptum fuerit, Filio Pater ad sinistram erit."

16 *Contra sermonem Arianorum* XII: PL XLII, 692: "non secundum lineamenta corporis quae in Deo non sunt, sed secundum effectivam virtutem. ..."

Later, Augustine deals with the text from John, "As I hear, so I judge" (Jn 5:30), which the Arians understood as indicating the subjection of the Son. He cites the text, "The Son cannot of himself do anything except what he has seen the Father doing" (Jn 5:19). After warning that Jn 5:30 is more difficult to understand than the Arians suppose, he cites John's words, "The Father does not judge anyone, but has given all judgment to the Son" (Jn 6:22). Then he asks, "How is it that 'the Son cannot of himself do anything except what he has seen the Father doing' (Jn 5:19), though he judges and does not see the Father judging?"[17] While the Arians, Augustine would contend, have tried to imagine the Son observing the Father in action so that he could do what he sees the Father doing, Augustine insists that, if one takes all the texts together, one is forced to transcend the imagination. He says,

> Let them attend to these things; let them think of them; let them ponder them, and in some way let their intention as far as possible become removed from the flesh (*excarnetur*). For by their carnal thought they strive to separate the one and identical nature of the Trinity in a distinction of substances and to arrange it in degrees of power.[18]

Still later, in dealing once again with Jn 5:30, which the Arians took as evidence of the subordination of the Son, Augustine says, "If they would think [of what Augustine has just said], they would not in their carnal thoughts arrange the powers or functions of the Trinity in unequal degrees, making the Father the emperor, the Son the judge, and the Holy Spirit the advocate like three men of unequal and unlike

---

17 *Contra sermonem Arianorum* XIV: PL XLII, 693: "Quomodo igitur 'non potest Filius a se facere quidquam, nisi quod viderit Patrem facientem,' cum judicet, nec Patrem videat judicantem?"

18 *Contra sermonem Arianorum* XIV: PL XLII, 693: "In ista intendant, ista cogitent, ista considerent; et eorum quodam modo, quantum fieri potest, excarnetur intentio, qui carnalibus cogitationibus moliuntur unam Trinitatis eamdemque naturam et substantiarum separare distantia, et potestatum gradibus ordinare." The verb "*excarnare*" is used by Augustine only one other time; in *Sermo* CXL 6: PL XXXVIII, 775, he says, "Exercet mentis Evangelium Ioannis, limat et excarnat, ut de Deo non carnaliter, sed spiritualiter sapiamus."

dignity."[19] On the other hand, Augustine turns back upon them their own argument and explains that

> even by such carnal thinking they cannot demonstrate a diversity of natures—which is the main point at issue between them and us. They compare these things to human practices and do not withdraw from things familiar to the human race that they can grasp in thinking. For the animal person does not perceive what belongs to the Spirit of God (1 Cor 2:14).[20]

After all, Augustine insists that, in the Arian comparison of the Father, Son, and Holy Spirit with the emperor, judge, and advocate, the latter three are all humans with the same nature, despite their different powers and functions.[21]

Later Augustine again accuses the Arians of carnal thinking. He first cites the Arian text, "The Father begot the Son, willing this without change or passion; the Son made the Holy Spirit without labor or exhaustion by his own power alone."[22] Among other things, Augustine states that the Arians should attend to their claim that the Son made

---

19 *Contra sermonem Arianorum* XVIII: PL XLII, 696: "Haec isti si cogitarent, non carnalibus cogitationibus sic Trinitatis potestates vel officia gradibus imparibus ordinarent, ut tamquam tres homines inaequalis ac dissimilis dignitatis facerent, tanquam imperatorem Patrem, judicem Filium, advocatum Spiritum sanctum." In *Sermo Arianorum* 9: PL XLII, 680, the relationship is stated less bluntly. After citing Jn 5:30, it says of Christ, "Unde et in judicando Patris praesentiam praeponit, dicens:'Venite, benedicti Patris mei' (Mt 25:34). Ergo justus judex est Filius; judicantis vero honor et auctoritas, Patris imperiales leges; sicuti et Spiritus sancti officiosa advocatio et consolatio."

20 *Contra sermonem Arianorum* XVIII: PL XLII, 696–697: "Qua sua cogitatione carnali, tamen naturae diversitatem, de qua inter nos et ipsos maxima quaestio est, in his tribus personis demonstrare non possunt. Cum enim ad humanos mores ista referunt, et ab humani generis consuetudine quam cogitando possunt capere non recedunt (animalis enim homo non percipit quae sunt Spiritus Dei (1 Cor 2:14). ..."

21 *Contra sermonem Arianorum* XVIII: PL XLII, 697: "quid aliud nos admonent, nisi quia et imperator, et judex et advocatus, homines sunt? Proinde judex imperatore etiamsi potestate minor est, non minus homo est."

22 *Contra sermonem Arianorum* XXVIII, 26: PL XLII, 702: "Pater, inquiunt, immobiliter et impassibiliter volens Filium genuit: Filius sine labore et fatigatione sola virtute sua spiritum fecit." See *Sermo Arianorum* 26: PL XLII, 681.

the Holy Spirit by his own power, for "in that way they are forced to say that the Son did something that he did not see the Father doing."[23] Augustine continues to press them, asking whether the Father also made the Holy Spirit, for, if he did, then the Son did not make him by his own power alone.[24] Worse yet, did the Father perhaps first make another Holy Spirit so that the Son could make the one he made? After all, the Son cannot do anything that he has not seen the Father doing.[25] However, the second hypothesis runs directly counter to Jesus' words, "Whatever the Father does, those same things the Son does in a like manner" (Jn 5:19). Hence, Augustine adds, "If they would try to think of these things, all those things that they make up for themselves in their carnal thought would assuredly be thrown into confusion."[26] Augustine elsewhere explains that such confusion is not meant to be the goal, but should rather be the path that leads to healing. In *Sermo CXXVI*, he points to the confusion that results from imagining that the Son watches what the Father does and then does the same thing, if one adds to such imagining of John 5:19 the content of John 1:3, namely, that all things were done through the Word. Here Augustine points out that the remedy for this carnal thinking lies in the confusion.

> Certainly you are confused, you heretic; certainly you are confused. But like one who has taken hellebore, you are confused in order to be healed. Now you are no longer yourself; you too condemn, as far as I can see, your carnal opinion and your carnal view.[27]

---

23 *Contra sermonem Arianorum* XXVIII, 26: PL XLII, 703: "Isto enim modo coguntur fateri, aliquid fecisse Filium quod non viderit Patrem facientem."

24 *Contra sermonem Arianorum* XXVIII, 26: PL XLII, 703: "An placet eis dicere, quod etiam Pater fecerit Spiritum sanctum? Non ergo eum sola virtute sua fecerit Filius."

25 *Contra sermonem Arianorum* XXVIII, 26: PL XLII, 703: "An alterum fecit prior Pater, ut posset Filius facere quem fecit, qui non potest facere nisi quod viderit Patrem facientem?"

26 *Contra sermonem Arianorum* XXVIII, 26: PL XLII, 703: "Si haec cogitare conentur, procul dubio turbabuntur eis omnia quae sibi carnali cogitatione componunt."

27 *Sermo* CXXVI, 10: *RB* 69 (1959), 188: "Certe turbaris, haeretice, certe turbaris; sed tamquam helleboro accepto turbaris, ut saneris. Iam te non inuenis, sententiam tuam et carnalem intuitum tuum, quantum arbitror, etiam ipse condemnas." Though hellebore (*helleborum*) was a drug used to

That is, the image of the Father and of the Son, the one unable to do anything by himself and watching the other's activity, like the apprentice observing the master carpenter, is shattered by the image of the Father doing all things by his Word so that one is forced to transcend thinking in images and arrive at understanding.[28] Hence, Augustine tells the Arians to place the eyes of the flesh behind them, raise up their heart, and gaze upon things divine.[29] If they do this, then their carnal intention is confused, hidden, destroyed.[30]

In his *Contra Maximinum Arianum*, Augustine frequently accuses the Arian bishop of thinking of God in carnal or imaginative terms. In the first book, Augustine twice accuses Maximinus of such carnal thinking. First, when Maximinus appealed to the ineffable groans of the Holy Spirit to prove that the Holy Spirit adores the Father,[31] Augustine interprets these groans as the prayers of the saints and says of the Arian interpretation, "No one thinks of the Holy Spirit in that way unless he thinks of him in terms of the flesh and not in terms of spirit."[32] Later Augustine accuses Maximinus of believing that the Son is mutable.

> Of course, you would not believe this, if as a Catholic you believed that the form of the servant was assumed by the form of God and not that the form of God was changed into the form of the servant. Then you would think—not in a carnal, but in a spiritual manner—

---

cure mental diseases, its cognate verb (*helleboro*) means "to purge." Either sense (or both) could be applicable here.

28 In the Oxford paper I suggested that Augustine was using against the Arians the Plotinian technique of correcting one image by another or of shattering one image against another in order to move beyond imagery to understanding. See Robert J. O'Connell, *St. Augustine's Early Theory of Man, A.D. 386-391* (Harvard: Belknap Press, 1986), p. 58, for a description of Plotinus's use of images to transcend the corporeal realm.

29 See *Sermo* CXXVI, 10: *RB* 69 (1959), 188: "Repone oculos carnis post te, erige si aliquid habes in corde, diuina intuere."

30 See *Sermo* CXXVI, 12: *RB* 69 (1959), 189: "Ubi est ergo intentio ista carnalis? Confundatur, abscondatur, perimatur."

31 See Rom 8:26.

32 *Contra Maximinum* I, ix: PL XLII, 750– 51: "Nemo enim sic de Spiritu sancto sapit, nisi qui secundum carnem, non secundum spiritum sapit."

that he remained the invisible God after having assumed the visible man. ...³³

In the second book Augustine deals with a number of texts from the debate in which he points to carnal thinking as the source of the Arian position. At one point Maximinus stated that the Son "sees the Father, but he sees the incomprehensible. The Father, on the other hand, sees the Son as one who holds and has the Son in his embrace. ..."³⁴ Augustine replies that only the carnal-minded think that way and accuses him of imagining to himself "an embrace, that is, some capacity of the greater Father by which he grasps and contains the smaller Son, as a home holds a human being in a bodily fashion or as a nurse's bosom holds an infant."³⁵ Augustine continues to jab away at his opponent, adding with irony that this way of thinking leads one to include among the marvelous things about Christ that "he grew in the form of the servant and became larger than he had been in the form of God so that, though he was first carried in his Father's embrace, he now sits at the Father's right hand."³⁶ Hence, he cries out, "Cast such childish or old womanish phantasms from your heart. ..."³⁷ Later Augustine accuses Maximinus of thinking of the Son's being born from the

---

33 *Contra Maximinum* I, xix: PL XLII, 758: "Quod utique non crederes, si formam servi a forma Dei esse susceptam, non formam Dei in formam servi esse mutatam, tanquam catholicus crederes; et visibili homine assumpto, permansisse invisibilem Deum, non carnaliter, sed spiritualiter cogitares. ..."

34 *Collatio cum Maximino* II, 9: PL XLII, 728: "Vidit ergo Patrem sed vidit incapabilem. Pater autem sic vidit Filium, ut tenens in sinu suo et habens. ..." Maximinus had conflated Jn 6:46: "Not that anyone has seen the Father except he who is from God; he has seen the Father" and Jn 1:18: "No one has ever seen God; the only begotten God who is in the Father's embrace, he has revealed him."

35 *Contra Maximinum* II, ix, 2: PL XLII, 764: "Sic non sapiunt, nisi qui carnaliter sapiunt. Sinum quippe tibi fingis, ut video, aliquam capacitatem majoris Patris, qua Filium minorem capiat atque contineat: sicut hominem corporaliter capit domus, aut sicut sinus nutricis capit infantem."

36 *Contra Maximinum* II, ix, 2: PL XLII, 764: "Ergo inter mirabilia Christi et hoc deputabitur, quia in forma servi crevit, et major est factus quam in forma Dei fuerat, ut cum prius portaretur in sinu Patris, nunc sedeat ad dextram Patris."

37 *Contra Maximinum* II, ix, 2: PL XLII, 764: "Abjice ista puerilia vel anicularia phantasmata de corde tuo. ..."

Father in a carnal manner and of rejecting, for this reason, the Son's generation from the Father. "Filled with carnal thoughts, you think that the substance of the Father could not beget the Son out of itself without undergoing what the substance of the flesh undergoes when it begets."[38] Shortly thereafter, he urges the Arian, "Remove the corruption; cast aside from the light of the mind any carnal passions and see the invisible reality of God that is known through what has been made."[39] That is, as God gave to human parents the ability to generate offspring of the same substance as themselves, so the Father has from his substance begotten a Son of the same substance. One must "purify" the concept of generation of any corruption and carnal passion; once one has done so, one "will not fail to believe out of contentiousness, but see as a result of understanding."[40]

Once Augustine uses a human analogy precisely "on account of the weakness of the carnal ones."[41] He asks us to think of a human child who obeys his parent, asks his parent for something, thanks the parent, is sent somewhere by the parent where the child states that he has come to do the parent's will. Then he asks, "Does this show that the child is not of the same substance as the parent?"[42] So too, Augustine accuses Maximinus of thinking in carnal terms of the Son's veneration and worship of the Father.[43] Later Augustine, arguing that the Holy Spirit is seated with the Father and the Son, warns that we should not think of their being seated in a carnal fashion. Otherwise, we would think that the Father is seated in the less honorable position at the Son's left or that the Holy Spirit is denied what Scripture promises to

---

38 *Contra Maximinum* II, xiv, 2: PL XLII, 771: "Carnalibus quippe cogitationibus pleni substantiam Dei de se ipsa gignere posse Filium non putatis, nisi hoc patiatur quod substantia quando gignit patitur carnis."

39 *Contra Maximinum* II, xiv, 3: PL XLII, 772: "Corruptionem de medio tollite, passiones carnales a lumine mentis adjicite, et invisibilia Dei, per ea quae facta sunt, intellecta conspicite" (Rom 1:20).

40 *Contra Maximinum* II, xiv, 3: PL XLII, 772: "non contendendo diffideres, sed intellegendo conspiceres."

41 *Contra Maximinum* II, xiv, 8: PL XL, 776: "Ut enim humanum aliquid dicam propter infirmitatem carnalium. ..."

42 *Contra Maximinum* II, xiv, 8: PL XLII, 776: "numquid hinc ostenditur non ejusdem cujus pater est esse substantiae?"

43 *Contra Maximinum* II, xviii, 3: PL XLII, 786: "Quodlibet de veneratione et obsequio Filii erga Patrem carnaliter sentias. ..."

the saints.⁴⁴ Finally, Augustine accuses the Arians of not hearing with faith Dt 6:4: "Hear, O Israel, the Lord is your God, the Lord is one," and, thus, of being Israel carnally, like the Jews, and not spiritually, like Christians.⁴⁵

Hence, there is ample evidence that Augustine accused the Arians not merely of thinking of the Father and the Son in terms of images, but also of falling into their error because of such image-thinking. However, he also points out that, if they accepted as true not merely that the Son cannot do anything by himself that he does not see the Father doing, but also that the Father does everything through his Son, the Word, they would be forced to transcend their image-thinking and would come to understand what one must first accept as true in faith. There remains the more difficult question of whether the Arians did indeed allow such image-thinking to control their theology.

II. MAXIMINUS AS AN IMAGE-THINKER

In the first part of this paper, I have shown that Augustine accused the Arians in general and Maximinus in particular of being "carnal" in their thinking about God. Augustine did not, of course, think that one became a heretic simply because one thought of God as bodily or by imagining him. The little ones in the Church also think of God in terms of bodily images, but they humbly believe what they do not understand. The Arians, Augustine claims, were too proud merely to remain at the level of faith and thought that they understood when they did not understand.⁴⁶

---

44 *Contra Maximinum* II, xxi, 3: PL XLII, 792: "Cum ipsa sessio non sit utique cogitanda carnaliter: alioquin opinaturi sumus honorabilius Filium sedere quam Patrem; honorabilius quippe sedetur ad dexteram: et videbitur esse consequens ut Pater sedeat ad sinistrum. Postremo qualis vobis persuaserit spiritus, ut sancto Spiritui denegetis quod sanctis hominibus sancta Scriptura concedit, vos videritis."

45 *Contra Maximinum* II, xxiii, 1: PL XLII, 796: "Quod et vos utique audiretis, si Israel esse velletis, non carnaliter ut Judaei, sed spiritualiter ut Christiani."

46 See *Enarratio in Psalmum* CXXX 9: CCL XL, 1905: "uolunt se extendere ad id quod capere non possunt; et si aliquid utcumque ceperint, aut uisi sibi fuerunt capere quod non ceperunt, extolluntur inde. et superbiunt inde; uidentur sibi quasi sapientes."

It is more difficult to show that Maximinus did in fact think of God in a carnal fashion as Augustine claims. Yet, there are, I believe, indications in the *Collatio cum Maximino* that Augustine's accusation was well grounded. There is, first of all, some indirect evidence that Maximinus thought of God as bodily and as able to be pictured in the imagination. The Homoian Arianism that Maximinus espoused shunned any philosophical learning and insisted upon a fidelity to the Scriptures and to the Scriptures alone.[47] When Maximinus stated for Augustine what he believed, he immediately added, "I state this on the basis of the Scriptures."[48] He not merely accepted the authority of the Scriptures, but refused to accept "those words which are not found in the Scriptures."[49] Maximinus surely intended to exclude the non-biblical language of the Council of Nicaea, but his claim clearly goes beyond that. In fact, he claims that to use words not contained in the Scriptures is to fall into the wordiness condemned by the Scriptures.[50] He insists that the use of testimonies from the Scriptures is the only admissible form of proof. "The truth is not attained by argumentation, but is proved by certain testimonies."[51]

Though Maximinus appeals to the Council of Ariminum, the authority of that Council stems from the fact that the fathers gathered there declared "in accord with the divine Scriptures the faith that they learned from the divine Scriptures."[52] So too, Maximinus points out

---

47 See R. P. C. Hanson, *The Search for the Christian Doctrine of God. The Arian Controversy 318-311* (Edinburgh: T. & T. Clark, 1988), 557–558.

48 *Collatio cum Maximino* 4: PL XLII, 711: "Et hoc de divinis Scripturis assero."

49 *Collatio cum Maximino* 1: PL XLII, 709: "eae vero voces quae extra Scripturam sunt, nullo casu a nobis suscipiuntur. ..."

50 See Prv 10:19 and Mt 12:36, as well as *Collatio cum Maximino* 13: PL XLII, 718: "Quamvis etiam etsi per totum diem quisque de divinis Scripturis proferat testimonia, non in verbositate illi imputabitur revera: quod si aut litteraria arte usus, aut expressione spiritus sui quisquis concinnet verba quae non continent sanctae Scripturae; et otiosa sunt et superflua."

51 *Collatio cum Maximino* 15, 21: PL XLII, 736: "Veritas non ex argumento colligitur, sed certis testimoniis comprobatur."

52 *Collatio cum Maximino* 4: PL XLII, 711: "Non ad excusandum me Ariminensis concilii decretum interesse volui, sed ut ostendam auctoritatem Patrum, qui secundum divinas Scripturas fidem nobis tradiderunt illam quam a divinis Scripturis didicerunt."

that Augustine's charges arise from the art of philosophy and warns Augustine against the dangers of using the rhetorical figure of metonomy as a means of exegesis.[53] Thus, in opposition to the Nicaean interpretation of texts concerning Christ's obedience to the Father, Maximinus insists that "the divine Scripture has not come as a source of our instruction so that we might correct it."[54] Hence, Maximinus not merely rests his theological position on the Scriptures, but also refuses to make any use of any non-biblical language or philosophical thought to interpret the Scriptures.[55]

The concept of a non-bodily or spiritual reality, however, is a philosophical concept. The ability to understand that God is incorporeal involves more than being able to speak of God as invisible or simple or spiritual—all terms that Maximinus admits.[56] To understand that God is incorporeal is to grasp that he is whole everywhere, that there is not more of him in a larger place and less of him in a smaller place, but that wherever he is—and he is everywhere—he is whole and undivided.[57] The *Confessiones* reveal to us the long struggle that Augustine underwent in coming to a concept of a spiritual substance—a concept that he came to from reading the *libri Platonicorum* within the Christian Neoplatonist circle of the church of Milan. What is all too often forgotten is that the concept of a spiritual or incorporeal substance is

---

53 See *Collatio cum Maximino* 15, 5 and 13: PL XLII, 725 and 718.

54 *Collatio cum Maximino* 15, 20: PL XLII, 736: "Nec enim in nostrum magisterium devenit divina Scriptura, ut a nobis emendationem accipiat."

55 It is, of course, very difficult to remain with the language contained in the Scriptures and to avoid all non-biblical language. Indeed, Maximinus does not succeed in doing so. See *Contra Maximinum* II, ix, 2: PL XLII, 763, where Augustine points out that Paul did not say that the Father was incomprehensible (*incapabilis*). Similarly, Augustine reminds Maximinus that the terms "*ingenitus*," "*innatus*" and "*incomparabilis*" are not biblical; see below note 66.

56 Though Maximinus holds that the Father is alone invisible, he admits that the Son is also invisible; see *Collatio cum Maximino* 9: PL XLII, 727–728. He speaks of both the Father and the Son as spirits; see *Collatio cum Maximino* 15, 15: PL XLII, 733. In *Collatio cum Maximino* 10: PL XLII, 728–729, he says that the Father is simple power; see below note 63.

57 See *Confessions* VII ,I, 2: CCL XXVII, 92–93 and *Epistula* CLXVI II, 4: CSEL XLIV, 550–553, for Augustine's realization of the non-corporeal nature of God and his description of the soul's incorporeality.

not found in the Scriptures or in any of the Western Fathers prior to Augustine in a fully articulated form.[58] For, apart from the Neoplatonist circle in the church of Milan, the corporealism of Stoic philosophy remained the common philosophical patrimony of the West.[59] Indeed, even after the time of Augustine, there were learned bishops, such as Faustus of Riez, who, like Tertullian in an earlier century, insisted that the soul was bodily.[60] Hence, given Maximinus's rejection of all philosophy and his insistence upon the *sola Scriptura* principle, it is not surprising that he lacked a concept of incorporeal reality and could only think of God as bodily and in terms of what can be imagined.

All the passages in which Augustine accuses Maximinus of thinking of God in a carnal manner, of course, count as evidence that Maximinus conceived of God in bodily terms. But there is at least one other passage that, I believe, confirms the evidence presented so far. In Maximinus's long final discourse, he insists "that the Father alone is the one God, not one along with a second and a third, but that he alone is the one God."[61] Maximinus goes on to argue the point. "If he alone is not the one [God], he is a part."[62] That is, Maximinus sees no way that the Son can also be the one God without the Father being

---

58 See G. Verbeke, *L'évolution de la doctrine du pneuma du Stoïcisme à s. Augustin* (Paris and Louvain, 1945) and F. Masai, "Les conversions de saint Augustin et les débuts de spiritualisme en Occident," *Moyen Âge* 67 (1961), 1-40.

59 For the distinction between corporealism and materialism, see E. Weil, "Remarques sur le 'matérialisme' des Stoïciens," in *Mélanges Alexandre Koyré. II. L'aventure de l'esprit* (Paris: Herman, 1964), pp. 556–572.

60 For Tertullian"s position, see *De carne Christi* XI, 4: CCL II, 895: "Omne, quod est, corpus est sui generis. Nihil est incorporeale nisi quod non est" and *De anima* VII, 3: CCL II, 790: "Nihil enim, nisi corpus." Though Tertullian admitted that God was a spirit, he nonetheless held that he was a body; see *Aduersus Praxean* VII, 8: CCL II, 1166: "Quis negabit Deum corpus esse, etsi Deus spiritus est." For the continued debate about the nature of the soul in 5th century Gaul, see Thomas Smith, "Augustine in Two Gallic Controversies: Use or Abuse?" in *Collectanea Augustiniana* III (New York: Peter Lang, 1993), pp. 43–55.

61 *Collatio cum Maximino* 15,10: PL XLII, 728: "Ego Patrem solum secundum antelata testimonia, non cum altero et tertio dico quod unus est, sed quod solus unus est Deus."

62 *Collatio cum Maximino* 15,10: PL XLII, 728: "Si vero solus unus non est, pars est."

merely a part of the one God, for, if the Son is also the one God, then the Father cannot be the whole of the one God. Moreover, Maximinus gives a reason why the Father cannot be a part: "I deny... that the one God is composed of parts; rather, what he is is unbegotten simple power."[63] Maximinus's argument, namely, that either the Father alone is the one God or the Father is a part of the one God, presupposes that a plurality in God can only be a plurality of parts—and of the sort of parts that compose a whole greater than any of the parts. And that, of course, is precisely what it is to be a body. What Maximinus lacks is the grasp of the spiritual or non-bodily reality of God that Augustine has and that allows him to say that the Father, the Son, and the Holy Spirit are one God.

> One is not a third of this Trinity, nor are two of them a greater part than one, and all of them are not something greater than each of them, because their greatness is spiritual, not corporeal."[64]

III. CONCLUDING REFLECTIONS

I have shown that Augustine accuses the Homoian Arians and Maximinus of thinking of God in a carnal fashion, that is, of thinking of God in bodily terms or in terms of what can be imagined. Indeed, he claims that their heresy arises from interpreting Jn 5:19 in terms of imagining the Father and the Son like a master craftsman and his apprentice. There is ample evidence that Augustine made this claim against the Arians. I have also tried to argue that, given Maximinus's insistence upon a biblical theology and upon the avoidance of all non-biblical language, he could hardly be expected to have the sort of concept of incorporeal reality that Augustine acquired only after years of struggle and then only from the works of the Neoplatonists. There is also some direct evidence from Maximinus's long final discourse that indicates that he could not think of God except as bodily, though the evidence for the absence of a concept can at best be tenuous.

---

63 *Collatio cum Maximino* 10: PL XLII, 728–729: "Nec enim ex partibus compositum unum dico Deum: sed ille quod est, virtus est ingenita simplex."

64 *Contra Maximinum* II, x, 2: PL XLII, 765: "nec hujus Trinitatis tertia pars est unus, nec major pars duo quam unus est ibi; nec majus aliquid sunt omnes quam singuli, quia spiritualis, non corporalis est magnitudo."

Contemporary theologians at times bemoan the Hellenization or the Platonization of the Christian doctrine of God and the loss of the biblical doctrine of the Father, Son, and Holy Spirit.[65] Maximinus's attempt to rely on the Scripture alone and to avoid all philosophical terms might be thought to aim at such a purely biblical formulation of the faith. However, as Augustine points out, Maximinus does introduce non-biblical terminology at times.[66] Furthermore, in supposing that he has avoided all philosophy in his theology, Maximinus has simply and unreflectively adopted the philosophy that was the common patrimony of his age, namely, Stoic corporealism, which was just as much a Hellenization of the biblical faith as the spiritualist metaphysics that Augustine learned from the Neoplatonists. Hence, in confronting Arianism, Augustine certainly thought out the Christian doctrine of God with the aid of a spiritualist metaphysics he learned

---

[65] See Hans Küng, *On Being a Christian*, trans. by E. Quinn (Garden City, NY: Doubleday, 1976), pp. 472–477. Küng refers to the trinitarian thought of the Cappadocian fathers as "almost ... a kind of higher trinitarian mathematics" that "scarcely reached any lasting solutions" and compares "this Greek speculation, remote from its biblical roots," to the flight of Icarus (p. 473). Augustine, of course, took over and worked out the trinitarian thought of the Cappadocians. But "[t]he real difficulties of the specifically Western doctrine of the Trinity arise from the fact that Augustine, its founder, . . . *started out, not like the Greeks, from the triplicity of persons, but from the unity of the divine nature*. In this respect Augustine had against him not only the Greeks and—for instance—Hilary of Poitiers in the West, but also the New Testament" (p. 475). See also M. Schmaus, "Die Spannung von Metaphysik und Heilsgeschichte in der Trinitätslehre Augustins," *Studia Patristica* VI. Texte und Untersuchungen 81 (Berlin: Akademie Verlag, 1962), pp. 503–518, especially 508–510. For further discussion of this question, see the introduction to Augustine's anti-Arian works in *Obras completas de San Augustín* XXXVIII (Madrid: Biblioteca de Autores Cristianos, 1990), pp. 240–251.

[66] Augustine points out that both Arians and Catholics use the non-biblical terms "*ingenitus*" and "*innatus*" of the Father and that the Arians make the non-biblical claim that the Father is incomparable to the Son. "Tu ubi legisti Patrem Deum ingenitum vel innatum. Et tamen verum est. Quod vero aliquoties dixisti, etiam Filio esse imcomparabilem Patrem, nec legis, nec verum est" (*Contra Maximinum Arianum* II, iii: PL XLII, 760). To Maximinus's claim that the Scriptures do not say that the Holy Spirit is adored, Augustine replies, "quasi non ex iis quae legimus, aliqua etiam quae non legimus, intelligamus" (ibid.).

from the Platonists. The alternatives he faced were not a Hellenized versus a non-Hellenized understanding of God, but a Stoic corporealist versus a Neoplatonic spiritualist understanding of God.

Moreover, it is arguable that Maximinus had operative in the articulation of his Trinitarian faith an unreflective philosophical principle, ultimately derived from Platonism, that subordinates whatever is derived from another to that other from which it is derived.[67] Such a philosophical principle held unreflectively, while he supposes himself innocent of all philosophy, leads Maximinus to the conclusion that the Son, though a great God, is inferior to the Father.[68] In this case, a philosophical principle, though held unwittingly, is the norm by which the content of the biblical revelation is judged. For Augustine, on the other hand, philosophy was not the norm or standard by which the word of God was judged, but a means by which it was understood. However important philosophical reflection was for coming to an understanding of the faith, for Augustine believing came first and faith remained the norm. Indeed, Augustine is quite insistent that one who desires to understand desires to understand precisely what he believes, not something else.[69]

---

67 Maximinus, for example, says, "Saepius aequalem Filium asseris Patri: cum ipse unigenitus Deus semper et in omnibus auctorem suum praedicet Patrem, a quo, ut paulo ante dixi, et vitam se consecutum hoc modo professus est" (*Collatio cum Maximino* 14: PL XLII, 731).

68 Thus, from the statement that Christ "a genitore suo omnia haec consecutus est, et vivit propter Patrem," Maximinius draws the conclusion that "Filius Patri subjectus est, ut charissimus, ut obediens, ut bonus a bono genitus" (*Collatio cum Maximino* 10: PL XLII, 714).

69 See *Epistula* CXX I, 2: CSEL XLIV, 706, where Augustine explains to Consentius that one who desires to understand his faith desires to understand that which he believes or to see with the light of reason that which he holds with the firmness of faith: "ut quod credis intellegas ... ut ea quae fidei firmitate iam tenes, etiam rationis luce conspicias."

THE DEFINITION OF SACRIFICE IN THE DE CIUITATE DEI

In his *Contra aduersarium legis et prophetarum*, written in 419 or 420 in reply to the work of an unidentified heretic, most probably someone in the Marcionite tradition, Augustine of Hippo was forced to deal with the topic of sacrifice because the anonymous heretic strongly objected to the animal sacrifices of the Jewish religion and cited Saint Paul as maintaining that all who offer sacrifice offer sacrifice to demons.[1] In a communication for the Oxford Patristics Conference in 1995, I summed up what Augustine said about sacrifice in that seldom read work and pointed out that Augustine presented in it a short, but brilliant treatise on sacrifice in which he showed the relationship between the sacrifices of the Old Law, the sacrifice of Christ on Calvary, and the sacrifice of the Church.[2] I was particularly struck by his apparently universal claim that visible sacrifices—whether of the Old Law or of Christ or of the Church—are signs of divine realities and in fact all signify the same great divine reality: "the grace of God through Jesus Christ our Lord."[3] Augustine says, for example, that David's sacrifice in 1 Kgs 2:4 by which he asked that God would spare the people was a sign that "God shows mercy regarding the salvation of the people through the one sacrifice of which David's was the symbol."[4] Hence, when I was invited to contribute a paper to a

---

1 The heretic's text of 2 Cor 10:20 read: 'Sed qui sacrificant, daemonibus sacrificant' instead of the text that Augustine had: 'Sed quia quae immolant daemonibus, et non Deo immolant." See *Contra aduersarium legis et prophetarum* I, xix, 38: CCL 49, 68.

2 See my translation of the work in *Augustine: Arianism and Other Heresies* (Hyde Park, N.Y.: New City Press, 1995).

3 See my "Sacrifice in Augustine's *Contra aduersarium legis et prophetarum*," in *Studia Patristica* XXXIII, ed. E. A. Livingstone (Leuven: Peeters, 1997), pp. 255–259.

4 *Contra aduersarium legis et prophetarum* I, xviii, 37: CCL 49, 67: "Unde illud quod Dauid obtulit, ut populo parceretur, umbra erat futuri, qua significatum est, quod per unum sacrificium, cuius illa figura erat, saluti populi spiritaliter parcitur."

volume in honor of Frederic W. Slatterer, SJ, I thought that it would be appropriate as an offering of one Jesuit priest to another to return to the topic of sacrifice in Saint Augustine and examine some of the aspects of its treatment in book ten of *De ciuitate Dei*, a passage which Gerald Bonner has described as "a wonderful *tour de force* ... one of the most profound discussions of the nature of sacrifice in Christian literature."[5] In particular, I want to look at the definition of sacrifice that Augustine, it seems, presents in book ten, a definition that has been the subject of considerable controversy. In fact, one distinguished theologian has forcefully argued that Augustine did not offer—and did not intend to offer—a definition of sacrifice in the passage,[6] though almost all other scholars who have written on chapters five and six of book ten have, nonetheless, taken Augustine as having presented there a definition of sacrifice.[7] Moreover, the definition that he apparently offers, along with his further claim that every act of mercy done for the sake of God is a sacrifice, seems to present a view of true sacrifice as something without any obvious relation to the two actions which the Church has consistently spoken of as sacrifices, namely, the death of

---

5 Gerald Bonner, "The Doctrine of Sacrifice: Augustine and the Latin Patristic Tradition," in *Sacrifice and Redemption. Durham Essays in Theology*, ed. S. W. Sykes (Cambridge: Cambridge University Press, 1991), 101–117, here 105.

6 Guy de Broglie, "La notion augustinienne du sacrifice 'invisible' et 'vrai,'" *Recherches de science religieuse* 48 (1960): 135–165.

7 Studies on sacrifice in the *De ciuitate Dei* are many. Besides Bonner's and de Broglie's, among the best I have found there are: Joseph Lécuyer, "Le sacrifice selon saint Augustin," in *Augustinus Magister* (Paris: Études augustiniennes, 1946) II, 905–914; Yves de Montcheuil, "L'unité du sacrifice et du sacrement dans l'Eucharistie," in *Mélanges théologiques* (Paris: Aubier, 1946), 49–70; Bernard Quinot, "L'influence de l'Épitre aux Hébreux dans la notion augustinienne du vrai sacrifice," *Revue des études augustiniennes* 8 (1962): 129–168; Ghislain Lafont, "Le sacrifice de la Cité de Dieu. Commentaire au *De Civitate Dei* Livre X, ch. I–VII," *Recherches de science religieuse* 53 (1965): 177–219; John F. O'Grady, "Priesthood and Sacrifice in 'City of God,'" *Augustiniana* 21 (1971): 27–44; Basil Studer, "Das Opfer Christi nach Augustins 'De civitate Dei' X, 5–6," in *Lex Orandi, Lex Credendi. Miscellanea in onore di P. Cipriano Vagaggini*, ed. G. Békés and G. Franedi (Rome: Editrice Anselmiana, 1980), 93–107; and Marcel Neusch, "Une conception chrétienne du sacrifice: Le modèle de saint Augustin," in *Le sacrifice dans les religions. Sciences théologiques et religieuses* 3, ed. by Marcel Neusch (Paris: Beauchesne, 1994), 117–138.

Christ on Calvary and the Mass.[8] Augustine's definition of true sacrifice in fact sounds as though it fits any act of mercy that anyone might do for one's fellow human beings for the sake of God.[9] Hence, I have chosen to examine the definition of sacrifice found in these chapters as the subject of this paper.

I. A FIRST LOOK AT THE DEFINITION OF SACRIFICE

In chapter five, while discussing the sacrifices of the Jewish people recorded in scripture, Augustine points out that we are to understand that the animal sacrifices offered by the patriarchs of old signified "the things which are done among us in order that we might cling to God and assist our neighbor toward the same end. The visible sacrifice, then, is the sacrament, that is, the sacred sign of the invisible sacrifice."[10] In

---

8 Such is the heart, I take it, of de Broglie's objection to taking what Augustine says here as a definition of sacrifice. He says, "Il suffit, comme on voit, d'interpréter le dogme catholique en partant de la définition dite 'augustinienne', pour voir s'envoler presque tous les problèmes, parfois délicats, que la théologie catholique du 'sacrifice' peut conduire à poser; et peut-être cette considération n'est-elle étrangère au succès que cette définition a quelquefois rencontré—Mais il reste permis de se demander si une si merveilleuse simplication de la théologie ne menaçerait pas le contenu du dogme lui-même. Car, si toute action inspirée par l'amour de Dieu et qui fait avancer l'humanité dans la voie du salut, méritait *proprement, pleinement, et indistinctement,* le nom de 'sacrifice', on comprend mal que l'Église puisse attacher quelque importance à nous entendre qualifier de ce vocable *deux* actions particulières, *et deux seulement*: celle qui s'accomplit jadis sur la Croix et celle qui se renouvelle quotidiennnement sur nos autels" (de Broglie, "La notion augustinienne," p. 140).

9 Such a view was articulated by John F. O'Grady in "Priesthood and Sacrifice in 'City of God,'" when he spoke of "[t]he notion of Augustine on sacrifice as any work which unites us with God, or any work directed to our final end" (p. 43). He says, "The Christian accepts the same demands of the Jew and of any other religious person. God wishes the offering of self, the interior sacrifice animated by charity, essentially involved in works of mercy in favor of others. ... True sacrifice unites man to God in a holy society; the invisible sacrifice forms the heart of sacrifice and signifies the offering of man himself. Further it was seen that these notions are not limited to Christianity nor even to Judaism, but Augustine sees them involved in man's nature as a person called to union with his God" (pp. 40–41).

10 *De ciuitate Dei* X, 5: CCL 47, 276–277: "Nec quod ab antiquis patribus alia sacrificia facta sunt in uictimis pecorum, ... aliud intellegendum est,

support of this claim he cites Psalm 50 to show that God is not pleased with holocausts, but that "sacrifice to God is a contrite spirit," for God will not reject "a heart that is contrite and humbled."[11] He points out that God speaking through the Psalmist does not reject sacrifice, but substitutes one sort of sacrifice by another. "He does not, then, want the sacrifice of a slaughtered animal, and he does want the sacrifice of a contrite heart."[12] Similarly, Augustine uses Psalm 50 to show that God did not demand animal sacrifices for their own sake, but to show that they were signs of the sacrifices that God does require.[13] He quotes the Prophet Micah to show what God does require of us, namely, "to practice justice and to love mercy and to be ready to walk with the Lord your God."[14] So too, he cites Hebrews 13:16, "Forget not to do good and to be generous, for God is pleased by such sacrifices."[15] Hence, he interprets the statement in Hosea 6:6, "I desire mercy rather than sacrifice," not to mean that God rejected sacrifice, but to mean that he preferred one sort of sacrifice to another.[16] "For what everyone calls a sacrifice," Augustine explains, "is a sign of the true sacrifice. Mercy is, in fact, the true sacrifice."[17] He adds that "all the sacrifices which we read that God commanded to be offered in many ways in the ministry of the tabernacle or the temple are directed to the love of God and of

---

nisi rebus illis eas res fuisse significatas, quae aguntur in nobis, ad hoc ut inhaereamus deo et ad eundem finem proximo consulamus. Sacrificium ergo uisibile inuisibilis sacrificii sacramentum, id est sacrum signum est."

11 Ibid: CCL 47, 277: "*Sacrificium Deo spiritus contritus; cor contritum et humiliatum Deus not spernet*" (Ps 50:19).

12 Ibid.: "Non uult ergo sacrificium trucidati pecoris, et uult sacrificium contriti cordis."

13 Ibid.: CCL 47, 277–8: "Et in huius prophetae uerbis utrumque distinctum est satisque declaratum illa sacrificia per se ipsa non requirere Deum, quibus significantur haec sacrificia, quae requirit Deus."

14 Micah 6:8 in *De ciuitate Dei* X, 5: CCL 47, 277: "*Aut quid Dominus exquirat a te nisi facere iudicium et diligere misericordiam et paratum esse ire cum Domino Deo tuo.*"

15 *De ciuitate Dei* X, 5: CCL 47, 278: "*Bene facere ... et communicatores esse noliter obliuisci; talibus enim sacrificiis placetur Deo.*"

16 Ibid.: "Ac per hoc ubi scriptum est: *Misericordiam uolo quam sacrificium* nihil aliud quam sacrificium sacrificio praelatum oportet intellegi."

17 Ibid.: "illud, quod ab omnibus appellatur sacrificium, signum est ueri sacrificii. Porro autem misericordia uerum sacrificium est. ..."

the neighbor."[18] Hence, at the beginning of chapter six, he says, "Thus true sacrifice is every work by which it is brought about that we cling to God in a holy society, every work, that is, which is directed to that final good by which we can be truly happy."[19] Augustine adds, "Hence, even an act of mercy itself by which a human being is helped is not a sacrifice if it is not done for the sake of God."[20] Augustine explains, "For even if a human being performs or offers it, sacrifice is, nonetheless, a divine reality (*res diuina*), so that the ancient Latin people even referred to it by that name."[21] Still later in this chapter Augustine repeats that "true sacrifices are works of mercy either toward ourselves or toward our neighbors that are referred to God."[22]

Augustine's discussion of sacrifice raises several questions: One, did he mean to offer a new definition of "true sacrifice" as an interior act of mercy or love such that visible acts of sacrifice are not genuinely sacrifices? Two, does his definition of sacrifice apply to every work of mercy done on account of God, even if the one who performs the act of mercy is not a Christian? And three, how are many true sacrifices related to the one and only true sacrifice of Christ? For elsewhere Augustine is quite clear that the sacrifice of Christ is the one true sacrifice. For example, in *De trinitate* IV, xiii, 17, he speaks of Christ's death as "the

---

18 Ibid.: "Quaecumque igitur in ministerio tabernaculi siue templi multis modis de sacrificiis leguntur diuinitus esse praecepta, ad dilectionem Dei et proximi significando referuntur."

19 Ibid. X, 6: CCL 47, 278: "Proinde uerum sacrificium est omne opus, quo agitur, ut sancta societate inhaereamus Deo, relatum scilicet ad illum finem boni, quo ueraciter beati esse possimus."

20 Ibid.: "Unde et ipsa misericordia, qua homini subuenitur, si non propter Deum fit, non est sacrificium."

21 Ibid.: "Etsi enim ab homine fit uel offertur, tamen sacrificium res diuina est, ita ut hoc quoque uocabulo id Latini ueteres appellauerint."

22 Ibid.: CCL 47, 279: "Cum igitur uera sacrificia opera sint misericordiae siue in nos ipsos siue in proximos, quae referuntur ad Deum. ..."

one most true sacrifice"²³ and in *De spiritu et littera* XI, 18, he clearly refers to the Eucharist as "the singular and most true sacrifice."²⁴

II. A NEW DEFINITION OF SACRIFICE?

In his study of the meaning of "true sacrifice" in this book of *De ciuitate Dei*, Guy de Broglie has strongly argued that Augustine did not intend to offer a new and better definition of sacrifice, since such a move would imply that the visible sacrifice—"what everyone calls a sacrifice"—is not a true sacrifice. As de Broglie sees it, such a move would, after all, imply that the visible death of Christ on Calvary and the visible offering of the Mass are not "true sacrifices."²⁵ De Broglie distinguishes three senses in which Augustine uses the term "true" of various things. First, in its basic or elementary meaning the term "true" means that a thing embodies the given idea in the proper sense as opposed to something which embodies it only in an improper or merely apparent sense. With this meaning Augustine spoke, for example, of a "true Catholic" as opposed to a "false Catholic."²⁶ Second, in its pregnant meaning the term "true" presents as "true" something that not merely realizes the idea in its proper sense, but also possesses such a degree of perfection

---

23 *De trinitate* IV, xiii, 17: CCL 50, 164: "Morte sua quippe uno uerissimo sacrificio pro nobis oblato quidquid culparum erat unde nos principatus et potestates ad luenda supplicia iure detinebant purgauit, aboleuit, exstinxit, et sua resurrectione in nouam uitam nos praedestinatos uocauit, uocatos iustificauit, iustificatos glorificauit."

24 *De spiritu et littera* XI, 18, CSEL 60, 170: "Unde et in ipso uerissimo et singulari sacrificio, Domino Deo nostro, agere gratias admonemur."

25 De Broglie's article, "La notion augustinienne," was written in opposition to the claims of Yves de Montcheuil in *Mélanges théologiques* (Paris: Aubier, 1946), 49–70, in which de Montcheuil presented, as de Broglie saw it, "le don spirituel que l'homme fait de soi à Dieu par la charité comme le seul 'sacrifice', *au sens plein et complet du terme*" (de Broglie, "La notion augustinienne," p. 138, note 10). De Broglie saw it as dangerous to suppose "qu'en parlant de 'vrai' sacrifice le grand Docteur entendait nous fournir du 'sacrifice' en tant que tel *une définition plus propre, plus profonde et plus satisfaisante* que toutes celles auxquelles le vulgaire était préparé à souscrire" (p. 141). For such an interpretation of Augustine would imply that the sacrifice of Calvary and the sacrifice of the Mass were something less than *true* sacrifices.

26 De Broglie, "La notion augustinienne," p. 144; Augustine, *De natura et origine animae* III, 2: BA 22, 522.

that the thing is thought to embody the proper sense of the term in a richer or doubled sense. With this meaning the Gospel speaks of Nathaniel as a "true Israelite," and in this sense Augustine says that the only true life is the happy life.[27] Third, in its typological meaning the term "true" transfers to the reality symbolized the name of the symbol. In this sense Christ is not merely called the Lamb of God, but is said to be the true Lamb of God, or the true light, the true manna, and the true vine.[28] Here de Broglie comments, "But nothing is also more in harmony with the Platonic tendencies of the great African Doctor, for whom the interest of the sensible world is reduced—or almost—to that of the spiritual realities that it symbolizes."[29] In this sense, Augustine not only speaks of Christ as the "true light" or of the Church as the "true temple," but claims that "true health" is not what the doctors tell us about and that "true freedom" is what sets us free from slavery to sin.[30] De Broglie claims that the originality of the typological sense of "true" lies in the fact that it in no sense calls into question the appropriateness of the ordinary meaning of the term, though many things that fit that ordinary meaning are said to be less true than some other reality quite different from them and of which they are merely the signs or symbols.[31]

When Augustine says that a true sacrifice is what is signified by the visible sacrifice, he is, then, not denying that the visible sacrifice is a sacrifice in the proper sense, but stressing that it is the interior act that in the pregnant sense realizes the proper meaning in a fuller or richer way and that in the typological sense the term "sacrifice," which properly applies to the visible sign, is transferred to the reality symbolized. Though Augustine does not, as de Broglie has shown, deny that the visible sacrifice—"what everyone calls sacrifice"—is properly a sacrifice, he clearly does place the emphasis upon the interior act of the one

---

27 See Jn 1:47 and Augustine, *Enchiridion de fide, spe, et caritate* XXIII, 92: CCL 46, 98.

28 See John 1:9, 6:32, 15:1. So too, Heb 8:2 speaks of the true tabernacle.

29 De Broglie, "La notion augustininne," p. 147: "Mais rien aussi n'était plus conforme aux tendances platoniciennes du grand Docteur africain, pour qui l'intérêt du monde sensible se réduit, ou peu s'en faut, à celui des réalités spirituelles qu'il figure."

30 Ibid. See Augustine, *De ciuitate Dei* XI, 9: CCL 48, 330; *Enarrationes in Psalmum* 130, 2: CCL 40, 1899; *Sermo* 385, 6–7: PL 39, 1693–1694.

31 De Broglie, "La notion augustininne," p. 148.

who offers sacrifice rather than upon the external and visible sign. An examination of the larger context of the discussion of sacrifice can, I believe, provide a plausible explanation of this fact.

III. THE CONTEXT OF THE DISCUSSION OF SACRIFICE

Augustine's discussion of sacrifice in *De ciuitate Dei* is found in book ten, the final book of the first part of the work which he himself described as *"magnum opus et arduum."*[32] The context of the definition of sacrifice in this work, which is every bit as large and difficult for the contemporary reader as it was for its author, offers, I believe, a key to understanding what Augustine was about. Its author left explicit instructions in a letter to Firmus, who served as a sort of literary agent for him in Carthage, about how the twenty-two books of the work were to be divided for future publication, if they could not be published as a whole.[33] The bishop explained that the work falls into two parts: the first ten books, which refute the vanities of the unbelievers and the last twelve, which defend the Christian religion.[34] The first five books of the first part argue "against those who maintain that the worship not of the gods, but of demons contributes to the happiness of this life," while the next five argue against "those who think that either such gods or many gods of any sort ought to be worshiped by ceremonies and sacrifices on account of the life that is to come after death."[35] Central to the first ten books, then, is the question of the

---

32 *De ciuitate Dei* I, Praefatio: CCL 47, 1.

33 The Letter to Firmus was published for the first time by Dom C. Lambot in "Lettre inédité de saint Augustin relative au 'De Civitate Dei,'" *Revue Bénédictine* 51 (1939): 109–121; it now numbered as *Epistula* 1A in CSEL 88. *Epistula* 2A, one of the letters discovered and first published by Johannes Divjak in 1981 in CSEL 88 and newly edited in BA 46ᴮ as *Epistula* 2*, reveals that the Firmus in question is not, as had been supposed, a Carthaginian priest and disciple of Augustine, but a pagan who was hesitating about receiving baptism.

34 *Epistula* 1A, 1: CSEL 88, 7: "decem quippe illis uanitates refutatae sunt impiorum, reliquis autem demonstrata atque defensa est nostra religio. ..."

35 Ibid.: "Si autem corpora malueris esse plura quam duo, iam quinque oportet codices facias, quorum primus contineat quinque libros priores quibus aduersus eos est disputatum qui felicitati uitae huius non plane deorum sed daemoniorum cultum prodesse contendunt, secundus sequentes

proper object of worship. The final twelve books, on the other hand, describe, in three clusters of four books each, the origin of the two cities, their development, and their ends.[36]

The discussion of sacrifice is found in the final, climatic book of the first part. In it Augustine continues to confront the Platonists who had in so many ways hit upon the truth about God and about human existence, though they ultimately rejected the incarnation of the Word. In praise of the Platonists, Augustine says, for example,

> We have chosen the Platonists who are rightly the most noble of all the philosophers, precisely because they were able to know that the human soul, though immortal and rational or intellectual, could be happy only by participation in the light of that God who created it and the world, and they claim that none will attain that which all human beings desire, that is, the happy life, unless by the purity of chaste love they cling to that one perfect Good, which is the immutable God.[37]

Augustine's praise for the achievements of the Platonists whose philosophy had earlier made possible the intellectual dimension of his conversion to Catholic Christianity could hardly be more fulsome.[38]

---

alios quinque <aduersus eos> qui uel tales uel qualescumque plurimos deos propter uitam quae post mortem futura est per sacra et sacrificia colendos putant."

36 Ibid.: "Iam tres alii codices qui sequuntur quaternos libros habere debebunt; sic enim a nobis pars eadem distributa est, ut quattuor ostenderent exortum illius ciuitatis totidemque procursum, siue dicere malumus, excursum, quattuor uero ultimi debitos fines."

37 De ciuitate Dei X, 1: CCL 47, 271–272: "Elegimus enim Platonicos omnium philosophorum merito nobilissimos, propterea quia sapere potuerunt licet inmortalem ac rationalem uel intellectualem hominis animam nisi participato lumine illius Dei, a quo et ipsa et mundus factus est, beatam esse non posse; ita illud, quod omnes homines appetunt, id est uitam beatam, quemquam isti assecuturum negant, qui non illi uni optimo, quod est incommutabilis Deus, puritate casti amoris adhaeserit."

38 For a recent and excellent discussion of the role of the Neoplatonists in Augustine's conversion and intellectual formation, see Robert J. O'Connell, *Images of Conversion in St. Augustine's Confessions* (New York: Fordham University Press, 1996), especially pp. 93–203 in which O'Connell describes Augustine's gradual absorption of the philosophical insights of the Platonists.

In book eight he explained that he prefers the Platonists to all other philosophers because

> they agree with us about the one God who is the author of this universe, who is not only above all bodies insofar as he is incorporeal, but is also above all souls insofar as he is incorruptible, who is our principle, our light, our good.[39]

Later in book ten Augustine even credits Porphyry with having come to a knowledge of "God the Father and God the Son, whom he called in Greek the paternal Intellect or paternal Mind,"[40] and with having admitted the need for grace for those few who come to God by the power of their intelligence.[41] In fact, according to Augustine, Porphyry acknowledged that a universal way for the liberation of the soul existed, though he had not found it—the way that Augustine maintained is found in the Christian religion and that is ultimately the Way, Christ himself.[42] On the other hand, Augustine clearly reproaches Porphyry for refusing to accept the incarnation of the Son of God, the one mediator between God and human beings, the one Way by whom alone we are to be saved.[43]

In the beginning of book ten, Augustine is engaged in confrontation with the Platonists on the subject of sacrifice. Though they agreed with the Christians that human happiness is only to be found in clinging

---

39 *De ciuitate Dei* VIII, 10: CCL 47, 277: "In quo autem nobis consentiunt de uno Deo huius uniuersitatis auctore, qui non solum super omnia corpora est incorporeus, uerum etiam super omnes animas incorruptibilis, principium nostrum, lumen nostrum, bonum nostrum, in hoc eos ceteris anteponimus." See also my "Ultimate Reality according to Augustine of Hippo," *Journal of Ultimate Reality and Meaning* 18 (1995): 20–33.

40 *De ciuitate Dei* X, 22: CCL 47, 296: "Dicet enim Deum Patrem et Deum Filium, quem Graece appellat paternum intellectum uel paternam mentem. ..."

41 *De ciuitate Dei* X, 29: CCL 47, 304: "Confiteris tamen gratiam, quando quidem ad Deum per uirtutem intelligentiae peruenire paucis dicis esse concessum."

42 *De ciuitate Dei* X, 32: CCL 47, 309–311: "Haec est religio, quae uniuersalem continet uiam animae liberandae, quoniam nulla nisi hac liberari potest. ... Unde tanto post ex Abrahae semine carne suscepta de se ipso ait ipse Saluator: *Ego sum uia, ueritas et uita.*"

43 *De ciuitate Dei* X, 29: CCL 47, 304: "sed incarnationem incommutablis Filii Dei qua salvamur ... non uultis agnoscere."

to the one God, which is the goal of sacrifice in Augustine's definition, they, nonetheless, held that in some cases immortal spirits inferior to God deserved the worship that Greek Christians called *latreia*, the worship which is owed only to the one true God.[44] Against this view Augustine argues that any immortal spirit that worships God and loves us will not want to be worshiped in place of God and that any such spirit that does not worship God is wretched and undeserving of our worship. Moreover, whatever may be the case with other acts of worship, Augustine argues that "no one would dare to claim that sacrifice ought to be offered to anyone but God."[45] He also argues that God has no need of the sacrifices we offer him, whether these be the animal sacrifices of the Old Law or the sacrifice of our own righteousness, for everything we do as part of the correct worship of God benefits us, not God. Augustine then explains, as we have seen above, that the animal sacrifices offered by the patriarchs signified the same actions that we carry out in order that we might cling to God and bring our neighbor to that same end. And there follows his definition of true sacrifice as "every work by which it is brought about so that we cling to God in a holy society, every work, that is, which is referred to that ultimate good by which we can be truly happy."[46] Given that definition, Augustine goes on to list things that are sacrifices and, in fact, true sacrifices.

IV. EXAMPLES OF TRUE SACRIFICES

Augustine first offers three examples of true sacrifices. First, he states that "a human being consecrated by God's name and dedicated to God insofar as one dies to the world in order to live for God is a sacrifice. For this belongs to the mercy one shows to oneself."[47] Second, our body

---

44 Augustine discusses at length the lack of a single Latin term suitable to translate *latria* and points out the shortcomings of *cultus, servitus, religio,* and *pietas*. See *De ciuitate Dei* X, 1: CLL 47, 271–274.

45 *De ciuitate Dei* X, 4: CCL 47, 276: "Nam, ut alia nunc taceam, quae pertinent ad religionis obsequium, quo colitur Deus, sacrificium certe nullus hominum est qui audeat dicere deberi nisi Deo."

46 *De ciuitate Dei* X, 6: CCL 47, 278: "Proinde uerum sacrificium est omne opus, quo agitur, ut sancta societate inhaereamus Deo, relatum scilicet ad illum finem boni, quo ueraciter beati esse possimus."

47 *De ciuitate Dei* X, 6: CCL 47, 278: "Unde ipse homo Dei nomine consecratus et Deo uotus, in quantum mundo moritur ut Deo uiuat, sacrificium est. Nam et hoc ad misericordiam pertinet, quam quisque in se ipsum facit."

is a sacrifice, when we chastise it with temperance "if we do this as we ought on account of God so that we do not offer our members to sin as weapons of wickedness, but to God as weapons of righteousness."[48] So too, and for even better reasons, our soul is a sacrifice

> when it is offers itself to God so that, enkindled with the fire of his love, it loses the form of worldly love and is reformed for him, now subject to the immutable Form and pleasing to him because it has received some of its beauty.[49]

Each of these sacrifices, whether of the whole human being, or of the body, or of the soul, might at first glance seem to involve nothing specifically Christian, even though the mention of each of these sacrifices is followed by a text of scripture that justifies our calling it a sacrifice. Yet this absence of anything specifically Christian is more apparent than real, for the words "consecrated by God's name" connote baptism, as a search of the Augustinian corpus readily shows.[50] Moreover, Augustine wrote *De ciuitate Dei* during the height of the Pelagian controversy so that, when he mentioned the virtue of temperance, he certainly had in mind the Christian virtue that was rooted in faith and in the love of God poured out in the heart by the Holy Spirit.[51] Yet, there is nothing in the description of these sacrifices that a non-Christian

---

48 *De ciuitate Dei* X, 6: CCL 47, 278: "Corpus etiam nostrum cum temperantia castigamus, si hoc, quem ad modum debemus, propter Deum facimus, ut non exhibeamus membra nostra arma iniquitatis peccato, sed arma iustitiae Deo, sacrificium est."

49 *De ciuitate Dei* X, 6: CCL 47, 278: "quanto magis anima ipsa cum se refert ad Deum, ut igne amoris eius accensa formam concupiscentiae saecularis amittat eique tamquam incommutabili formae subdita reformetur, hinc ei placens, quod ex eius pulchritudine acceperit, fit sacrificium!"

50 See, for example, *Epistula* 23, 4: CSEL 34/1, 67: "Cur non dicis: ego unum baptismum noui Patris et Filii et Spiritus Sancti nomine consecratum atque signatum; hanc formam ubi inuenio, necesse est ut adprobem; non destruo, quod dominicum agnosco, non exsufflo uexillum regis mei?" or *Sermo* 352: PL 39, 1551: 40: "Sed quia baptismus, id est, salutis aqua non est salutis, nisi Christi nomine consecrata, qui pro nobis sanguinem fudit, cruce ipsius aqua signatur."

51 See *De nuptiis et concupiscentia* I, iv, 5: CSEL 42: 216, for Augustine's use of Rom 14:23 and Heb 11:6 to argue that there is no true virtue without faith. The fact that the specifically Christian elements are understated rather than explicit may explain how O'Grady missed them; see above note 9.

would necessarily find unacceptable. I want to suggest that Augustine emphasized the interior and spiritual character of true sacrifice as part of his strategy to convert contemporary Platonists to Christianity and specifically to the worship of the Christian God in the Church. I suggest that a Platonist exploring the possibility of becoming a Christian would not necessarily find anything off-putting or incompatible with Platonic spiritualism at its best.

Later in book ten Augustine mentions certain people who wanted to offer visible sacrifices to the lesser gods, but wanted to offer to the one God who is invisible, who is the greatest and the best, only the invisible sacrifices of a pure mind and a good will. There the bishop of Hippo insists that visible sacrifices are the symbols of invisible offerings and that "visible sacrifice must be offered only to him to whom we ourselves ought to be an invisible sacrifice in our hearts."[52] Gerald Bonner suggests that Porphyry is the "most obvious subject of these remarks" and points to a saying ascribed to Apollonius of Tyana which Porphyry cites to the effect that "the highest god has no need of sacrifices at all, and that the only fitting offering is man's reason."[53] Bonner rightly, I believe, concludes that, though Augustine was influenced by Neoplatonic thought, "It is not necessary, and may indeed be positively misleading, to emphasize that influence at the expense of the more obviously immediate influence of the Bible, on which his mature theology is fundamentally based."[54]

What I would like to suggest, on the other hand, is that Augustine's emphasis upon the interior and invisible forms of sacrifice in *De ciuitate Dei* is not due so much to his being under the influence by Neoplatonist thinking as to his concern to present the Christian understanding of sacrifice in a way that would be most acceptable to some contemporaries who were deeply attracted to the spiritualism of

---

52 *De ciuitate Dei* X, 19: CCL 47, 293: "ita sacrificantes non alteri uisibile sacrificium offerendum esse nouerimus quam illi, cuius in cordibus nostris inuisibile sacrificium nos ipsi debemus."

53 Bonner, "The Doctrine of Sacrifice," p. 102, where he refers to Prophyry's *De abstinentia* II, 34. See *Porphyre. De l'abstinence* II. Livres II et III, ed. and tr. J. Bouffartique and M. Patillon (Paris: Belles Lettres, 1979), 100–101: θύσομεν τοίνυν καὶ ἡμεῖς. ἀλλὰ θύσομεν, ὡς προσήκει. ... διὰ δὲ σιγῆς καθαρᾶς καὶ τῶν περὶ αὐτοῦ καθαρῶν ἐννοιῶν θρησκεύομεν αὐτόν.

54 Bonner, "The Doctrine of Sacrifice," p. 104.

Platonism. In his recent study of *De ciuitate Dei* Johannes van Oort has argued that the work was basically a work of Christian apologetics meant to prepare converts—educated ones, we must suppose—for the reception of baptism.[55] In this light, one can maintain, I believe, that, while in no sense being unfaithful to the understanding of sacrifice he learned in the teachings of scripture and in the writing of such patristic authors as Tertullian and Cyprian,[56] Augustine may have emphasized the spiritual and interior character of the Christian understanding of sacrifice in a way that would allow contemporary Platonists to see that Christianity was capable of incorporating the highest ideals of Platonic spiritualism.

V. THE UNIVERSAL SACRIFICE

After the three examples of true sacrifice, Augustine repeats his claim that "true sacrifices are works of mercy, whether toward ourselves or toward our neighbors, which are offered to God," and points out that "works of mercy have no other purpose than that we may be set free from misery and, in this way, be happy."[57] He adds that we can be happy only by clinging to God. Hence, he concludes that

> the whole redeemed city, that is, the assembly and society of the saints, is offered to God as the universal sacrifice through the great priest who also offered himself for us in his Passion in the form of the servant so that we might be the body of so great a head.[58]

---

55 Johannes Van Oort, *Jerusalem and Babylon: A Study into Augustine's City of God and the Sources of the Doctrine of the Two Cities* (Leiden: E. J. Brill, 1991), especially Chapter Three: "The 'City of God' as an Apology and a Catechetical Work." See pages 173–175 where Van Oort points to Letter 2* in which Augustine urges Firmus to enter the city of God by baptism if he wants to enjoy the fruits of the work: "neque enim ille fructus est eorum, quod delectant legentem, nec ille, quod multa faciunt scire nescientem, sed ille, quod ciuitatem dei persuadent vel incunctanter intrandam uel perserueranter habitandam" (*Epistola* 2*, 3: BA 46B, 64).

56 For the influence of Tertullian and Cyprian upon Augustine's thought on sacrifice, see once again Bonner, "The Doctrine of Sacrifice," pp. 107–111.

57 *De ciuitate Dei* X, 6: CCL 47, 279: "Cum igitur uera sacrificia opera sint misericordiae siue in nos ipsos siue in proximos, quae referuntur ad Deum; opera uero misericordiae non ob aliud fiant, nisi ut a miseria liberemur ac per hoc ut beati simus. ..."

58 *De ciuitate Dei* X, 6: CCL 47, 279: "profecto efficitur, ut tota ipsa redempta ciuitas, hoc est congregatio societasque sanctorum, uniuersale sacrificium

The truly great work of mercy, then, is the work of our salvation, the universal sacrifice by which we are set free from the misery of sin and reconciled to God through the great priest.[59] In all his writings Augustine used the expression "universal sacrifice" only in this passage, and the most frequent use of the "*universalis*" in all his works is as adjective with "*via*" in the same book of *De ciuitate Dei*.[60] Such a pattern of usage suggests that Augustine linked in his mind the universal sacrifice with the universal way, the existence of which Porphyry acknowledged, but did not discover, and which Augustine knew was the incarnate Christ. Again we have evidence that in his discussion of sacrifice Augustine has the great Platonist in mind, not, of course, to convert Porphyry, but to nudge contemporary Platonists, those who were in agreement with the Christians on so many important points, to take the step and enter the city of God and become part of the universal sacrifice that is the people of God. Such, after all, was Augustine's message to Firmus in *Letter* 2*.[61]

---

offeratur deo per sacerdotem magnum, qui etiam se ipsum obtulit in passione pro nobis, ut tanti capitis corpus essemus, secundum formam serui."

59 In "Das Opfer Christi," Basil Studer points out the puzzling fact that Augustine does not explicitly apply his definition of sacrifice to the sacrifice of Christ on the Cross. He says, for example, "Es ist schwer auszumachen, warum Augustin selbst nicht auf die naheliegende Möglichkeit aufmerksam geworden ist, seinen ohne Zweifel persönich tiefempfundenen Opferbegriff auf das Verständnis des Sterbens Christi auzudehnen" (p. 104). He does not explicitly apply his definition to Christ's death, I suggest, because he sees that death as the chief part of the universal sacrifice by which the whole Christ, head and body, is offered to the Father.

60 The adjective "*universalis*" appears in Augustine's works 75 times. It occurs most frequently with "*via*"—19 times and 18 of these in book ten of *De ciuitate Dei* where the context is Porphyry's search for a universal way of salvation. Sixteen times the adjective accompanies "*concilium*," and another 6 times "*ecclesia*."

61 *Epistula* 2*, 3: BA 42^B, 62–64: "Nam quod in alia tua epistola te ab accipiendo sacramento regenerationis excusas, totum tot librorum quos amas fructum recusas; neque enim ille fructus est eorum, quod delectant legentem, nec ille, quod multa faciunt scire nescientem, sed ille, quod ciuitatem dei persuadent uel incunctanter intrandam uel perseueranter habitandam; quorum duorum primum regeneratione, secundum iustitiae dilectione confertur."

Yves de Montcheuil commented on the meaning of "*opus*" in Augustine's definition of sacrifice with these insightful words,

> If we take things from the point of view of human history in its entirety, as God sees them, we must say that there is but one sole sacrifice in the complete sense: the act by which predestined humanity ... passes from the sin in which it is found to the full reality of salvation. "Opus"—"the great work" of human history, that by which humanity attains its goal: "that we cling to God in a holy society," so that we may be truly happy.[62]

This universal sacrifice, then, is not merely a work of mercy, but the one all-inclusive work of mercy, because it is the sacrifice that Jesus Christ offered on Calvary in the form of the servant as the head of his body, the Church, and which is re-presented in each Eucharistic sacrifice. Christ as head offered that sacrifice in the form of the servant so that the whole city of God might as his body be the universal sacrifice offered to God.[63] In accord with his theme of the unity of sacrament and sacrifice, de Montcheuil adds,

> "A work" that is broken down into a series of "works," because humanity itself is made up of distinct and successive human beings, because each human beings is also subject to time and it is not by one single "action" that one realizes perfect society with God. ...[64]

---

62 Yves de Montcheuil, "L'unité du sacrifice et du sacrement dans l'Eucharistie," in *Mélanges théologiques* (Paris: Aubier, 1946), p. 51: "Si nous prenons les choses du point de vue de l'histoire humaine dans son ensemble, comme Dieu les voit, nous devons dire qu'il n'y a qu'un seul sacrifice au sens total: l'acte par lequel l'humanité prédestinée ... passe du péché où elle se trouve à la consommation du salut. 'Opus', 'grand oeuvre' de l'historie humaine, celui par lequel l'humanité parvient à sa fin: 'ut sancta societate inhaereamus Deo,' en sorte qu'elle soit vraiment heureuse."

63 The Latin "*societas*" in Augustine definition of sacrifice, which has often been translated into English as "fellowship," loses the power of the Latin term, which here clearly refers to the whole Christ, the City of God, for there is no other "sancta societas qua inhaereamus Deo." See Donald J. Keefe, *Covenantal Theology: The Eucharistic Order of History*. 2 vols. (Lanham, MD: University Press of America, 1991), II, p. 369.

64 Ibid.: "'Opus' qui se décompose en une série d'opera', parce que l'humanité se compose elle-même d'hommes distincts et successifs, parce qu'aussi chaque homme est soumis au temps, et que ce n'est pas par une seule 'action' qu'il réalise sa société parfaite avec Dieu. ..." Yves de Montcheuil, SJ, a member of the faculty of the Institut Catholique de Paris, was executed

In his discussion of sacrifice in book ten Augustine mentions the sacrifice of Calvary only here, and he does not explicitly say that it is an act of mercy, though it is surely implied.[65] The sacrifice of Calvary is THE work of mercy, the work of our redemption by which we are reconciled to God, for as Augustine puts it in book ten: "Human being are, after all, separated from God only by sins, which in this life are washed away not by our strength, but by God's compassion, by his pardon, not by our power. ..."[66] And he explains, "the forgiveness of sins is brought about in him as priest and sacrifice, that is, through the mediator of God and human beings, the man Jesus Christ, through whom we are reconciled to God by the washing away of sins."[67] Because Augustine stressed the reality of the unity between Christ the head and his members, he saw every act of mercy performed by a member of the whole Christ as part of that universal sacrifice, the great act of mercy offered by Christ to reconcile us to the Father.[68]

---

on the night of August 10–11, 1944 at Vecors, France, after his capture during a Nazi attack upon a group of young resistance fighters. He was visiting the group during his summer vacation in order to provide them with some spiritual care. During the attack he remained behind with the wounded and was subsequently executed—an end which surely fits the Augustinian characterisation of sacrifice as a work of mercy toward other human beings for the sake of God. See the Préface to *Melanges théologiques*, 7–12, by H[enri] de L[ubac].

65 See Basil Studer, "Das Opfer Christi," 95.

66 *De ciuitate Dei* X, 22: CCL 47, 296: "Non enim nisi peccatis homines separantur a deo, quorum in hac uita non fit nostra uirtute, sed diuina miseratione purgatio, per indulgentiam illius, non per nostram potentiam. ..."

67 *De ciuitate Dei* X, 22: CCL 47, 296: "in ipso sacerdote ac sacrificio fieret remissio peccatorum, id est per mediatorem dei et hominum, hominem christum iesum, per quem facta peccatorum purgatione reconciliamur deo."

68 The theme of the whole Christ (*totus Christus*) underlies the unity of the many acts of sacrifice with the one sacrifice of Christ. See, for example, *Enarrationes in Psalmum* 26, enar. 2, 2: CCL 38, 155: "Sacrificium obtulit Deo non aliud quam seipsum. Non enim inueniret praeter se mundissimam rationalem uictimam, tamquam agnus immaculatus fuso sanguine suo redimens nos, concorporans nos sibi, faciens nos membra sua, ut in illo et nos Christus essemus. . . . Inde autem apparet Christi corpus nos esse, quia omnes ungimur; et omnes in illo et christi et Christus sumus, quia quodammodo totus Christus caput et corpus est."

THE IMAGE AND LIKENESS OF GOD IN ST. AUGUSTINE'S *DE GENESI AD LITTERAM LIBER IMPERFECTUS*

Augustine began *De Genesi ad litteram liber imperfectus* around 393.[1] He tells us in *Retractationes* 1,18 that he wanted to try his hand at the arduous task of a literal interpretation of Genesis, but that he was still a novice in Scriptural exegesis and was unable to carry out his project. Augustine did, however, manage to work his way through the first chapter of Genesis up to verse 26, "And God said, 'Let us make man to our image and likeness.'" And with that verse he gave up on a literal interpretation of the text. In reviewing his works in 427 he came upon this unfinished and unpublished work and intended to destroy it since he had written the twelve books of *De Genesi ad litteram* in the intervening years. After examining it, however, he decided to preserve it as "a useful indication" of his first attempts at Scriptural interpretation.[2]

Little attention has been paid to the *Liber imperfectus*, which has been rightly overshadowed by the twelve books of *De Genesi ad litteram*, to which Augustine refers us in order to judge what he might have found unsatisfactory or worth defending in the unfinished commentary.[3] Though for Augustine's considered views on Genesis we must turn to his later masterpiece, for understanding the development of his thought it is at least equally important to examine his first efforts and those points at which "in explaining the Scriptures [his] novice efforts collapsed beneath the magnitude of the burden."[4]

The final sections of this unfinished work are, I think, especially interesting for the study of the development of Augustine's thought. In 16, 55–60 Augustine presents an interpretation of Gen 1:26 in accord with which the Word, the only-begotten Son, is the Image and Like-

---

1 See G. Bardy, *Les Revisions*, BA 12, p. 571.
2 See *Retractationes* 1, 18.
3 *Retractationes* 1, 18.
4 Ibid.

ness of God the Father, while man is made unto or according to this Image and Likeness, that is, unto or according to the Son or Word. Du Roy has pointed out that the preposition "*ad*" has a twofold sense, signifying both an orientation or movement of return to the principle and a relation of resemblance.⁵ Furthermore, though all of creation participates in the Likeness and is made through the Image and Likeness of God, only man in his rational mind is also made "*ad imaginem et similitudinem Dei*." Hence, man's likeness to God is understood in terms of his participation in and orientation toward the Likeness, who is the Word and the Son of the Father.⁶

Augustine later came to reject this interpretation of "unto the image and likeness of God," replacing this anagogical approach to the economic Trinity with an analogical approach to the immanent Trinity—a change that Du Roy claims had grave consequences for Augustine's *intellectus fidei* with regard to the Trinity.⁷ In this paper I first examine Augustine's interpretation of "*ad imaginem et similitudinem Dei*."

---

5 "Le 'ad' signifie donc à la fois une relation particulière de resemblance ('selon') et une orientation, un mouvement de retour vers le Principe, l'Unité, mouvement pour lequel nous ne trouvons pas de préposition adéquate en français ('a', 'vers')." (See Olivier du Roy, *L'intelligence de la foi en la Trinité selon saint Augustin: Genèse de sa théologie iusqu'en 391* (Paris: Etudes Augustiniennes, 1966), p. 361. One might add that we do not have a single preposition in English either that does justice to the senses of the Latin. The Greek has *kat' eikona kai homoiosin*, which would be more literally translated into Latin as *secundum imaginem et similitudinem*, thus bringing out man's being formed to or in accord with the Image. In any case Augustine clearly saw man's being made *ad imaginem et similitudinem* as his being conformed to the Son; see *De diversis quaestionibus 83*, qu. 23 (cited below, p. 8).

6 Augustine derived this interpretation of Gen 1:26 from Origen, it seems, via the preaching of Ambrose. For example, in *Contra Celsum* 6, 63, "*Eita phēsin ho Kelsos mē enidōn tēi diaphorai tou 'kat' eikōna theou' kai 'tēs eikōnos autou.*'" See Gerald A. McCool, SJ, "The Ambrosian Origin of St. Augustine's Theology of the Image of God in Man," *Theological Studies* 20 (1959): 62–81. For Origen's doctrine on man as *kat' eikona*, see Henri Crouzel, SJ, *Théologie de l'image de Dieu chez Origène* (Paris: Aubier, 1956) and *Origène* (Paris: Lethielleux, 1985), especially pp. 130–137.

7 "Ce changement aura de graves conséquences sur son *intellectus fidei* de la Trinité car, venant à point pour le sortir des impasses de l'anagogie trinitaire (où on va au Pere par le Fils), elle va l'acheminer à la théologie analogique de l'image trinitaire en l'homme. Et au fur et à mesure que celle-ci se pré-

in *De Genesi ad litteram liber imperfectus*. Then I suggest an explanation of why Augustine gave up on his project of a literal interpretation of Genesis at this point. Finally, I suggest even more tentatively some reasons why he gave up this view of man as made unto or according to the Image.

In dealing with Gen 1:26, Augustine notes that an image is always like that of which it is an image, but that not everything like something else is an image of that other thing. For X to be an image of Y, X must be like Y and be derived from Y. Why then does Genesis say "image and likeness" since an image cannot fail to be a likeness? Augustine tentatively suggests that something like (*simile*) and likeness (*similitudo*) differ as someone chaste and chastity or someone brave and bravery. Thus likeness is that by which all like things are like, as chastity is that by which all chaste things are chaste. Hence, an image of us is not properly our likeness, though it is like us. Rather, Augustine continues, the likeness by which all like things are like is found where there is the chastity by which all chaste things are chaste. This likeness is in God where there is that wisdom that is not wise by participation, but by participation in which every wise soul is wise.[8]

> Hence, the Likeness of God, through which all things were made, is properly called likeness, because it is like not by participating in some likeness, but it itself is the first Likeness, by participation in which whatever things God has made through it are like.

Hence, "image" signifies origination or generation from the Father, and "likeness" signifies that the Image is not merely like, but Likeness itself.

> As nothing is more chaste than chastity itself and nothing more wise than wisdom itself and nothing more beautiful than beauty itself, so nothing can be said or can be thought or can be more like than likeness itself. Thus we understand that the Father's likeness is so like him that it fully and perfectly embodies his nature.

This Likeness of God, through which all things have been made, is able to impose its form (*species*) upon every nature, for every nature

---

cisera, c'est le lien économique avec la Trinité créatrice et salvatrice qui ira en s'affaiblissant" (Du Roy, *L'intelligence*, p. 358).

8 H. Somers points out the anti-Arian tenor and roots of this position. See H. Somers, SJ, "Image de Dieu. Les sources de l'exégèse augustinienne," *Revue des études augustiniennes* 7 (1961) 105–125.

has parts like each other. Augustine argues that in order that an individual thing be one of the elements, e.g., fire or air, each of its parts must be like the rest. So too, he claims that any body whether animate or inanimate must be like others of its kind and have parts like one another, and such bodies are more beautiful in proportion to the greater likeness of their parts. So too, friendship between souls is built up by like conduct, and in an individual soul constancy demands like actions and virtues, which, in turn, are the marks of happiness. Thus the universe is composed of things that are like, but they are not the Likeness, through which they were all made.

All things have been made through the wisdom of God, but only souls—and not cattle, trees and inanimate elements—are called wise.[9] So too, only the rational substance is made both through the Likeness and unto the Likeness. For there is no nature that comes between the rational substance and the Likeness.[10] Though it is aware of this only in its purest and happiest state, the human mind clings to nothing but the truth itself, which is called the Father's likeness and image and wisdom. Augustine briefly entertains the idea that man's body bears a likeness to God insofar as, being erect, he is not turned away from heaven, just as the Likeness is not turned away from the Father.[11] Yet he notes that our body is very different from heaven, while the Likeness that is the Son is in no respect unlike the Father. "Whatever other things are like each other are unlike in some respect, but the Likeness itself is in no respect unlike." The Father is only the Father, and the Son is only the Son. When the Son is said to be the Likeness of the Father, we see that no unlikeness enters in, and yet the Father is not alone, if he has the Likeness.

At this point Augustine left the work unfinished until the time of the *Retractationes*; then he repeated Gen 1:26 and added,

---

9 Likeness extends to everything that God has made, just as, in *De libero arbitrio* 2, 11, 31 number extends to all things, while wisdom is limited to souls.

10 See Paul Aubin, "L'Image dans l'oeuvre de Plotin," *Recherches de science religieuse* 41 (1953): 348–379, for elements in Plotinus's treatment of image and likeness that surely influenced Augustine's thought.

11 This interpretation was almost a commonplace in ancient literature. It is also found in Augustine's writings from early to late. See H. Somers., "L'image de Dieu," pp. 112–114 for the texts in Augustine and for a list of secular and patristic authors in which the theme is found.

What we have written above sufficiently explains these words of Scripture, "Let us make man to our image and likeness," so that the likeness of God, unto which man was made, can be understood as the very Word of God, that is, the only-begotten Son, not, of course, that [man] is the same image and likeness equal to the Father.

From 1 Cor 11:7 Augustine sees that a man (*vir*) is the image of God, though he adds, "This image made unto the Image of God is not equal to and coeternal with him, of whom he is the image, and it would not be, even if he had not sinned." Thus, man himself is clearly called the image of God and is not merely made unto the Image, that is, unto the Son of God. Still not satisfied, Augustine insists that the preferable meaning in this passage involves our taking account of the plurals, "*faciamus*" and "*nostram*." "For man was made to the image not of the Father alone or of the Son alone or of the Holy Spirit alone, but to the image of the Trinity."

Hence, Augustine argues that God did not say to the Son, "Let us make man unto your image," or "unto my image," but in the plural, "unto our image and likeness," and we should not remove the Holy Spirit from that plurality. Hence, we should understand the singular in the next line of Genesis, "And God made man to the image of God," not as if God the Father made man to the image of God, that is, of his Son. "Otherwise, how could the words, 'to our image' be true, if man was made to the image of the Son alone?" Hence, Augustine insists that the words "to the image of God" should be understood as "to his own image," because God is the Trinity.[12]

Hence, the apparent reasons for Augustine's dropping his earlier interpretation of Gen 1:26, which du Roy refers to as the anagogical approach to the economic Trinity are, first, that 1 Cor 11:7 speaks of man as the image of God and, second, that "*nostram*" demands that man was made to the image of God the Trinity. Initially, Augustine does not claim that the first interpretation is wrong, but only that the

---

12 Augustine notes that some have thought that man was originally created to the image of God and will attain the likeness of God in the resurrection of the body. Clement of Alexandria similarly reports that there are "among us those who think that man received the image by his very origin, while he will receive the likeness later by being made perfect" (*Stromata* 2, 22). Augustine scorns the idea of an image that is in no way like what it images, but invokes the authority of James the Apostle to avoid the appearance of relying on reason alone (James 3:9).

second is preferable (*potius eligendus*), but ultimately he implies that "*ad imaginem nostram*" could not be true, if man was made to the image of the Son.

Augustine had previously commented on Gen 1:26 in *De Genesi contra Manichaeos*; there he was concerned primarily with warding off the anthropomorphic interpretation with which the Manichees charged Catholic believers.[13] At that point Augustine regarded the image and likeness of God as lying in the incorporeal human mind in virtue of which man is superior to the other animals, but there is no hint that he thought of the Word as the Image and Likeness, unto or according to which man was made. Yet in *Soliloquia* 1, 1, 4 Augustine prays to the Father, "who made man to your (*tuam*) image and likeness," thus leaving the text at least open to this meaning. And in *De vera religione* 43, 81 Augustine clearly identifies the image and likeness with the Son, while 26:49 links man's perfect form that he will attain in eternal life with his being made unto the image and likeness of God. Hence, in some of his earliest writings we find God's image and likeness identified with the Son so that man's being made unto the image and likeness of God is his being made unto and according to the Son.

What then led Augustine to break off his commentary on Genesis at this point? It seems reasonable to suppose that he was encountering difficulties in giving a literal interpretation of the creation of man to the image and likeness of God.[14] Yet up to the point where the original text breaks off, there is no sign of a problem, none of the hesitancy and doubt that he expressed on so many previous points. Why then did he break off his exegesis at this point?

I suggest that the problem that led Augustine to break off his first literal exposition of Genesis lay, not in 1:26, but in 1:27, specifically in the words, "male and female he created them." Why should that verse bring to a halt the literal interpretation of the text? Because at that point Augustine thought that man as he was created by God was an

---

13 For further evidence on this point, see Somers, "Image de Dieu," pp. 111-112, which cites texts on this theme from Origen, Chrysostom, Basil and Ambrose; see also my "The Aim of Augustine's Proof that God Truly Is," *International Philosophical Quarterly* 26 (1986): 253–268, especially 255–257, for Augustine's concern with the anthropomorphism in the African church.

14 He did, after all, admit that he collapsed under the burden of literally interpreting Genesis; see *Retractationes* 1, 18.

incorporeal soul with at most a spiritual body such that a literal interpretation of the two sexes was impossible.[15]

After all, when Augustine dealt with Gen 1:27 in *De Genesi contra Manichaeos* 1, 19, 30, he maintained that we certainly may interpret this verse and the subsequent blessing "spiritually so that we believe it was turned into carnal fecundity after sin."[16] In speaking of "the chaste union of male and female" and "the spiritual offspring of intelligible and immortal joys," he anticipates the allegorical interpretation that he will give in *De Genesi contra Manichaeos* 2, 12, 16 of Gen 2, where man and woman are seen as the contemplative and active sides of the incorporeal soul. Moreover, Augustine's clear debt to Ambrose's *Hexaemeron* on other points regarding the doctrine of man as made unto God's Image suggests that he may here too be following Ambrose who emphasizes that man was made unto the image and likeness of God in his incorporeal soul or mind, while passing over Gen 1:27.[17] Furthermore, Augustine directed us to *De Genesi ad litteram* for what he approved and disapproved in the *Liber imperfectus*.[18] In 3.22.34 Augustine returns to Gn 1:26-27 and mentions that some exegetes have interpreted Gn 2 as describing the formation of man's body, while they held that Gn 1:26-27 refers to the creation of his spirit.[19] Of these he says, "They do not realize that making them male and female is possible only with respect to the body." Augustine does mention a subtle interpretation that explains "male and female" as referring to the contemplative and

---

15 For further evidence on the claim that Augustine viewed man before the fall as an incorporeal soul with at most a spiritual body, see Robert O'Connell, *The Origin of the Soul in St. Augustine's Later Works* (New York: Fordham University Press, 1987), especially the chapter on *De libero arbitrio* III.

16 See my "Spirituals and Spiritual Interpretation in St. Augustine," *Augustinian Studies* 15 (1984): 65–81, especially 75–77, for the claim that to interpret a text spiritually involves understanding terms that seem to signify corporeal realities as signifying incorporeal or spiritual realities.

17 See Ambrose, *Hexaemeron* 3, 7, 32 and 6, 7, 40–8.48 (CSEL 32.1, pp. 80 and 231–240).

18 See *Retractationes* 1.18.

19 Augustine mentions this position in *De Genesi contra Manichaeos* 2, 7, 9 without any sign of disapproval. Somers, "Image de Dieu," pp. 116–117, cites Basil's *De structura hominis* 2, as a possible, though indirect, source of this idea.

active sides of the incorporeal soul; however, such an interpretation, which was his own in *De Genesi contra Manichaeos* 2.12.16 is certainly not a literal interpretation of the text. Hence, I suggest that, because he viewed man as God created him as a soul who fell into his mortal body only after sin, he was unable to continue with a literal interpretation of Genesis when confronted with "male and female he created them." Hence, at this point he left his work unfinished.[20]

Why did Augustine come to reject this interpretation of Gen 1:26? There is, of course, his professed reasons, namely, that he did not see how Genesis could employ the plurals, *"faciamus"* and *"nostram,"* if God made man to the image of the Son. However, there may be a better explanation that can be teased from the texts. In *De diversis quaestionibus 83*, qu. 23, Augustine again takes up the participation theme in much the same language as in the *Liber imperfectus* passage. That is, Augustine uses Plato's argument from Phaedo that, if something varies in its essential elements, then it does not have them from itself.[21] Augustine says,

> Therefore, those things which are like by participation admit unlikeness, but likeness itself can in no way be unlike in any respect. The result is that, when the Son is called the likeness of the Father, he cannot in any respect be unlike the Father. (For whatever things are like either among themselves or to God are like by participation in [the likeness], since it is the first species by which they are, so to speak, specified and the form by which all things are formed). He is then the same as the Father though he is the Son and the

---

20 Further support for this contention might be derived from *Confessions* 13, 24, 37 where Augustine again gives a spiritual interpretation to the command to increase and multiply, which he interprets in terms of the multiplicity of senses of Scripture. Moreover, Augustine had early held that "we would not have any such temporal relationships which arise by being born or dying, if our nature remained in the precepts and image of God and was not dismissed to this corruption" (*De vera religione* 46, 88). In *Retractationes* 1, 10, 2 Augustine completely disapproved of the idea implied in *De Genesi contra Manichaeos* 1, 19, 30 that the first parents would not have had children, had they not sinned. So too, in *Retractationes* 1, 13, 8, commenting on the above text from *De vera religione*, Augustine admits that at that time he "had not yet seen that it was possible that offspring not destined to die would be born from parents not destined to die, if human nature were not changed for the worse by that great sin."

21 *Phaedo* 100d–102a.

other is the Father, that is, he is the likeness, and the other the one whose likeness he is. He is substance and the other one is substance, though there is one substance. For if [the substance] is not one, the likeness admits unlikeness, and every true reasoning rejects this possibility.

Earlier in this question Augustine had argued that everything chaste is chaste by chastity, everything beautiful is beautiful by beauty, and so on with regard to goodness, eternity and wisdom. In the case of wisdom, he tells us, God is wise not by participation in wisdom, "but because he generated that wisdom by which he is said to be wise." Now, if he generated the wisdom by which he is said to be wise, it would seem that the Father also generated the likeness by which he, i.e., the Father, is said to be like. That is, the Father is surely just as much likeness as is the Son. What we are faced with is a confusion of essential and personal terms. In dealing with this passage in the *Retractationes* 1,26, 2, Augustine simply points out that he dealt with this question better in *De trinitate* 6, 2, 3. By that time he had worked out the theory of the trinitarian relations and had at hand such lapidary formulae as, "Whatever then they are said to be non-relatively, the one is not said to be without the other, that is, whatever they are said to be that manifests their substance, they are both said to be," and "Only what both of them are not cannot be said of them in the formula, X from X. Thus we cannot say: Word from Word, since both are not the Word, but only the Son is." The point is that at the time of the *Liber imperfectus* and *De diversis quaestionibus 83* Augustine had not yet worked out the doctrine of trinitarian relations.[22] Hence, he could speak of the Son as the Likeness, though later he came to see that likeness is an essential term.

Furthermore, it seems that Augustine was exploiting most explicitly at this period a doctrine of participation. And while participation dif-

---

[22] In his classic study, *S. Augustin et la pensée grecque: Les relations trinitaires* (Fribourg: Librairie de l'université, 1940, Irenée Chevalier holds that the whole of the *De trinitate* was written between 400 and 419 and dates Books V–VII, the central books on the doctrine of the relations, between 413 and 416. O'Connell argues for a later date for the beginning of the work, namely, 404, and argues that it was not the doctrine of relations that held up the completion of the work, but problems with the origin of the soul; see *Later Works*, pp.177–178.

fers from Plotinian emanation, it is not efficient causality either.[23] That is, I tentatively suggest that without a clear idea of efficient causality and without having worked out the trinitarian relations, it was possible for Augustine to link man's being made unto the Image of God with the Son in a way that was no longer possible once he had worked out the doctrine of the trinitarian relations and once he had come to a clearer grasp of efficient causality and had come to see that the effects of the divine efficient causality are common to all three persons. Though du Roy points to grave consequences for Augustine's theology of the Trinity that stem from his move to an analogical approach to the immanent Trinity, Augustine's development of the doctrine of the trinitarian relations brought to the theological understanding of the mystery of the Trinity an intelligibility that subsequent theology has rightly found indispensable.

---

23 Of. *De diversis quaestionibus 83*, qu. 23, the notes in the BA edition point out, "Il ne s'agit pas de l'émanation plotinienne, mais non plus d'une efficience, quoique saint Augustin n'y repugne pas comme Platon." See the note by J. A. Beckaert in BA 10, *Mélanges doctrinaux* (Paris: Desclee de Brouwer, 1952), p. 702.

BIBLIOGRAPHY

WORKS OF SAINT AUGUSTINE CITED

Collatio cum Maximino. PL 42, 709–742.

Confessiones. PL 32, 659–868; CSEL 33, 1–388; CCL 27, 1–273.

Contra Academicos. PL 32, 905–958; CCL 29, 3–61.

Contra adversarium legis et prophetarum. PL 42, 603–666; CCL, 49, 35–131.

Contra Cresconium. PL 43: 445–594 ; CSEL 52: 325–582.

Contra epistulam Manichaei quam vocant fundamenti. PL 42, 173–206; CSEL 25.1, 193–248.

Contra Faustum. PL 207–518; CSEL 25:1, 252–797.

Contra Felicem Manichaeum. PL 42, 519–552; CSEL 25.2, 801–852.

Contra Fortunatum Manichaeum. PL 42, 111–130; CSEL 25/1, 251–797.

Contra Iulianum opus imperfectum. PL 1049–1608; CSEL 85.1, 1–506 and 85.2, 1–506.

Contra Maximinum. PL 42, 709–742.

Contra mendacium. PL 40, 517–548; CSEL 41, 469–528.

Contra Priscillianistas et Origenistas. PL 42., 669–678; CCL 49, 165–178.

Contra Secundinum. PL 42, 577—602; CSEL 25.2, 905–975.

Contra sermonem Arianorum. PL 42: 683–708.

De anima et eius origine. PL 44, 475–548; CSEL 60, 303–419.

De animae quantitate. PL 32, 1035–80; CSEL 89, 131–231.

De beata vita. PL 32, 959–976, CSEL 63, 89–116; CCL 29, 65–85.

De civitate Dei. PL 41, 13—804; CCL 47.1, 1–314; 47.2, 321–866.

De consensu Evangelista rum. PL 34, 1041–1230; CSEL 43, 1–418.

De continentia. PL 40, 349–372; CSEL, 41, 139–183.

De diversis quaestinibus ad Simplicianum. PL 40, 349–372; CCL 44, 1–91.

De diversis quaestionibus octoginta tribus. PL 40, 11–100; CCL 44A, 11–249.

De doctrina christiana. PL 34, 15–122; CSEI. 89, 3–169; CCL 32, 1–167.

De duabus animabus. PL 34, 15–122; CSEL 25.1, 51–80.

De fide et symbolo. PL 40, 181–196; CSEL 41, 3–32.

De Genesi ad litteram. PL 34, 245–486; CSEL 28.1, 3–435.

De Genesi ad litteram imperfectus liber. PL 34, 219–246; CSEL 28.1, 457–503.

De Genesis contra Manichaeos. PL 34, 173–220; CSEL 91, 67–172.

De haeresibus. PL 32, 593–656; CCL 45, 283–351.

De immortalite animae. PL 32, 1021–1034; CSEL 89, 101–128.

De libero arbitrio. PL 32, 1221–1310; CSEL 74, 3–154; CCL 29, 2.11–321.

De magistro. PL 32, 1193–1220; CSEL 77.1, 3–55; CCL 29, 157–203.

De mendacio. PL 40, 487–578; CSEL 41, 413–466.

De moribus ecclesiae Catholicae et de moribus Manichaeorum. PL 32, 1309–1378;CSEL 90, 3–156.

De musica. PL 32, 1081–1194.

De natura boni. PL 42, 551–572; CSEL 25.2, 855–889.

De opere monachorum. PL 40, 547582; CSEL 41: 531–597.

De ordine. PL 32, 977–1020; CSEL 63, 121–180; CCL 29, 89–137.

De patientia. PL 43: 611–626; CSEL 41: 663–691.

De peccatorum meritis et remissione et de baptismo parvulorum. PL 44, 109–200; CSEL 60, 3–151.

De praedestinatione sanctorum. PL 44, 959–992.

De sermone Domini in monte. PL 34, 1229–1308; CCL 35, 1–188.

De spiritu et littera. PL 44, 201–246; CSEL 60, 155–229.

De trinitate. PL 42, 817–1098; CCL 50, 25–380; 50A, 381–535.

De utiliate credendi. PL 42, 65–92; CSEL, 25.1, 3–48.

De utilitate jejunii. PL 40, 707–716.

De vera religion. PL 34, 121–172; CSEL. 77.2, 3–81; CCL 32, 187–26

Ennarationes in Psalmos. PL 36, 67–1028; 37, 1033–1966; CCL, 38, 1–616; 39, 623–1417; 40, 1425–2196.

Enchiridion ad Laurentium. PL 40, 231–290; CCL 46, 49–114.

Epistulae. PL 33, 61–1094; CSEL 34.1, 1–125; 34.2, 1–746; 57, 1–656; 88, 3–138.

In Johannis epistulam. PL 35, 1977–2062.

In Johannis evangelium tractatus. PL 35, 132–1975; CCL 36, 1–688.

Retractationes. PL 32, 553–656; CSEL 36, 7—204; CCL 57, 5–143.

Sermones. PL 38, 23–1484; 39, 1493–1638, 1650–1652, 1655–1659, 1663–1669, 1671–1684, 1695–1697, 1701–1736.

Soliloquia. PL 32, 869–904; CSEL 89, 3–98.

Speculum. PL 34, 887—1040; CSEL 12, 3–285.

TRANSLATIONS CITED

Augustine: Arianism and Other Heresies. Translated with an introduction and notes by R. J. Teske. Hyde Park, N.Y.: New City Press, 1995.

Augustine: De Doctrina Christiana. Edited with an introduction, translation, and notes by R. P. H. Green, Oxford Early Christian Texts. Oxford: Clarendon Press, 1995.

Oeuvres de saint Augustin: La Genèse au sens littéral. Translated with introduction and notes by P. Agaësse and A. Solignac, Bibliothèque augustinienne BA 48–49. Paris: Desclée de Brouwer, 1972.

Saint Augustine. Against the Academics. Translated by John J. O'Meara. Westminster, MD: Newman, 1950.

Saint Augustine, *On the Free Choice of the Will*. Translated by Anna S. Benjamin and L.H. Hackstaff, with an introduction by L.H. Hackstaff. Indianapolis: Bobbs-Merrill, 1964.

Saint Augustine on Genesis: Two Books on Genesis against the Manichees and On the Literal Interpretation of Genesis: An Unfinished Book. Translated by Roland J. Teske. Washington, D.C.: Catholic University of America Press, 1991.

Saint Augustine, *Les Révisions. Bibliothèque Augustinienne*. Vol. 12. Translation, introduction, and notes by G. Bardy. Paris: Desclée, De Brouwer et Cie, 1950.

Saint Augustine, *La Trinité. Deuxiéme Partie: Les Images. Bibliothèque Augustinienne*. Vol. 16. Translation by P. Agaësse, notes by P. Agaësse and J. Moingt. Paris: Desclée, De Brouwer et Cie, 1955).

The Works of Aurelius Augustine, Bishop of Hippo. Translated by Marcus Dods. Volume VI. *The Letters of Saint Augustine*. Edinburgh: T. and T. Clark, 1872.

SECONDARY SOURCES

BOOKS

Adams, Marilyn McCord. *What Sort of Human Nature? Medieval Philosophy and the Systematics of Christology.* The Aquinas Lecture, 1999. Milwaukee: Marquette University Press, 1999.

Alfaric, Prosper. *L'évolution intellectuelle de saint Augustin: I. Du Manichéisme au néoplatonisme.* Paris: Nourry: 1918.

Ambrose. *Expositio evangelii secundum Lucam.* CCL XIV: 1–400.

———. *Hexaemeron.* CSEL 32.1, 3–261.

Aquinas, Thomas. *Summa contra Gentiles.* Rome: Leonine Commission, Romae, 1934.

———. *Summa theologiae.* 3 Vols. Turin: Marietti, 1952.

Basil the Great. *De structura hominis oratio.* Patrologia graeca 32.2.

Bierwaltes, Werner. *Regio Beatitudinis: Augustine's Concept of Happiness.* Villanova: Villanova University Press, 1981.

Bourke, Vernon J. *Augustine's Quest for Wisdom: Life and Philosophy of the Bishop of Hippo.* Milwaukee: Bruce, 1945.

Boyer, Charles. *Christianism et néoplatonisme dans la formation de saint Augustin.* Paris: G. Beauchesne, 1920.

———. *L'idee de vérité dans la philosophie de saint Augustin.* Paris: Beauchesne, 1940.

Brown, Peter. *Augustine of Hippo: A biography.* Berkeley: University of California Press, 1969.

Butler, Cuthbert. *Western Mysticism: The Teaching of Augustine, Gregory and Bernard on Contemplation and the Contemplative Life.* 2nd ed., with Afterthoughts. New York: Harper and Row, 1966.

The Catholic Study Bible. Edited by D. Senior et al. (New York: Oxford University Press, 1990).

Chadwick, Henry. *Augustine.* Oxford: Oxford University Press, 1986.

Chevalier, Irenée. *S. Augustin et la pensée grecque: Les relations trinitaires.* Fribourg: Librairie de l'université, 1940.

Clement of Alexandria. *Les stromates.* Sources chrétiennes 30, 38, 278–79, 428, 446, 463. Paris, Éditions du Cerf, 1951–

Collingwood, R. G. *An Essay on Metaphysics.* Oxford: Clarendon Press, 1940.

Comeau, M. *Saint Augustine exégète du quartième évangile.* Paris: Beauchesne, 1930.

Courcelle, Pierre. *Recherches sur les "Confessions" de saint Augustin.* Paris: E. de Boccard, 1950.

Crouzel, Henri. *Origène*. Paris: Lethielleux, 1985.

———. *Théologie de l'image de Dieu chez Origène*. Paris: Aubier, 1956.

Decret, François. *Aspects du Manichéisme dans l'Afrique romaine: Les controverses de Fortunatus, Faustus, et Felix avec saint Augustin*. Paris, Études augustiniennes, 1970.

De Lubac, Henri. *Catholicism: Christ and the Common Destinay of Man*. Translated by L. C. Shepherd and E. England. San Francisco: Ignatius Press, 1988.

———. *Histoire et esprit. L'intelligence de l'Ecriture d'apres Origène*. Theologie 16. Paris: Aubier, 1950.

Documents of the 31st and 32nd General Congregations of the Society of Jesus. Edited by John W. Padberg. Saint Louis: The Institute of Jesuit Sources, 1977.

Du Roy, Olivier. *L'intelligence de la foi en la trinité selon s. Augustin. Genèse de sa théologie trinitaire jusqu'en 391*. Paris: Etudes augustiniennes, 1966.

Epiphanius of Salamis. *Panarion Haereseon* 1–33, ed. K. Holl (Leipzig: J.C. Hinrichs'she Buchhandlung, 1915), 234–237; *Panarion Haereseon* 34–64, ed. K. Holl and J. Dummer (Berlin: Akademie Verlag, 1980), 1-4, 211-214, and *Panarion Haereseon*. 65-80, ed. K. Holl and J. Dummer (Berlin: Akademie Verlag, 1985), or PG 42, 853–873.

Flew, Antony. *The Presumption of Atheism and Other Essays*. New York: Barnes and Noble, 1976.

Frankena, William. *Ethics*. Engelwood Cliffs, NJ: Prentice-Hall, 1973.

Gilson, Etienne. *The Christian Philosophy of St. Augustine*. New York: Random House, 1960.

Gryson, R. *Scolies ariennes sur le councile d'Aquilée*. Sources chrétiennes 167. Paris: du Cerf, 1980.

Hansen, R. P. C. *The Search for the Christian Doctrine of God: The Arian Controversy 318–381*. Edinburgh: T. & T. Clark, 1988.

Hume, David. *An Enquiry concerning Human Understanding*. Edited by L. A. Selby-Bigge. Oxford: Clarendon Press, 1902.

Irenaeus of Lyons. *Adverus haereses*. Sources Chrétiennes 210–211.

Kant, Immanuel. *Fundamental Principles of the Metaphysics of Morals*. In *Basic writings of Kant*. Edited by Allen W. Wood. New York: Modern Library, 2001.

Keefe, Donald J. *Covenantal Theology: The Eucharistic Order of History*. 2 vols. Lanham, MD: University Press of America, 1991.

Kenny, Anthony. *The God of the Philosophers*. Oxford: Clarendon Press, 1979.

Lawless, George. *Augustine of Hippo and his Monastic Rule*. Oxford: Clarendon Press, 1987.

Le Blond, J.-M. *Les conversions de saint Augustin*. Paris: Aubier, 1950.

Lonergan, Bernard. *Insight: A Study of Human Understanding*. New York: Philosophical Library, 1957.

Mandouze, André. *Saint Augustin: L'aventure de la raison et de la grâce*. Paris: Etudes augustiniennes, 1968.

Maritain, Jacques. *St. Thomas and the Problem of Evil*. Milwaukee: Marquette University Press, 1942.

Marrou, Henri-Irénée. *Saint Augustin et la fin de la culture antique*. Paris: de Boccard, 1938.

Meslin, M. *Les ariens d'Occident*. Paris: Editions du Seuil, 1967.

Nash, Ronald. H. *The Light of the Mind: St. Augustine's Theory of Knowledge*. Lexington: University of Kentucky, 1969.

O'Connell, Robert J. *Images of Conversion in St. Augustine's* Confessions. New York: Fordham University Press, 1996.

———. *The Origin of the Soul in St. Augustine's Later Works*. New York: Fordham University Press, 1987.

———. *St. Augustine's Confessions: Odyssey of Soul*. Cambridge: Harvard University Press, 1969.

———. *St. Augustine's Early Theory of Man, A.D. 386–391*. Cambridge: Harvard University Press, 1968.

O'Donnell, James J. *Augustine*. Boston: Twayne, 1985.

O'Meara, John J. *The Young Augustine. The Growth of St. Augustine's Mind up to his Conversion*. New York: Longmans, 1954.

Origen, *Homélies sur s. Luc*. Introduction, translation, and notes by Henri Crouzel. *Sources Chrétiennes* 87. Paris: Editions du Cerf, 1967.

Philaster of Brescia. *Diversarum heresion liber*. CCL 9, 207–324.

Plantinga, Alvin. *God and Other Minds*. Ithaca: Cornell University Press, 1967.

Plato. *Phaedo*. In *Plato 1*. With an English translation. Cambridge, MA: Harvard University Press, 1947.

Possidius. *Vita Augustini*. PL 32, 33–66

Punzo, Vincent. *Reflective Naturalism*. New York: Macmillan, 1969.

Quintillian, *Institutionis oratoriae libri duodecim*. Edited and annotated by M. Winterbottom Oxford.Clarendon Press, 1970.

Rahner, Karl. *Karl Rahner in Dialogue: Conversations and Interviews 1965 – 1982*. Edited by Paul Imhof and Hubert Biallowons. Translated by Harvey Egan. New York: Crossroad, 1986.

Smith, Gerard. *Freedom in Molina*. Chicago: Loyola University Press, 1966.

Stoop, J. A. A. A. *Die deificatian hominis in die Sermones en Epistulae van Augustinus*. Leiden, 1950.

Tertullian, *De praescriptione haereticorum* PL 2, 9–74; CCL I, 187–224.

———. *De carne Christi*: PL 751–792; CCL 2, 873–917.

Thimme, W. *Augustins geistige Entwicklung in den ersten Jahren nach seiner "Bekehrung" (386–391)*. Berlin: Trowitzsch and Son, 1908.

Tyconius. *The Book of Rules of Tyconius*. Edited by F. C. Burkitt. Cambridge: University Press, 1894; repr. Nendeln, Liechtenstein: Kraus, 1967..

Van der Meer, F. *Augustine the Bishop: Church and Society at the Dawn of the Middle Ages*. New York: Harper, 1965.

Van Oort, J. *Jerusalem and Babylon: A Study of St. Augustine's City of God and the Sources of his Doctrine of the Two Cities*. Leiden: E. J. Brill, 1991.

Verbeke, G. *L'évolution de la doctrine du pneuma du Stoïcisme à s. Augustin*. Paris: D. de Bouwer; Louvain: Institut supérieur de philosophie, 1945.

Von Balthasar, Hans Urs, and M. E. Korger, *Aurelius Augustinus, Psychologie und Mystik. De Genesi ad litteram 12*. Coll. Sigillum 18. Einsiedeln: Johannes, 1960.

Weinandy, Thomas. *In the Likeness of Sinful Flesh: An Essay on the Humanity of Christ*. Edinburgh: T&T Clark, 1993.

ARTICLES

Agaësse, P. and A. Solignac. "'Spiritus' dans le levre XII du De Genesi." In *Bibliothèque augustinienne* 49. Paris: Institut des études augustiniennes, 2001. Pp. 559–66.

Aubin, Paul. "L'Image dans l'oeuvre de Plotin." *Recherches de science religieuse* 41 (1953): 348–379.

Bonner, Gerald. "The Doctrine of Sacrifice: Augustine and the Latin Patristic Tradition." In *Sacrifice and Redemption. Durham Essays in Theology*. Edited by S. W. Sykes, 101–117. Cambridge: Cambridge University Press, 1991.

Cipriani, N. "Echi antiapollinaristici e aristotelismo nella polemica di Giuliano d'Eclano." *Augustinianum* 21 (1981): 373–89.

Cousineau, Robert-Henri. "Creation and Freedom: An Augustinian Problem: 'Quia voluit'? or 'Quia bonus'?" *Recherches Augustiniennes* 2 (2963): 253–71.

Daniélou, Jean. "Le Bon Samaritan." In *Mélanges bibliques rédigés en honneur de André Robert*. Paris: Travaux de l'Institut Catholique, 1956. Pp. 457–65.

De Broglie, Guy. "La notion augustinienne du sacrifice 'invisible' et 'vrai.'" *Recherches de science religieuse* 48 (1960): 135–65.

De Montcheuil, Yves. "L'unité du sacrifice et du sacrement dans l'Eucharistie." In *Mélanges théologiques*. Paris: Aubier, 1946. Pp. 49–70.

Fitzmyer, J. A. *The Gospel according to Luke*. Introduction, translation, notes by J. A. Fitzmyer. New York: Doubleday, 1985.

Folliet, Georges. "'Deificari in otio.' Augustin, Epistula X, 13." *Recherches augustiniennes* 2 (1962): 225–36.

Kannengieser, Charles. "Apollinaris of Laodicea, Apollinarism." In *The Encyclopedia of the Early Church*. 2 vols. Edited by Angelo di Berardino; translated by Adrian Walford, I, 58–59. New York: Oxford University Press, 1992.

Karris, Robert J. "The Gospel according to Luke." In *The New Jerome Biblical Commentary*. Edited by R. E. Brown, J. A. Fitzmyer, and R. E. Murphy, 676–721. Englewood Cliffs, NJ: Prentice-Hall, 1990/

Korger, M. E. "Grundprobleme des augstinischen Erkenntnisselehre. Erläutert am Beispiel von de genesi ad litteram XII." *Recherches augustinienness* 2 (1962): 33–67.

Küng, Hans. *On Being a Christian*. Translated by E. Quinn. Garden City, NY: Doubleday, 1976.

Lafont, Ghislain. "Le sacrifice de la Cité de Dieu. Commentaire au *De Civitate Dei* Livre X, ch. I–VII." *Recherches de science religieuse* 53 (1965): 177–219.

Lambot, Dom C. "Lettre inédité de saint Augustin relative au 'De Civitate Dei.'" *Revue Bénédictine* 51 (1939): 109–121.

Lécuyer, Joseph. "Le sacrifice selon saint Augustin." In *Augustinus Magister*. Paris: Études augustiniennes, 1946. II, 905–914.

Lienhard, Joseph T. "'The Glue Itself is Charity': Ps. 63:9 in Augustine's Thought." In *Presbyter Factus Sum*. Edited by E. Muller, J. Lienhard, and R. Teske, 375–84. New York: Peter Lang, 1993.

Lossky, Vladimir. "Éléments de 'Théologie Négative' chez Saint Augustin." *Augustinus Magister* I, 575–82.
Madec, Goulven. "Connaissance de Dieu et action de grâces. Essai sur les citations de *Ép. aux Romains* I, 18–25 dans l'oeuvre de saint Augustin." *Recherches augustiniennes* 2 (1962): 273–309.
Maréchal, Joseph. "La vision de Dieu au sommet de la contemplation d'après saint Augustin." *Nouvelle Revue Théologique* 58 (1930): 89–109 and 191–214.
Markus, Robert. "Augustine." In *The Cambridge History of Later Greek and Medieval Philosophy*. Edited by A. H. Armstrong. Cambridge: Cambridge University Press, 1967.
Mayer, Cornelius. "Allegoria." In *Augustinus-Lexikon*. Edited by C. Mayer, I, 1/2, 234–39. Basel-Stuttgart: Schwabe, 1986).
Masai, François. "Les conversion de saint Augustin et les débuts du spiritualisme en Occident." *Moyen âge* 67 (1961): 1–40.
McCool, Gerald. "The Ambrosian Origin of St. Augustine's Theology of the Image of God in Man." *Theological Studies* 20 (1959): 62–81.
McEvoy, James J. "Neoplatonism and Christianity: Influence, Syncretism, or Discernment?" In *The Relationship betrween Neoplatonism and Christianity*. Edited by Thomas Finam and Vicent Twomey, 7–32. Dublin: Four Courts, 1992.
Moreau, Madeleine. "Lecture due *De doctrina christiana*." In *Saint Augustin et la Bible*. Edited by Anne-Marie la Bonnardière, 253–85. Paris: Beauchesne, 1986.
Neusch, Marcel. "Une conception chrétienne du sacrifice: Le modèle de saint Augustin." In *Le sacrifice dans les religions. Sciences théologiques et religieuses* 3. Edited by Marcel Neusch, 117–138. Paris: Beauchesne, 1994.
O'Connell, Robert J. "Augustine's Rejection of the Fall of the Soul." *Augustinian Studies* 4 (1973): 1–31.
———. "Faith, Reason, and Ascent to Vision in St. Augustine." *Augustinian Studies* 21 (1990): 83-126 .
O'Grady, John F. "Priesthood and Sacrifice in 'City of God.'" *Augustiniana* 21 (1971): 27–44.
Pépin, Jean. "A propos de l'histoire de l'exégèse allégorique: l'absurdité, signe de l'allégorie." In *Studia Patristica* 1 (= *Texte und Unter-*

suchungen 63). Edited K. Aland and F. L. Cross, 395–413. Berlin: Akademie Verlag, 1955.

Peters, E. "What Was God Doing Before He Created Heaven and Earth?" *Augustiniana* 34 (1984): 53–74.

Quinot, Bernard. "L'influence de l'Épitre aux Hébreux dans la notion augustinienne du vrai sacrifice." *Revue des études augustiniennes* 8 (1962): 129–68.

Refoulé, François. "Julien d'Éclane, théologien et philosophe." *Recherche de science religieuse* 53 (1964): 42-84 and 233–47.

Sanchis, D. "Samaritanus ille: L'exégèse augustinienne de la parabole du bon Samaritain." *Recherches de science religieuse* 40 (1961): 406–25.

Schmaus, M. "Die Spannung von Metaphysik und Heilsgeschichte in der Trinitätslehre Augustins." In *Studia Patristica* 6 (= Texte und Untersuchungen 81). Edited F. L. Cross, 503–18. Berlin: Akademie Verlag, 1962.

Sheppard, Gerald T. "Canonical Criticism." In *The Anchor Bible Dictionary*. Edited by David. N. Freedman. 6 vols. I, 861–66. New York: Doubleday, 1992.

Simonetti, M. "Agustin e gli Ariani." *Revue des études augustiniennes* 13 (1967): 55–84.

Smith, Thomas. "Augustine in Two Gallic Controversies: Use or Abuse?" In *Collectanea Augustiniana* III. New York: Peter Lang, 1993. Pp. 43– 55.

Somers, H. "Image de Dieu. Les sources de l'exeéèse augustinienne." *Revue des études augustiniennes* 7 (1961) 105–25.

Studer, Basil. "Das Opfer Christi nach Augustins 'De civitate Dei' X, 5–6." In *Lex Orandi, Lex Credendi. Miscellanea in onore di P. Cipriano Vagaggini*. Edited by G. Békés and G. Franedi, 93–107. Rome: Editrice Anselmiana, 1980.

Taylor, John H. "The Text of Augustine's *De Genesi ad litteram*." *Speculum* 25 (1950): 87–93.

Teske, Roland J. "The Aim of Augustine's Proof that God Truly Is." *International Philosophical Quarterly* 26 (1986): 253–68.

———. "Augustine, Jansenius, and the State of Pure Nature." In *Augustinus in der Neuzeit*. Edited by Kurt Flasch and Dominique de Courcelles, 161–74. Turnhout: Brepols, 1998.

———. "A Decisive Admonition for St. Augustine?" *Augustinian Studies* 19 (1988): 85–92.

———. "The *De Libero Arbitrio* Proof for the Existence of God." *Proceedings of the Jesuit Philosophical Association* (1987): 15–47; in revised form in *Philosophy and Theology* 2 (1987): 124–42.

———. "Heresy and Imagination in St. Augustine." In *Studia Patristica* 27. Edited by Elizabeth Livingstone, 400– 404. Leuven: Peters, 1993.

———. "*Homo spiritalis* in St. Augustine's *Confessions*." In *Augustine: From Rhetor to Theologian*. Edited by Joanne McWilliam, 67–76. Waterloo, Ont.: Wilfrid Laurier University Press, 1992.

———. "*Homo spiritalis* in St. Augustine's *De Genesi contra Manichaeos*," *Studia Patristica* 22. Edited by Elizabeth Livingstone, 351–55. Leuven: Peters, 1989.

———. "The Link between Faith and Time in St. Augustine." In *Augustine: Presbyter Factus Sum*. Collectanea Augustiniana II. Edited by R. Muller, J. Lienhard, and R. Teske, 195–206. New York: Peter Lang, 1993.

———. "The Motive for Creation according to Saint Augustine." *The Modern Schooman* 65 (1988): 245–53.

———. "Omniscience, Omnipotence, and Divine Transcendence." *The New Scholasticism* 53 (1979): 283–94.

———. "Sacrifice in Augustine's *Contra aduersarium legis et prophetarum*," in *Studia Patristica* 33. Edited by E. A. Livingstone, 255–59. Leuven: Peeters, 1997.

———. "Spirituals and Spiritual Sense in St. Augustine." *Augustinian Studies* 15 (1984): 65–81.

———. "St. Augustine as Philosopher. The Birth of Christian Metaphysics." *Augustinian Studies* 23 (1992): 7–32.

———. "St. Augustine's View of the Original Human Condition in *De Genesi contra Manichaeos*." *Augustinian Studies* 22 (1991): 141–55.

———. "St. Augustine's Use of '*manens in se*.'" *Revue des études augustiniennes* 39 (1993): 291–307.

———. "Spirituals and Spiritual Interpretation in Augustine." *Augustinian Studies* 15 (1984): 65–81.

Van Fleteren, Frederick. "Augustine's Ascent of the Soul in Book VII of the Confessions: A Reconsideration," *Augustinian Studies* 5 (1974): 29–72.

———. "The Early Works of Augustine and his Ascents at Milan." In *Studies in Medieval Culture* X. Edited by John R. Sommerfelt and Thomas Seiler, 19–23. Kalamazoo: The Medieval Institute, 1977.

———. "A Reply to Robert O'Connell." *Augustinian Studies* 21 (1990): 127–37.

Von Jess, W. Gundersdorf. "La simplicidat de Dios en el pensiamento agustiniano." *Augustinus* 19 (1974): 45–52.

Weil, E. "Remarques sur le 'matérialisme' des Stoïciens." In *Mélanges Alexandre Koyré. II. L'aventure de l'esprit*. Paris: Herman, 1964. Pp. 556–72.

INDEX OF NAMES

A

Adam, 12, 15, 17, 74-76, 103, 134, 155, 173, 177, 198, 231-233
Adams, M.,15, 215, 283
Agaësse, P., 61-63, 127, 155-156, 164, 283, 287
Alfaric, P., 22, 25, 284
Alypius of Thagaste, 98
Ambrose of Milan, 14, 21, 23, 26, 121-122, 130-132, 134, 138, 164, 166, 168, 192, 217, 272, 276-277, 284
Apollinaris of Laodocea, 223-228, 288
Apollonius, 265
Aquinas, Thomas, 15, 22, 40-41, 43, 48, 50-55, 57-60, 77-78, 83, 145, 215, 232, 283-284, 286
Aristotle, 77-78, 231
Aubin, P., 274, 287

B

Baius, M., 233
Bardy, G., 61, 63, 97, 271, 283
Basil of Caesarea, 254, 267, 269, 276-277, 284, 290
Bierwaltes, W., 35, 284
Bonaventure, 215
Bonafacius, 237
Bonner, G., 254, 265-266, 287
Bourke, V., 24, 53, 121, 284
Boyer, C., 22, 148, 284
Brown, P., 10, 38, 114-115, 167, 284, 288
Butler, C., 145-148, 160, 165, 284

C

Caelestinus, 24
Chadwick, H., 111, 120, 284
Chevalier, I., 279, 284
Cilleruelo, L., 101
Courcelle, P., 22-23, 77, 95, 122, 155, 284
Cicero, M. T., 23, 35, 67, 111
Cipriani, N., 226, 287
Collingwood, R., 56, 284
Comeau, M., 129, 165, 284
Consentius, 91-94, 251
Cousineau, R., 33, 287
Crouzel, H., 272, 284, 286
Cyprian of Carthage, 266

D

Daniélou, J., 167, 288
Decret, F., 115-116, 285
de Broglie, G., 16, 254-255, 258-259, 288
de Lubac, H., 139, 168, 285
de Montcheuil, Y., 16, 254, 258, 267-269, 288
Descartes, 53, 69
Divjak, J., 260
du Roy, O., 32, 150, 272, 275, 280, 285

E

Epiphanius of Salamis, 223-225, 285
Evodius of Uzalis, 33, 42-44, 46-47, 83-86

F

Faustus, the Manichee, 111, 114, 116-117, 120, 124, 248, 285
Faustus of Riez, 248
Firmus, 149, 260, 266-267
Fitzmyer, J., 167-168, 177, 288
Flew, A., 5, 9, 11-12, 39-42, 49-50, 53, 55-60, 285
Folliet, G., 97, 103-105, 107, 288
Frankena, W., 58, 285

G

Gilson, E., 12, 36, 61, 63-64, 66-67, 69-71, 76, 82, 154, 285
Gregory of Nyssa, 28, 145, 284
Gryson, R., 237, 285
Gundersdorf, W., 26, 292

H

Hanson, R., 237, 246
Hermaniuck, M., 167
Hilary of Poitiers, 250
Honoratus, 112, 127, 220
Hoskyns, E., 167
Hume, D., 42, 285

I

Irenaeus of Lyons, 168, 192, 285
Isaiah, 93, 151, 158-160, 217, 220

J

Jansenius, C., 233, 290
Jerome of Bethlehem, 22, 89-90, 167, 288
John, the Apostle 16, 22, 28-29, 34, 37, 39, 81, 104, 116-117, 129, 145, 158-160, 164-165, 190, 203, 215-216, 218, 231-232, 236, 239, 241, 254-255, 259, 283, 285-286, 289-291
Julian of Eclanum, 15, 220, 223-233

K

Kannengieser, C., 223, 288
Keefe, D., 268, 285
Kenny, A., 50, 285
Korger, M., 146, 164, 287-288
Küng, H., 250, 288
Kurz, W., 190

L

La Bonnardière, A.-M., 129, 193-194, 289
Lafont, G., 254, 288
Lambot, C., 260, 288
Lawless, G., 98, 105-107, 285
Le Blond, J.-M., 62, 286
Licentius, 195
Lienhard, J., 37, 141-142, 288, 291
Lombard, Peter, 215
Lonergan, B., 59, 82, 286
Lossky, V., 62-63, 69, 288
Luther, M., 41, 215

M

Madec, G., 30, 289
Mandouze, A., 97-98, 101, 104-105, 107, 286
Mani, 115-117, 123, 224, 228
Maritain, J., 48, 54, 286
Markus, R., 63-64, 66, 289
Marrou, H.-I., 128-129, 140-142, 286
Masai, F., 28, 248, 289
Maximinus, the Arian, 5, 9, 11, 15-16, 235-237, 242-251
McEvoy, J., 24, 289
Meslin, M., 237, 286
Monica, 21, 79, 130

INDEX OF NAMES

Moreau, M., 129, 289
Moses, 14, 29, 82, 123, 125, 157, 160-165, 185-186

N

Nash, R., 35, 62-63, 286
Nebridius, 13, 65, 68, 97-101, 105, 107-108
Neusch, M., 254, 289

O

O'Connell, R., 45, 66, 72, 93, 122, 209-210, 242, 261, 277, 279, 286, 289, 292
O'Donnell, J., 190-191, 209, 286
O'Grady, J., 254-255, 264, 289
O'Meara, J.J., 22, 115, 283, 286
Origen of Alexandria, 72, 128-129, 139, 168, 192, 272, 276, 284-286
Orosius, Paul, 31

P

Paul, the Apostle, 14, 31, 82, 115-119, 123-124, 141, 143, 146, 148, 155-157, 163-165, 170-171, 176, 181, 183, 218, 221-222, 231-232, 247, 253, 274, 286-287
Pelagius, 180
Pépin, J., 14, 127-129, 289
Peters, E., 112, 290-291
Philaster of Brescia, 224, 286
Plantinga, A., 11-12, 39, 41, 53, 56, 286
Plato, 11, 30, 32, 36-37, 62, 66, 70-72, 76-79, 83, 108, 148, 154, 278, 286
Plotin, 155, 274, 287
Plotinus, 11, 15, 21-23, 29, 31-32, 38, 45, 72, 93, 95, 103, 108, 122, 148, 209-212, 242, 274
Possidius, 38, 237, 286

Porphyry, 11, 21-22, 103-104, 107, 122, 148, 155, 262, 265, 267
Punzo, V., 58, 286
Pythagoras, 71

Q

Quinot, B., 254, 290

R

Rahner, K., 218, 286
Refoulé, F., 226, 231-232, 290
Romanianus, 23, 127
Rosmini-Serbati, A., 81

S

Sanchis, D., 168, 290
Schmaus, M., 250, 290
Scotus, Duns, 215
Secundinus, the Manichee, 114
Shepherd, G., 168, 192, 285
Sigisvult, 237
Simonetti, M., 237, 290
Smith, Thomas, 290
Smith, Gerard, 287
Socrates, 12, 66, 218
Solignac, A., 127, 155-156, 164, 210, 283, 287
Somers, H., 273-274, 276-277, 290
Studer, B., 254, 267, 269, 290
Stoop, J., 97, 287
Swetnam, J., 25

T

Taylor, J. H., 155-156, 290
Tertullian, 112-113, 248, 266, 287
Theodorus, 26-27, 131, 151
Theodore of Mopsuestia, 226
Thimme, W., 97, 287
Thonnard, F. J., 87
Tyconius, 219-220, 222, 287

U

Ubaghs, C., 81
Ulfila, the Arian, 237

V

Van Bavel, T. J., 194
Van der Meer, F., 97-98, 105, 287
Van Fleteren, F., 9, 122, 145, 154, 210, 291
Van Oort, J., 115, 266, 287
Verbeke, G., 248, 287
Vergil, 67
von Balthasar, H. U., 164, 287

W

Weil, E., 113, 248, 292
Weinandy, T., 229, 287
William of Auvergne, 141